COVER-UP OF CONVENIENCE

COVER-UP OF CONVENIENCE

The Hidden Scandal of Lockerbie

John Ashton and Ian Ferguson

MAINSTREAM
PUBLISHING

EDINBURGH AND LONDON

First published in Great Britain in 2001 by
MAINSTREAM PUBLISHING COMPANY (EDINBURGH) LTD
7 Albany Street
Edinburgh EH1 3UG

This edition 2002

ISBN 1 84018 389 6

A catalogue record for this book is available from the British Library

Typeset in Garamond and Gill

The Random House Group Limited supports The Forest Stewardship
Council (FSC®), the leading international forest certification organisation.
Our books carrying the FSC label are printed on FSC® certified paper.
FSC is the only forest certification scheme endorsed by the leading
environmental organisations, including Greenpeace. Our
paper procurement policy can be found at
www.randomhouse.co.uk/environment

Printed and bound in Great Britain by Clays Ltd, St Ives PLC

CONTENTS

FOREWORD BY TAM DALYELL MP

Seldom can an act of terrorism have had so many layers of sinister intrigue as the Lockerbie bombing. It was ten days after the disaster, on the evening of 31 December 1988 – Hogmanay – that I first became aware something very odd was afoot. A constituent, who I knew was an off-duty Lothian and Borders Police officer, pulled me aside at a function. He told me in confidence about disturbing events he had witnessed in the preceding days, while assigned to the Lockerbie crash site helping the Dumfries and Galloway force search the site. He described how American agents were swarming around the area, openly removing items of debris. He was concerned, not only because they appeared to be riding roughshod over the rules of evidence gathering required of a criminal investigation, but also because the police were doing nothing to stop them. My initial reaction was, 'Well, one can hardly deny the Americans, since they've lost 175 citizens.' During the following weeks I talked to more officers, some of whom had been left seething by similar experiences with the mysterious Americans.

Five years later, because I had repeatedly raised Lockerbie issues in the Commons, I was introduced to Allan Francovich, a remarkable American film-maker who had just begun to make his landmark Lockerbie documentary *The Maltese Double Cross.* His dogged investigation suggested that the 'official version' of the bombing (which insisted it was, in the words of one US official, a 'Libyan government operation from start to finish') was a sham and that the real culprits lay outside of Libya. More worryingly, he presented compelling evidence that the CIA was complicit in the disaster and, in so doing, made sense of the troubling accounts of my police sources. Although not the first investigator to advance this 'alternative version', he did so with a degree of detail that was too great to be ignored. The British and American governments' extraordinary joint campaign to discredit the film was both an indicator of how close Francovich had got to the truth and a disturbing reminder of the lengths to which some of those in authority would go to keep the lid on the affair.

Francovich's sudden death in 1997 came as a massive blow, but thankfully his deputy John Ashton has kept alive his spirit of inquiry.

In 1999 I became aware of another earnest seeker after the truth, Ian Ferguson, who was at the time producing a documentary for US National Public Radio. He is one of those rare individuals who, like Francovich and Ashton, is prepared to ask the awkward questions and devote many long hours to the search for answers. His reporting of the events surrounding the trial, for Scotland's *Sunday Herald* newspaper and on his website thelockerbietrial.com, has been unsurpassed and has frequently rattled the cages of authority. I was delighted to learn that he and Ashton had collaborated to produce this book.

As an MP, I have seen it as my role to complement the efforts of the various investigators and the equally remarkable work of the British Lockerbie victims' relatives, by raising questions in Parliament, and to that end I have so far initiated 16 adjournment debates. The sixth of these, held on 1 February 1995, was answered by the then Foreign Secretary Douglas Hurd. I am told it was the only occasion since the war that a senior cabinet minister had replied to a backbencher's adjournment debate. I am a creature of instinct and I sensed that he and the other ministers who have replied over the years were uncomfortable with having to peddle the official line. Later that day, Douglas spotted me talking to his then shadow and eventual successor Robin Cook MP. My diary entry for the day reads:

> Douglas swooped down on Robin and myself in the corridor by the window opposite the clerk's assistant's office. He said, 'I really do ask you two to believe that as Foreign Secretary I cannot tell the [Scottish] Crown Office [which was in charge of the Lockerbie case] what to do, nor does the Foreign Office have detailed access to evidence which they say they have. You must understand that law officers really are a law unto themselves.' Robin and I agreed that Douglas Hurd was not unfriendly towards us, and was probably correct in outlining the rules. Robin said that he guessed that Hurd was being honest with us and did not know the full story. I shrugged my shoulders, and told Robin he was probably right.

One of the most remarkable, but least reported, revelations in the recent trial of the two Libyans was that even the Crown Office did not know the 'full story' when it indicted the pair in 1991. Indeed, it was not until the trial was underway that it learned that its star witness was highly unreliable. The CIA had known this for well over a decade, yet had not seen fit to make available the crucial paperwork documenting this man's failings. Evidence heard at the trial also confirmed the long-held suspicion that CIA agents were involved in the highly irregular activities at the crash site witnessed by my police sources.

In my view, these facts alone warrant the full independent inquiry that has always been the demand of the British victims' relatives. I have no doubt that there is much else in this book that will add weight to that demand. My government colleagues promised such an inquiry when in opposition and I trust that, as men of honour, they will make good that pledge.

Tam Dalyell
April 2001

PREFACE

Our e-mails crossed somewhere in cyberspace.

Ashton to Ferguson: '*Can you believe this?*'

Ferguson to Ashton: '*This has to be a joke!!! I can hardly believe what I am reading.*'

The focus of our incredulity was a document we were scouring simultaneously on our respective sides of the Atlantic. It was a document for which we, and others, had waited many years; the judgment in Britain's largest-ever criminal trial, for the country's worst mass murder.

A few hours earlier Abdel Basset Ali Al-Megrahi had been convicted, at Camp Zeist in Holland, by a panel of three Scottish Law Lords, of the murders of the 270 people who died when Pan Am Flight 103 exploded over the town of Lockerbie on 21 December 1988. Megrahi's associate Lamin Khalifah Fhimah, who was also accused of the murders, had been acquitted.

It was mid-afternoon, UK time, on Wednesday, 31 January 2001, and the judgment had been available on the internet for a couple of hours. As we read the document between e-mails, our sense of amazement grew. It would be understandable had a lay jury delivered a wrongful verdict in such a complex case, but for some of Britain's finest legal brains to have made the same error was, to say the least, disappointing. At almost every turn, their lordships had employed strange arguments and leaps of logic, in a manner that also startled some legal observers.

And yet.

And yet, while we remained shocked by the judgment, we both had a hunch there might be a guilty verdict. We had each spent years investigating Lockerbie and the experience had taught us that this was a story in which the truth lay buried and that persistent scratching away at the surface reveals a very different picture to the one presented to casual observers. That picture can be summed up in one line: innocent people have been blamed for the bombing and the guilty remain free.

Nevertheless, there can seldom have been a story in which the journalist's cliché, 'the devil is in the detail', was better employed. We had each worked on substantial broadcast documentaries about the bombing (in Ashton's case, Allan Francovich's controversial two-and-a-half-hour epic *The Maltese Double Cross* and in Ferguson's an hour-long programme for American public radio), but we both knew the broadcast media were not always capable of conveying the welter of detail necessary to understand the complex story. We agreed that we could only do justice properly to the subject in a book. What follows, we believe, is the fullest account of the Lockerbie saga yet published.

That said, we do not offer conclusive proof, either of Megrahi's innocence or of what really happened. Rather, we have assembled a circumstantial case which, we maintain, is at least as compelling as the prosecution case against the two Libyans. At times we speculate, just as the prosecution did at Camp Zeist, and we leave it to the reader to judge which of those speculative elements they accept and which they reject.

This book by no means marks an end of our investigations. Anyone who has further information to offer can contact us via Mainstream Publishing, or can e-mail John Ashton at ja162@hotmail.com and Ian Ferguson at ianfergus@yahoo.com.

John Ashton
and Ian Ferguson,
April 2001

ACKNOWLEDGEMENTS

A multitude of people warrant acknowledgment, far too many, in fact, to list here.

The relatives of the Lockerbie victims deserve particular thanks, chief among them Martin and Rita Cadman, Pam Dix, John and Lisa Mosey, Sanya Popovic and Jim and Jane Swire. So too do all our sources, whose help was invaluable. Many of them had much to lose by talking to us and therefore cannot be named. Among those we can name who gave particular help were Hasan Assali, Juval Aviv, Jim Berwick, Professor Robert Black, John Brennan, Charles Byers, Tam Dalyell MP, Dr David Fieldhouse, Mike Jones, Owen Lewis, Herman Mathews, Nan McCreadie, Michael Meehan, Dan Perrault, Denis Phipps, Dr Michael Scott, Teddy Taylor MP and Frederic Whitehurst.

Bill Campbell of Mainstream Publishing had the courage to commission the book and his colleagues, Sharon Atherton, Fiona Brownlee, Neil Graham, Tina Hudson, Deborah Kilpatrick, Peter MacKenzie, Becky Pickard and Jess Thompson helped bring it to fruition. Arthur Davidson provided valuable legal advice prior to publication.

Many fellow journalists gave generous help, including: Helena Bengsston, Jan-Olof Bengtsson, Ronen Bergman, John Coates, John Cooley, Con Coughlin, Don Devereux, Rob Evans, Paul Foot, Drago Hedl, Bjorn Hygstedt, David Jessel, Shelley Jofre, David Johnston, Jürgen Krönig, Gunther Latsch, John Loftus, Neil Mackay, Joe Mifsud, David Milne, Mats-Eric Nilsson, Margaret Renn, Murdoch Rodgers, Frank Ryan, Kjetil Stormark, Phillip Wearne, Terry Wrong and David Yallop.

John Ashton adds: I would like to thank Celia, Ellis and Rachel Ashton, Leslie, Lois and Eva Clifton and all my friends for their enduring love and support. The production team of *The Maltese Double Cross* also deserve special mention, in particular the late Allan Francovich, who, more than anyone, inspired me to produce this book. Melanie McGrath gave me faith that publication was not a pipe dream, Peter Gartside made not a murmur of protest when I took over the kitchen and computer to write it and Claire Logan dispensed sound editorial advice. The directors and staff of Just Television were wonderfully tolerant of both my obsession with the subject and my lengthy absences. Finally, thanks to Ian Ferguson, a fine journalist and newfound friend, who advanced this investigation well beyond what I was capable of and put up with my e-mail tantrums.

Ian Ferguson adds: For their friendship, support and for being extraordinarily tolerant of me during the research and writing of this book – my friend and partner Lisa, Cecile Bedor, Marco Caruana, Chris and Connie Coleman, Deo Cuschieri, Claudia Daly, Fred DeVere, Des Dillon, Vinka Drezga, Nick Hayes, Wilf James, Euan and Jane Kerr, Stan Kusunoki, Mamie Lang, Sarah Penman, Hall and Donna Sanders, Martin Schoen and David Schroeder. I would also like to give special thanks to Bill Buzenberg, John Biewen, Stephanie Curtis and the production team at *American Radio Works*, all of whom showed great support during the making of the radio documentary *Shadow over Lockerbie*. And finally to John Ashton, my co-author. Having stretched his patience to the limit many a time, it's a tribute to his many qualities as a fine writer and man that he is still talking to me.

Finally, apologies to all those people we forgot to mention.

NOTES ON SOURCES

In the early months of 1994, when researching the Lockerbie documentary *The Maltese Double Cross*, John Ashton spent many weeks trailing across southern Scotland and northern England, interviewing mountain rescue volunteers who had given up their time in the aftermath of the bombing to comb the vast crash site for debris. Many were happy to talk on the record, while others were more wary, citing the Official Secrets Act and the presence of unidentified 'heavies' at the time. A number of them spoke of one particular search volunteer, whom we will call 'Peter', who, they said, had been party to a quite extraordinary find. No one knew what he had seen, because so shaken was he by the experience that he had always refused to go into detail about it. Everyone painted Peter as a down-to-earth and honest man, who was not the type to engage in flights of fancy.

Ashton eventually tracked down Peter and arranged for an off-the-record meeting, which was also attended by one of Ashton's colleagues. Without revealing what the other searchers had said about him, the pair gently probed Peter about his experiences at the crash site. It soon became clear that he wasn't going to say what, if anything, had so disturbed him and his inquisitors concluded that the rumours were simply the product of Chinese whispers. By then, however, Peter had, quite matter-of-factly, described something else that was potentially of the utmost importance. He said that shortly after the crash, he had found on Lockerbie golf course a package of what appeared to be drugs in white powder form.

Five years later, before the authors had teamed up to write this book, Ian Ferguson learned through his own sources about Peter's drug find. He too made contact with him and arranged an off-the-record meeting in which he asked Peter directly about the find. Peter now denied it. They changed the subject, but some while later he said to Ferguson, unprompted, 'I've not been got at you know.'

We relate this anecdote because it illustrates the difficulties of researching a story like Lockerbie. Maybe Peter hadn't been 'got at' – maybe no one has. But the fact remains that, to this day, many people with evidence about the bombing remain reluctant to come forward publicly. Some of our account, therefore, is based on these unattributable sources. We have only included accounts corroborated by other evidence. Some of those who spoke on condition of anonymity have been given aliases.

As far as possible we have referenced our sources, either in the body of the text or as endnotes. Some events that have been widely reported and are commonly accepted are not sourced.

It may jar with some readers that we often cite other media stories about Lockerbie. We have done this not out of laziness, but rather because the way the story has evolved through the media is an important element of the overall picture.

I. FIRST SUSPICIONS

No one thought to ask how they had got there so quickly. The middle-aged Americans wandering around Lockerbie town centre were clearly not bewildered tourists. Dressed in cream trench-coats, the men exuded an air of purpose which could only mean they were there on official business. With hindsight their presence was the first public clue that the bombing of Pan Am Fight 103 was no straightforward act of terrorism; but to the mountain rescue volunteers who encountered them, their strange accents and formal dress were just one more bizarre element in an already surreal scene.[1]

Like the rest of the small army of volunteers who had arrived in the town on the night of Wednesday, 21 December 1988, the rescue teams had far more important matters on their minds. It was around 9 p.m. Just two hours earlier Pan Am Flight 103 had fallen out of the skies from 31,000 feet, shortly after crossing the border between England and Scotland: 7.03 p.m. was the exact time that Alan Topp, air traffic controller at Prestwick airport, saw the radar image of the Boeing 747 Clipper *Maid of the Seas* fragment silently as its height readout disappeared from his display.[2]

Flight 103 was heading from Heathrow to Detroit, via New York's JFK airport. Although the jumbo jet had begun its journey in London, a smaller Pan Am Boeing 727 had earlier carried passengers from Frankfurt to Heathrow on a feeder flight numbered 103A. Somewhat unusually for a flight so close to Christmas, the plane was only around two-thirds full. Of the 243 passengers and 16 crew members – a total of 259 people – 175 were Americans, most of whom were heading home from Europe to spend Christmas with their families. They included servicemen stationed in West Germany and a party of 35 Syracuse University students who had spent the previous semester studying in London. There were 20 other nationalities represented on the flight, including 32 Britons.

British Airways pilot Robert Chamberlain, flying a few miles away, was the only person actually to witness the moment of destruction: a brief orange flash which penetrated the night-time clouds, rather like a gas flare. Shortly afterwards he saw a huge explosion as the Jumbo's fuel-laden wings hit the ground.[3]

The people of Lockerbie had no warning of the disaster. A community of around 2,500 set amid low hills a few miles north of the English border, the town was quite prosperous and, until that terrible night, peaceful. Many locals were occupied with pre-Christmas preparations, while others had settled down to watch *This Is Your Life* on television. The first indication of the imminent nightmare was a screaming, roaring sound. Seconds later came the explosion, which many likened to an earthquake.

Had the plane broken up a few seconds later the point of impact would probably have been the fields to the west of the town. However, by a tragic stroke of ill fortune, it occurred at Sherwood Crescent, a quiet street of modern bungalows next to the A74, the main Carlisle–Glasgow road. The blast killed 11 residents, bringing the death toll to 270, and obliterated 6 of their homes, leaving a 40-foot crater.

The heaviest part of the wreckage, the wings, marked the western extremity of the crash site, with the westerly wind spreading an ever-widening plume of lighter wreckage many miles eastwards. Half a mile away, at the Rosebank Estate, a large section of the fuselage containing 60 bodies smashed into the red-brick houses. Miraculously, no residents were killed. Three miles east of the town, at Tundergarth, the plane's cockpit landed in a field opposite the parish church. Lying on its side, like a beached whale, the crumpled structure rapidly became the abiding image of the tragedy.

As the winter solstice dawned the morning after the crash, the cockpit became the centrepiece of a weird and grim tableau. For miles around, incongruous objects peppered the landscape as a hideous reminder of the previous night's carnage: a Pan Am drinks trolley complete with undamaged miniatures; Christmas presents carefully wrapped and labelled; brightly coloured clothes and baggage and suitcases of all shapes and sizes. Worst of all, of course, were the bodies. Some were still strapped into their seats, clinging to each other, the terrifying moment of the explosion frozen on their faces, while others simply looked asleep.

As if the horror of being confronted with such sights was not enough to endure, the local people suffered the further agony of media intrusion. There were few places to hide from the ubiquitous reporters and cameras, so private grief became a commodity to be captured and traded in the name of 'human interest'. For those genuinely interested in human responses to disaster there were some shining examples on display in the aftermath of the crash. Local policemen saw notorious troublemakers turn up at the town hall volunteering to give whatever help they could; townsfolk offered shelter to people whose homes had been destroyed; and a band of protectors rallied around the 13-year-old Steven Flannigan from Sherwood Crescent, who lost his parents and sister, to shield him from the media sharks. Over the following months the quiet generosity and caring of the people of Lockerbie provided a reassuring antidote to the depravity of the people who had carried out the bombing.

Amid the tragedy and the quiet heroism a still stranger story was unfolding in the fields and hills of Lockerbie's bleak midwinter and Americans, rather than Scots, were at its core. Given that the plane belonged to a US carrier and had many Americans on board, it is understandable that the US would wish to have an official presence at the crash site, but it was odd that the first Americans reached the scene so quickly. It is possible that they had travelled down from one of the US naval bases on the Scottish coast, but if that were the case, they had got to Lockerbie with remarkable speed. Even if they had come by helicopter, they must have scrambled almost immediately the news of the crash came through. The US government would later officially deny that any of its employees had reached the town before around 11 p.m. The first arrival, it claimed, was the Consul General from Edinburgh.[4] However, US officials privately acknowledged that two agents were dispatched to the crash site within an hour.[5]

By midnight the numbers of Americans were swelled even further by officials who had arrived on a specially arranged flight from Heathrow to Carlisle. Pan Am's London-based manager of corporate security, Jim Berwick, remembers about 20 of them on the flight. Who they were, and what their jobs were, he was never told.[6] A senior official from Carlisle airport who witnessed the arrival of the flight believes that Berwick significantly underestimated the number of American officials on board. Two coaches had been hired to drive them up to Lockerbie, he recalls, both of which were more or less full. Around 20 of the arrivals were wearing Pan Am uniforms, but the remainder were in plain clothes.[7]

At Lockerbie Academy, which had rapidly been converted into an emergency response centre, Inspector George Stobbs (of the local Dumfries and Galloway police force) was surprised to see that, by midnight, an FBI agent had set up a desk. According to Stobbs, the agent 'came in, introduced himself and just sat there most of the night, observing what was happening'.[8] The US government was again reluctant to acknowledge that so many of its people had arrived so soon, subsequently claiming that the London plane did not arrive until 3 a.m.[9]

The following day a further set of Americans arrived, this time from the USA, among them the forensic expert Tom Thurman of the FBI and Walter

Korsgaard of the Federal Aviation Authority (FAA). Thurman had been dispatched to Lockerbie within hours of the crash by the FBI's head of counter-terrorism, Oliver 'Buck' Revell, who later said he had learnt of the disaster via a CNN newsflash.[10]

In theory the Americans had no jurisdiction over the crash investigation. Since it had occurred on Scottish soil, primary responsibility fell to the local police force – in this case, Dumfries and Galloway Constabulary. The smallest force in Britain, it had only 333 officers and 26 stations. In the years since the crash praise has been heaped on the tiny force for its thorough and determined investigation. In the semi-official mythology of Lockerbie they have been patronisingly portrayed as fiercely independent Celts who would tolerate no outside interference. Some of those with inside knowledge of the investigation tell a different story, in which the Americans were heavily involved from day one.

Among the first outsiders to be alerted was the veteran Scottish Labour MP for Linlithgow Tam Dalyell, whose dogged efforts to expose the darker side of state activity made him a trusted confidant for whistle-blowers in government and the public services. On 31 December 1988, Dalyell's Hogmanay celebrations were interrupted by an officer from his local police force, Lothian and Borders Constabulary, who wanted to speak to him in confidence. The officer had spent most of the previous nine days in Lockerbie with colleagues, helping the Dumfries and Galloway police search for bodies and debris. He said that he had been greatly disturbed by some of the events he had witnessed at the crash site. The countryside around Lockerbie was crawling with unsupervised Americans, he said, and they appeared to be conducting their own searches. In doing so they were going through evidence that should have been left alone until it could be dealt with by the Scottish police. It was clear that the Americans were operating with an official sanction, because there were no orders that they be stopped, and in some instances they were even accompanied by police officers.

Over the coming weeks other disgruntled policemen contacted Dalyell, some raging at the Americans' dealings with the vital physical evidence. 'I'm not pretending that they said they are from the FBI or the CIA,' Dalyell later recalled. 'They were just Americans who seemed to have arrived extremely quickly on the scene.'[11]

It was quite obvious to others that many of the Americans were indeed agents of the CIA. At two consecutive morning briefings a police inspector told a mountain rescue team leader from the north of England that American agents would be joining his party in their searches of the area to the east of Tundergarth. Some of the agents turned up dressed in Pan Am overalls.[12] Another policeman remembers accompanying one of them on 24 December, again in the Tundergarth area. 'He was no more working for Pan Am than I was,' the officer later commented.

The same officer was ordered to accompany a group of Americans to the area around where the cockpit of the plane had landed. Their instructions were to look for a bundle of documents which, he was told, had been given to the captain of Flight 103, and a black hard-sided Samsonite case. Despite their efforts, however, they were unable to find either item.[13]

Many more strange tales were to emerge from the army of volunteer searchers who scoured the hills for bodies and debris. Three days after the disaster Eric Spofforth, a search dog-handler from Hebden Bridge in Yorkshire, was out in the fields near Tundergarth when he was circled by a white civilian helicopter. Looking up, he saw one of the occupants peering at him through the telescopic sights of a gun. A keen marksman, he recognised the weapon as a high-powered rifle.[14] Another Yorkshire dog-handler, Alison Collau, had a similar experience a short distance away. When the marksman first spotted her, she was on her own in open countryside and her dog was buried in undergrowth and therefore not visible from the air. As the helicopter hovered above her she feared that she might be mistaken for a looter. It was only when the reappearance of the dog confirmed that she was a bona fide searcher that the helicopter flew away.[15] No one in authority ever referred to the helicopter, or to what it was that the marksman was assigned to protect.

The secrecy extended to the radio amateurs of the so-called 'Raynet' network who helped the police in the aftermath of the disaster. With the police airwaves swamped and the hilly terrain creating communication difficulties, they became essential to the search effort, supplying vital lines of communication between the police headquarters in Lockerbie and the various parties of searchers out in the fields. They were subsequently required to sign the Official Secrets Act.[16]

A former very senior Scottish legal officer, who was intimately involved in the case, later described the FBI and CIA as 'duplicitous bastards'. He was speaking about the information they had held back during various parts the investigation and he regarded them as unhelpful.[17]

The authorities were undoubtedly desperate to find certain highly sensitive items. At a morning briefing a day or so after the crash, police and mountain rescue team leaders were told to look out for a particular item, without being told what it was. When they asked the obvious question, 'How do we know what we should be looking for?', they were told only, 'You will know what it is when you find it.'[18]

No doubt one of the things that the authorities were keen to find was cash. Two bags full of US dollars were found in the police's search sector D, which covered the Tundergarth area. The first was found in a large holdall by a mountain rescue team from Scotland, who estimated its contents added up to around $500,000.[19] The second was in an attaché case discovered in a woodland to the south of the Langholm Road, at the approximate map reference 285 810.[20]

A third find was made in the Kielder Forest in Northumbria, by members of the Teesdale Mountain Rescue team, who searched the area from 27 December 1988 until early January 1989. Dave Thomson, the team member who signed for all the items handed over to the police, saw two or three brown paper packages within a few yards of each other. Each contained a very large sum in new, large-denomination dollar bills.[21]

A fourth find occurred near Elsdon in Northumberland, a full 40 miles away from Lockerbie. Carl Hamilton from the Northumbria National Park Wardens' mountain rescue team spotted a sodden bundle of dollars by the side of a quiet road.[22]

Three days after the crash local teenagers Stuart and Robbie Dodd, and their friend Alan Hyslop, found half a million dollars in traveller's cheques whilst searching the fields on the Dodd family's farm. The cheques, some of which were for several thousand dollars, were in a battered brown envelope which had marked on it the figure '$547,000'.[23]

None of these finds was ever confirmed by the authorities, who instead went out of their way to deny them. They said there was nothing found other than 'what might ordinarily be regarded as personal money'[24], whilst the young boys had mistaken the traveller's cheques for expired banker's drafts which were being flown back from Europe to their originating banks in the USA.[25] Such disinformation was understandable during the vital days after the crash when it was necessary to deter looters, but there was no obvious reason for the fiction to continue after everything of importance had been found.

The authorities also denied a number of major drug finds. A whole suitcase full of cannabis was found in search sector D. Everything recovered from the area was supposed to be logged at a temporary police post that had been set up there, but the suitcase was not. Instead, it was sent straight down to the central police warehouse that had been established at the disused Dexstar chemicals factory in Lockerbie.[26]

Far more significant and, in the years to come, far more controversial, was the discovery of large quantities of what appeared to be heroin. On the first terrible night a search volunteer combing Lockerbie golf course saw a search-

and-rescue dog running around a cellophane packet about half the size of a bag of sugar; on inspection, the packet clearly contained white powder.[27]

Police in the Tundergarth area were also ordered to be on the lookout for heroin. Some were told unofficially that it was suspected as belonging to a young Arab passenger. They weren't told the passenger's name, but the flight manifest showed that there was only one Arab person on the plane: 20-year-old Khalid Jaafar, an American citizen born in Lebanon, who had begun his journey in Frankfurt on Flight 103A.[28] Within a couple of days more heroin had turned up in a field of the nearby Tundergarth Mains farm. Concerned that a suitcase that had landed in his field had been overlooked, Farmer Jim Wilson contacted police headquarters and shortly afterwards an officer arrived, who, with Wilson's help, emptied out the case's contents into a plastic sack. One of the items in the case was a wide belt with large pouches around it, into which had been stuffed clear polythene packages containing white powder. The officer commented to Wilson something like, 'Uh, oh. I know what we've got here . . . We know about this one.'[29] Rather than taking the sack away, he contacted headquarters once more. Shortly afterwards some Americans arrived in a four-wheel-drive vehicle to take the suitcase away, apparently annoyed that it had not been recovered sooner.[30]

In July 1989 the first concrete account of a heroin find was published in *Lockerbie: the Real Story*, a book written by Scottish radio reporter David Johnston, one of the first reporters on the crash scene. As a ten-year veteran of Edinburgh's Radio Forth, he had excellent contacts among the Lothian and Borders policemen who were assigned to the Lockerbie search. Johnston assumed that, like virtually all transatlantic flights, Flight 103 was bound to have carried drugs. When his enquiries were met with official denials, he became suspicious and checked with his trusted sources among the police rank and file. Independently of each other, four different sources confirmed that large quantities of heroin had been found and that a section of the Dexstar warehouse had been set aside for drug finds.

Drugs and money were not the only items on board Pan Am 103 about which the authorities wished to keep quiet. A couple of days after the crash – he can't remember exactly when – a mountain rescue leader from North Yorkshire was guiding his team across a field a few miles east of Tundergarth, just to the north of the Langholm Road. As his team approached the eastern boundary of the field, he was approached by a policeman who warned him that they must on no account enter the field. A few hundred yards away the team could see that something had been covered with a large red or orange tarpaulin at the approximate map reference 293 817.[31]

In 1995 *Private Eye* reporter Paul Foot was sent an anonymous note alleging that a Mr Ron Smith, who worked for Scottish Woodlands at Castle Douglas in Galloway, had also come across the tarpaulin and had been warned off by army personnel. Foot checked with Smith, who told him that he was not involved in the incident, but knew someone who was. The story, as reported to him, was that someone had got close enough to see that the sheet covered a large box or container – far too big to have been the aircraft's black box voice recorder. The account tallied with the separate observations of Eric Spofforth and Alison Collau, because there was a helicopter hovering over the site, carrying a marksman who waved away anyone who got too close to the sheet. Soon after this incident the container vanished, apparently taken away by air, since there were no tyre tracks across the field to indicate the presence of a lorry.

A few miles away another no-go area was temporarily established on the top of a hill to the east of Carruthers Farm, near the village of Waterbeck. A day or so before Christmas, farmer Innes Graham was checking his sheep when he was approached by two plainclothed Americans, who ordered him not to go up on to the hill. He never asked why, and just assumed that something important lay there.[32] On the night of the crash a searcher had found US State Department papers on the farm marked 'sensitive', so the Americans were perhaps worried that more papers were at large on the hill.[33] A number of suitcases had landed on the farm, which Graham and his family stored in a barn. A couple of nights after the crash they heard someone snooping around the building.

These events were probably connected to a bizarre episode concerning a suitcase belonging to one of the plane's passengers, US Army Major Charles McKee. Sometime before Christmas a dog-handler had found McKee's battered case on the ridge above the farm. Shortly afterwards it had been removed by Americans who ignored the strict rules of evidence-gathering required under Scottish law and took the case away, replacing it some while later in a slightly different location, minus some of its contents.

On Christmas Eve a party of Scottish police officers based at Tundergarth were asked to accompany two Americans to the site where the case had been recovered. They were told that the Americans were employees of Pan Am, but the policemen strongly suspected they were intelligence agents. After trudging through the thick mist for half an hour, it dawned on the officers that the purpose of the venture was to find the 'cleansed' case, as if for the first time. Aware that they were being used, and fearing the consequences of colluding with anyone not observing the strict rules of evidence, they insisted that they should return to base, using the excuse of the deteriorating weather. Later the same day two British Transport Police dog-handlers from Glasgow duly obliged the Americans, no doubt unaware that they were not the first people to find the case.[34]

Exactly what had been taken from McKee's case after its initial removal, only the American agents can know for sure, but there are some clues.

Pan Am Heathrow ground hostess Linda Forsyth was one of the last people to see McKee alive. She was on duty in the Clipper lounge (so called because it catered for passengers flying Clipper class). As Flight 103 was checking in, she received a call from a colleague at the check-in area, informing her that a party of three Americans was about to come up to the lounge, one of whom was hoping for an upgrade to Clipper class, and one of whom was travelling Economy class. The person wanting the upgrade was McKee and he was delighted that she could organise it for him.

The two colleagues were Matthew Gannon, the CIA's deputy station chief at the US Embassy in Beirut, and Ronald Lariviere, a security officer at the embassy. All three had flown together from Cyprus, having left Beirut early in the morning. Forsyth recalls they were in high spirits, seemingly very glad to be returning home. Shortly before the flight was due to board they were joined by a fourth colleague, Daniel O'Connor, a security officer from the US Embassy in Nicosia, who had taken a later flight from Cyprus.

Forsyth was rather surprised when the four men asked to be seated separately – and even more so when they claimed not to know each other. Since they were giggling as they told her, she assumed they were fooling around, but in fact it was standard operating procedure for intelligence personnel to travel separately and the four men were still on active duty.[35]

A senior source within the US Defense Intelligence Agency has told the authors that McKee was the coordinator of a Special Forces group who were poised to make a rescue attempt on the American hostages held in Beirut. The source, who spoke on condition of anonymity, said the operation was at an 'advanced' stage, with extraction vehicles and air transport support arranged. Without any explanation the operation, which involved an American Delta Force unit, was called off. McKee, who had been involved in the intricate planning of what would have been a very daring rescue attempt, was said to be furious. When he questioned who had given the order to abandon the operation, he was told that it came from the top. When McKee asked how high, his commander told him the order had come from the White House. It is believed that McKee was returning with part of his unit to confront those whom he felt had put all of his men in jeopardy. By all accounts McKee would never have returned from a posting without authorisation and on this occasion he had no such authority, such was his concern.

Searchers in the Newcastleton Forest, near the English border, found documents which appeared to relate to the location of hostages in Lebanon. One policeman had a close look at these documents when they were being held at one of the temporary storerooms and found that they included detailed maps and plans which appeared to show the location of Western hostages. He also found part of what appeared to be a handwritten transcript of an interview.[36] Could McKee's case have included such material? Or maybe something even more sensitive?

The authorities' desperation to conceal the truth about McKee and his colleagues was illustrated by a strange incident involving David Johnston. On 1 February 1989 he filed a story for Radio Forth based on information from a reliable source, revealing the presence of the intelligence team on the plane and suggesting that they might have had the bomb planted in their luggage in Beirut. The story was broadcast at 8 a.m. By 9 a.m. two senior officers of Lothian and Borders Police had arrived at the offices of Radio Forth demanding to see Johnston. It puzzled him that they should know he was responsible for the story, because the report had not actually carried his voice. Since all his information had come from official sources in Britain and elsewhere, it was not as if he knew something that the police did not. When he eventually sat down to talk to the officers, it became clear that their real concern was to find out who was behind the leak. For six hours they repeatedly demanded to know his source, but he refused to disclose it.

In desperation, the police offered a strange solution to the impasse. They said they would take him, there and then, to see Prime Minister Margaret Thatcher so that he could reveal his source to her, in private. He was warned that if he refused the offer he could be sent to prison for contempt. When Johnston declined, the case was referred to the prosecuting authorities, but not the local Procurator Fiscal's office, which would normally handle obstruction of justice offences. Due to what the police described as the 'extraordinary' circumstances of the case, it was sent directly to the Lord Advocate Lord Fraser of Carmyllie. If the authorities had hoped to stifle the story, their efforts had by now backfired; the media had hold of the story and Johnston was fast becoming a journalistic *cause célèbre*. On 3 February the Lord Advocate announced he would not proceed with charges.[37]

This was by no means the last tussle the reporter was to have with the Scottish authorities. When he published *Lockerbie – The Real Story* in July 1989, he caused both the Lord Advocate, Lord Fraser, and the recently appointed Chief Constable of Dumfries and Galloway, George Esson, to be up in arms. Most of the controversy was caused by Johnston's allegation that the authorities had covered up a horrendous mistake which resulted in the families of two of the American victims being sent the wrong remains for burial. The author's sources told him the bodies that *should* have gone to the two families, although completely intact, were quietly incinerated, along with pieces of flesh and bone which could not be positively linked to any of the victims. The information about one of the bodies was very precise: it was a young man in his 30s wearing Union Jack underpants. The other body, Johnston alleged, was a woman's.

Lord Fraser said the book made interesting reading but contained 'much which is inaccurate or speculative'. George Esson was more outspoken, claiming that much of the book was 'factually inaccurate or simply untrue' and calling some of it 'totally outrageous'. It was notable, however, that neither man was able to refute any of the specific claims in the book. Esson declared that he was 'not prepared to divert the resources of this criminal investigation in order to respond to, or to publicise material which is so widely off the mark that it is offensive'.[38]

Whether Esson liked it or not, Johnston's account tallied with one of the oddest of all the many unusual episodes to unfold on the Scottish hillsides in the grim days after the crash. It centred on Dr David Fieldhouse,[39] a police surgeon from Bradford in West Yorkshire, who offered his services to the police after learning of the crash from the BBC *Nine O'clock News*. With 19 years' experience, Fieldhouse was used to dealing with dead and injured; moreover, having been on hand at the 1985 Bradford City fire disaster, he knew the type of procedures necessary when the number of casualties was large.

The police were grateful for the offer and he immediately made his way up to Lockerbie, reaching the town by eleven o'clock that evening. Once it was clear that no one would be found alive, he was asked to attend the Shawhill area near to the Tundergarth, where it had been reported that there were two or three bodies. On arrival, he found that volunteer search dog-handlers had already been busy finding bodies.

His grim task was to declare the bodies as dead and leave labels on them carrying his initials and a number. Under Scottish legal procedures a police officer had to be in attendance when each body was declared dead, so Dr Fieldhouse was allocated an officer who remained with him all night, before being replaced by three officers from the Cumbria force.

For the next 15 hours he worked virtually non-stop. The Dumfries and Galloway Constabulary could not provide him with enough labels, but he had his own supply. To protect them from the foul weather, he put each one inside a disposable plastic glove and tucked it somewhere that it was unlikely to blow away. Having received no instructions about how to number the bodies, he gave each one its own number, prefixed with his initials 'DCF'. At the same time he kept a written record of his DCF codes and the order in which he had seen the bodies, as well as a decription of them and their location.

By nightfall on 22 December Fieldhouse had certified 59 bodies dead. Of those, how many had been given a 'DCF' number and an additional one already had a police label on it. During that entire time he had just one biscuit to eat. Exhausted, he returned to Lockerbie to report on his activities. A debriefing meeting took place that evening, from which he was excluded, but afterwards he spoke to Detective Chief Inspector Gordon Alston, the officer in charge of the Tundergarth search area. He explained where he had been searching and how many bodies he had found, using a map to show their approximate location. He then arranged to meet Alston by Tundergarth Church at nine o'clock the following morning.

When Dr Fieldhouse arrived at Tundergarth Church well before 9 a.m. on the 23rd, he was told that Chief Inspector Alston had been delayed. Another police officer told him that, despite what he had done, all the bodies he had found were to be re-coded. Recognising that Alston would have more pressing tasks to attend to, and knowing that there was nothing more he could do, after waiting an hour and a quarter he decided to return to Bradford.

On arriving home he immediately wrote a letter for the attention of the senior investigating officer at Lockerbie, giving a full report and enclosing the notes he had made about the 59 bodies. On 30 December he wrote another letter to Leslie Sharp, Chief Constable of Cumbria, to congratulate him on the conduct of the officers who had accompanied him on 22 December. On 5 January Sharp wrote back to thank him for his words of praise and to express his gratitude for all his efforts. In April he received a request from the Lockerbie police to provide a statement about his activities on 21 and 22 December. He immediately obliged with an eight-page formal statement which he sent on 22 April, together with a covering letter and maps.

In the early weeks of 1989, Fieldhouse had given up five or six days to sit with police officers at a computer at the Lockerbie Incident Centre. Together they tried to match his records with those of the police and with medical, dental and other personal information provided by relatives. The situation was complicated by the fact that the police had initiated their own numbering system, using their own labels. The 'DCF' numbers from Fieldhouse's own labels appeared to have been ignored, which meant he had to match the bodies with those relabelled by the police. Had the details from his original labels been recorded on the computer this task would have been relatively easy, but they were not. To further complicate matters, there were a number of discrepancies between the map references worked out by Dr Fieldhouse and those recorded by the police officers who had relabelled the bodies.

Despite these hurdles, after a few sessions at the computer, it was possible to match the records for the vast majority of victims and come up with a conclusive identification. There were two notable exceptions. The first was the body labelled by Fieldhouse as DCF 50. The notes written at the time by Fieldhouse read, 'Male 20s, blue jeans, red-&-white blue-striped pants. Field going north from the monument.' The police had given the body their own number, B170, and their notes recorded it as being found at map reference 177 802. Whereas all the other body numbers on the police list had names next to them, B170 was marked 'unident. male'. From the description it seemed very much as if DCF 50 was the young man in the Union Jack underpants whom David Johnston claimed was secretly cremated along with the unidentified remains. Even if it was not, the police there could be in no doubt from the note that an intact body remained unidentified.

The second case involved a body that Dr Fieldhouse had labelled DCF 12. He noted that it was male, found 'N. East of farm, top field.' On checking the map afterwards, he worked out that it had been lying at approximate grid reference 197 801. Unlike all the 58 bodies he had found, none of the bodies relabelled by the police matched DCF 12. Nor did the police have any records casting light on the identity of the victim; as far as they were concerned, DCF 12 did not exist. Fieldhouse was nevertheless sure of his information, because DCF 12 was one of three bodies that he found to the east of the road that runs south from Bankshill to Stockbridgehill. Had it been in a cluster of 50, Fieldhouse recognised that a mistake would have been possible, but he believed it extremely unlikely that he would make a mistake with one that was found in a group of only three. Furthermore, of those three, it was the only one that lay to the north of a wall that ran eastward from the road. After many hours on the computer at Lockerbie Academy, Dr Fieldhouse was confident enough of his information to tell the police in his sworn statement of 22 April: 'I am absolutely certain that the body coded DCF 12 . . . was in the fields just east of Shawhill Farm.'

The mystery of DCF 12 becomes even more intriguing when considered in the light of another of the strange tales to emerge in the hours after the crash. On the afternoon of 22 December, the senior official at Carlisle airport, who witnessed the large influx of American agents the previous evening, was on hand when a second specially arranged flight arrived. Like the earlier flight, it carried plainclothed Americans, but this time they brought with them a single hefty coffin. On discovering that they were being filmed by a cameraman from the local Border Television station, they became agitated and demanded that he stop. However, since the local police had granted permission to film, the airport official allowed him to continue.[40] The pictures were broadcast that evening, but no explanation was ever given for the coffin. Could it have been used to spirit DCF 12 back to the US?

Such speculation was of no concern to Dr Fieldhouse. He assumed the discrepancies in the records were due to problems with map reading. Having provided his statement to the police, as far as he was concerned, the matter was closed.

As we will see, he was in for a rude shock. Like many of the people who stumbled across Lockerbie's sinister secrets, he would fall victim to official smears and distortions. The authorities on both sides of the Atlantic would never concede the existence of the extra body, the drugs, the cash, the red tarpaulin, and the mysterious Americans. Some of these finds would remain a mystery, while others were pointers to a very nasty scandal. From day one an altogether more palatable reality was evolving which would keep the lid on the scandal of Flight 103.

2. WARNINGS OF DISASTER

Not everyone was surprised by the Lockerbie bombing. Indeed to those sections of the Western intelligence services responsible for monitoring Middle East terrorism, it probably seemed inevitable. For them the second half of 1988 was an unusually busy time. They were all braced for trouble.

In November the PLO leader, Yasser Arafat, made the historic announcement that the organisation was ending its campaign of terrorism against Israel. Hardline Palestinian groups viewed the move as an appalling sell-out and it was anticipated that they would step up their terrorist activities in order to discredit the initiative.[1]

But it was an event months earlier that had first triggered the bout of nerves. On 3 July 1988 a civilian airliner making the short journey across the Persian Gulf, from Bandar Abbas in Iran to Dubai, was shot out of the sky by two surface-to-air missiles fired from a US Navy battlecruiser, the *Vincennes*. Iran Air Flight 655 was carrying 290 passengers and crew, most of whom were making their way to Mecca for the festival of *Hajj*, the most sacred day in the Muslim calendar. There were no survivors.

According to the crew of the *Vincennes*, the ship's computer-controlled command information centre had shown the plane to be rapidly descending towards it, which made them fear it was an Iranian F-14 jet fighter. In the minutes before he ordered the attack, the ship's commander, William C. Rogers III, sent out ten warning messages but received no response. By the time he realised that he had made a monstrous error, it was too late. By coincidence a television crew was present on the ship when the attack took place. Footage beamed around the world showed the exultant crew as the radar registered a hit and then captured their embarrassed silence as it became apparent that they had killed innocent civilians.

The shoot-down understandably caused outrage in Iran. To a nation fed on a diet of anti-Western propaganda, it seemed to confirm all its worse fears about America. Iranian television declared it 'the greatest war crime of our era' and called for attacks on US targets. President Ali Khamenei declared that Iran would use 'all our might . . . wherever and whenever we decide'[2] and Tehran Radio declared that the attack would be avenged in 'blood-spattered skies'.[3]

If the US government hoped to calm the situation, it went precisely the wrong way about it. Appearing on national television a few hours after the shoot-down, President Ronald Reagan, rather than apologising to Iran, said the mistake had arisen as a result of attacks by Iranian gunboats. Speaking at a Pentagon press conference, Chair of the Joint Chiefs of Staff Admiral William Crowe suggested such incidents, coupled with the belief that they were about to be attacked by a hostile warplane, gave the *Vincennes* a legitimate right to self-defence, believing the gunboats to have been joined by a hostile warplane. This glossed over the fact that, even if the crew had been correct, they would not have faced significant danger, since F-14s are thought to be ineffective against warships, particularly those as heavily armoured as the *Vincennes*.

Two weeks after the incident the US government gave further justification for the ship's actions. Addressing the United Nations, Vice President George Bush declared that the shoot-down had occurred 'in the midst of a naval attack initiated by Iranian vessels against a neutral vessel and subsequently against the *Vincennes* when she came to the aid of an innocent ship in distress'.

William Rogers was praised and the whole crew were awarded the Combat Action Ribbon. The ship's anti-air warfare officer was even congratulated for managing an 'exceptionally smooth flow of information' and for efficiently carrying out the missile-firing procedure. Further salt was rubbed into Iranian wounds when Rogers was later decorated. The citation praised his 'tactical skills' in dealing with Iranian gunboats, but made no mention of Flight 655. Such generosity was not extended to the relatives of the flight's victims, who never received an apology for the awful blunder and had to wait eight years for compensation.

As time went by, disturbing evidence emerged to support an Iranian government allegation that the downing of Flight 655 was an act of aggression by the US.[4] A US Navy frigate, *Sides*, had been about 20 miles away at the time of the attack. Its computer system showed that Flight 655, far from descending towards the *Vincennes*, was actually still climbing after take-off. It was also discovered that seven out of the ten messages sent by the *Vincennes* were on a frequency unobtainable by civilian aircraft. Even the remaining three messages were unlikely to have been received. The only message likely to have got through was from the *Sides*, but it was sent just 39 seconds before the *Vincennes* let loose her missiles. The commander of the *Sides*, David Carlson, was particularly disturbed by the affair. He revealed that a number of fellow commanders considered the *Vincennes* to be overly aggressive and that even before the 3 July incident, they had given it the nickname 'RoboCruiser'.

Four years on, Admiral Crowe, who was by then retired from the US Navy, made the startling admission that at the time of the incident the *Vincennes* was violating Iranian territorial waters. The House Armed Services Committee demanded that Crowe reappear before its members, who were understandably anxious to discover why the public had not been told this crucial fact at the time. Crowe implied that no one had previously asked the right question.

Following the hearing, on 6 August, the chair of the committee, Les Aspin, declared that his investigative staff would continue to look into the affair, but the initiative was short-lived. The following month Crowe announced that he was supporting candidate Bill Clinton in the forthcoming presidential election. Following Clinton's victory, he was appointed Chair of the President's Foreign Intelligence Advisory Board; Aspin was appointed Defense Secretary. A few months later Crowe was made Ambassador to the UK; Aspin resigned as Defense Secretary and was appointed to Crowe's former position.

Were it not for David Carlson and others, the truth might well have remained buried. By piecing together video footage, the ship's data tapes, and interviews with crew members, it was discovered that the excuses offered by George Bush were nonsense. The Iranian gunboat did not start the skirmish by firing on the *Vincennes*, but rather fired back when it found the cruiser bearing down on it with all guns blazing. It tried to retreat into Iranian territorial waters, but the *Vincennes* ignored the boundary and continued firing.

The Iranian government at the time of Ayatollah Khomeni, although usually painted as fanatically pursuing an unrelentingly hardline interpretation of Muslim law, harboured a range of political leanings, from extremists to pragmatists. Despite its wish to promote Islam on a global scale, it also recognised the realities of international politics. Many times it had threatened to wage war on the West, and for the most part the threats turned out to be hot air. But, after the downing of Iran Air 655, elements within the regime were determined to back up words with action.

The US authorities were well aware of this. Just two days after the plane was downed, the US Air Force's Military Airlift Command issued a warning to its civilian contractors: 'We believe Iran will strike back in a tit-for-tat fashion – mass casualties for mass casualties.' The warning continued, 'We believe Europe is a likely target for a retaliatory attack. This is due primarily to the large concentration of Americans and the established terrorist infrastructures in place throughout Europe.' On 7 July the warning was picked up by the State Department and disseminated via its computer bulletin board.[5]

Nearly four months later Iran's revenge mission was unearthed. On 26 October 1988 the West German Federal police, the *Bundeskriminalamt* (BKA), arrested a cell of suspected members of a Syrian-based radical Palestinian group, the Popular Front for the Liberation of Palestine – General Command (PFLP-GC). These events, which are described in detail in the next chapter, were to become of central importance to the Lockerbie saga. The group had blown up airliners in the past and were known to have discussed a revenge attack with anti-Western militants in the Iranian government over the previous months. Most importantly of all, they were caught red-handed with a bomb built into a Toshiba radio-cassette player that was designed to detonate at altitude.

The arrests had at least put paid to Iran's plans. Or had they? The cell's leader, Hafez Dalkamoni, and the bomb-maker himself, Marwan Khreesat, confessed to having made a number of other aircraft bombs. What was more, these bombs were still at large because the BKA had failed to spot what lay under their noses. Furthermore, most of those arrested were released and it seemed likely that other group members and sympathisers had avoided the BKA's attentions. A classified security bulletin issued by the US Defense Intelligence Agency (DIA) on 1 December 1988 stated:

> Although there have been no recent publicised threats of retaliation against the US for the 3 July Iranian airbus shootdown, Tehran's general intent to conduct terrorist attacks against the US continues . . . Some Middle Eastern terrorist groups have conducted assassinations and bombings in West Germany and have the infrastructure to conduct both bombings and assassinations.[6]

The BKA also knew there was no room for complacency. In the wake of the Autumn Leaves raids, details of the Toshiba bomb had to be disseminated to all interested parties. The obvious priority was to make sure that the international airline industry was warned of the threat.

On 9 November the BKA released a warning through Interpol, and other security channels, about the PFLP-GC's bombs and, six days later, hosted a meeting to brief the international authorities concerned with airline safety about the radio-cassette bomb. British representatives were among those in attendance and on 17 November they passed on details of the briefing to security officials in the Department of Transport. The following day the Department also received a copy of a bulletin containing the same information that had been issued to US airlines by the American Federal Aviation Authority (FAA). On 22 November the Department of Transport sent a telex to UK airports warning about the Toshiba bomb and pointing to the possible existence of other barometric bombs. The following day the authorities at London's Heathrow airport distributed their own warning to security staff about the Toshiba bomb, stating it was 'imperative that when screening or searching radios, radio-cassette players, and other electrical equipment, staff are to be extra vigilant'.

The Heathrow authorities built a dummy radio-cassette bomb and circulated it among their staff, along with photographs, for training purposes. Over the next three or four weeks, the Department of Transport received additional information and photographs of the Toshiba bomb from the German authorities. On the basis of these its officials began to prepare a circular for the British aviation industry, which was signed by the department's Principal Aviation Security Adviser, James Jack, on 19 December. However, problems over obtaining reproduction colour photographs, coupled with delays in the Christmas post, meant that most airlines did not receive the circular until the New Year of 1989, well after the Lockerbie bombing.

By the time the circular was being prepared, the airline industry had been put on alert by another major development. On 5 December an anonymous Arab man telephoned the US Embassy in the Finnish capital, Helsinki, and warned of an imminent bomb attack on a US airliner. He said that it would take place some time during the next fortnight and that the target would be a Pan American flight from Frankfurt to the US. Two people were implicated in the alleged plot, both of whom were described as members of the Abu Nidal Organisation (ANO). 'Abu Nidal' was the *nom de guerre* of Sabri Al Banna, whose group was probably the most notorious Middle East terrorist organisation of the 1980s. Like the PFLP-GC, it was opposed to Yasser Arafat's PLO.

One of those named in the warning was Yassan Garadat who, the caller claimed, was an Arab man based in Finland; the other, who was said to be living in Frankfurt, was referred to only as 'Abdullah'. The caller said that Abdullah would provide Garadat with a bomb and Garadat would in turn plant it on an unidentified Finnish woman.[7]

Another name to be dropped by the caller was a 'Mr Soloranta'. This was particularly intriguing, because a notorious ANO bomber, Samir Kadar, had married a Finnish woman whose maiden name was Soloranta. Kadar was reported to have died in a botched bomb attempt in Athens the previous July, but there were rumours that he had escaped death and gone to ground.[8]

The official who took the call was acting Regional Security Officer

Kenneth Luzzi. He informed his security colleagues, including a CIA officer based at the embassy, and also alerted the Finnish intelligence service. The warning was passed on to Washington DC and, like the earlier 'Toshiba warning', to Interpol. Two days later the FAA issued a security bulletin to all US airlines and embassies. Given that the warning was of particular relevance to Pan Am, on the morning of 8 December the airline's headquarters telexed its Heathrow-based Corporate Security Manager, Jim Berwick, with instructions to travel to Helsinki as soon as possible to investigate the warning. Berwick flew to Helsinki that evening and met Luzzi at the airport the following morning.

Four days on, the warning appeared to have been thoroughly checked out and Berwick left the meeting with the impression that it was a hoax. He was told that the caller was involved in drug smuggling and that Yassan Garadat, who was implicated in the bomb plot, was in fact part of a rival smuggling operation. The purpose of the call, it seemed, was simply to undermine the rival. The name of the caller was never officially acknowledged, but he was later revealed to be Samra Mahayoun, a young Palestinian living in Helsinki on a student visa.[9]

The seemingly relaxed attitude of the Helsinki embassy did not permeate through to Moscow, where the US Embassy's administrative counsellor, William Kelly, drafted a memo for the staff notice board. Addressed to 'All Embassy Personnel', it read:

> Post has been notified by the Federal Aviation Administration that on 5 December 1988, an unidentified individual telephoned a US diplomatic facility in Europe and stated that sometime within the next two weeks there would be a bombing attempt against a Pan American airliner flying from Frankfurt to the United States. The FAA reports that the reliability of the information cannot be assessed at this point, but the appropriate police authorities have been notified and are pursuing the matter. Pan Am also has been notified. In view of the lack of confirmation of this information, post leaves to the discretion of individual travellers any decisions on altering personal travel plans or changing to another American carrier. This does not absolve the traveller from flying an American carrier.

In disseminating the warning in this way, Kelly appeared to be in breach of the FAA's guidelines. When asked subsequently to explain the possible breach, embassy staff said they had been unsure of those guidelines and that the FAA had failed to respond to their request for clarification. The ambassador concurred with senior staff that it was unfair to keep their juniors in the dark about the warning, so on 13 December the notice was posted up.[10] Had the warning genuinely been a hoax, the Moscow staff's anxiety could have been minimised by a simple phone call to Kenneth Luzzi in Helsinki, but whether or not anyone made one remains a mystery. Karen Decker, a young consular official working in the Moscow embassy at the time said, 'There was a real push in the Embassy community to make sure that everybody was aware that there had been a terrorist threat made, and that people flying Western carriers going through such points as Frankfurt should change their tickets.'[11] It has also never been properly established how many people changed their travel plans as a result of the embassy notice.

Pan Am staff at all airports had already been told to be on the lookout for radio-cassette players following the earlier Toshiba warning, but Jim Berwick knew that, despite Luzzi's reassurances, he could not afford to ignore this additional bomb threat. He ordered special screening of all women passengers from Finland transferring to transatlantic flights in Frankfurt.

At the time, Pan Am was given no evidence to suggest that the Toshiba warning, like the Helsinki warning, might be linked in any way to a planned attack on its aircraft; but, incredible as it may seem, the US authorities were in possession of just such information. US intelligence officials would later concede that, prior to the Autumn Leaves raids, members of the PFLP-GC cell had monitored Pan Am's facilities at Frankfurt airport. Furthermore, a few days before the Helsinki warning, the US State Department's Office of Diplomatic Security received a specific warning that Palestinian radicals were planning to target the airline. When the department's digest of the warning was eventually made public its source was concealed, but the relevant section read:

> Team of Palestinians not assoc [iated] with Palestinian Liberation Organisation (PLO) intends to atk [attack] US tgts [targets] in Europe. Time frame is present. Tgts specified are Pan Am airlines and US mil[itary] bases.[12]

The PFLP-GC was, of course 'not associated' with the PLO. Moreover, by the time the warning was issued, the PFLP-GC had assembled a number of bombs in Germany designed to blow up aircraft, all but one of which remained at large. Yet the intelligence services chose to keep this information from Pan Am and the public – the warning remained a secret until it slipped out, possibly by accident, six and a half years later.

The source of the warning may well have been the Israeli secret service, Mossad. It has been reported that Mossad informed MI6 in late November 1988 that an anti-Arafat, pro-Syrian group would attempt to sabotage a civilian airliner flying out of Europe near the Christmas holiday season. MI6 allegedly dismissed the warning as 'alarmist rubbish',[13] but may still have passed it on to the Americans.

And this was not the only information that was received by MI6 but withheld from the world's airlines. In late November 1988, the respected investigative author David Yallop travelled to Libya to interview Colonel Gadafy and Abu Nidal (who at that point was based in Libya). Before leaving, Yallop had spoken to Brian Crozier, the former head of the London-based Institute for the Study of Conflict, who has made no secret of his affiliations to the CIA and MI6. He asked Yallop to put three or four specific questions to Nidal and Yallop duly obliged. Nidal answered the questions, but the author assumed that Crozier would be more interested in another snippet of information. Nidal revealed that he was being put under great pressure by both Syria and Iraq to resume terror tactics. The reason, he explained, was that both countries hoped to blame the attack on the PLO, and so discredit Yasser Arafat's recent peace initiative.

On returning to London, Yallop asked Crozier to meet him as soon as possible with an MI6 officer present. Yallop presented Crozier with an eight-page report. This covered a variety of subjects, including Nidal's veiled warning, then elaborated, telling them the attack would probably be against an American target in Europe and would almost certainly emanate from Damascus. To Yallop's astonishment, the MI6 officer seemed more interested in Nidal's personal habits than this potentially vital piece of intelligence. He insisted that Crozier pass on the information to the CIA, in the hope that the agency would take it more seriously. Weeks later Crozier would confirm that he had shared the warning with the CIA, but, much to Yallop's chagrin, the information apparently went no further and certainly not as far as the world's airlines.[14]

In the early hours of 9 December 1988 a unit of the elite Golani Brigade of the Israeli Army launched a surprise attack on the PFLP-GC's Southern Lebanon headquarters at Al-Na'ameh, near Damour, about ten miles south of Beirut. During a bloody three-hour battle the Israeli troops were able to gain access to part of the warren of underground tunnels that made up the base. Two days later the *Jerusalem Post* newspaper reported that they managed to seize documents relating to the PFLP-GC's planned terrorist activities. A number of intelligence sources have claimed that these included a plan to attack a Pan American flight out of Frankfurt during that same month of December and that the Israelis warned West German and American intelligence.

None of the published warnings specified Pan Am Flight 103 from Frankfurt to Detroit via London and New York; none mentioned the date of 21 December. As that date approached a number of Western government employees who were scheduled to take the doomed flight – besides the US embassy employees in Moscow – changed their travel plans. These included Chris Revell, a US Army combat engineer, returning from his posting in West Germany. He and his wife had been due to fly on Flight 103 on 21 December, but they changed the booking and travelled a few days earlier.[15] By coincidence his father, Oliver 'Buck' Revell, was Executive Assistant Director of the US Federal Bureau of Investigation (FBI): effectively number-three man in the Bureau, he had overall responsibility not only for its criminal investigations, but also for combating terrorism.

Another group risked travelling with Pan Am even though they, or their deputies, would almost certainly have had knowledge of the Helsinki warning. South African Foreign Minister Pik Botha, the Defence Minister Magnus Malan, intelligence service chief General Nils van Tonder, Assistant Director of Foreign Affairs Rusty Evans and eight other senior South African government officials were travelling to the United Nations headquarters in New York to sign the Namibia peace accord. It was originally intended that they should take Flight 103, but their plans were changed. Having arrived in London on the morning of 21 December, they took the earlier Pan Am Flight 101,[16] which, unlike Flight 103, received special security checks at Heathrow.[17]

Some American government officials played down reports that they had been booked to travel on Flight 103. Among them was Steven Greene, Assistant Administrator in the Office of Intelligence of the US Drugs Enforcement Administration (DEA). On 21 December he was due to travel back to the US from Europe, where he had been attending a meeting. A 1989 US government memorandum stated that he had been due to take Flight 103, but was forced to make a late cancellation.[18] Greene said that the author of the memorandum had been mistaken.

The US ambassador to Lebanon, John McCarthy, also claimed that government officials had misinterpreted his travel plans. On the morning of the 21 December he flew by helicopter from Beirut to Cyprus, along with his secretary, his bodyguard Ronald Lariviere and the CIA's deputy chief of station in Beirut, Matthew Gannon. Risking separation from his bodyguard, McCarthy allowed him to fly on with Gannon to London and that same evening he and Gannon were able to connect with Flight 103. The ambassador and his secretary stayed on in Cyprus for a day and returned to the US on 22 December. Shortly afterwards, the State Department's intelligence chief Ronald Spiers told journalists: 'My understanding is he [McCarthy] was scheduled to be on that plane, but got held up in Nicosia.'[19] McCarthy would later describe this claim as a 'misunderstanding',[20] but, as we shall see, his account of events did not fit with other facts. Spiers may also have had a lucky escape, telling the reporters, 'Ironically, I might have been on [Flight 103] myself since I just got back from Europe last night.'[21]

By virtue of their involvement with US intelligence, Matthew Gannon and Ronald Lariviere may have known about the various warnings that had been circulated in recent weeks. Perhaps life in war-torn Beirut had made them used to terrorist risks, or perhaps they had been told they need not take the warnings seriously. As they joined Pan Am Flight 103 at Heathrow airport, just before 6 p.m. on 21 December, they perhaps figured to themselves that their superiors would not have allowed them to travel if the flight was at serious risk.

No doubt their fellow passengers had similar faith in the Western intelligence services. Had these people known that a number of sophisticated bombs, designed to blow up aircraft, were at large in the country where the flight originated, they would probably have felt much less comfortable. Had they also known that, within the past three weeks, there had been a number of strong indications that radical Palestinians were planning to attack Pan Am, they would most surely have chosen to fly with another airline.

3. AUTUMN LEAVES

Iran, the PFLP-GC and the group's Syrian hosts were the prime suspects for the Lockerbie bombing. And with good reason. Within days of the shoot-down of Iran Air Flight 655 by the USS *Vincennes*, on 3 July 1988, the first signs emerged of a possible Iranian counter-strike. US intelligence learned that the PFLP-GC's leader, Ahmed Jibril, had met government officials in Iran. The CIA later acknowledged that Jibril had offered his services to avenge Flight 655.[1]

This was a particularly disturbing development: not only was the PFLP-GC one of the most ruthless terrorist groups in the Middle East, but also it had a track record in blowing up aircraft. The group was formed by Jibril in 1968 after he broke away from George Habash's Popular Front for the Liberation of Palestine (PFLP). Although born in Palestine, Jibril had lived in Syria since 1948 and was trained by the Syrian military as an engineer. In 1964 he began terrorist operations against Israel and shortly afterwards was among the founders of the National Front for the Liberation of Palestine. In 1967 this metamorphosed into the PFLP, but the alliance was short-lived as Jibril believed Habash was too concerned with ideology and not sufficiently committed to armed struggle.[2]

On 21 February 1970 the PFLP-GC joined the major league of international terrorism when it planted bombs aboard two European airliners destined for Israel. The first was an Austrian Airlines flight from Frankfurt via Vienna. As the plane climbed to 10,000 feet, the device exploded in the baggage hold and blew a two-foot hole in the fuselage. The pilot was able to keep control and made an emergency landing back at Frankfurt; all those aboard escaped unhurt. Those on board Swissair Flight 330 from Zurich to Tel Aviv were not so lucky. Once again a bomb had been planted in the luggage hold, but this one did not explode until the plane had reached 14,000 feet. Initially the pilot seemed to cope, but the damage was too great and the plane plummeted into a forest, killing all 47 passengers and crew.

In August 1972 the group again targeted a civilian airliner, this time one belonging to the Israeli national airline El Al. The plane was heading from Rome to Tel Aviv, with 140 people on board, and had reached around

15,000 feet when a bomb exploded. Fortunately the pilot was able to return safely to Rome and there were no casualties. The subsequent investigation established that the device had been built into a record player carried by two young and unsuspecting British women: they told the police it had been given to them as a gift by a pair of Arab men who had befriended them in Rome.

Investigators discovered that the two earlier bombs had been built into transistor radios. All three appeared to have been detonated by barometric switches, activated by the drop in pressure that accompanies gains in altitude. They therefore had the advantage over conventional timing devices in that they would not detonate the bomb while still on the ground if the flight was unexpectedly delayed. A new departure in high-tech terrorism, the bombs were the handiwork of young PFLP-GC operative Marwan Khreesat. When Italian police arrested the two men who had given the record-player bomb to the English girls in Rome, they confessed that Khreesat had handed it to them in Yugoslavia. Yet despite this, and other damning evidence, Jibril's technical wizard remained at large. Over the next 16 years he appeared to go into retirement, living quietly in the Jordanian capital Amman where he worked repairing televisions.

Ever the military engineer, Khreesat's old boss Ahmed Jibril retained his penchant for technical innovations. In November 1987, mounting one of the most audacious operations in the history of Middle East terrorism, two of his men used motorised hang-gliders to fly over the Israeli border from Lebanon. Once again their destination was an Israeli army base in Qiryat Shemona. They were equipped with radio transmitters, infra-red binoculars, and armed with hand grenades and machine guns fitted with silencers. The element of surprise allowed them to kill six Israeli troops before one of them was gunned down. The other died when his glider crashed.

The previous year, Israeli security officials at Heathrow airport foiled an attack that had chilling echoes of the PFLP-GC's earlier airline bombings. On 17 April a young pregnant Irish woman, called Anne-Marie Murphy, was stopped at El Al's check-in counter and found to have a bomb built into her suitcase. Murphy was as surprised as anyone. She told security guards that the case had been given to her by her fiancé, a Jordanian called Nezar Hindawi. He had told her to fly to Israel with it and wait for him to join her a few days later. It turned out that Hindawi was working under the direct instructions of Syrian intelligence and had been scheduled to fly to Damascus at around the time the El Al flight had been due to explode. When his Syrian handlers learned that the bomb had been discovered, they ordered him not to fly and took him to the Syrian Embassy. A safe-house and change of identity was arranged, but Hindawi was beginning to panic. Believing the Syrians might kill him in order to cover their tracks, the following morning he broke free and turned himself in to the police.

A number of Western intelligence reports have claimed, without proof, that Hindawi was affiliated to the Abu Nidal Organisation. Others have suggested the whole operation was masterminded by Mossad, utilising deep cover agents, in order to discredit Syria. Whatever the truth of these allegations, there is compelling circumstantial evidence that the PFLP-GC was involved in the affair. It had a track record of mid-air bombings and of utilising young, European women as dupes. Hindawi's controller was Lieutenant-Colonel Haitham Sayid of Syrian Air Force intelligence. In turn, he answered to Brigadier-General Mohammed Khouli, one of the country's top intelligence chiefs and an extremely close confidant of President Hafez Al Assad. Khouli was reportedly closer to Ahmed Jibril than any other terrorist leader and Western intelligence estimated that they would brief each other at least once a week.

On 25 October 1986, six months after Hindawi's arrest, *The Times* obtained a letter, to his brother Awni, which he had attempted to have smuggled out of prison. It read:

> Go to Damascus and talk to brother Abu and Ahmed-Haitham of the following: Ahmed Jibril has two Israeli prisoners. Haitham has his word. Thatcher will be visiting Israel next Sunday. He has two Israeli prisoners. Abu has their words as well. A prisoner exchange should be organised which must include my brother Hazi. If necessary this can be accomplished in Thatcher's visit. Tell Haitham if necessary to include some foreigners from Beirut in exchange.[3]

Despite the group's intimate ties with the Assad regime, Syria was not the PFLP-GC's sole sponsor. During the mid-1980s the group is alleged to have received $20–25 million a year from the Libyan government of Colonel Gadafy. It is claimed that, in return, Jibril's troops and intelligence agents helped Libya in its war against its southern neighbour, Chad. As 1988 approached, however, Libyan funding was becoming less reliable. Since launching air raids on the Libyan capital, Tripoli, and the second city, Benghazi, in April 1986, the US had led an economic blockade against the country from which Gadafy was anxious to escape. Despite his fierce anti-Western rhetoric, he was shrewd enough to know that he had to keep groups like the PFLP-GC at arm's length. It was reported that Gadafy stopped funding the PFLP-GC, while his support for PLO leader Yasser Arafat's renunciation of violence in November 1988 put further distance between himself and Jibril.[3]

A far more significant ally for Jibril was Iran. When Iran went to war with its neighbour Iraq in 1980, most Arab nations sided with their fellow Arabs in Iraq – as did the PLO, which received financial support from Baghdad. Having historically been hostile to Iraq, Syria proved to be an exception and forged strong ties with Iran. The Syrian-controlled Palestinian groups followed suit, none more so than the PFLP-GC.

Shortly after the Iranian revolution Jibril announced, 'We have been in touch with Iranian activists since 1970. We have trained tens of their leaders, giving them arms and experience.' Given this background, it was perhaps inevitable that, during the early '80s, the PFLP-GC would continue to nurture contacts among the Iranian Revolutionary Guards and in due course develop a strong relationship with the new Iranian- and Syrian-backed Lebanese radical Islamic group Hizbullah.[4]

According to some reports, the strategic alliance between Syrian-backed Palestinian groups and Iranian-backed Shi'ites eventually came to fruition in a terrorist coalition called Interror. Its members, which included the PFLP-GC, Hizbullah and the Abu Nidal Organisation, pledged to wage war on Israel, Saudi Arabia and the West. Syria and Iran both promised to give extensive support. The Interror pact was allegedly formalised in a treaty signed at the Carlton Hotel, Beirut, on 20 December 1988 – the day before the Lockerbie bombing.[5]

In Jibril's case his embrace of the radical Islam was as much about the continuing need for financial support as it was about forging strategic alliances. Unlike the PLO, the PFLP-GC did not have widespread investments to provide it with a sound financial base. Instead, it relied on handouts from various governments. By July 1988 the need for funds was reportedly acute: Libyan support was dwindling and the group may also have been still feeling the effects of a drastic reduction in the financial support from the Assad regime from 1986 to 1987, the consequence of a sharp economic downturn brought about by economic sanctions imposed on Syria after Nezar Hindawi's attempt to blow up the El Al flight from Heathrow.

Jibril would have been well aware that the Iranian government wanted to avenge the downing of Flight 655, but that it needed to be discreet and would therefore be looking for terrorist proxies to do its dirty work. He must also have known that the contract would be very lucrative. His close relations with Tehran, coupled with his group's long-standing expertise and experience in aeroplane bombings, meant they were the hot favourites to win the contract.

US intelligence was tipped off about Jibril's movements by the Israeli intelligence service Mossad, which naturally had more reason than any other spy service to keep close tabs on him. Shortly after the *Vincennes* incident, Mossad allegedly intercepted several messages between Jibril's headquarters in Damascus and the Sheik Abdulah barracks, which was the Revolutionary Guards' main base in Lebanon's Bekaa Valley. Jibril was apparently desperate to set up a meeting with Iranian hardliners and a week or so later he travelled to Tehran. For the next few months, it seems, Israeli, US and other Western intelligence services kept a very close watch on the PFLP-GC's activities. US intelligence sources revealed that, in the wake of the initial visit to Tehran, there were further meetings in the Iranian capital, and in Beirut and the Bekaa Valley. They claimed the US National Security Agency intercepted a telephone conversation, on a non-secure line, between Jibril and Iranian Interior Minister, Ali Akbar Mohtashemi, in which Jibril made oblique references to a number of US targets in Europe that his group could hit, for the right price.[6]

Mohtashemi was the most obvious point of contact for Jibril. Not only was he the leading hardliner in the Iranian Government, but his prior experience as ambassador to Syria, and his role in nurturing Hizbullah, meant he was uniquely well qualified to assess the capabilities of terrorist groups. Although the haggling continued for some weeks, Mohtashemi knew that Jibril was a man he could trust, and by September he appeared to have given the go-ahead for an operation which would exact revenge on the basis of 'an eye for an eye.'[7] Liaison with Tehran was to be carried out through the Iranian Revolutionary Guards in Lebanon.

One of the participants in discussions with Iran was Jibril's right-hand man, Hafez Kassem Dalkamoni. Born in Palestine in 1945, he had been a loyal member of the PFLP-GC since its foundation in the late 1960s. In 1969 his lower right leg was blown off when a bomb exploded prematurely during a commando raid on an electricity supply line in northern Israel. At the time of the negotiations with Iran, Dalkamoni was running the PFLP-GC's European operation. In January 1988 the job had taken him to the German town of Neuss, a town on the western edge of the massive industrial conurbation of the River Ruhr which centres on Düsseldorf. He stayed in an apartment at 16 Isarstrasse which was owned by his brother-in-law, local greengrocer Hashem Abbasi. The German intelligence service was aware of his presence, but apparently believed him to be on a weapons-buying mission. It is suspected that the Germans secretly agreed with Syria to leave Palestinian suspects alone, so long as no actual terrorist actions were launched on German soil. Whether this is true or not, the Germans initially seemed none too concerned by Dalkamoni's presence, only keeping him under intermittent surveillance.[8]

Mossad was far more vigilant. On 2 February 1988 it warned the BKA that the PFLP-GC had been training to blow up US military trains in Germany. On 26 April a bomb exploded on a railway line near the village of Hedemünden as a US troop train was passing. No one was hurt, but the bombing left major question marks over the German authorities' attitude towards the PFLP-GC. Incredibly, the train bombing was the second such incident to take place in Hedemünden in less than a year. The previous August another trainload of US troops had a lucky escape when a bomb exploded on the line. No one was arrested for either bombing. While the Germans stepped up their surveillance on Dalkamoni, it was not until much later that he was charged and convicted for his involvement in the bombings. In the meantime he went about his business unhindered for a further six months.

Those six months turned out to be one of extraordinary activity. In July, following Jibril's initial contacts with the Iranian government, the German foreign intelligence service, the *Bundesnachrichdienst* (BND) warned the BKA that 'a joint commando of PFLP-GC and Hizbullah' could be about to attack American installations in West Germany. The tip-off probably came from Mossad, who the following month alerted the Germans to a possible PFLP-GC strike against an Israeli handball team that was touring West Germany.[9] The attack did not take place, but, as the weeks passed by, it was clear something major was afoot.

In September, following the finalisation of the deal between Ahmed Jibril and the Iranian government, Dalkamoni travelled to the Yugoslavian town of Krusevac, where the PFLP-GC had a safe-house containing an arms cache. On 5 October he entered Germany once more and headed for his brother-in-law's apartment at 16 Isarstrasse. By this time the BKA decided that it must act seriously on the growing number of warnings it was receiving about the PFLP-GC and its associates. In early October one of its most senior anti-terrorist officers, Manfred Klink, met with the West German Federal prosecutor in Karlesruhe in charge of large-scale anti-terrorist operations. They agreed on a huge surveillance operation, to be code-named '*Herbslaub*', or 'Autumn Leaves', involving 24-hour monitoring of 16 targets in 6 cities.

Inevitably the most important target for Operation Autumn Leaves was 16 Isarstrasse. Within days of the surveillance beginning, a stream of visitors began to arrive there. The first of these visitors was Hashem Abassi's younger brother Ahmed, who was visiting from his adopted home of Sweden. For a few days he stuck closely with Dalkamoni, apparently acting as his translator. On 7 October they travelled to Berlin, and two days later to Frankfurt. On, or around, 13 October a white Volvo with Swedish licence plates was seen outside the flat, driven by someone of Arab origin. Along with two other unidentified Arab men, the driver took packages to and from the building. The following day all three left in the car.

Interest in these three men was overshadowed by the arrival of another Arab visitor to Dalkamoni's temporary apartment on 13 October. He had flown into Frankfurt with his wife earlier that day from the Jordanian capital, Amman. If they weren't already aware of it, the BKA surveillance unit would soon know the man's identity. He was none other than Marwan Khreesat, the PFLP-GC's master aeroplane bomber from the early 1970s. His sudden reunion with the man chosen by Ahmed Jibril to help negotiate a revenge attack with the Iranians was a chilling sign that the attack was imminent.

On 15 and 16 October the BKA discreetly followed Dalkamoni as he drove to visit various associates in cities to the south of Neuss. According to the BKA's surveillance log, one of those he called on was Martin Khadorah, who lived in a block of flats at 68 Bernadottstrasse, Frankfurt. Originally called Mahmoud Khadorah, he was Palestinian, but had changed his name on becoming a German citizen. The BKA suspected him of being involved in an aborted terrorist attack in 1983. Their suspicions were strengthened in August 1986, when two alleged PFLP-GC members, arrested in London, were found to have his name and telephone number among their contacts.

Shortly after Dalkamoni's visit Khadorah drove to the Yugoslav town of Maribor, where he was reported to have met Dalkamoni's brother, Bilal.

According to the BKA log, after visiting Khadorah on 15 or 16 October, Dalkamoni called on Yasim Kam-Nakche, a 59-year-old Syrian-born German citizen listed as living in Lambsheim and Bürstadt (both towns near Mannheim). The BKA log contained few other details about Kam-Nakche, other than that in December 1985 he had supplied a member of the Libyan News Service with information about the simultaneous gun massacres carried out that month by members of the Abu Nidal Organisation at Rome and Vienna airports.

On 16 October Dalkamoni and Kam-Nakche visited a Palestinian called Ahmed Kaplan, who lived at 40 Hauptstrasse in Hockenheim. The BKA surveillance team noted that, on arrival, 'they loaded up Dalkamoni's car with plastic bags and cartons'. One of the plastic bags, they recorded, 'had a brown unidentifiable substance in it'.

Dalkamoni must have travelled back to Neuss that same day, because the BKA eavesdropped on telephone calls he made from 16 Isarstrasse. The first was to a contact in Cyprus who was later identified as Habib Dajani, the Syrian proprietor of the King's Take-Away restaurant in Nicosia. Dajani told Dalkamoni he had recently obtained a German visa and that he would be travelling to Berlin the following Monday, 24 October. Questioned months later, Dajani claimed that his contacts with Dalkamoni had concerned the import and export of cars and that his planned trip to Germany was to swap his left-hand-drive car for a right-hand-drive one. However, Dajani admitted that he had for some time passed on messages on Dalkamoni's behalf. He told the police that among those to have left messages was Abu Nidal. It was concluded that the restaurateur was a 'willing participant' in Dalkamoni's operation, rather than an active terrorist.

Another whom Dalkamoni telephoned on 18 October was a person in Damascus, whom he called 'Abed'. Dalkamoni told him that everything would be ready in a couple of days and then put another person on the line, whom he referred to as 'Safi'. It was clear to the BKA that Safi was in fact Marwan Khreesat. The veteran bomb-maker told Abed that he had 'made some changes to the medicine' and added that it was now 'better and stronger'. On the basis of what he had been told, Abed concluded that 'things are under way'.

At 6.10 p.m. that same day Dalkamoni met a man described by the BKA as being in his early thirties, 170 cm tall, slim, bearded, with black hair and 'remarkably big ears'. After the meeting the man drove off in a car which it was discovered belonged to Bassam Ahmad Mustafa Radi, a 34-year-old Jordanian national who lived in Hamburg. According to the BKA's log, Radi had originally come to their attention in December 1986, when they were tipped off about a terrorist plot to distribute marker pens ingeniously booby-trapped with small explosive capsules to two of Berlin's Jewish community centres. The BKA's source named Radi as a member of the terrorist cell and an associate, Adnan Younis, as its ring-leader. Younis, who also went under the name 'Abu Tarek', was an intriguing character. A longstanding member of the PFLP-GC, he had lost a hand and an eye in an accidental explosion while undergoing training in Lebanon during the early '80s. At the time of the exploding pens incident he was running a pizzeria in Berlin and, despite the apparently damning evidence against him, he was never convicted.

By 20 October Dalkamoni was back in Frankfurt. He called Khreesat in Neuss to tell him that he was about to take delivery of 'three black tins with lids', 'gloves' and 'paste' from someone called 'Masoud'. Masoud, it would later be claimed, was a cover name for another PFLP-GC member, Abdel

Fattah Ghadanfar. The 47-year-old Jordanian held a number of passports under various aliases, including, bizarrely, Ronald John Bartle, of Redruth in Cornwall. Up until recently he had lived in Damascus, but the BKA was reportedly told that he moved to West Germany on the orders of his superiors in the PFLP-GC. After Dalkamoni, he was probably the most important member of the group's German network and had been entrusted with setting up covert financial arrangements, which could be used discreetly to fund the group's European operations from Syria. His West German base was an apartment above a shop at 28 Sandweg in Frankfurt.

The BKA log states that on 22 October Dalkamoni and Khreesat 'drove to Frankfurt and visited two electrical shops'. No details were given of what they may have bought. At 2 p.m. the same day he was observed to meet up with 'the same stranger that he met on 18 October'. Whether or not this was the big-eared Arab is not clear, as the stranger was identified as 'Ramzi'. Whereas the previous stranger appeared to live in Hamburg, 'Ramzi' had been contacted on a Frankfurt telephone number. 'Ramzi' turned out to be Ramzi Diab, another member of the PFLP-GC. After the meeting, Dalkamoni visited Ghadanfar's flat at 28 Sandweg.

Sources within the BKA confirmed that Diab's real name was Salah Kwikas and that he was a Palestinian. In the early 1980s he was reportedly captured by Israeli commandos while on a terrorist mission inside Israel and released in 1985 as part of an exchange deal for three Israeli reservists captured by the PFLP-GC in 1982.[10]

The following day Dalkamoni was back in Neuss, where he received a call from someone called Abu Hassan in Damascus. Dalkamoni explained that 'things' were now nearly ready and that he would be with Abu Hassan by Friday, which was five days later.

On 24 October Dalkamoni and Khreesat again went shopping, this time in Neuss. They were accompanied by Dalkamoni's young brother-in-law, Ahmed Abassi, who acted as translator. At the Huma-Markt store, they appeared to buy four clocks, three of which were mechanical and the fourth digital. They then visited the Kaufhalle shopping centre, where they were observed buying glue, some screws, 16 small, thin 1.5 volt batteries and some electrical switches. Later that day the BKA eavesdropped on a telephone conversation, in which Khreesat told someone in Amman that he had started the work yesterday and needed another two to three days before he could return home.

It was obvious from these latest developments that an attack could be imminent. On the morning of 26 October the BKA observed Dalkamoni and Khreesat walk out of the Isarstrasse apartment and climb into

Dalkamoni's silvery-green Ford Taunus. They drove to a nearby street, Hafenstrasse, where Khreesat made a call as Dalkamoni waited outside. It was time for the BKA to pounce. As Khreesat emerged from the phone box over a dozen agents sprung out to arrest the two men, neither of whom attempted to resist. In the Ford the police found blank Spanish and Syrian passports and, lying under a blanket, a Toshiba 453 'Bombeat' model radio-cassette player.

A raid on the Isarstrasse apartment confirmed BKA suspicions. As well as more blank passports, they found a mini-production line for home-made bomb-making: electronic components, soldering irons, and, most significantly, time-delay and barometric fuses and a detonator. Equally alarming were the discoveries made later the same day, during a raid of Abdel Faltah Ghadanfar's safe-house at 28 Sandweg, Frankfurt. Among the finds were six automatic rifles, a bazooka, thirty hand grenades and a launcher, five kilos of Semtex explosive, six kilos of TNT and fourteen sticks of dynamite. Announcing the raid to the media, the German Federal Prosecutor's office described the terrorist arms cache as the largest ever found in the country.

Also discovered in the Sandweg apartment were luggage tags from the West German state airline Lufthansa, 14 airline timetables, a Sanyo cassette player and a Yugoslavian airlines carrier bag.[12]

Besides Dalkamoni, Khreesat and Ghadanfar, 14 other suspects were rounded up in Operation Autumn Leaves. They included the Abassi brothers, Hashem and Ahmed, Yasim Kam-Nakche, Ahmad Kaplan, Bassam Radi, Adnan Younis and Ramzi Diab. Another of those arrested was Martin Khadorah, although accounts vary as to whether he was in Germany or Yugoslavia at the time. A few weeks after the Autumn Leaves raids the Yugoslav police raided the Krusevac safe-house apartment that Dalkamoni had visited at the beginning of October and seized seven and a half kilos of Semtex, two kilos of Soviet-manufactured dynamite, nearly five hundred detonators and large quantities of fuse. The occupant, Palestinian Mobdi Goben, escaped arrest and fled back to Syria.

Shortly after the arrests of 26 October, the BKA discovered an example of Khreesat's handiwork. Opening up the Toshiba cassette recorder found in Dalkamoni's car boot, they saw that it contained 300 grammes of Semtex, carefully moulded to the inside, plus a detonator and four pencil batteries. The switching mechanism was of particular interest, containing as it did two distinct elements: a simple time-delay switch and a barometric pressure switch. A technical analysis showed that the time switch would only be activated when pressure inside the barometric switch's tiny vacuum chamber had fallen to around 950 millibars. Such levels are only found at about 2,500 feet, which led to the inescapable conclusion that the bomb was designed to blow up an aircraft. Some airlines put luggage through pressure chambers in order to trigger such devices, but the incorporation of a timer meant the trigger could be delayed, allowing the terrorists to fool the pressure chamber – the timer would activate the bomb after 35 or 45 minutes. The Semtex inside the bomb was eventually analysed and found to be part of the same batch discovered in the Frankfurt and Krusevac safe-houses.

The operation appeared to be a success, but it later emerged that the BKA had made a major blunder. At least three other barometric bombs were in the Isarstrasse apartment at the time of the raids but were not seized. Two were built into tuners and the third into a Sanyo monitor. These only came to the BKA's attention in April 1989, four months after Lockerbie. Furthermore, among other items the BKA failed to seize were numerous radio-cassette players. According to notes made at the time, these included 12 stereo models. Only one radio-cassette player was seized, a Toshiba 453 'Bombeat' model identical to the one found in the car boot. It was found to have extra holes drilled into it, a clear sign that it was being modified to be a bomb.[12]

Most of the Autumn Leaves suspects were released without charge within days, but Dalkamoni, Khreesat and Ghadanfar continued to be held under conditions of strict security. As their interrogations got under way, it became clear to the BKA officers that their earlier suspicions had been fully justified.

Dalkamoni admitted that he had taken explosives to the Isarstrasse apartment, adding that the material had been smuggled into West Germany from the Krusevac safe-house by Martin Khadorah. It didn't ring quite true that a professional terrorist like Dalkamoni would risk allowing such material to be carried across two or three international borders, where it could easily have been discovered by routine inspections. It would have been far safer for the PFLP-GC's Syrian or Iranian sponsors to have smuggled it in the diplomatic baggage, which was exempt from security checks.

Whichever way the explosive found its way into his hands, Dalkamoni confessed to his role in the bomb-making, telling the police that he had supervised Khreesat as he built bombs into a Toshiba radio-cassette player, two radio tuners and a monitor screen. He said that a Toshiba radio-cassette player had been brought by Khreesat from the PFLP-GC's Damascus offices, via Amman, inside which were concealed two clocks – to be used as electronic timers – and two barometric pressure switches. A second Toshiba radio-cassette player, also containing two clocks and two pressure switches, he said, had been handed over by Ramzi Diab during their Frankfurt meeting on 18 October.

Like Dalkamoni, Ghadanfar was forthcoming about the fact that the group was planning terrorist attacks in Germany, and about Khreesat's bomb-making. He confirmed to the BKA that he took his orders from Dalkamoni and described his role in funding the group's European operations.

Khreesat also confirmed that he knew of a terrorist plot – he could hardly have denied it – but insisted that he was unaware of specific targets. He gave details of the PFLP-GC's structure and membership, but was reluctant to say much else. He explained that he could not give details of his own background.

The reason for Khreesat's reticence soon became clear. On 5 November he asked to make a telephone call to Amman. The BKA placed the call for him and Khreesat spoke at length with someone about the need to 'expedite legal matters in Germany'. Five days later Khreesat appeared before Judge Christian Rinne at the Federal High Court in Karlesruhe. A prosecutor applied on behalf of the BKA for a new arrest warrant to keep Khreesat in custody. The application should have been a mere formality, but instead Judge Rinne delivered his own bombshell. He told the court:

> The accused is certainly suspected of the alleged charge, but the strong suspicion of crime necessary for warrant of arrest is, however, lacking. It is not possible to prove at present a connection between the residence at 28 Sandweg in Frankfurt, in which weapons of warfare and explosives have been secured, and the accused. No weapons, or similar, were found in the residence at 16 Isarstrasse in Neuss, where he stayed. It has not been possible to discover a target or location for a crime of explosion. Also, the involvement of the accused as regards the purpose of his stay in the Federal Republic, the nature of his relationship with the other accused parties, and his ignorance of the preparations for the crime, have not been so clearly refuted that a strong suspicion of crime can be confirmed.

The astonishing judgment flew in the face of all the facts. Khreesat had admitted to being party to a terrorist plot; his two senior accomplices had told the BKA that he had prepared bombs in the Neuss apartment; that apartment had been raided and found to contain bomb components and traces of explosives; and he had been caught red-handed with a bomb designed to blow up aircraft. But such matters were now academic, for Khreesat was out of the BKA's grasp. He flew directly back to Jordan, never to return.

So why was so much of the patient work of Operation Autumn Leaves undone? Khreesat, it emerged, was no ordinary terrorist. It was later admitted that he was, all along, an undercover agent for the Jordanian intelligence service, the Mukabarat, which has historically been very close to Western intelligence services – in particular the CIA, which played a central role in its creation. Small wonder, then, that he should have been quietly let off the hook by the German authorities. Subsequent to his release, various sources inside Western intelligence told journalists that he was an asset of the CIA, the German foreign intelligence service the BND, and Mossad.

Ramzi Diab has also been named as a mole, most likely for Mossad. He disappeared after being released and is believed to have returned to Syria, where he was executed on the orders of Ahmed Jibril.[13] Khreesat was more fortunate. Ever since his release, he has lived under extremely close protection in Amman.

Khreesat's PFLP-GC colleagues, Hafez Dalkamoni and Abdel Ghadanfar, fared rather differently, but the outcome of their story was no less strange. Despite the overwhelming evidence that they were planning future attacks on German soil, they were never charged with such offences. Having spent months languishing in high-security prisons, they were eventually charged with involvement in the Hedemünden troop-train bombings of August 1987 and April 1988. It was never adequately explained why, given the specific intelligence provided by Mossad two months before the second train bombing, they had not been arrested earlier for these offences. They were not convicted until 1991, with Dalkamoni receiving a 15-year prison sentence and Ghadanfar 12 years.

4. THE PRESS CRACK THE CASE

The police were keeping an open mind. At least, that was the official line peddled in the days following the Lockerbie disaster. But by the end of the week all the smart money was on this being an Iranian-sponsored revenge attack for the American downing of Iran Air Flight 655 six months earlier.

The day after the crash an anonymous caller contacted the London offices of Associated Press and United Press International and declared: 'We, the Guardians of the Islamic Revolution, are undertaking this heroic execution in revenge for the blowing-up of the Iran Air plane by America a few months ago and keeping the Shah's family in America.'[1] Little was known about this group in the West, but, according to a DIA internal report, the group was organised in February 1979 following a directive issued by the Islamic Revolutionary Committee in Tehran. Synonymous with the Iranian Revolutionary Guards, its duties were described as 'assisting in internal security, fighting counter-revolutionaries and carrying out verdicts of the Revolutionary Courts'.[2] It was common for Middle East terrorist groups, particularly those connected to the Revolutionary Guards, to adopt a variety of names which displayed their allegiance to Iran.

By the time the anonymous call was made, news had leaked of the Helsinki warning and the world's media had begun to make connections between Lockerbie, Flight 655, the Autumn Leaves raids and Marwan Khreesat's aircraft bombs.

Exactly a week after the disaster, on 28 December, Dumfries and Galloway Constabulary made the announcement most observers had anticipated: Flight 103 had been destroyed by a bomb. For many months the Scottish police and volunteer searchers would continue to search 845 square miles of southern Scotland and northern England for further evidence, but within weeks solid clues had emerged which pointed the finger at the PFLP-GC. On 16 February 1989 the head of the Lockerbie investigation, Detective Chief Superintendent John Orr, announced that the bomb had been housed in a radio-cassette recorder. Peter Claiden, a scientist with the Ministry of Defence's Royal Armaments Research and Development Establishment (RARDE), had found a small fragment of the recorder's circuitry embedded in a manufacturer's ID plate which had been attached to one of the aluminium luggage containers from the plane's front cargo hold.[3] On examination it turned out to be from a Toshiba device: a twin-speaker model, according to the manufacturer. Although the bomb found in the boot of Dalkamoni and Khreesat's car was built into a single-speaker model, the BKA had noted that there were 12 stereo radio-cassette players in the cellar of Hashem Abassi's Isarstrasse apartment where his brother-in-law Hafez Dalkamoni and bomb-maker Marwan Khreesat were staying. In April 1989 three more barometric bombs were found in Abassi's greengrocer's shop, two of which had been built into tuners and the third into a Sanyo monitor. Abassi told the BKA that the devices had been at the Isarstrasse apartment when they were raided on 26 October.

One of the tuner bombs exploded during examination by a BKA technician, killing him and badly injuring a colleague. As a precaution the BKA disabled the remaining tuner bomb by spraying it with a water cannon.

If these three bombs had been overlooked by the BKA, who was to say that they had not also overlooked a further bomb built into one of those stereo radio-cassette players that had not been seized on 26 October? And who was to say that such a bomb, or an unmodified stereo radio-cassette player, had not subsequently been removed from the Isarstrasse apartment by Dalkamoni and Khreesat's associates? The second Toshiba radio-cassette player, which Dalkamoni confessed was handed to him by Ramzi Diab, had never been found and it was possible that the group had acquired further Toshibas.

By the end of March 1989 it was being reported as fact that the attack had been carried out by the PFLP-GC, with Iranian backing. The *Sunday Times*'s front-page headline on 26 March, for example, read 'PAN AM BOMBERS IDENTIFIED'. Referring to anonymous US intelligence sources, the article stated:

> They know that the organisation behind the bombing, which killed 270 people, was a Palestinian splinter group, the Popular Front for the Liberation of Palestine – General Command, led by Ahmed Jibril, a Damascus-based PLO renegade who opposes Yasser Arafat's current peace drive.

PLO sources told the newspaper that the group had been paid US $10 million for the bombing. They believed, but could not prove, that 'the money came from Iranian radicals seeking revenge for the downing of an Iran airbus by the American cruiser *Vincennes* in the Gulf last summer'.

On 28 March 1989 an International Coordination Meeting of the Lockerbie investigation took place. According to a 'confidential' report of the meeting obtained by the authors, John Orr told his colleagues in the FBI and the German BKA: 'To date 14 pieces of explosive-damaged baggage have been recovered and enquiries to date suggest that on the balance of probability, the explosive device was likely to be amongst the Frankfurt passengers' baggage items. Of all the currently identified explosive-damaged baggage, all but one item originated from Frankfurt.'

Orr also told the meeting of the 'evidential connection between the murder of 270 persons at Lockerbie and activities of the PFLP-GC in Germany', and continued: 'There were a number of important factors to be considered, including the history of this organisation (PFLP-GC); the fact that a Toshiba-make radio-cassette recorder packed with 300 grammes of Semtex Explosive was found in West Germany; at least one hardshell suitcase, possibly Samsonite, was traced to a member of the PFLP-GC in West Germany in October 1988; and the previous conduct of this organisation, which makes it clear that the group is prepared to make repeated attacks on similar targets with identical modus operandi.' The group's *modus operandi* in aircraft bombings, dating back to the mid-'70s, was, of course, to plant the bombs on unsuspecting dupes.

In May the German magazine *Quick* reported that it had seen minutes of a secret meeting in Tehran, after the downing of the Iranian airbus by the US *Vincennes*, at which it was agreed to carry out a revenge attack. It also stated that the Iranians had paid Ahmed Jibril US $1.3 million to carry out the job.

On 30 July 1989 *The Observer* also nailed the Iranian connection in a front-page exclusive containing a detailed account of the events which supposedly led up to the bombing. It reported that, just a few days after the *Vincennes* incident, the Iranian chargé d'affaires in Beirut, Hussain Niknam, invited Ahmed Jibril and other terrorists to a meeting at the Iranian Embassy. Further meetings followed in Tehran and Beirut – some of which were attended by representatives of the Iranian Revolutionary Guards and Hizbullah, and at least one of which involved the Iranian interior minister Ali Akbar Mohtashemi. During these meetings it was agreed to target US airlines flying out of Europe. At first hijacking was considered, but this was dropped for logistical reasons in favour of bombing. The final meeting of all the various parties was held at the Carlton Hotel in Beirut between 18 and 20 December 1988. At the meeting, according to the article:

> Ahmed Jibril is said to have spoken of 'three aims': the liberation of
> Palestine through the elimination of PLO leader Yasser Arafat and

'other American collaborators'; the continuation of the fight against America; and the need to remain in the shadows behind any terrorist action.

Niknam was alleged to have added that 'a major event against American imperialists would take place within days'. The article was almost entirely based on anonymous intelligence sources, but the degree of detail was compelling. Furthermore, the description of the Carlton Hotel meeting tallied with other accounts, which claimed that the so-called Interror pact between radical Palestinian and Islamic terrorists had been signed at the hotel on 20 December.

On 11 September 1989 there was virtually official confirmation of the PFLP-GC's role in the bombing. The FBI's anti-terrorism chief, Buck Revell, told a congressional committee that the Bureau believed it had identified the group responsible for the bombing.[4] Although he did not name the PFLP-GC, everyone knew it was that group to which he was referring.

On Christmas Eve 1989, in the last major Lockerbie scoop of the year, the *Sunday Times* reported that British forensic scientists had identified white plastic residue from the Lockerbie crash site and believed it matched material in alarm clocks that had been purchased by Dalkamoni and Khreesat in Neuss shortly before their arrests on 26 October 1988.

So, by the end of 1989, just over a year after Lockerbie, anyone who had paid close attention to the case was sure that the bombing was carried out by the PFLP-GC on behalf of Iran. There was also good reason to believe that the operation was carried out with assistance from the Syrian authorities and Hizbullah.

But how did they get the bomb onto the plane?

The BKA's forensic experts cast doubt on the assumption that it had been planted in Frankfurt. They compared the Toshiba radio-cassette bomb found in the car boot with the device built into the Sanyo monitor and the remains of the second tuner bomb. All three were fitted with a barometric switch and a timing mechanism, which they determined would be activated once the air pressure had fallen to 950 millibars. There would then be a delay of around 35 to 45 minutes before the timer activated the bomb's detonator. If the pressure rose above 950 mb as a result of the aircraft descending, the timer would effectively return to zero.

The BKA calculated that air pressure would reach 950 mb about seven minutes after take-off. Given that the flight from Frankfurt to London was 1 hour 18 minutes, they concluded – quite correctly – that if a bomb with similar barometric and timing mechanisms had been loaded on Flight 103 in Frankfurt it would have exploded before reaching Heathrow.[5] But no one knew what kind of mechanism the Lockerbie bomb contained and the PFLP-GC had access to bomb-makers smart enough to design a device that could be planted in Frankfurt but not blow up until *after* take-off from Heathrow.

Having let a number of bombs and stereo radio-cassette players slip through their hands, the BKA arguably had good cause to find reasons why the bomb could not have originated in Frankfurt. Within days of the disaster strong clues were emerging that the opposite was true. On 22 December, ITN broadcast a very brief interview with a woman called Yasmin Siddique, who had been a passenger on the Frankfurt–London leg of the doomed flight the previous day. While queuing for the flight at Frankfurt airport she had seen something suspicious. 'The man in front of me was getting very agitated, very nervous,' she recalled. 'The policeman was taking a very long time checking his passport. He had an American passport, he was of Middle East descent, I couldn't tell you which country. But he was getting very upset. He looked at me, he looked at the floor, he looked everywhere, but he wouldn't look at the policeman. He turned round, watching everybody while he was putting his passport away, and he seemed very agitated.'

The only Middle Eastern passenger on Flight 103 was Khalid Jaafar, the 20-year-old, Lebanese-born US citizen. Siddique later confirmed that it was him she had seen.[6] Jaafar held both a Lebanese and American passport and, although official records show that his US passport was not found at Lockerbie, this is not to say he was not carrying it at Frankfurt airport. It may simply have been lost in the Scottish hills, or it could have disappeared for less straightforward reasons. Perhaps the young man's nervous disposition was simply down to the fact that the German authorities were giving him a difficult time because of his Arab origins.

Eight days after Yasmin Siddique's television interview Khalid Jaafar was named as the person who took the bomb on the plane. The allegation came in the *Washington Times*, a paper known for its many sources within the US government's intelligence services. The article reported claims that Jaafar was an innocent victim who had been duped by the terrorists into carrying the bomb. Ironically, in years to come, the *Washington Times* would be a forum for certain individuals to attack those who suggested that the bombers had duped Jaafar into carrying the bomb.

The day after the *Washington Times* story a British newspaper weighed in. The *Daily Express* carried a front-page picture of Khalid Jaafar next to the banner headline, 'THE BOMB CARRIER'. Since Jaafar was the only Arab on the plane and had recently been in the terrorist cauldron of Lebanon, it was perhaps inevitable that the finger of suspicion would be pointed at him. But the *Express* was not merely parroting the *Washington Times* story; reporters Ross Mark and Bill Greig had sources of their own in the FBI and Scotland Yard.

As soon as the two stories appeared, other sources attempted to play down the Jaafar link. On 1 January 1989, the day after the *Daily Express* story, the *Mail on Sunday* carried an article in which his father, Nazir, denied that the boy had been the terrorists' dupe. He was sure, he said, because Khalid only had two carry-on bags and did not have any luggage in the hold of the plane. On the same day the *Sunday Telegraph* reported that 'sources close to the investigation in London' had dismissed reports that Jaafar had been identified as the bomb carrier. Two days later *The Independent* reported claims that his carry-on bags had been found and that they showed no signs of bomb damage. The source for the story was an anonymous searcher who had had supposedly contacted the paper in order to counter the claims that Jaafar had taken the bomb on the plane. He or she did not wish to be identified, the article explained, 'because of police rulings against speaking to the press'. These denials seemed compelling, but Pan Am documentation which emerged subsequently from Frankfurt airport revealed Jaafar had in fact checked in two bags which may well have been placed in the luggage container in which the explosion took place.

Pan Am was also receiving information about Jaafar. On 2 January Ingrid Olufsen, not her real name, the airline's director of passenger services in Oslo, received a telephone call from a man who introduced himself as Mr Goldberg, a Danish chemical engineer in Oslo on business. He said that he had important information about a young Arab man whom he had seen pictured on the front cover of that day's *Dagbladet* newspaper (which had repeated the *Daily Express*'s story of two days earlier). Aware that this was a potentially important witness, Olufsen arranged to meet Goldberg after work in a hotel near to her office in Oslo. He said that on 19 December, two days before the Lockerbie disaster, he had met Jaafar in Sweden when they were both travelling on the 1710 train from Gothenburg to Stockholm. He then provided her with a photocopy of a page from his address book in which he had recorded notes of the apparently chance meeting.

Goldberg said he had spent much of the journey talking to the young man, who had told him he was called Rabe Khalid Jaafar, but that he also used the name Said Ali Jaafar. He told Goldberg that he had been visiting an acquaintance in Gothenburg and was off to Stockholm to see another. Goldberg noted the addresses of each of the acquaintances.

Goldberg agreed to accompany Olufsen to a police station to make a statement, but before they left Olufsen had to nip back to her office to collect some warmer clothes. While there she took the opportunity to fax the information to her Pan Am colleagues in London. By the time she returned to the hotel Goldberg had disappeared into the night, never to be seen or heard of again.

It was a strange episode. Despite volunteering his information freely, Goldberg struck Olufsen as being rather furtive. His name further heightened the mystery: Goldberg is a common name in Israel or the USA, but unusual in Scandinavia. It was odd that he had chosen to relay the information to Pan Am rather than to the police. Moreover, his account did not fit with any of the press stories that had appeared up until then, all of which suggested Jaafar had been in West Germany immediately prior to the bombing.

The day after Goldberg's brief appearance a front-page article in the British *Daily Star* newspaper suggested a means by which the bomb had got onto the plane. Running to just a few column inches, it suggested that illicit drugs deals were involved in the disaster. It began: 'A crooked baggage-handler at Frankfurt airport may have planted the Pan Am jumbo jet bomb. Police suspect that he was duped into loading a suitcase containing the Semtex explosive, believing it was cocaine.' The article was written by Barry Gardner, whose source was within a British law enforcement agency. Were it not for the fact that the more sober news media tend not to take the *Daily Star* very seriously, they might have probed the drug connection with greater vigour.

Gardner was not the only one tipped off about a possible Frankfurt drug connection. Not long before the bombing Pan Am's Jim Berwick, who was responsible for security in Europe, the Middle East and Scandinavia, attended a regular meeting of Heathrow airline security officers with a Pan Am colleague, security manager Mike Jones. The meeting was also attended by an HM Customs investigator, Philip Connelly, whom Berwick had known for over 20 years – and whom he knew to be, at the time, a 'head of the heroin squad'. Berwick later recalled, 'Phil took me aside and gave me the indication that he had been the British Customs representative at a meeting in Germany with representatives of German Customs and DEA, when it became known to Phil that Pan Am was in fact being used as a conduit or a route through which drug shipments were being moved from Europe to the US.'[7] According to Mike Jones, two days after the bombing

Connelly phoned him at his office at Heathrow looking for Berwick. Jones told Connelly that Berwick was 'up at Lockerbie' and that he could not reach him. According to Jones, Connelly then asked if Pan Am had considered a bag switch at Frankfurt airport, involving Turkish baggage-handlers. Jones recalls, 'I took this to mean a switch of the drugs bag.'[8]

On 30 July 1989 *The Observer* carried a front page 'exclusive' which echoed Connelly's tip-off and the *Daily Star*'s earlier scoop. Under the headline, 'LOCKERBIE: TURKS "PLANTED BOMB"', the article claimed that Ahmed Jibril had utilised Islamic fundamentalists among Frankfurt airport's Turkish baggage-handlers to get the bomb onto the plane. It also reported that, prior to the bombing, someone had made suspicious inquiries at Frankfurt airport, which could have been an attempt to reconnoitre the airport's security arrangements. Curiously this person was thought to be an American, who used the alias David Lovejoy. It was alleged that he had played a key role in helping transfer funds from Iran to the PFLP-GC. His was a name that would appear elsewhere.

The drug connection resurfaced in a brief *Sunday Times* article of 16 April 1989, headed '"DRUGS COURIER" LINKED TO LOCKERBIE BOMBING'. Written by Washington correspondent Mark Hosenball, a journalist renowned for his intelligence contacts, it reported 'Washington sources' had revealed that traces of heroin had been found in the wreckage of Flight 103. The implication was that the drug was close to the source of the explosion. According to the article, this lent weight to 'a theory that the person who planted the bomb on the plane may have been a drug courier duped by the bomb-makers into taking it on board by being told that he was smuggling drugs'. Khalid Jaafar was mentioned, but the article did not directly suggest that he was the drug-smuggling dupe. As with the *Daily Star*'s story, no one in the media chose to follow up the report.

It had been widely rumoured among the rank-and-file police officers who searched the Tundergarth area that a young Arab passenger had been carrying drugs. They may not have known it, but the rumours were not without justification. The only Arab on the plane was Khalid Jaafar, some of whose clan had historically been one the most important drug-producing dynasties in the Lebanon's Bekaa Valley. During the 1920s they had supplied Lucky Luciano's Mafia mob in the US. Following the Syrian invasion of Lebanon in 1976, they reportedly developed strong ties with the occupying forces. They had developed particularly close ties with the Syrian military intelligence, whose commander in Lebanon was General Ghazi Kenaan. According to a July 1992 report by the US House of Representatives Republican Task Force on Terrorism and Unconventional

Warfare, the clan was involved in the large-scale smuggling of heroin and Iranian counterfeit dollar bills to Western Europe.[9]

In November 1992 another report appeared about Syrian involvement in Lebanese drug production. Entitled 'Syria, President Bush, and Drugs – the Administration's Next Iraqgate', it was a staff report for the sub-committee on Crime and Criminal Justice of the US Congress's Committee on the Judiciary. The section of the report on Kenaan's boss, the overall head of Syrian Military Intelligence, General Ali Dubbah, stated: 'He is connected with the Jaffar [sic] clan.'

Another drug connection surfaced in the British press on 12 February 1989. An article in the *Sunday People* claimed that a Syrian called Monzer Al-Kassar was among those being investigated by the FBI in connection with the Lockerbie bombing. As the article explained, Al-Kassar stood trial twice at the Old Bailey in 1977, accused of being involved in an international drug ring. Eventually jailed for two and a half years, he was released almost immediately because he had spent over two years on remand in Brixton prison.

One of four brothers, Al-Kassar was the brother-in-law of General Dubbah, and also featured prominently in the November 1992 Congressional staff report.

In 1985, he was being used by the White House to supply arms to the Contra guerrillas in Nicaragua. Records which came to light after the Iran–Contra scandal became public showed that he was paid handsomely for his services. In 1987 President Reagan's former National Security Adviser, Admiral John Poindexter, one of the architects of Iran–Contra, was asked by a Congressional committee to explain the National Security Council's dealings with Al-Kassar. In a masterpiece of understatement he said, 'When you're buying arms on the world's arms market . . . you often have to deal with people you might not want to go to dinner with.'[10]

The most detailed early account of the Lockerbie bombing appeared in the Arabic *Al-Dustur* newspaper on 22 May 1989. The writer, Dr Ali Nuri Zadeh, told a compelling and highly detailed account of the planning of the attack on Pan Am 103. His source was a highly placed Iranian cleric who was close to the Ayatollah Montaseri, seen by many as the successor to Ayatollah Khomenei. The article was reprinted in English on 23 June in the Joint Publication Research Service (JPRS), a publication of the government for 300 top-level government officials. The story followed a dateline theme and started off on 8 July 1988. The report's account of 20 December 1988 opened with the following:

> (an engineer employed by the Frankfurt Airport authority at
> Frankfurt Rhein-Main Airport) received the green light to carry out

the operation from [an Iranian Diplomat]. The morning of 21 December was chosen for carrying out the operation, after the Iranian embassy in Beirut had received information to the effect that five American intelligence were setting out for America via Frankfurt and via a Pan Am flight on its morning flight overflying Britain.

Obviously the timing of the flights was not accurately reported. The story reported the following for 4 November 1988:

An American agent known in Iranian circles as 'David Love-boy' contacted the Iranian Embassy in Beirut from Junieh and informed Mohsen Armin (Iranian Intelligence Beirut) that a group consisting of five experts from American Intelligence had arrived in East Beirut. Its purpose was to collect information on the places where hostages were held. It is worth mentioning that the American agent who had struck bargains on weapons to the benefit of Iran disappeared from sight three days after the bombing of the American aircraft over Lockerbee [sic]. According to some sources, he had an appointment in a hotel near the area 'Wulaag Mini' in Athens and an unknown group kidnapped him as soon as he entered the hotel.

This document, when distributed by the government JPRS had a number of surprising omissions from the original *Al-Dustur* article, such as the following from 17 November:

'David Love-Boy' contacted the Iranian Embassy in Beirut a second time to inform Armin that CIA agents had left Beirut, but that they would return to it in the beginning of December.

Love-Boy/Lovejoy would prove elusive and it was not the last time that US government agencies would censor information about the link between Pan Am 103 and the CIA's secret hostage-release efforts.

5. OFFICIAL INQUIRIES, OFFICIAL WHITEWASH

It seemed to be an open-and-shut case. So much had leaked from official sources within the first few months after the Lockerbie bombing to make it certain that the bombing was Iran's revenge for the downing of Iran Air Flight 655 and that it had been carried out by a terrorist alliance in which Ahmed Jibril's PFLP-GC was to the fore. There were also strong indications that the bomb had been planted on an unwitting Khalid Jaafar, and that drug running was somehow involved.

Most upsetting of all to the relatives of the Lockerbie dead was the revelation that a number of warnings had been circulated prior to the bombing. The relatives trusted the authorities on both sides of the Atlantic to bring the culprits to justice as soon as possible, but as news of the warnings spread, they also wanted to know why their loved ones were ever allowed onto Flight 103.

Within weeks the need for mutual support and the desire to uncover the truth galvanised the British-based relatives into a campaign group with two women at its forefront. The first was Elizabeth Delude-Dix, an American living in London who had lost her British husband, Peter Dix. The second was Linda Mack, a part-time masters student at Cambridge University: she did not lose a relative on Flight 103, but rather a college friend, 25-year-old American Julian Benello, whom she had known for only a few months.

The two women organised the first meeting of British victims' relatives in February 1989. Much of their initial campaigning targeted the British government's Transport Secretary Paul Channon, who was faced with the unenviable task of justifying his department's decision not to make public the Helsinki and Toshiba warnings. Addressing the House of Commons on 10 January, he reiterated that the Helsinki warning was one of a large number of hoaxes received by his department every year and argued that if every warning was made public the whole airline industry would grind to a halt.

Within a month Mack had exposed his position as distinctly threadbare. She discovered that the FAA had issued only sixteen security bulletins during 1988, and that none of them were as specific as the Helsinki warning. She drafted a letter to *The Independent* which was signed by 21 other 'relatives or friends'. Printed on 23 February, it called for Channon to resign over his misrepresentation of the warning, concluding:

> We ask now that Mr Channon accept ministerial responsibility . . .
> His resignation will not bring back the people we have lost; it will,
> however, ease our sense of betrayal at the actions and omissions of
> our government. It might also ensure that a similar chain of events
> is not repeated.

The relatives soon brought more trouble for the minister. Elizabeth Delude-Dix obtained a copy of the original FAA security bulletin dealing with the Helsinki warning. As described above in Chapter Two it revealed far more than the notice posted up in the Moscow Embassy. It not only gave the names of the people mentioned by the caller, but also mentioned their alleged membership of the Abu Nidal Organisation and the method by which they would attempt to get the bomb onto the plane.

It appeared amazing that so detailed a warning had seemingly resulted in so little action. Channon was thrown on the defensive. Pressed by the parliamentary opposition on 14 March, he stuck to the line that the Helsinki warning had 'very little credence', but the following day yet more disturbing evidence emerged, this time concerning the Toshiba bomb warning circulated by the German authorities in the wake of the BKA's Autumn Leaves raids.

The Department of Transport had known about the warning since November, yet it was not until two days before Lockerbie that a fully detailed description of the bomb – along with photographs – were sent out to airlines. To make matters worse, it was revealed that the material had been sent through the post at a time when the inevitable Christmas delays ensured that many airlines did not receive it until after the Lockerbie disaster.

In the midst of this débâcle, news emerged that provided the grieving relatives with some considerable comfort. On 17 March a rash of headlines in the tabloid press proclaimed that the criminal investigation had effectively been solved. The *Daily Mail*'s front page declared: 'PAN AM KILLER TRACKED DOWN'. The article added that 'the terrorist who planted the Lockerbie jet bomb may be named within a few days. He has been tracked down to a desert hideout.' *The Sun* blasted off with 'WE KNOW JUMBO BOMB KILLER' and reported: 'Detectives probing the Lockerbie jet disaster now know WHO planted the bomb, HOW he did it and WHERE he put it on the plane.' The now defunct *Today* went even further, claiming that 'the terrorist who planted the bomb was under close arrest last night'.

The *Daily Mail* attributed the information to 'a senior government official' and *The Sun* to 'Whitehall sources'. In fact the source of the story could hardly have been more authoritative: it was none other than Paul Channon. The previous day the minister had invited a handful of senior lobby correspondents to lunch in a small private room at the Garrick Club. They were Robin Oakley of *The Times*, Ian Aitken of *The Guardian*, Julia Langdon of the *Daily Mirror*, Chris Buckland of *Today* and Geoffrey Parkhouse of the *Glasgow Herald*. The group were told that the brilliant work of the Scottish police had cracked the Lockerbie case and that arrests were imminent. Predictably, the culprits were all members of the PFLP-GC. The reporters knew that they were being offered a major scoop, but on strict lobby terms – in other words, the source of the story must not be named.

Channon's disclosure was a ploy designed to distract attention at a time when the opposition parties and Fleet Street were baying for his blood. Unfortunately for him, not everyone in the media was as respectful of the conventions of Westminster reporting as his lunch guests. The day after the briefing the American ABC Television network named him as the source of the story. The British press picked up on the ABC report, laying bare the diversionary ruse. Two days later he was once again named as the mole in the House of Commons and accused of creating a deliberate smokescreen to divert attention from the government's handling of the warnings. The minister vainly denied the allegations, but was fatally wounded. Although he resisted opposition calls to resign, he was quietly dropped from the cabinet during a summer reshuffle a few months later.

The substance of Channon's claim – that there was overwhelming evidence to show the PFLP-GC were responsible for the bombing – was never denied. Although he was clearly prepared to limit what he was prepared to say, it is highly unlikely that he would have chosen to give the reporters such a strong steer if it were untrue. The weeks passed by. No killers were named. No arrest warrants were issued. And none of Channon's government colleagues sought to ease his discomfort by confirming that the Lockerbie case had been cracked.

It was not until many months later that light came to be shed on the strange official silence. In their syndicated *Washington Post* column of 11 January 1990, journalists Jack Anderson and Dale Van Atta reported on a telephone conversation between Margaret Thatcher and President George Bush in mid-March 1989 – exactly the same time that Paul Channon was declaring the case solved. The two leaders agreed that the Lockerbie investigation should be toned down. Among the reasons cited was the need to avoid prejudicing negotiations with Syrian- and Iranian-backed terrorists who were holding Western hostages in Lebanon.

On 24 March 1989 there were yet further revelations about warnings. *The Independent* reported that another FAA security bulletin, dated 7 December 1988, had described a suspected attempt to test the security procedures of TWA airlines at Frankfurt airport. Reporter Nick Cohen appeared to have got his scoop from Linda Mack, who was quoted as saying: 'A public inquiry is now needed to establish why the Department of Transport or other ministries did not collect and collate this information. Frankfurt is mentioned explicitly three times within a period of nineteen days. Yet we know that baggage and passengers arriving from Frankfurt were not screened at Heathrow airport.'

Mack's success in exposing such information helped land her a job with ABC Television, where she worked on some major investigations of the bombing. Somewhat surprisingly, given her track record, in years to come she would turn her fire on certain other journalists who cried 'cover-up'.

Her efforts in the early days helped convince the families of the British Lockerbie victims that the blunders over warnings should be the subject of a full independent inquiry. The government did not grant them an audience until 19 September 1989, when they met with Channon's replacement as Transport Secretary, Cecil Parkinson MP. The results were encouraging. Parkinson was very receptive to their arguments and, by the end of the 90-minute meeting, seemed persuaded. Careful not to raise their hopes too high, he nevertheless promised to recommend to government colleagues that a Scottish judge be appointed to lead an inquiry. The relatives accepted that, since it would be dealing with intelligence matters, the inquiry would have to be held in private. Satisfied that progress was finally being made, the relatives' spokesman, Dr Jim Swire, declared that Parkinson represented 'a fresh face and a fresh mind'.

Several weeks later the relatives' fragile optimism was shattered. An embarrassed Parkinson told them that he was sorry, but a judicial inquiry of the type he outlined had been blocked by Downing Street.

On 16 December the government announced that an inquiry would be held in Scotland, but that it would only be a fatal accident inquiry (FAI). The Scottish equivalent of English inquests, FAIs are only empowered to determine the cause of death and the precautions that might have been taken to avoid such death. All the truly important questions surrounding Flight 103, such as who actually carried out the bombing and what advanced warning the authorities had had of the terrorists' plans, would remain untouched. Evidence that might impact on the criminal investigation would be disallowed. So, too, would evidence relating to the operations of the intelligence services and those which lay in the political arena – including issues such as public expenditure on aviation security.

The Lord Advocate, Lord Fraser of Carmyllie, justified this limited form of inquiry on the grounds that it was important not to raise any matters that might prejudice a future criminal trial of the bombers. This ignored the fact that the judicial inquiry suggested by Parkinson could not, since it would have sat in camera, have prejudiced the criminal inquiry. Moreover, as we shall see, when indictments were subsequently issued against the two Libyans accused of the bombing, the Lord Advocate's office would not prevent the widespread dissemination of the apparently irrefutable evidence gathered by the Scottish police.

It was clear to many of the British relatives that the real reason a judicial inquiry had been blocked was that the judge might uncover facts embarrassing to the British and American governments. Margaret Thatcher and her former Transport Secretary, Paul Channon, both invoked parliamentary privilege to resist successfully a legal attempt by Dr Jim Swire to compel them to give evidence to the FAI. The government also opposed an application by the families' legal representatives to have 13 Pan Am employees from Frankfurt airport provide evidence to the inquiry.

When the FAI finally got under way on 1 October 1990, it soon became apparent that the government would keep the inquiry on a very tight rein. On the third day the former Chief Constable of Dumfries and Galloway, John Boyd, was asked by Stephen Pounian (a US lawyer representing the American relatives) if the warning about a bomb threat against Pan Am received by the US Embassy in Helsinki had mentioned a Toshiba radio-cassette device. Before Boyd had a chance to answer, the Lord Advocate immediately intervened to ask Sheriff Principal John S. Mowat QC to disallow the question, on the grounds that it impinged on the criminal investigation.[1]

Despite such setbacks, many of the victims' relatives reasoned that the FAI was preferable to no inquiry at all; they resolved to make the best of it and hoped that at least some of their nagging questions would be answered. For Martin and Rita Cadman, in particular, it offered the chance to raise matters that had been troubling them for over 18 months. In the immediate aftermath of the bombing the couple repeatedly offered to help find and identify the body of their son, Bill, but were told by the police that no visual identification would be necessary. They had assumed that his body would not be found, that it had been destroyed, perhaps in the crater in Sherwood Crescent, Lockerbie.

Martin Cadman wrote to the Dumfries and Galloway police to ask when Bill's body had been found and on 31 January 1989 the police wrote back informing him that the date was 24 December, three days after the bombing. In March 1989 the Cadmans received Bill's death certificate which confirmed that his death was registered on '2/1/89' and that he was 'Found dead 1988 December twenty-fourth 1700 hours Tundergarth, Lockerbie'.

On 1 June 1989 two police officers from Lockerbie visited the Cadmans' house in Surrey to hand over some of Bill's possessions. Martin asked about the date his body was found. One of the officers, a PC Hope, referred to some papers he had with him and said it was found on 22 December – not the twenty-fourth, as shown on the death certificate. On 7 June Martin wrote to the Chief Constable of Dumfries and Galloway Constabulary asking him to confirm the date on which Bill's body was found.

The letter was passed on to the Procurator Fiscal who replied on 9 June: 'I have had enquiries made and can confirm that his body was recovered on 24 December, and this date has been recorded on all the official records.' He added, 'I have established that the papers Constable Hope was referring to were unofficial documents on which a typing error had been made in relation to the date.'

There the matter rested until Wednesday, 10 October 1990, the fifth day of the FAI and the first of five days of testimony by Sergeant David Johnston of Strathclyde Police (no relation of the Radio Forth reporter). Johnston's evidence detailed where each of the victims was found, how they died, and – critically for the Cadmans – when they were certified dead and when they were removed to the mortuary. The couple arrived early to give the Lockerbie Air Disaster Group's team of solicitors notes on which to cross-examine Sergeant Johnston on the date Bill's body was found.

Just before the day's proceedings were to start at 10 a.m. their solicitor gave them a copy of a four-page death schedule relating to Bill. This showed that police surgeon Dr David Fieldhouse, the Bradford police surgeon who had volunteered his services to search for bodies in the Tundergarth area in the hours after the disaster, pronounced life extinct on 22 December, and that the body was photographed *in situ* on the 24 December and recovered and removed to the mortuary on the twenty-fourth. This was the first confirmation they had that Police Constable Hope was correct when he told them on 7 June 1989 that Bill was found on the twenty-second. So why had the Procurator Fiscal indicated otherwise? And why was the body left for two days after being found by Dr Fieldhouse, a period during which it would be exposed to the weather and to interference by animals?

According to Sergeant Johnston's evidence, Bill Cadman was one of many victims who were pronounced dead on 22 December by Dr Fieldhouse, but not removed to the mortuary until 24 December. Pressed by counsel for the families, Brian Gill QC, as to what had gone wrong, Johnston put the blame firmly with Dr Fieldhouse. Johnston claimed that bodies pronounced dead by Dr Fieldhouse had been left simply because the police had no knowledge of his activities. He stated that Fieldhouse had gone out 'on his own', and that 'the officer in charge at the time did not realise which area he was going to'. It was not until search teams had found Bill Cadman's body on 24 December that they realised Fieldhouse had already made an examination two days earlier. The exchange went on:

> *Gill:* May I take it, therefore, that when the search teams who were covering the Tundergarth fields came upon William Cadman's body on the twenty-fourth, they were at the time in possession of no information showing that that body had already been looked at by Dr Fieldhouse?
>
> *Johnston:* They realised because in fact of the label Dr Fieldhouse had attached to the victim that this victim had been examined by Dr Fieldhouse, yes.
>
> *Gill:* But prior to finding the body and seeing that label, am I to take it that they were completely unaware that Dr Fieldhouse had been there before them?
>
> *Johnston:* That is correct.
>
> *Gill:* And therefore they had been given no opportunity by him to find William Cadman's body at any earlier time?
>
> *Johnston:* That is correct sir.

Johnston compounded the distorted picture by claiming that he had returned home on 22 December and then not reported his activities until 'some months later'. When Gill observed, 'It is clear, Sergeant, that this is scarcely a very satisfactory state of affairs,' Johnston replied: 'It was not very satisfactory, sir.'

As each case was described, Fieldhouse's integrity was further impugned. The following exchange gives a flavour:

> *Sheriff Principal Mowat:* Sergeant, this is one of those unfortunate cases, is it not, similar to the last one in which the body has been found first by Dr Fieldhouse?
>
> *Johnston:* It is.

Mowat: And may I take it that again in relation to this victim Dr Fieldhouse has failed to give the police the fullest possible explanation as to his investigations at the earliest possible date? *Johnston:* That is correct.[2]

In the eyes of the inquiry Dr Fieldhouse had impeded the meticulous work of the police and caused unnecessary anguish to the grief-stricken relatives. Of course nothing could be further from the truth: he had reported to the police as soon as he arrived in Lockerbie and it was they who assigned him to look for bodies in the Tundergarth area. At all times during his searches he had been accompanied by at least one police officer and, as soon as he returned home to West Yorkshire, he provided the police with a full report of his activities. It was strange that Sergeant Johnston should give such a distorted picture. Although he was not involved in the case until 25 December, four days after the bombing, he was one of the officers with whom Dr Fieldhouse had spent hours poring over computer records at the Lockerbie Incident Centre in order to identify the victims.

Dr Fieldhouse might have remained ignorant of the inquiry's criticisms had his son, Nicholas, not spotted a report in *The Times.* By coincidence on the same day he received a letter from the solicitor representing the British Lockerbie victims' families asking to meet. He agreed and at the meeting expressed his desire to give evidence to correct the impression given by Sgt Johnston. Sheriff Mowat accepted that Dr Fieldhouse should give evidence and on 22 January 1991 he took the witness stand. He was soon able to demonstrate that he had acted at all times under police supervision and that he had provided the police with a full account of his activities as soon as he had returned home from the crash site. In his final determination on the FAI, Mowat stressed that Fieldhouse had at all times followed the appropriate procedures. He offered his apologies and suggested that the mix-up had arisen because the information he had provided to the police was overlooked.

The doctor had been vindicated, but the claim that Sergeant Johnston's testimony was a simple mistake was difficult to follow. The police were in possession of all the facts concerning Dr Fieldhouse's involvement and Johnston, of all people, must have known that the doctor had made every effort to assist the police investigation.

Moreover, Johnston's assertion that the search teams had not 'found' Bill Cadman and others for the second time until the twenty-fourth did not fit other known facts. Bill was one of six victims listed at the FAI as having been found at map reference 179 809. This spot is just to the south of the

Langholm Road and a couple of hundred yards away from where the aeroplane's cockpit landed in an area where, according to Johnston's own evidence, many other bodies were listed as having been found. From within a couple of hours of the plane coming down, and for many days after, this entire area was swarming with police and volunteer rescue workers. Even if Fieldhouse had been as negligent as Sergeant Johnston had implied, the idea that Bill Cadman's body would not have been found until three days after the crash was rather odd. Twelve years on, his parents still do not know what happened to his body during the two days between being found and removed to the mortuary; nor do they know why it was not removed sooner.

Dr Fieldhouse had, of course, certified dead both the extra, 271st, body (DCF 12) and the unidentified young man in the Union Jack shorts. As the reaction to the book *Lockerbie: The Real Story* by Johnston's namesake showed, the police were undoubtedly sensitive about this issue. The author had claimed that two intact bodies had been quietly cremated along with unidentified remains. Chief Constable George Esson condemned the book, but refused to respond to its specific claims. Shortly before commencing his slight on Dr Fieldhouse, Sergeant Johnston revealed information which appeared to vindicate the book. While he was being questioned by the Lord Advocate about the individual files, or packs, in which information about the victims was kept, the following exchange took place:

> *Lord Advocate:* How many of these victim packs were there in all?
>
> *Johnston:* Two hundred and seventy-two.
>
> *Lord Advocate:* How does it come to that?
>
> *Johnston:* There were 255 victims recovered, which left 15 missing presumed dead. Of the 255 we also had two unidentified male victims. These male victims therefore were included in the recovered victims and also included in the missing presumed dead. This is for administrative purposes.
>
> *Lord Advocate:* I wondered about that. It is not that there is any confusion about the number of victims. The number is 270, but for administrative purposes it is 272.
>
> *Johnston:* Yes.

So, there were, after all, two unidentified bodies. One was obviously the young man in the Union Jack boxer shorts found by Dr Fieldhouse; but who was the second one? Could it have been the unidentified male DCF 12? According to reporter David Johnston's sources, the second body was female – but, according to the policeman of the same name, it was male. Of course there was no way that the police would confirm that it was DCF 12, because the official line remained that there were only 270 people on the plane. Nevertheless, Sergeant Johnston's revelation posed some serious questions. At least one of the Lockerbie victims was identified on the basis of a severed hand alone, yet despite all the potential means of identification open to them, including the victims' relatives and dental records, the police were unable to identify two of the victims. How could they be so sure that there were not one or two extra people on the plane? The manifest for Flight 103 was not released to the media until at least a day after the disaster. This raised the suspicion that it might have been inaccurate.

The mistaken claims about Dr Fieldhouse's activities had provided the FAI with a ready explanation for why the victims' bodies were left out in the open for two days. If the inquiry was to accept that proper procedures had been thrown out of kilter by an irresponsible freelance, then the failure to recover the bodies sooner might be deemed excusable. There were, of course, no valid procedural reasons for the delay in removing the bodies, because Dr Fieldhouse had done everything by the book.

The delay may simply have been the result of a simple cock-up, and the police may genuinely have thought Fieldhouse had not followed the correct procedures. Maybe they believed they should wait until a second doctor had pronounced life extinct before allowing the removal of the bodies. This scenario was unlikely, though, because Chief Constable John Boyd was under immense pressure to get the bodies to the mortuary as soon as possible. Horrific pictures of bodies lying in fields had been flashed around the world by the media from first light on 22 December. But even if it were true, why couldn't the police simply admit their mistake to the FAI?

A far more plausible reason for the delay was the shadowy activities of the American agents who had flocked to Lockerbie within hours of the bombing. The policemen and volunteer searchers who encountered these spooks had been left in no doubt – by the cavalier way in which they disregarded the strict rules of evidence-gathering required by Scottish law – that it was they, despite the valued efforts of the police, who regarded themselves as running the show. In those first few days after the crash they were desperate to find certain items, among them the suitcase belonging to the US Army's intelligence specialist, Major Charles McKee, and the packages of drugs. In these circumstances they are likely to have tried to ensure that nothing be removed until they had found what they wanted.

The authors wrote to the Chief Constable of Dumfries and Galloway with the following questions about Dr Fieldhouse and the delay in recovering bodies:

(1) In view of Sherrif Mowat's observations [that Dr Fieldhouse had at all times followed the appropriate procedures], how could it have come about that [his] information [had] been overlooked? The question is asked in light of the fact that: (i) Dr Fieldhouse had reported to the police as soon as he arrived in Lockerbie on the night of 21 December; (ii) it was the police who assigned him to look for bodies in the Tundergarth area; (iii) at all times during his searches he had been accompanied by at least one police officer; (iv) as soon as he returned home, he provided the police with a full report of his activities.

(2) Can you confirm whether or not Sgt Johnston was one of the officers with whom Dr Fieldhouse had spent many hours at the Lockerbie Incident Centre in the weeks following attempting the identies and location of the victims?

(3) From within a couple of hours of the plane coming down, the entire area around where Bill Cadman was found was flooded with police and volunteer rescue workers, a situation which continued for many days. Even if Dr Fieldhouse had been negligent as Sgt Johnston had implied, how could it be the case Bill Cadman was not found until three days after the crash?

(4) How could Sgt Johnston claim that on 24 December 'no-one knew exactly when Mr Cadman's body had been examined by Dr Fieldhouse'? The 22 December was the only day that Dr Fieldhouse had been searching for bodies in the Tundergarth area and the police knew this because he had reported it to the Inspector in charge of the Tundergarth search area.

(5) Who was the 'officer in charge at the time' who, according to Sgt Johnston, 'did not realise which area' Dr Fieldhouse was going to?

The following reply was sent on behalf of the Chief Constable, by Detective Chief Superintendent Tom McCulloch:

At the briefings to the search teams on 21–22 December, staff were instructed to keep a documented log of the bodies discovered by them in their respective sectors and therefore submit this record on their return to the Incident Control Centre.

A police officer who accompanied Dr Fieldhouse assisted him to maintain a log of the bodies examined and thereafter returned this record to him on completion of their search. Dr Fieldhouse did not immediately submit this record to the Incident Control Centre, but took it with him when he returned to his home on 22 December [*sic*]. Unfortunately, a copy of the log was not provided to the Police Control Centre by Dr Fieldhouse before he returned home. Dr Fieldhouse thereafter prepared a statement and posted it to the Lockerbie Incident Control Centre on 23 December 1988.

It is not clear when the police received the statement, but it is not unreasonable to assume that the postal service would have been delayed by the increased demand of Christmas and the disruption caused by the air disaster. According to our records, the statement provided by Dr Fieldhouse was registered on the Holmes system on 5 January 1989. It would therefore appear that this record was not available when the Police Search Team subsequently recovered the body of William Cadman on 24 December 1988.

The extensive operation to recover the bodies of the deceased was carried out in a methodical and systematic manner to ensure that all the requirements of the Scottish legal system were fully complied with so that this evidence could be properly admitted at any future judicial proceedings. Although this was a relatively painstaking and time consuming process, the procedures employed by the police at this time subsequently allowed for this evidence to be agreed by the Defence Teams at the recent criminal trial. This significantly reduced the number of witnesses called by the Prosecution and more importantly avoided causing any further distress to family members.

I am also able to confirm from our records that Dr Fieldhouse subsequently assisted the police staff at the Lockerbie Incident Centre to identify the bodies he had examined on 21–22 December 1988.

The authors showed Mr McCulloch's response to Martin Cadman, who commented, 'McCulloch has not explained why the original death certificate had the wrong date (24 December); nor why the procurator fiscal who replied to my letter in June 1989 kept up the fiction by saying PC Hope was reading from an informal document in which there was a typing error in respect of the date . . . And no one has explained why we had to wait until October 1990 to know that PC Hope had told us the truth.'

The relatives hoped the FAI would resolve unanswered questions about drugs. Some were aware that the farmer, Jim Wilson, had seen a substantial quantity of white powder in a suitcase that landed in his field and were puzzled by the authorities' failure to explain (or even acknowledge) the find. When Jim Wilson and his wife, June, were called to give evidence on the second day of the inquiry, the relatives naturally assumed that they would be asked about the drugs. But they were not.

Reverend John Mosey was keen to have this issue aired. The clergyman from Oldbury in the West Midlands and his wife, Lisa, lost their 19-year-old daughter Helga on Flight 103. His surprise turned to unease as he heard police witnesses, on two separate occasions, tell the FAI that there were no major drug finds at the crash site. He subsequently asked the relatives' legal counsel, Brian Gill QC, to raise the question of the drugs. Gill was non-committal; but when Mosey asked a second time some days later, via the group's solicitor, Peter Watson, Gill refused. A few days later he asked Gill directly once again. This time, according to Mosey, Gill became 'quite annoyed' and threatened to cease representing Mosey if he continued to press him. Mosey retained a great liking and respect for Gill and his skills and conduct of the enquiry, but, looking back on the incident, he said: 'I sensed that I was embarrassing him, that he didn't want to raise it, and wasn't prepared to give his reasons.'[3]

Over the following days Mosey lost sleep agonising over the issue. On 30 January 1991 he decided to put his views on the record in a letter to Gill, his deputy, Colin Campbell QC, and Peter Watson. It formally notified them of the drug find and then went on:

> I have, twice, asked you as my legal representatives at this inquiry, to look into this matter. You have refused. I did not raise this before the inquiry because I believed that the Police would certainly produce this evidence and who was I to tell them how to carry out their job anyway. I have raised it during the Inquiry because, regardless as to whether it is peripheral or very central to the business in hand, I cannot continue to hold this knowledge in the light of police statements in this court. Having spoken to you, my legal representatives at this Inquiry, on two occasions and now having committed myself to paper, I feel that my own conscience is clear. The moral responsibility of this information is now yours.

Mosey gave the letters in person to Gill and Campbell, then lodged a copy with his own solicitor in Birmingham. Later the same day Peter Watson told Mosey that the letter had been passed on to the Lord Advocate, Lord Fraser. The Lord Advocate had in turn given it to John Orr, the former head of the

Lockerbie investigation, who in January 1990 had been promoted to Deputy Chief Constable of Dumfries and Galloway. After that day's proceedings one of the legal team took Mosey to meet Orr and Lord Fraser. Mosey was told that, subsequent to giving evidence to the inquiry, Jim Wilson had been interviewed again and had nothing to add to that evidence. Mosey had no reason to doubt this, but felt the issue of the drug find had still not been properly addressed. He again explained that he had asked on a number of occasions for the issue to be raised and that the request was now in writing. According to Mosey, Orr then assured him in the presence of the Lord Advocate that it would be looked into: 'I can remember his exact words", Mosey later recalled: "A senior police officer will be sent to interview Mr Wilson".'[4]

More than a year after the FAI Rev Mosey learned that Jim Wilson was still to be re-interviewed. In 1992 Tam Dalyell MP wrote to the Lord Advocate about the issue. In a reply, dated 3 July 1992, Lord Fraser stated that no drugs had been found at the Lockerbie crash site, except for a small quantity of cannabis.

The authors wrote to Brian Gill QC, Lord Fraser and John Orr to request their responses to Rev Mosey's recollections. Brian Gill, now a Scottish Law Lord replied: 'The questions that you raise relate to an Inquiry that took place more than ten years ago. I have not retained any correspondence or other confidential papers from that time . . . In any event, since your questions relate to my role as senior counsel for a number of the relatives of the Lockerbie victims, I do not think it would be proper for me to engage in correspondence with you on the point.'

Lord Fraser replied that he did not remember the exact words recalled by Rev. Mosey, but went on: 'I do recall, however, agreeing to a further interviewing of Mr Wilson to ascertain whether he had further relevant evidence to offer. Such agreement would not necessarily mean the involvement of a senior police officer. At that stage of proceedings the more appropriate person to conduct such as interview might well have been a member of the Procurator Fiscal Service and I would be surprised if, in my presence Mr Orr would have taken on the singular responsibility of instructing a police officer to carry out the interview. I understood Mr Wilson was interviewed again and offered no evidence to support the account of the discovery of a large quantity of heroin in one of his fields.'

The letter to John Orr, who, subsequent to the fatal accident inquiry, was knighted and promoted to Chief Constable of Strathclyde, was passed on to Detective Chief Superintendent Tom McCulloch of the Dumfries and Galloway Police for reply. He wrote back: 'There is no evidence to support the allegation that a large quantity of drugs landed in a field following the destruction of Pan Am 103. Apart from a small quantity of cannibas, no other drugs were found during an extensive and thorough search of the crash site by the police.'

Although there is no suggestion that Lord Gill, Lord Fraser and Sir John Orr had acted in any way inproperly, most of the questions arising from Rev Mosey's claims, remained unanswered.

Jim Wilson never publicly acknowledged the drug find. Always a private man, he and his wife were understandably upset by the tragedy and by the subsequent media intrusion.

The authorities' reluctance to have the FAI hear evidence of the drug finds was in contrast to their approach to evidence concerning Khalid Jaafar. By the time the inquiry took place, it was known that the bomb had been placed in a bronze Samsonite suitcase, the remaining fragments of which could not be positively linked to any of the victims. Nevertheless the Pan Am documentation, which showed that, contrary to his father's earlier denials, the young man had checked in two bags, inevitably added to the speculation that someone had conned him into taking an extra bag or two – one of which could have contained the bomb. At the FAI, however, the two carry-on bags transformed into the checked-in bags. Given that only two bags belonging to him were found, neither of which showed signs of blast damage, it followed, according to Sheriff Mowat's final report, that they must have been the checked-in bags; this in turn meant he could not be the bomb carrier.

It was somewhat straightforward reasoning, which overlooked the obvious possibility that the two intact bags were unscathed because one, or both, of them were carried on and were therefore nowhere near the bomb blast. If he checked in an additional bag, which either contained the bomb, or was swapped by the terrorists for one that did, surely the terrorists would take precautions to prevent it being linked back to him? And if he checked in a second case that survived the blast, who was to say that it wasn't lost, or quietly removed from the crash site by the mysterious American agents who scoured the hillsides around Lockerbie? Sadly neither the FAI, nor the attendant media, bothered to explore such issues.

The US government was as unwilling as its British counterpart to allow a full inquiry into Lockerbie. Two official inquiries were announced in 1989, but both would focus on aviation security issues, rather than who was actually behind the bombing. The first was carried out by the House of Representatives Committee on Government Operations' Sub-committee on Government Activities and Transportation. A remarkable sub-committee memorandum leaked to *The Independent* referred to a Pan Am internal telex which suggested that 'about 80 per cent' of Christmas holiday flight bookings had changed as a result of the Helsinki warning. The memo suggested the airline should be asked for 'the details of lost revenue, since Pan Am was obviously keeping track of threat-related cancellations'.[5] The document undermined sensationally the US government's earlier assurances that the Helsinki warning had not saved the lives of its employees.

By the time the sub-committee got round to having public hearings on 25 and 26 September, the awkward questions raised by the memo appeared to have been forgotten. The report of the hearings, entitled *The Bombing of Pan Am Flight 103: A Critical Look at American Aviation Security*, ran to almost 500 pages, but contained little of interest. The central question of why, despite so many warnings, US security agencies had failed to save Flight 103, remained unanswered.

By the time the report appeared, President George Bush had issued an Executive Order declaring the establishment of a 'President's Commission on Aviation Security and Terrorism to review and evaluate policy options in connection with aviation security, with particular reference to the destruction on December 21, 1988, of Pan American World Airways Flight 103'.

Chaired by Ann McLaughlin, former Secretary of Labor in President Ronald Reagan's government, the seven-member commission also included two members from the House of Representatives and the Senate (representing both parties equally), a former Navy Secretary and a retired US Air Force General. They were backed up by 33 staff, including nine investigators, drawn from various government departments and the private sector. Between November 1989 and March 1990 the commission held five public hearings and interviewed scores of witnesses. The Lockerbie victims' relatives were generally impressed by the tough questioning of airline and security executives, by McLaughlin in particular.

On 16 February 1990 some of the British relatives met members of the commission at a specially arranged meeting at the US Embassy in Grosvenor Square, London. Among those who went along were Martin and Rita Cadman, who had suspected the British and American governments of covering up the truth ever since discrepancies had arisen over their son Bill's death certificate. At the end of the meeting Martin was taken aside by a commissioner who, out of earshot of the rest of the room, urged him to 'keep up the fight'. The commissioner then added that the British and American governments knew exactly who was responsible for the bombing and how they had carried it out, but that they would never make the facts public. He added that much of the 'wilder speculation' that had appeared in the press was accurate, but that no one in authority would acknowledge what was true and what was not.[6]

The only warnings dealt with in detail by the commission's report were the so-called Helsinki and Toshiba warnings. Repeating the familiar line that the Helsinki warning was a hoax, it also contained a series of graphs and tables designed to demonstrate that the warning had not caused significant numbers of people to avoid Flight 103. This appeared to contradict the Pan Am internal telex which suggested 80 per cent of bookings made through the Moscow embassy were changed as a consequence of the warning. The telex had been sent by Jennifer Young, Pan Am's Director of Operations in the Soviet Union, to her security supervisor in Frankfurt. By the time she testified before the commission, Young appeared to have backed down. She explained that the telex had been written following a conversation with a part-time Pan Am employee based at the embassy who had asked for guidance on how to respond to questions from customers who had seen the warning. Young said that she needed a quick answer from the security supervisor and therefore used the 80 per cent figure to grab his attention. Young added that she had 'no specific numbers' of people who re-booked and had no knowledge about any cancellations resulting from the notice being posted.

The commission's report claimed that its staff had conducted a thorough investigation into all the rumours and allegations concerning changes in travel plans by American personnel. They found only one passenger who had been due to fly to the United States, via Frankfurt, and had changed instead to a direct flight. Since the original booking was for 16 December, rather than 21 December, it was not a decision that saved his, or her, life. However, there was one person whose life may have been saved. The part-time Pan Am employee at the embassy told commission staff that she had booked an American journalist on an airline other than Pan Am on 21 December, without telling him the reason – but commission staff were 'unable to substantiate' the claim.

Whatever the truth about the number of people who re-booked or avoided Pan Am, the commission's report acknowledged that the warning had been far more widely distributed than had been previously imagined. Initial reports had implied that one copy had been put on the staff notice board. In fact it had been posted on many bulletin boards within the embassy, some of which could be viewed by visitors. In addition it had been passed on to all the internal offices within the embassy (including the press office) and also to contracting companies, the US Information Service, the

American Community Association and to the Anglo-American School. 'Ultimately,' the report said, 'the notice was available to most of the approximately 2,000 members of the US community in Moscow.' Given that none of these people ended up on Flight 103, it is hard to believe that their travel plans were not influenced by the warning.

The report raised other suspicions. In particular, it stated that the Finnish police had concluded the warning was a hoax by 10 December. As the relatives were well aware, it was not until three days later, on 13 December, that it was displayed in the Moscow embassy. The explanation, the commission reported, was that senior US officials (presumably intelligence officials) had deliberately not informed the FAA of the Finnish police's discovery. This made little sense because in 1988 Moscow, of all the US embassies in the world, would have been packed with intelligence agents. It would have taken only a telephone call from one of these agents to their counterparts in Helsinki to check whether or not the FAA's warning was credible.

The report stated that the FAA was not informed that the warning was a hoax because the officials involved were 'concerned the carriers would misinterpret the information as a signal to relax their security precautions'. This too was somewhat strange. Since it was the only airline to be named in the warning, Pan Am was clearly by far the most important carrier. As we have seen, shortly after the warning the Helsinki Embassy's Regional Security Officer Kenneth Luzzi assured Pan Am's Jim Berwick it was a hoax. This was even before the 10 December date cited by the President's Commission. If Pan Am could be told it was a hoax, why not the other carriers, through the FAA?

There was a strange postscript to the story. In July 1992 Martin and Rita Cadman read in their newspaper that a man called Stephen Docherty had been sent to prison for four years for making a hoax call to police about a bomb at Victoria station. Martin Cadman wrote at once to the Finnish embassy in London asking who had been prosecuted for the hoax call about the Pan Am airliner and what punishment they received. A reply dated 17 November 1992 stated: 'The identity of the caller cannot be disclosed, as sufficient evidence has not been assembled to convict the chief suspect, a foreigner who obtained Finnish citizenship.'

If this was the case, why, shortly after the Lockerbie disaster, were the US authorities sufficiently confident of the caller's identity to name him off the record as Samra Mahayoun, a Palestinian student residing in Finland? If the official line was that the caller had not been identified, the Cadmans understandably reasoned, who could say for sure that the call was a hoax?

The Cadmans wrote another letter, this one to the Earl of Caithness, who was then junior Minister for Transport, asking for a further inquiry into the Helsinki warning. Caithness replied that he had 'nothing to add, and had not got the authority to release the name of the hoax caller'. When the Cadmans pointed out that no hoaxer had yet been identified, they got a couple of testy letters from the director and coordinator of transport security at the Department of Transport, Mr Harry Ditmas. 'This warning was a hoax,' he parroted, without proof or explanation.

6. UGLY RUMOURS AND BLANKET DENIALS

What were the US and British authorities so afraid of? So afraid that they didn't dare hold full independent inquiries into Lockerbie; so afraid that US agents were dispatched to the crash site to remove items such as Major Charles McKee's suitcase; that the drug and cash finds were denied; and that they tried to show Khalid Jaafar could not have carried the bomb. In the face of official silence and denials, it was left to others to probe these sensitive areas.

The first person independent of the British and American authorities and the media to investigate the bombing was Juval Aviv, president of Interfor, a New York private investigations firm. Born in Israel in 1947, Aviv claims to have spent ten years as an agent of the Israeli secret service, Mossad, and has spoken of his work in assessing security at high-risk Israeli establishments in Europe. He also claims to have led a Mossad hit squad that was dispatched to hunt down the Palestinian terrorists responsible for a massacre of Israeli athletes at the 1972 Munich Olympics.

Aviv settled in New York in the late '70s and in the early '80s formed Interfor. Calling on his own intelligence connections as well as staff who had worked for a number of Western intelligence and police agencies, the company was designed to service corporate and government clients. Aviv's first brush with controversy came in 1984 when he was the main source for the book *Vengeance*, by Canadian journalist George Jonas, which first alleged the Munich revenge mission (and which was the basis for a feature film, *Sword of Gideon*). The book was dismissed by some as fantasy and for many years the Israeli Government denied the squad had ever existed. The Israeli Prime Minister's counter-terrorism advisor, Yigal Carmon, went further, stating categorically that Aviv had never had any connection to Mossad. The US authorities were nevertheless satisfied by his credentials. By the time of the Lockerbie bombing, Interfor was established as a highly capable outfit with clients such as the United States Internal Revenue Service (IRS). According to US government documents declassified over a decade later, Aviv had also been asked by the Secret Service in 1982 and 1983 to assess potential threats to the US President.[1]

In May 1989 Interfor came to the attention of James Shaugnessy, a New York attorney who represented Pan Am and the US Aviation Insurance

Group (USAIG), their insurers, after he was recommended by several of the city's leading law firms. By this time the airline and USAIG were facing a civil action brought by families of the victims of Flight 103, which claimed that the airline's faulty security procedures had brought about the tragedy. USAIG wanted to know whether the civil action was worth contesting and therefore required a wide-ranging investigation of the bombing. Shaugnessy and his team checked out a number of investigators and terrorism experts. Aviv came out top of the pile.[2]

Starting in June 1989, he began a three-month investigation which took him to Europe and the Middle East, and in mid-September 1989 delivered a preliminary report. The Interfor Report, as it came to be known, was based largely on six intelligence sources. Although not named, Aviv's descriptions made impressive reading. 'Source 1', for example, was described as comprising of 'six persons working in different units of the intelligence community of a Western government . . . The very number of separate sources in these agencies, (not necessarily sympathetic to each other), all sharing the conclusion, as well as the depth of the intelligence gathered, and the agencies' considerable resources and special interest in the matter, justifies rating this information as very good.'

The report confirmed the bombing had been commissioned by Iran and carried out by Ahmed Jibril's PFLP-GC with the help of their Syrian sponsors and various other terrorists. This was hardly sensational, but the other claims made in the report were; in particular its account of how Jibril's men executed the Iranian contract and its explanation of why so many warnings had failed to save Flight 103. Aviv's sources had independently told him the same appalling story. They suggested the bombing was the result of some of the insane US covert foreign policy initiatives of the governments of President Reagan and his deputy, and eventual successor, George Bush. It also explained the rumours that had circulated among the police at Lockerbie, and backed up the early press stories.

By the time of Reagan's election in 1980, America was reeling from the successive humiliations of Vietnam and the mid-'70s oil crisis which brought to an abrupt end decades of economic stability. Further humiliation followed the 1979 Iranian revolution, when the puppet US regime of the Shah was replaced by the radical, Islamic, anti-Western government of Ayatollah Khomeni. The seizure of 52 hostages in the American Embassy in Tehran became the dominant issue in the latter stages of President Jimmy Carter's government, its apparent impotence further underlined when a planned helicopter rescue mission came to grief in the Iranian desert with the loss of eight US servicemen.

As Carter's Republican challenger in the 1980 presidential election, Ronald Reagan profited from such blunders. Years later, evidence emerged that in October 1980 some members of his campaign team had colluded with Iran, during secret meetings in Paris, to keep the hostages in captivity until after the election. The so-called 'October Surprise' mission was master-minded by his campaign manager William Casey and also involved Reagan's running-mate George Bush.[3] Despite its immediate success, October Surprise prefigured the crisis of the mid-'80s, known as Iran-Contra, which was to become the Reagan government's Achilles heel.[4]

Iran-Contra was triggered by the capture of a few US citizens in Lebanon in the early '80s. Given its earlier manipulation of the hostage issue, the Reagan White House was especially sensitive to its political potency. The March 1984 seizure of the CIA's Beirut Station Chief William Buckley, who ironically had been sent to Beirut to coordinate hostage rescue operations, caused the tremors of anxiety to give way to full-blown panic.

In response to the growing problem Reagan's henchmen, led once again by William Casey, who had been appointed CIA Director, reverted to the same covert deals that had served them during October Surprise. These involved the secret, illegal supply of weapons to Iran in return for help releasing the hostages. Iran was by then involved in its eight-year war with Iraq and weapons sales to either side constituted a breach of United Nations agreements. The profits from the deals went towards the illegal supply of weapons to the right-wing Nicaraguan Contra guerrillas. US government support for the Contras had been outlawed by Congress in 1984, but Reagan's administration was convinced that the left-wing Sandanista government of the small Central American state posed a threat to US interests in the whole region.

Although initiated by William Casey, the operation was run on a day-to-day basis by a hitherto obscure NSC staff member, Lieutenant-Colonel Oliver North. When the operation was exposed in November 1986, most media coverage focused on the gung-ho super-patriot and on how much President Reagan and his deputy George Bush knew. The fact that the White House inner-circle had had dealings with a number of controversial Middle-East figures, such as the Iranian arms dealer Manucher Ghorbanifar and the Syrian arms dealer Monzer Al-Kassar passed by with rather less comment.[5]

According to the Interfor Report, in 1988 – well after the Iran Contra deals had come to light – the CIA became involved in another strange hostage deal with Middle East heroin traffickers. The report claimed that the Agency learned of a major heroin trafficking operation being run on behalf of the same groups who were holding the hostages in Lebanon. It involved consignments of the drug being transported from Lebanon and Syria to Europe and sometimes onwards to the US. Aviv claimed the West German BKA was tipped off about the smuggling and in turn informed a locally based CIA unit and the DEA. The CIA unit approached the drug dealers and offered to allow them to continue the drug shipments, especially to the US, if they helped arrange the release of the American hostages in Lebanon. They agreed, aware that by protecting the drug shipments the CIA was, in effect, making the operation risk-free. The shipments became what is known in law enforcement parlance as 'controlled deliveries'; they were monitored and, through cooperation with the authorities in other countries, allowed to pass through security and customs checks unhindered.

Aviv stated that the CIA unit answered to a control in Washington DC, but he was unsure whether its activities were sanctioned by CIA headquarters. According to his report, the drug-running operation frequently utilised Frankfurt airport, which employed a number of Turkish Islamic fundamentalists recruited to the cause at mosques in Cologne and Bonn. Drug mules would board flights with a checked-in suitcase containing innocent items, which a baggage-handler would then switch for an identical case containing heroin. One of the mules used in the operation, the report claimed, was Khalid Jaafar.

Aviv reported that the drug dealers informed their terrorist associates of the CIA-protected drug pipeline. Realising that it provided a security loophole which perfectly suited his plans, Ahmed Jibril called upon the drug dealers' loyalty, demanding that he be allowed to exploit it. The arrest of Hafez Dalkamoni and bomb-maker Marwan Khreesat in the October 1988 Autumn Leaves raids interrupted Jibril's plans, but Aviv claimed he was able to call upon the technical assistance of a Libyan bomb-maker known as 'The Professor' and a Syrian known as 'Patel' to construct the Lockerbie bomb. Thereafter it was simply a matter of putting the bomb in the suitcase to be switched with the case checked in by Khalid Jaafar as part of an apparently routine controlled delivery.

The only potential threat to the sordid dealings, according to Aviv's report, was the small team of intelligence specialists led by Major Charles McKee and CIA Beirut deputy station chief Matthew Gannon, who had been assigned to locate Western hostages in Lebanon. The team had stumbled on the secret deals with the drug dealers and McKee in particular was appalled. He reported back to CIA headquarters, but nothing was done. Believing that the CIA double-dealing was jeopardising both the hostage rescue mission and the lives of his team, he planned to return to the

US unannounced to blow the whistle. Had he been successful, the CIA and President-elect Bush would be faced with an almighty scandal. Unbeknown to McKee's team, the drug dealers got wind of his travel plans and reported back to their CIA contacts.

Aviv detailed a number of very specific warnings about the bombing, some of which came from Israeli intelligence. The last warning came only an hour before the feeder flight left Germany, when BKA agents, who normally monitored the controlled drug deliveries, saw a bag being put on the plane which was different to the one usually used to carry drugs. According to Aviv they warned the CIA unit, which in turn reported to its control. It was told: 'Don't worry about it. Don't stop it. Let it go.' They issued no instructions to the BKA, so the BKA did nothing. In short, the Interfor Report alleged, the CIA allowed the death of 270 people, including American agents, in order to protect its own murky deals.

It seemed too crazy to be true. And some of the report's details were indeed bizarre. It claimed, for example, that Jibril personally met Khalid Jaafar and 'The Professor' in Bonn on 13 December 1988, though quite why it was necessary to introduce the unwitting mule to the bomb-maker was unclear. Despite such peculiarities, the degree of detail in the 27-page report was compelling. If, as was later alleged, it was a complete fabrication, then it was a very clever and intricate one.

For the senior executives of Pan Am and their insurers, the Interfor Report must have made uncomfortable reading. Already facing the civil compensation claim brought by the Lockerbie victims' relatives, they were now confronted with a document suggesting the airline's own baggage-handlers had been unwitting accessories to the bombing. Just how much was known about the secret drugs channel by the higher echelons within Pan Am, the Interfor Report did not reveal.

As the major US flag carrier, Pan Am had a cosy relationship with the US intelligence community going back decades. Cooperation in 'off the books' covert operations had taken place in Vietnam. Senior retired veterans of the CIA have stated that Pan Am was amenable and would be used by various government agencies who wished to ship personnel or cargo without disclosing it on a manifest. When asked why Pan Am cooperated with agencies such as the CIA, the answer was invariably that they were 'doing their national duty'.[6] Whilst it was manifestly clear that nobody within Pan Am knew Flight 103 was going to be blown up, it was inconceivable that a CIA-protected, regular drugs shipment could have occurred without the cooperation of someone in a position of authority within the airline.

Rather than probing these sensitive areas, Aviv chose to emphasise how real culpability for the disaster lay with the US government. He suggested that in defending the civil action, Pan Am and their insurers should subpoena the CIA, the State Department and other Federal agencies for all the information they held about the disaster. The lawyers followed his advice. In so doing, as we will describe in later chapters, they precipitated a Kafkaesque legal farce that would drag on for years.

The US government quickly moved to quash Pan Am's subpoenas before Chief Judge Thomas Platt of the US District Court, Eastern District of New York. Based on papers he was shown in camera Platt felt the government might have a valid claim that the documents in question were covered by state secrets privilege, but the government refused even this suggestion and offered no justification for its refusal to release the documents. In response, Judge Platt directed the government to search for all the documents relating to where the bomb was placed on the plane and to the warnings it had received prior to 21 December 1988.[7] Rather than responding in full to Pan Am's subpoenas, the US government distilled the specific allegations it had identified in the Aviv report and instructed each of the six agencies that James Shaugnessy had attempted to subpoena to respond to the distillation with a declaration that there was nothing to support it.

Not everyone in the federal institutions was so adamant that Aviv's claims were baseless. Joe Miano was a mid-level analyst for the DEA at the time. 'I was in my office at the DEA headquarters in downtown Washington when the news [Pan Am 103] came over the radio,' he recalled. 'There was something haunting in hearing the report. It stuck with me.'

Miano was reassigned in his duties as an intelligence analyst for the European/Middle Eastern Strategic Drug Intelligence office in 1989. He began working on assembling strategic intelligence about the drug situations throughout the Middle East.

In late 1989 Miano read Aviv's leaked Interfor Report, which implicated Middle East drug dealers in the bombing. This aroused his interest and with the knowledge of his superiors he contacted Aviv. He later wrote:

> I looked at Aviv's report and was very interested. It had a number of facts that seemed to be consistent with what we believed to be true about the dealers. I spoke with Aviv and he said there was more information that would prove conclusively that they were to blame.
>
> But I was hooked on the idea that perhaps the US government was hiding something. There was just too much information that suggested the dealers might have been involved.[8]

Miano drew his information from a variety of sources but will not reveal what he saw in DEA files, however what he saw convinced him that there were too many inconsistencies in the offical version of the crime.

As we will see in Chapter 11, Miano's suspicions were to cost him dear.

James Shaugnessy attempted to depose the officials who had signed the declarations that there was nothing to support his subpoenas, but the court ruled against him on a technicality. At a further conference in July 1990, Judge Platt finally ordered the government to produce the documents he had previously asked for so he could view them in camera. A few months later, Shaugnessy was astonished to learn that in the wake of the July conference Judge Platt had been confidentially briefed by government agents. As a result of this briefing, he had dropped his previous order for the government to produce its documents and quashed the Pan Am subpoenas. Shaugnessy was never told when the meeting took place, who the government agents were and what they told the judge. Undeterred, he obtained leave to commence a third-party legal action against the US government, alleging that its intelligence and law enforcement agencies were culpable in the bombing. The action would only proceed if the airline and their insurers lost the civil liability suit brought by the Lockerbie victims' relatives. Once again, he attempted to subpoena various government agencies.

Shaugnessy was to suffer for his tenacity. In applying for the third-party action to be dismissed, the government filed a memorandum recommending that substantial financial sanctions should be imposed on him for suggesting the government was at fault and for abusing court procedures.

The attorney persisted with the action against the government and once again subpoenaed the various agencies implicated in the bombing. Judge Platt ordered the government to respond to the subpoenas, but the government continued to play the secrecy card. At another in camera meeting in July 1991, government officials showed certain documents to Platt and asserted state secrets privilege. The judge subsequently informed Shaugnessy that on the basis of the documents he had seen, the contents of which were never disclosed, he accepted the government's claim for state secrets privilege. Somewhat contradictorily, he also denied discovery on the grounds that there was nothing in the documents that would assist the third-party action against the government.

Two years earlier, journalists Emma Gilbey of ABC Television and Tom Foster of the *Syracuse Post Standard* had independently attempted to use the US Freedom of Information Act in order to gain the information

Shaugnessy had sought in his original subpoenas of September 1989. Amongst other things, they requested information about prior warnings of attacks against American planes at Frankfurt airport; how the bomb was put on Flight 103 and by whom; and drug shipments through Frankfurt airport, including the Pan Am baggage area. The requests were turned down, but the answer received from the National Security Agency was revealing. It stated that the information was located in the records, but copies could not be supplied on the grounds of 'statutory privilege' and 'state secrets'. It was a strange response, given that Pan Am's lawyers were told that no such records existed.

Although Judge Platt refused the government's motion to quash Pan Am's third-party legal action, by denying discovery of the documents he effectively killed it off. In a last throw of the dice, Shaugnessy asked the court to either issue an order granting discovery or dismiss the suit altogether. Three days before Pan Am's civil liability trial was due to begin, on 24 April 1992, Platt finally dismissed it.

The frustration of Shaugnessy's team was all the greater because he had, by that time, accumulated evidence which he felt would help to corroborate the Interfor Report. It was evidence that the authorities, once again, seemed determined to ignore.

In January the team hired a highly experienced, retired US army polygrapher James Keefe, an Interfor employee, to conduct polygraph – or 'lie detector' – tests on three of its Frankfurt baggage-handlers. Initially Shaugnessy was apprehensive about using lie detector tests, but was persuaded by Aviv. Aviv's investigations suggested that the three, Kilnic Aslan Tuzcu, Roland E. O'Neill and Gregory L. Grissom, might have been involved in baggage switches as part of the alleged CIA-protected covert drug-running operation. Polygraphs can be unreliable and are not admissible as evidence in courts of law on either side of the Atlantic. The test, which all three baggage-handlers consented to voluntarily, indicated that Tuzcu and O'Neill had lied in denying that they were involved in a baggage switch. Grissom was ruled out as a suspect, because he was out on the airport's tarmac at the time Flight 103 was loaded. Richard Arther, of Scientific Lie Detection Inc, carried out a subsequent review of James Keefe's work on 28 February 1990. Arther was able to corroborate Keefe's results on Grissom and Tuzcu, but was unable to render an opinion on the test carried out on O'Neill.

James Shaugnessy immediately reported the results to the Scottish police, who asked him to sign a statement about the tests in the presence of the FBI. But in the wake of this potentially crucial lead, neither the Scottish police nor the American or German authorities sought to apprehend Tuzcu and O'Neill, and initiate inquiries of their own. To add to Shaugnessy's frustration, when Keefe returned to New York he was subpoenaed to defend his actions before a federal grand jury in Washington.

Having had a second polygrapher confirm Keefe's findings, at least in respect of Tuzcu, Pan Am arranged for a pretext to fly Tuzcu and O'Neill to Britain, believing that the Scottish police would be interested in detaining and questioning them. When the pair landed at Heathrow there were no police waiting to meet them and, despite the fact they were in London for a few hours, none of the authorities showed the slightest interest. No doubt rather perplexed, the two men returned to Frankfurt that evening. There remains no evidence to implicate any of the baggage handlers in the bombing.

Once again the only people to suffer for the initiative were the airline's legal team, this time at the hands of the German authorities. The BKA announced a criminal investigation of the polygraph team, for taking polygraphs illegally and for kidnapping the two subjects. Both allegations were plainly ludicrous and were eventually dropped, but not before the BKA had filed a complaint with the US State Department.

Shaugnessy claimed to have received other information, besides the polygraph tests, which indicated that the Interfor Report might be correct. In a sworn affidavit he described how he met with a number of informed sources, including four well-placed intelligence sources, who confirmed many elements of the report and provided additional information.

The first of these sources he described as 'a former agent for the United States Military intelligence and perhaps the DIA'. Shaugnessy spent a day interviewing this source in California, during which the source 'provided me with information and showed documentation concerning the involvement of the United States intelligence community in narcotics trafficking into the United States'. The second source, Shaugnessy said, was 'a former agent with [West] German Intelligence' who, like Juval Aviv, carried out an investigation and delivered a report to him. Shaugnessy described the third source as a former CIA employee 'who had spent many years working in the Middle East'. This individual provided information about 'the involvement of the United States' intelligence community in arms trafficking and narcotics trafficking.' The final of the four intelligence sources, according to Shaugnessy, was 'a then current senior analyst for the DEA' who told him that 'much of what was contained in Mr Aviv's report relating to narcotics trafficking, particularly narcotics trafficking through Frankfurt Airport, was true'.[9]

It would be almost exactly twelve months after the Interfor Report was leaked to the media before journalists produced their own evidence of US government involvement in the Lockerbie. However, when it came it could hardly have been more damaging to the government: the organisations involved were two of the country's largest broadcasters, NBC and ABC. On consecutive nights, 30 and 31 October 1990, the networks broadcast similar stories detailing how the protected drug-running operation had been central to the bombing. Significantly, unlike the Interfor Report, neither broadcast mentioned the CIA and the crazy deals it had allegedly struck with drug dealers. Instead they concentrated on the DEA, which the Interfor Report had only mentioned in passing. Rather than suggesting that Lockerbie was the fault of a maverick CIA operation, as Juval Aviv had done, the reports alleged that the bombers exploited an operation officially sanctioned by the DEA.

NBC was the first with the story on 30 October. Its report explained:

> NBC news has learned that Pan Am flights from Frankfurt, including 103, had been used a number of times by the DEA as part of its undercover operations to fly informants and suitcases of heroin into Detroit as part of a sting operation to catch dealers in Detroit. The undercover operation, code-named Operation Courier, was set up three years ago by the DEA in Cyprus to infiltrate Lebanese heroin groups in the Middle East and their connections in Detroit . . . informants would put suitcases on the Pan Am flights, apparently without the usual security checks, according to one airline source, through an arrangement between the DEA and German authorities. Law enforcement officials say the fear now is that the terrorists that blew up Pan Am 103 somehow learned about what the DEA was doing, infiltrated the undercover operation and substituted the bomb for the heroin in one of the DEA shipments.

The programme named Khalid Jaafar as the unwitting bomb carrier.

The ABC report the following evening was more specific, naming the front company established by the DEA in Cyprus:

> In 1987, the US Drugs Enforcement Administration set up a dummy company called Eurame here in Nicosia, on the Mediterranean island of Cyprus . . . The DEA recruited undercover couriers who would be monitored as they carried the drugs from Lebanon, through Cyprus and Europe and onto drug dealers in

Detroit. ABC news has confirmed that one of those couriers was a young Lebanese American named Khalid Jaafar.

Khalid Jaafar's name had, of course, cropped up before as the alleged dupe who had taken the bomb on the plane, but he had never been revealed as having been connected to a United States government agency. Neither report could be shrugged off lightly. Each had taken many months to complete and each was fronted by very well known and respected reporters; Brian Ross of NBC and Pierre Salinger of ABC. Furthermore, both reports were based on sources within the government's own law enforcement and intelligence structures.

One of the sources common to each broadcaster was an American called Lester Coleman. His story was to become one of the most controversial and distracting sub-plots to the entire Lockerbie saga. Originally a journalist, in the mid-'80s Coleman began to work as a contract consultant for the DEA's Cyprus office, the nerve centre of efforts to monitor drug production in Lebanon. It was no ordinary assignment because, while working for the DEA, Coleman was simultaneously employed by the US Defence Intelligence Agency (DIA). Attached to the Pentagon, the DIA is the ultra-secretive, combined intelligence arm of the US armed forces, with an estimated 57,000 employees and a budget five times that of the CIA. One of the reasons Coleman was chosen by the DIA was his ability to speak Arabic. He had learned the language as a child, when his family had moved to the Middle East where his father worked as an engineer. According to Coleman, the DIA was desperate for information about Lebanon, but it also wanted to keep a discreet eye on the DEA and CIA, both of which it viewed with suspicion. His primary duty, he says, was therefore to monitor a fellow government agency whilst keeping his true affiliations secret.

By the time Coleman arrived in Cyprus, the flow of drugs out of Lebanon was so great that the best the DEA could do was monitor where the supply was going in the US in order to catch the dealers there. In order to do this, he claims, it relied on controlled deliveries, but he insists that these were merely a fig leaf for the CIA's secret hostages agenda. The DEA had standing instructions to assist in supplying informants who might help locate hostages. Michael Hurley, the head of DEA Cyprus, attended weekly meetings with the CIA's Cyprus station chief.[10] The groups holding the hostages in Lebanon were, by and large, the same ones who were in control of drug production. It followed that the gathering of intelligence on drug production would also yield vital intelligence on the hostages. The DEA's network of confidential informants and sub-sources were, in effect, the

CIA's eyes and ears in Lebanon, a mixing of roles, Coleman claims, which may have proved fatal. To remain secure the operation required the complete loyalty of the network of informants, but in the frenetic atmosphere of war-torn Lebanon this could not be guaranteed. A myriad of different clans and political and religious factions were vying for power, all of whom had to cooperate with the Syrian military and intelligence forces, which kept an iron grip on the drug trade. Coleman alleges that the informants were not trained agents and, worse still, that some were reporting back to the Syrian-controlled terrorists.

He insists he tried to raise this security issue with Hurley but was ignored. Tension between the two men grew and Coleman eventually left the island in May 1988. He claims that prior to departing he had warned Hurley, in a taped telephone conversation, that the security situation was 'a disaster waiting to happen'.[11] Hurley does not deny rowing with Coleman over the phone, but accuses him of editing in the phrase and of concocting his claims of lax security. He also maintains that Coleman was sacked by the DEA for 'unsatisfactory behaviour.'

Despite his avowed prophecy, Coleman says it was not until months after Lockerbie that he realised the disaster might be connected to drug trafficking. He claimed the realisation had been triggered by the discovery that Khalid Jaafar was among the victims. 'The kid was one of those I saw coming through the office in Cyprus,' he later insisted. 'I knew from the conversations around me in '88 that he was involved in controlled deliveries – there's no doubt in my mind about that at all.'[12]

Coleman undermined his case by wrongly placing much of the blame for the bombing on Michael Hurley, against whom he held considerable personal animosity but no evidence. Having left Cyprus seven months before Lockerbie, he had no special knowledge of the bombing, nor did he have evidence that the alleged faulty security in the DEA's Cyprus operation contributed to the disaster. In any case, his theory that the bombers had planted the bomb on Khalid Jaafar as part of a controlled drug delivery operation, via the DEA office in Cyprus, fell at the first hurdle, for two simple reasons. Firstly, when Jaafar left Lebanon for the last time he flew directly to Germany, rather than passing through Cyprus. Secondly, he spent the six weeks prior to Lockerbie based in Germany.

By the time they got to speak to Coleman, the NBC and ABC investigations were well advanced. The DEA responded to the networks' subsequent broadcasts with an internal investigation. A month later its administrator, Robert Bonner, could announce that the investigation had found 'no connection' between a DEA undercover operation and the bombing.

In December 1990 a further investigation was held in the US Congress by the sub-committee on Government Information, Justice and Agriculture of the House Government Operations Committee. A sub-committee spokesperson explained that the purpose of the inquiry was 'to hear from the DEA and the FBI what they did to investigate the charges'. If that was the case, the hearings were a failure on their own terms. Making his opening statement on 18 December, the sub-committee's chairman, Robert Wise of West Virginia, put on record his disappointment that the DEA and Department of Justice did not see fit to make field agents available to the hearings and that written information from the DEA, particularly a closeout memo on the investigation, had not been received. The only cooperation the DEA gave was to allow two senior officials to testify: Stephen H. Greene, Assistant Administrator in its Operations Division, and David Westrate, Assistant Administrator for Planning and Inspection. As for the FBI, Wise said:

> I want to note that the FBI to this date has been totally uncooperative, and that they have been issued three invitations to appear . . . despite repeated invitations and at least one meeting with an FBI official and also a press release put out by the FBI, saying that they had completed their investigation and found nothing to link the DEA to the Pan Am Flight 103 bombing, they still refuse to make that presentation to Congress.

Wise noted that there had been something of a U-turn on the part of the FBI. When preparations for the hearings were taking place an FBI legislative representative had told sub-committee staff members that the Bureau's investigation of the allegations was separate from the overall investigation of Pan Am 103. This implied there would be no problem making details of that investigation available to the sub-committee but, Wise reported,

> Now we are told that the investigations are inextricable, and that the FBI does not feel comfortable coming forward on the allegations concerning DEA until the overall investigation of the Pan Am flight 103 bombing is concluded.

He was understandably perplexed that the FBI could see fit to issue a press release stating that it had found no evidence to link the DEA to the bombing, but could not explain to the sub-committee what the grounds were for having reached this conclusion.

The sub-committee's hearings barely investigated the allegations. Instead, its members had to be content with the assurances of the two DEA representatives that its own internal investigation had turned up no evidence to incriminate itself. The investigation was headed by Stephen H. Greene, who explained that it had reviewed over 1,600 case files opened in Europe and the USA during fiscal years 1984–89. Of those, he said, only three involved the transit of drugs through Frankfurt and none had taken place in December 1988, or matched the scenario described in the recent television reports. He went on to say that no connection had been found between individuals named in those reports and active and inactive DEA informants and that no one on Flight 103 was a 'DEA employee, informant or source of information'.

But what if, as Lester Coleman claimed, Khalid Jaafar was a DEA sub-source rather than an actual informant? David Westrate denied outright that sub-sources would be used as couriers in controlled drug deliveries. When pressed by Robert Wise to state categorically whether or not Jaafar was a sub-source, he replied,

> It is our conclusion that he was not an informant, certainly, or a sub-source, nor do we have any information that would indicate that he was operating in any way in a situation in which he would have sub-sources for us.

However, Westrate had just acknowledged that sub-sources are not generally known to the DEA. A little later Greene was also pushed on this point: 'I am saying again, not to our knowledge. We stated before, we cannot determine who all sub-sources are. Sub-sources are often known only to an informant.'

Wise quizzed Greene further about Jaafar, asking if the investigation had looked into Jaafar's family background and, if so, what it had found. He then inquired about the frequent trips the young man had reportedly made between Dearborn, Michigan and Lebanon. In reply to both questions, Greene asked that he be allowed to defer his answers to the closed executive session of the hearings. Nothing has ever been made public about what was said in that session. Greene would have given honest and frank answers and no doubt he would have, at the very least, told the sub-committee that some members of the Jaafar clan had been among the most important drug-producing dynasties of the Bekaa Valley.

Amid the obfuscation, two interesting facts emerged from the hearings. The first was the admission that the DEA used a front company on Cyprus called Eurame. ABC Television had identified it as the transit point for the DEA couriers who were used on the controlled drug deliveries. Greene claimed that it had been set up by the Cypriot police and that it was merely used by the DEA as a place to meet contacts away from the US Embassy.

The second revelation did not come out through the public session, but in a memorandum that was reproduced in the official transcript of the hearings. Written a year earlier on 22 December 1989 by Nicholas P. Geier, a staff investigator from the President's Commission on Aviation Security and Terrorism, it reported on a meeting with Richard P. Bly, Deputy Assistant Administrator in the DEA's office of intelligence. The meeting had clearly been called following the revelations of Juval Aviv's Interfor Report. Bly had assured Geier that there was no DEA operation involving a Pan Am plane on that date and that the DEA had no warning of the disaster. The memo went on to report that:

> Mr Steve Green [sic], Assistant Administrator, Office of Intelligence,
> was in Europe attending a meeting and was scheduled to return to the
> US on the ill-fated Pan Am flight 103. However, the meeting was
> extended for another day and he was forced to cancel his flight.[13]

The next major media investigation of Lockerbie came in a front-page article in *Time* magazine on 27 April 1992, headlined 'THE UNTOLD STORY OF PAN AM 103'. Veteran reporter Roy Rowan spent four months investigating the story, much of which was spent with Juval Aviv. Having met with Aviv's sources and after checking with sources of his own, Rowan concluded that the Interfor Report was substantially correct.

Like the Interfor Report the *Time* article claimed that a Middle Eastern heroin trafficking operation, conducted, with the blessing of a freewheeling CIA unit in Germany, was utilized by Ahmed Jibril in order to get the bomb on the plane. It also alleged a DEA-controlled drug delivery operation run from Cyprus. The article made no mention of Khalid Jaafar or Hizbullah, but it reported a means by which a rogue bag might have got onboard without being recorded in the airport's paperwork. Rowan had obtained an FBI telex dated 23 October 1989, from the US Embassy in Bonn to the Bureau's director in Washington. It was written following a visit to Frankfurt airport by FBI agent Lawrence Whitaker the previous month. According to the document, while being given a guided tour of the baggage area Whitaker and Detective Inspector Watson McAteer, of the Scottish police, 'observed an individual approach coding station 206 with a single piece of luggage, place the luggage in a luggage container, encode the destination into the computer and leave without making any notation on the duty sheet'.

Rowan also reported that a Samsonite case which should have been sent on Flight 103 was mysteriously left behind in Frankfurt. This strengthened the theory that the bomb suitcase had been switched with an innocent one by an airport insider who believed he was involved in a drug-smuggling operation. The Samsonite which was left behind belonged to a Pan Am pilot, Captain John Hubbard, and was one of two identical cases he was sending from Berlin back to his home town of Seattle. The airline had fixed the cases with so-called 'rush' tags, special labels designed to speedily reunite bags which become separated from their owners. Hubbard's rush tags were marked for Pan Am Flight 637 from Berlin to Frankfurt, Flight 107 from Frankfurt to London and Flight 123 from London to Seattle. When Flight 637 was delayed, 11 of the cases destined for Flight 107 were left behind, including Hubbard's two Samsonites. At Frankfurt airport they were therefore re-routed via Pan Am 103. However, only one of the suitcases ended up among the debris at Lockerbie, with the other remaining in Frankfurt and being forwarded to Seattle the next day. While this did not prove that the Samsonite containing the bomb was switched for one of Hubbard's Samsonites, it did indicate another means by which the bomb suitcase could have got onto Flight 103 without being recorded.

Most of Rowan's article concentrated on the Beirut hostage rescue team led by Major Charles McKee. Like Aviv, Rowan reported that at the time of his death McKee was heading back to Washington to expose the CIA unit's secret deal with the Middle East drug dealers, which McKee believed was undermining his team's efforts. The article also alleged that the team's plans were passed to the Iranian Embassy in Beirut by an American named David Lovejoy. The implication was that Lovejoy was part of a double-cross designed to thwart McKee's whistle-blowing and protect the CIA unit's dirty deals. *Time* printed a photograph of a former friend of Lester Coleman's called Michael Shafer, who it wrongly alleged was Lovejoy.

The Lebanese newspaper *Al-Dustur*, in its detailed article of 22 May 1989, claimed an American called 'David Love-Boy' had tipped off the Iranian about McKee's team. The name David Lovejoy also surfaced in *The Observer* article of 31 July 1989. The article claimed it was an alias used by an American, who allegedly reconnoitred security arrangements at Frankfurt airport and also helped transfer funds from Iran to the PFLP-GC.

It has been speculated that Lovejoy may have been Beirut-based British arms dealer Ian Spiro, who had sold weapons to Iran since the late 1970s and had developed good contacts with Iranian-backed Islamic radicals in Lebanon, such as Hizbullah. As these groups began to take Western hostages, he was paid by American and British intelligence for information. It is claimed that his greatest coup was to obtain a copy of William Buckley's confession via his Iranian contacts, who included Ali Akbar Mohtashemi.[14] Among his Western intelligence contacts was Oliver North, who arranged for him to meet the Archbishop of Canterbury's special envoy Terry Waite shortly before Waite went to Lebanon to negotiate with the hostage-takers.[15] Western intelligence reportedly severed their contacts with Spiro after North's secret arms-for-hostages deals were exposed[16] and, according to some reports, he then began working as a double agent for Iran.[17]

Throughout his time in Lebanon Spiro had five passports in different names[18] and was never known by his real name. He left Beirut in 1988 and, reverting to his real name, settled in California with his second wife Gail and their three children. In November 1992 Gail and the children were found murdered at the family home near San Diego. A few days later Spiro was found dead at the wheel of his car, seventy miles away in the desert, with a bottle of cyanide at his side. It appeared to be a classic murder-suicide. It was rumoured that his business had gone awry and that he was facing mounting debts.[19]

Some, including members of his immediate family, were convinced that he was murdered to maintain his silence. Having previously kept a very low profile, it was thought that financial pressures might have driven him to sell his story. Whether true or not, it was certainly the case that a few weeks before his death he had begun to contact journalists. One anonymous CIA insider said his colleagues 'were not very happy that Spiro's links with the agency had come into the open'.[20]

Another theory was that Spiro was killed by a Lebanese hit squad, either because he was about to betray his hostage-taking contacts to the US authorities or because he was trying to blackmail them. It was common for Lebanese gangs to wreak revenge by murdering whole families. The deaths coincided with the publication of full-page advertisements in the Arab press advertising a US government bounty scheme which promised substantial rewards for information that might lead to the capture of the hostage-takers.[21]

Whether murder or suicide, intelligence reports circulating in the Middle East at the time of Spiro's death suggested he was associated with Charles McKee's hostage rescue mission. One of those reports claimed he had tipped off the Iranians about the movements of McKee's team and their plans to return to the US on Flight 103.[22]

7. NEW CLUES IN MALTA

In the months after the Lockerbie disaster, pieces of the jigsaw fell steadily into place. Everyone seemed to accept that the bombing was a revenge attack for the downing of Iran Air Flight 655 and that Ahmed Jibril's PFLP-GC had executed the Iranian contract with back-up from his Syrian allies and fellow radicals' groups. Indeed, on 12 September 1989 there was virtually official confirmation of the PFLP-GC's role in the bombing when the FBI's anti-terrorism chief Buck Revell told a congressional committee that the Bureau believed it had identified the group responsible for the bombing.[1] Official leaks had also identified Khalid Jaafar as the unwitting bomb carrier. Drug finds at the crash site gave weight to the suggestion that the terrorists had exploited a Middle East heroin-smuggling operation.

Juval Aviv's Interfor Report had confirmed these findings and explained some of the outstanding mysteries: why the drug finds were kept quiet; why American agents were desperate to recover Major Charles McKee's belongings from the crash site; and why the governments on both sides of the Atlantic were unwilling to hold proper inquiries and release documents about the bombing.

The world did not know it at the time, but well before the Interfor Report's shocking scenario was leaked, the first crucial steps had been taken in the creation of a very different version of the Lockerbie story. A wholesale realignment of the official investigation would take place that would not only erase any suggestion of US complicity in the bombing, but would also eventually exonerate the PFLP-GC and their sponsors in Iran and Syria, shifting the blame to two obscure Libyans. Those first steps placed the focus of the investigation away from Germany to the Mediterranean island of Malta.

On 29 October 1989, just three days before the Interfor Report was leaked to the media, the *Sunday Times* ran a front page article headed: 'LOCKERBIE DISASTER TRAIL LEADS POLICE TO MALTA'. Reporter David Leppard revealed, 'Police investigating the Lockerbie air disaster have uncovered evidence that the bomb which destroyed the American jumbo jet was originally loaded on to the plane at Malta.' It was clear that Leppard had very generous sources within various law enforcement agencies and his articles were a reliable barometer of the official investigation.

The evidence that had led detectives to Malta, Leppard reported, was baggage records from Frankfurt airport which indicated that an unaccompanied bag had been loaded onto Flight 103, having been transferred from an Air Malta flight to Frankfurt on the morning of the disaster. Forensic examiners had determined that the bomb bag contained clothes made in Malta, so the police had concluded that the unaccompanied bag had contained the bomb. If this was true, Khalid Jaafar and the alleged botched CIA drugs-for-intelligence operation immediately became red herrings.

As Leppard's book *On the Trail of Terror* later revealed, the Frankfurt airport documents consisted of a computerised record from the airport's baggage transit system of all the bags delivered by that system to Flight 103A from Frankfurt to London. They also included a worksheet filled in by baggage-handlers at the so-called coding station 206, one of the points at which bags entered into the automated baggage transit system. From there the bags were automatically conveyed to computerised input counters, where they were recorded by the computer and dispatched to the relevant aircraft. Leppard claimed the Lockerbie investigators were able to match all but one of the bags recorded on the computerised list to passengers on Flight 103A. That bag, numbered B8849 on the computerised record, was apparently logged into the system at input counter S0009 at 1307 hours. Bags going through this counter were recorded as having been physically entered into the system at coding station 206.

The handwritten worksheet for station 206 was filled in by two baggage-handlers, Joachim Koscha and Mehmet Candar. It noted the originating flights of the various batches of baggage dealt with by the station 206, and appeared to show that between 13:04 and 13:10 they were dealing with bags from KM180, the Air Malta flight that had arrived from the island on the morning of 21 December.

The documents seemed to provide irrefutable evidence that an unaccompanied bag from Malta had made its way onto Flight 103. In fact, in years to come gaping flaws would be exposed in this evidence, but even at the time there were some very strange aspects to the story. Leppard reported that the documents were not handed to the Scottish police until August 1989, a full eight months after the disaster. Stranger still, they had apparently been in the possession of the West German BKA since February 1989.

Leppard suggested German bungling and the rivalry with the Scottish police was responsible for the mishap, but such factors could not account for another curious twist to the tale. When the BKA handed over the documents it also supplied two BKA internal memoranda, which analysed the baggage on board Flight 103. Based on the two airport documents, one of the memos clearly stated that a bag from Air Malta flight KM180 had ended up on the doomed jumbo jet. It could have shown that the BKA's definitive conclusion could not be sustained, yet when the Crown Office later announced indictments against two Libyans the documents would be central to its case.

The preservation of all baggage records from Frankfurt airport should have been a priority for the German authorities from the moment they learned of the crash. Although there was no immediate proof that the plane had been bombed, a thorough investigation of the crash would require all available records to be analysed. For reasons never adequately explained, other records were not preserved. The list, when analysed in tandem with the worksheet from coding station 206, enabled the BKA to surmise that the bomb suitcase had come unaccompanied from Malta. Vital records showing KM Flight 180's arrival time, how many bags were unloaded and by whom, all disappeared.

The story of the emergence of the computer list was peculiar. Rather than being preserved by the airport authorities as a matter of routine, it was allegedly only saved due to the diligent actions of a worker on the baggage system's computer, Bogomira Erac. Mindful of the fact that the computer automatically wiped its memory after a few days, she printed off a copy of the records for Flight 103 and placed it in her locker before going on holiday for two weeks. On returning she was apparently surprised to learn that no one had shown any interest in it. She handed it to her baggage section leader who passed it on to the BKA.

Arguably of greater importance than the airport's baggage records were those belonging to Pan Am itself. As a matter of routine the airline kept a file on every flight to and from the airport, the details of which could have been crucial in establishing which bags were loaded onto Flight 103 and by whom. On 23 January 1989 Michael Jones of Pan Am's European security team went to Frankfurt airport to look for these documents. In particular, he was hoping to locate the cargo- and baggage-loading plan, along with details of who was responsible for loading the plane. On arriving at the company's offices he discovered the documents were missing from the daily file. If they had been taken by the police, it would be normal practice for a copy to be retained in the file, but no such copy was present and Jones never found it.[2]

For all the oddities surrounding the Frankfurt airport documents, the emerging Malta link was bolstered by the forensic determination that the bomb suitcase had contained clothes manufactured on the island. The key item of clothing turned out to be a pair of trousers, a fragment of which carried a label of a Maltese manufacturer, the Yorkie clothing company. Scottish detectives who visited the company on 1 September 1989 were told by its owner, Victor Calleja, that by checking two other marks in the trousers against the company's order book he could trace the purchaser. On doing so he was able to state with absolute confidence that the trousers had been sold to a shop called 'Mary's House', in nearby Sliema.[3]

The small, quiet shop was owned by a Mr Edward Gauci, but was run on a day-to-day basis by his sons Tony and Paul. Tony Gauci was almost immediately able to confirm that he had sold the trousers to a customer about nine months previously. He remembered this because the customer had bought a hodgepodge of clothes which also included a pair of brown herringbone trousers, a cardigan, an imitation Harris tweed jacket, three pairs of pyjamas, a blue Babygro with a sheep's face design on the front and a black umbrella. Since similar items showing signs of blast damage were found at Lockerbie, Gauci's account represented a devastating breakthrough for the Scottish police.

Better still, Gauci could remember the man who had purchased the clothes, not least because of his apparent disregard for the size, colour or cost of his purchases. Furthermore, as he left the shop the man bought an umbrella because it had started to rain outside. Gauci recalled that the customer was of Arab descent, around 50 years old, well-dressed, about six foot or over in height, well-built with a big chest though not fat, clean-shaven and with very dark hair. He had come into the shop about ten minutes before it closed at 7 p.m. That day Gauci's brother Paul had left the shop early in order to watch a football match on television. Paul worked out that the date in question was 23 November.

Malta has a great many Arab residents and visitors, mostly from its near-neighbour Libya but also from Tunisia and the other north African countries. Gauci told the police that he was usually able to distinguish between the two because Tunisians often speak French when they have been talking for a while. He felt fairly sure that the customer was a Libyan.[4]

The new Malta connection seemed undeniable. An unaccompanied bag from the island had apparently been loaded onto Flight 103, and the clothes in the bomb suitcase had been bought on the island less than a month before the bombing by an Arab who had acted in a strange manner. Furthermore, there was the first hint of a Libyan connection to Lockerbie. But what of Hafez Dalkamoni's PFLP-GC cell in Neuss and Frankfurt – surely they could not be ruled out of the bombing? After all, only one of

Khreesat's bombs had been found before Lockerbie and some of the others had been found afterwards; it was surely feasible that a fifth had ended up on Fight 103.

As the first anniversary of Lockerbie approached, evidence emerged of a direct link between the island and the PFLP-GC's West German cell. This centred on the activities of a Swedish-based Arab man called Mohammed Abu Talb. He was rapidly to become the prime suspect in the bombing.

Abu Talb was born in Port Said, Egypt, in 1952. He joined the PLO in Sania in 1968 and then joined the Egyptian army, which sent him to the Soviet Union to be trained in the use of SAM 3 missiles. In 1970 he went to Lebanon and became a member of the Palestinian Popular Struggle Front (PPSF), which, like the PFLP-GC, was a hard-line Marxist-Leninist organisation. In 1972 he was imprisoned in Egypt but escaped towards the end of 1973 and fled to Lebanon where he worked for the PPSF. In 1976 he was shot in the leg and as a result walked with a pronounced limp.[5] The following year he became the personal bodyguard of the PPSF's leader, Sami Gusha.

In 1979 he married Jamilla Mograbi, a Palestinian whose family were veterans of the armed struggle. Her sister Rashidi had been killed while attempting to blow up an Israeli bus in the Gaza strip and another was serving a prison sentence in Britain for the attempted murder of the Iraqi Ambassador to the UK.[6]

In 1980, Abu Talb returned to the Soviet Union for just over a year, to receive training in 'organisation, training and recruitment techniques'.[7] He returned to Lebanon in 1981 then, after the Israeli invasion of Lebanon the following year, moved to Syria. In November 1983 he and his wife travelled to Sweden, with Abu Talb entering the country on a false Moroccan passport. They claimed political asylum and were allowed to stay, settling in Uppsala where Jamilla's brother Mohammed already lived. Two other brothers, Mahmoud and Mustafa, followed shortly after.

In 1988 Abu Talb ran a small business selling Arab videos from a café owned by a Palestinian from Syria called Hamid Al Wani who, according to the Swedish security police, the Säkerhetspolis (SAPO), was the PFLP-GC's commander for the middle region of Sweden. His brother Sadi Al Wani was reputedly a founder member of the PFLP-GC with Ahmed Jibril, and was expelled from Sweden in 1980. In August 1988 Abu Talb was stabbed in the café by an Arab man called Chamaoun Daher, following an argument.[8]

Abu Talb first came to the BKA's attention on 13 October 1988 as they monitored the apartment at 16 Isarstrasse in Neuss, where Marwan Khreesat was preparing his bombs. Having observed a white Volvo with

Swedish licence plates pull up outside, they watched some young Arab men go upstairs to the apartment and then carry parcels back and forth to the car. One of the men was Ahmed Abassi, the brother of the apartment's owner, Hashem Abassi. He shared a flat with Mahmoud Mograbi in Uppsala. The two others were identified as Jehad Chabaan and Samir Ourfali, brother and cousin respectively of Imad Chabaan, the car's owner.

Also a resident of Uppsala and a close associate of Abu Talb, Chabaan had a few years earlier changed his name to Martin Imandi. His two relatives had entered Germany on a flight from Damascus on 5 September, along with another of his brothers, Ziad Chabaan. Imandi had met them at Munich airport and attempted to drive them back to Sweden, but all four were arrested by the Danish police at the border town of Rodbyhavn and accused of carrying false documentation. After two days in custody Imandi was allowed to continue to Uppsala, but the others returned to Munich. Ziad Chabaan flew back to Syria while his brother and cousin remained in Germany.

At some point over the next couple of weeks they telephoned a contact – possibly Imandi – who advised them to travel to Neuss and call on Hashem Abassi. This they apparently did and were taken to the flat at 16 Isarstrasse where they were allowed to stay.

The driver of the white Volvo spotted at Isarstrasse on 13 October was Mohammed Mograbi, who Imandi had sent to Germany in another effort to bring his relatives to Sweden. In the event Mograbi returned empty-handed and the two men made their own way to Sweden via the Kiel to Gothenburg ferry.[9]

The BKA did not tell the Swedish police of the possible link between the Volvo's occupants and the suspected terrorists in Neuss until 30 October, four days after the Autumn Leaves raids. On 1 November SAPO, rounded up Martin Imandi, Mohammed Mograbi, Mohammed Abu Talb and several of their associates.

SAPO found four intact passports belonging to Abu Talb, plus two burnt ones which they were unable to reconstruct. At least two were Egyptian and one Moroccan.[10] Two of the passports were found at 35 Djaknegatan, the home of Mustafa Mograbi. Among the other items seized from the house were cables, an electrician's box, an electric switch and, most intriguingly of all, barometric instruments with the barometer missing and a series of wrist watches, some of which had various pieces missing. Abu Talb and Jamilla Mograbi's address was Dirigentvagen, but Abu Talb said Mustafa's house was a 'care of' address, which he stayed at as a result of 'a few family problems'.[11]

The local prosecutor filed charges alleging that Imandi and Mograbi had been preparing to smuggle explosives for use against aeroplanes. Mograbi insisted that the mysterious parcels taken from the Neuss apartment were merely clothing and gifts. With no supporting evidence forthcoming from the German police, all the suspects were released the following day.

He did not know it at the time, but Imandi had in fact been under surveillance by the Swedish police ever since he had attempted to smuggle his relatives into the country in early September. It was claimed that after arresting him at Rodbyhavn, the Danish border police had made a routine computer check on his fingerprints and scored a major hit. They appeared to match a single print found on an Arab newspaper that had been wrapped around a nail bomb intended to blow up the Copenhagen offices of the Israeli airline El Al. At the time of the incident, in June 1985, an unwitting passer-by had seen an Arab man place a bag in the doorway of the offices. Thinking he had forgotten it, she picked it up and chased him. Obviously panicked, he snatched the bag back and threw it in the nearest canal before running away. That same day two other bombs exploded in the city at a synagogue and at the offices of the Northwest Orient airline, killing one person and wounding twenty-two In April 1986, the same gang was believed to be responsible for a bomb which exploded at the offices of Northwest Airlines in the Swedish capital of Stockholm.

However unlikely it seemed that a single fingerprint could have been found on a piece of paper which had been underwater for hours, the trail led back to Imandi and his friends in Uppsala. Investigations continued over the next few months and on 18 May 1989 SAPO arrested 15 suspects during raids in Stockholm, Gothenburg and Uppsala, including Imandi, Abu Talb and his brothers-in-law Mustafa and Mahmoud Mograbi. All four were eventually charged with the Copenhagen and Stockholm bombings.[12]

The main evidence against them was a confession by Mahmoud Mograbi. Abu Talb insisted that his move to Sweden marked the end of his involvement in the Palestinian armed struggle, but Mahmoud claimed that in spring 1985 he was sent to Syria on Abu Talb's and Imandi's insistence to learn how to make bombs. He claimed that he returned to Sweden with US $5,000 and a letter, which he was under instruction not to open until his arrival. He said that on arrival he opened the letter and discovered the handle of the bag he had been carrying had been utilised to smuggle four detonators into Sweden. He claimed that three bombs were subsequently constructed in the bathroom of Abu Talb's house. Imandi also confessed, corroborating Mahmoud's story that the pair of them accompanied Abu Talb to Copenhagen, where they planted bombs at the synagogue and the offices of El Al and Northwest Orient airlines.[13]

News of the Lockerbie connection began to filter through to the British media shortly after the arrests, but it would be some months before the full extent of the link was known. The most remarkable discovery was that Abu Talb had been in Malta in October 1988, just a few weeks before Lockerbie. The first mention of the visit was buried deep in an article in *The Independent* on 30 October 1989, the day after David Leppard had broken the story of the Malta link in the *Sunday Times*. And *The Independent* made the further startling claim that Hafez Dalkamoni had also visited Malta in October 1988, and that both he and Abu Talb had met a group of Palestinians on the island who had been identified by intelligence sources as a PFLP-GC cell. So, for the first time, there was a concrete link between Malta and the terrorists in Germany.

Over the next few weeks a flood of stories appeared which dragged Abu Talb and Malta ever deeper into the Lockerbie conspiracy. It was clear from the extent of the leaks that there were people in the official investigation who were keen to link him to the bombing. On 31 October 1989 *The Independent* followed up the previous day's story by naming Abu Talb's and Dalkamoni's Malta contact as a PFLP-GC member called 'Saleem'. It claimed they had been linked to a bakery on the island and that intelligence sources had in turn linked the bakery's owners to Ahmed Kaplan, whom Dalkamoni had visited in Hockenheim on 16 October 1988. The report also stated that Abu Talb had been on the island from 19–26 October.

'Saleem', it later emerged, was Abdel Salem who actually ran the bakery. According to documents filed at Companies House in Malta, the bakery was owned by the Miska Trading Company of Old Steet, Valetta, which was established on 19 June 1987. Its directors included Imad Adel Hazzouri, who lived in Balzan with his uncle Ismail Hazzouri. Ismail was allegedly a friend of Ahmed Kaplan.[14] Abu Talb confirmed to SAPO that he spent his time in Malta with Abdel Salem and his brother Hashim Salem, who was in the clothes business. He said he went with Abdel Salem to the bakery in the morning and accompanied him as he delivered bread to his customers. He stressed that Adbel Salem was not his friend, and that he only knew him through his wife.[15] Abdel Salem added to the mystery, telling Lockerbie investigators he had only met Talb once in Malta and that was a chance meeting in Valetta in October 1988.[16]

Abu Talb also told SAPO that prior to travelling to Malta he had spent two weeks on Cyprus, saying he had gone to the island to aid his recuperation from the earlier stab wound. This trip was potentially highly significant, because the first three days of this visit coincided with Dalkamoni's presence on the island. Dalkamoni told the BKA that he made frequent trips to Cyprus because the PFLP-GC had a bank account there. After returning to Germany the BKA monitored his telephone conversation with Habib Dajani, the Syrian proprietor of the King's Take-Away restaurant in Nicosia.

During his first few days in Cyprus Abu Talb had stayed in a cheap hotel, but he later told SAPO that he had moved to one of the most expensive. Though there was no proof that he had met Dalkamoni whilst in Cyprus, it was speculated that the trip had been made in order to receive instructions and payment from Dalkamoni.

The SAPO interrogation revealed a curious turn of events as Abu Talb travelled from Cyprus to Malta. During an overnight stopover in Rome he decided to change his air ticket from Malta to Benghazi in Libya. According to him, he had called a friend in Libya who agreed to help smuggle him from Libya to Egypt so he could visit his family. Abu Talb said he was only able to afford to buy the ticket because he was lent about $20 by a helpful Libyan named Fawzi. When questioned in August 1989 about the Scandinavian bombing, he is reported to have told SAPO that Fawzi was a friend he had met in Libya in 1977, but when interviewed in April 1990 he said the encounter at Rome airport was the first time he had ever met Fawzi.

Abu Talb claimed that, having checked his bags onto the plane for Benghazi, he was kicked off the flight because he didn't have a visa for Libya. He reverted to his original plan and flew to Malta, but his bags remained on the flight to Benghazi and he was not able to recover them for two days. It was later suggested that this might have been a ruse to smuggle bomb components to him from Libya.[17]

On 1 November *The Times* claimed, sensationally, that Abu Talb had admitted to the Swedish police that some time between October and December 1988 he had passed to another person one of the bombs which had been prepared by the PFLP-GC in Germany. If true, it would be the first time that anyone had admitted a role in the Lockerbie bombing, but Abu Talb denied making the confession and the claim never reappeared in the media.

On 5 November, David Leppard delivered another major scoop for the *Sunday Times*. Headlined 'REVEALED: THE LOCKERBIE PLOT – THE PAYMASTER, THE BOMBER AND THE BUNGLING GERMANS', it provided the latest incarnation of the fast-developing Malta connection. According to the article, the Lockerbie bomb had been smuggled from Frankfurt to Malta by Ramzi Diab, the German PFLP-GC member whom the BKA observed meeting Dalkamoni in Frankfurt on 18 October 1988. Dalkamoni and Abu Talb then travelled to the island to instruct the cell there to put the bomb on an Air

Malta flight to Frankfurt. An unidentified member of the island cell had then bought the clothes which were put in the bomb bag from Mary's House.

The following week, Leppard reported that leaked Swedish police documents showed Abu Talb had made a second trip to Malta in November 1988, returning to Sweden on the 26th. If true, this meant he was almost certainly on the island on 23 November, the very date that Tony Gauci's brother Paul had given as the one on which the mystery clothes buyer had visited his shop. The article also revealed that Abu Talb's former wife, Jamilla Mograbi, had told the police that Abu Talb had been to Malta to buy clothes. Not only that, but surveillance records indicated he had visited a flat in Frankfurt where, according to the article, 'the bomb was almost certainly built', and that he owned a brown Samsonite suitcase, 'of the same type and colour that contained the bomb'.

In fact, as Leppard later reported in his book *On the Trail of Terror*, the brown Samsonite was still in Abu Talb's apartment in Uppsala. And Leppard was also wrong about the Swedish police document, which actually stated that Abu Talb had returned to Sweden from Malta not on 26 November but on 26 October. The mistake was due to a mistranslation of the Swedish word for October. If he didn't return to the island after 26 October then he clearly couldn't be the clothes buyer, but in a further article on 3 December 1989 Leppard reported that Abu Talb had been 'positively identified' as the person who bought the clothes from Mary's House. His article also revealed that the Swedish police had removed 15 bags of clothes from his apartment, which they believed he had brought back from Malta. Abu Talb's lawyer told Leppard it was now probable that the Scottish police would apply for the extradition of his client.

One problem with the story, not addressed by Leppard, was Abu Talb's age. At the time he is alleged to have bought the clothes he was 36, yet Tony Gauci had identified his mystery customer as around 50 years old. Furthermore, Abu Talb had a pronounced limp, which Gauci would surely have noticed if he was the clothes buyer.

On 21 December 1989, the anniversary of the Lockerbie disaster, Abu Talb and Martin Imandi were jailed for life for the Copenhagen and Stockholm bombings. Mahmoud and Mohammed Mograbi received lighter sentences as accessories to the plot. Before the trial, Mahmoud had given a full confession which implicated the others and was released immediately on conviction.

A few days before being convicted Abu Talb was interviewed by the Scottish police. He declined to answer questions about Lockerbie, but subsequently let it be known that he categorically denied any involvement with the plot to destroy Flight 103. He was interviewed again by the Swedish police, with the Scottish police in attendance, on 3–5 April and again denied any involvement in the bombing. And, while he acknowledged that he had heard the Al Wani brothers were connected to the PFLP-GC in 1980, he denied having any contact with the group. He also claimed that he had no knowledge of his brother-in-law Mohammed's trip to the 16 Isarstrasse flat in Neuss until he was informed by SAPO subsequent to his arrest on 1 November. Yet only a couple of days before his arrest he had telephoned Mohammed, who had by then returned from West Germany.[18]

Despite such denials, on the day prior to his conviction the Swedish newspaper *Dagens Nyheter* reported three new damning pieces of evidence. The first was that investigators who raided his flat found a diary in which the date of 21 December 1988 had been circled. The second was a telephone call between Abu Talb's ex-wife Jamilla and a Palestinian friend, which took place after the police had raided Abu Talb's apartment. Swedish police, who tapped the call, were alleged to have heard Jamilla tell her friends, 'Get rid of the clothes.' The third was the claim that someone calling themselves Abu Taleb had entered Malta in November 1988 using an Egyptian passport. If this was true then maybe Abu Talb had, after all, been on the island when the clothes were bought. This might account for his ex-wife's apparent sensitivity about the clothes.

Jamilla Mograbi subsequently denied having urged her friend to get rid of the clothes and insisted that there was nothing suspicious about the clothes Abu Talb had brought back from Malta. She said that while in Cyprus, he had met a friend who told him that a friend of his had a clothes factory in Malta. Abu Talb was interested, she said, because he had set up a small trading company in Uppsala and was looking for suppliers. Having been invited, he travelled to Malta to pick up some samples of his clothing. She confirmed that he returned to Sweden with a variety of clothes, including jeans, ladies sweaters and men's shirts. Some of the Maltese clothes that were confiscated by the police had never been returned to her.[19]

Abu Talb contradicted his wife's claim that he had returned to Sweden with samples of clothing. A leaked extract from the interview contained the following exchange:

Q: When did you buy clothes in Malta?
A: I didn't buy any clothes in Malta, the only items I got were the black pair of jeans and some shirts too from Jamilla, Abdel Salem's wife. I also got some shirts.
Q: Describe the clothes.

A: A pair of black jeans, a green shirt with a Malta label on it.
Q: Did anyone give you any further clothes?
A: No.

According to Mahmoud Mograbi's solicitor Annika Wallin, when he was first questioned about Abu Talb's visit to Malta, he was warned that he must not tell her. At first he went along with the order, but he cracked and told her during a prison visit. Concerned that someone might be listening to the conversation, he took the precaution of turning his music up very loud before telling her.[20]

Three days after Abu Talb's conviction David Leppard reported in the *Sunday Times* that Lockerbie investigators had matched plastic residue from the crash site with material from the alarm clocks purchased by Hafez Dalkamoni and Marwan Khreesat. So, with just over a year having passed since Lockerbie, the emerging official version of the bombing leaked to the media had three elements. The first was that the PFLP-GC's German cell had carried out the bombing; the second was that the bomb had started its journey in Malta; and the third was that Abu Talb was somehow deeply involved in the plot.

On second glance certain aspects of the Abu Talb story were rather strange. Quite apart from the incredible coincidence of Martin Imandi's fingerprint matching the one on the soggy magazine, there was the timing of the arrests. The 18 May swoop took place almost four years after the first of the alleged offences, yet just five months after Lockerbie. Then there was the diary with the date of Lockerbie circled. Would a ruthless terrorist, who was skilful enough to evade detection for four years, be so stupid as to mark in his diary the date of a major attack? And would he be so reckless as to leave it around his apartment for months after the attack? Likewise, if he had been the customer in Mary's House, would he be so short-sighted as to keep other clothes which might lead back to the shop, even at a friend's apartment? To the more sceptical observer, the spate of news stories about Abu Talb demonstrated that he was either deeply involved in the Lockerbie bombing or was being set up as a decoy. Evidence would eventually emerge that the truth lay somewhere between the two.

8. THE KNIVES COME OUT

By the first anniversary of Lockerbie, there were two very different theories about the bombing: the first was black-and-white; the second, murky-grey. The black-and-white version, in which the bomb came in an unaccompanied suitcase from Malta, presented the case as a victory of terrorist cunning over American innocence. By contrast, the grey version, which involved the bombers exploiting a CIA-protected drug-running operation, suggested there was also blood on Uncle Sam's hands. Over the coming years, a conflict would rage over the two versions in the media and courtrooms. Not surprisingly, it was the first version that the American and British governments expected the public to believe and, in seeking to uphold it, they would go to extraordinary lengths to stifle dissent.

The earliest incarnation of the alternative theory of the bombing was Juval Aviv's Interfor Report, which first became public in early November 1989. Its key findings were leaked to James Trafficant, a US congressman and member of the House of Representatives Aviation Committee, who released the pages to the press amid a blaze of publicity. Unaware of the identity of the report's author, most of the media coverage suggested its findings might help Pan Am avoid liability for the disaster. The airline protested that it was embarrassed by the leak, and that it would not subscribe to the report's findings until it could find evidence for them.

Three weeks after the leak, a serious backlash began. In its 26 November edition, *The Observer* ran a front-page article headed 'PAN AM LOCKERBIE REPORT A SHAM – HOW LOCKERBIE BOMB STORY WAS PLANTED'. Reporters John Merritt and Simon de Bruxelles revealed that the report had been written by 'an Israeli intelligence expert based in New York', who had 'failed to provide any evidence to substantiate a single claim in his report'. Moreover, the article claimed, the report was 'riddled with errors'.

It went on to give details of three of the alleged errors. The first was the claim that on 25 November 1988 the leader of the drug running operation had rented a car in Paris and driven to Frankfurt with components for the bomb. On checking with the rental firm in question, the reporters had been told that no car hired on 25 November had clocked up sufficient mileage to have reached Frankfurt. Aviv's claim that the man had personally driven the

Lockerbie bomb from Paris to Frankfurt always seemed rather far-fetched, but the rental firm's denial hardly constituted proof that he was wrong.

The second alleged error was the report's claim that the protected drug-running system exploited by the terrorists went under the code-name Corea. The article claimed that Corea actually referred to communications between the so-called Trevi group of European intelligence, customs and police forces that had been established to monitor terrorism, revolution and violence. This may well have been true, but it did not preclude the possibility that there was a quite separate operation called Corea, or that communications relating to the drugs-for-hostages operation described in the Interfor Report was hidden within the Trevi/Corea intelligence traffic. It is also possible that Corea was a misspelling of the word *khouriah*, the Lebanese slang word for shit which, as in the West, doubles as slang for heroin. Perhaps the real name of the operation was *khouriah*, or even courier, because of its use of couriers. Aviv could have been utterly mistaken about the name of the operation and that it was never called Corea, or anything like it, but that didn't mean the operation never existed.

The report's third alleged error was its claim that documents proving what was in the report were held in the safe of Kurt Rebmann, a German equivalent of an assistant attorney general, based in Berlin. The article pointed out that Rebmann denied Aviv's claim and that he was, in fact, a Federal prosecutor based in Karlsruhe. Mistakes concerning Rebmann's job description and location did not render the Interfor Report's central claims invalid. Moreover, if the report's claims were true, Rebmann could be forgiven if, he felt understandably that the correct thing to do was not to confirm to newspaper reporters that he was in possession of such important documents.

The Observer was, of course, correct to state that Aviv had produced no evidence to substantiate his report. He only ever claimed to have based it on unattributable intelligence sources, and the report's preamble clearly stated, 'From the perspective of intelligence analysis, our findings are conclusive. From the perspective of journalists, it is publishable speculation. From the perspective of trial lawyers, it probably remains inadmissible speculation or hearsay.'

The leaking of the Interfor Report and the subsequent *Observer* article ruined the Pan Am legal team's chances of being able to discreetly gather evidence to substantiate the report. To add to their difficulties, a US magistrate ordered an evidentiary hearing to examine the leak. Juval Aviv denied being the source of the leak, but following testimony from, among others, *The Observer*'s John Merritt, the magistrate declared his denial was 'not credible'.

Aviv claims the US authorities may have leaked the report pre-emptively in order to discredit him and Pan Am's lawyers. He points out that at the point the leak occurred, the airline's attorneys lacked any hard evidence to back up his intelligence findings. It was therefore easier to portray those findings as pure fantasy, leaked by Pan Am or Aviv, to get the airline off the hook for faulty security, than it might have been a year or so down the line, when the attorneys had gathered some of that hard evidence. He also claims that shortly before the leak to Congressman Trafficant his offices were broken into and his computer invaded, and that he was subsequently kept under heavy surveillance, rendering it impossible for him to carry out further investigations.[1]

For all the difficulties created by the leaking of the Interfor Report, Pan Am's lawyers, led by James Shaugnessy, continued to investigate the bombing. As we described in chapter four, in January 1990 they hired retired US army polygrapher James Keefe, an Interfor employee, to conduct polygraph – or 'lie detector' – tests on three of the airline's Frankfurt Airport baggage handlers,. The tests on two handlers suggested they had lied in denying that they were involved in switching a suitcase. Pan Am subsequently flew the two men to London, in the hope that they would be questioned by the British authorities.

Within a week, *The Observer* was once again on the case. The paper's 28 January edition carried an article by John Merritt headed 'LOCKERBIE: PAN AM MEN SUSPECTED AFTER TAKING LIE TESTS'. It pointed out that the timing of the interrogations and the circumstances surrounding them had refuelled suspicions about Pan Am's methods in defending the lawsuit brought by the Lockerbie victims' relatives.

Six months earlier, on 30 July 1989, Merritt's by-line had been on a front-page exclusive under the banner, 'LOCKERBIE: TURKS "PLANTED BOMB"'. Co-written with Farzad Bazoft, the article had claimed that unnamed Turkish Pan Am employees at Frankfurt airport had been responsible for getting the bomb on the plane.

It was not clear what had happened after July 1989 to change the reporter's mind. He had perhaps become convinced that the bomb had originated in Malta and ended up on Flight 103 because of Pan Am's faulty security procedures at Frankfurt airport, rather than the activities of baggage handlers involved in drug-running operations. His January article quoted Lee Kreindler, lead attorney in the Lockerbie victims' relatives' civil liability suit, whose case against Pan Am depended on the unaccompanied Maltese bag. Over the next couple of years, Kreindler and Merritt stayed on very good terms and Merritt wrote further articles for *The Observer* which broadly supported Kreindler's case by casting doubt on allegations of US government complicity in the disaster.

Juval Aviv resigned from the Pan Am case in May 1990, but hopes that this would put an end to his troubles were short-lived. Over the following months he was called back to court on several occasions to face allegations that he had conspired with the airline to concoct a bogus defence to counteract the civil action. He claims to have suffered a continuing campaign to intimidate and drive him out of business, alleging that on a number of occasions he and his employees arrived at the Interfor offices to find signs that someone had broken in overnight. Usually nothing had been taken, but the intruders had left signs of their presence; for example, leaving drawers open and computers and lights switched on. He claims his car was sometimes left in a slightly different position than where he had previously parked it and that on those occasions it would have clocked up a few extra miles since he last drove it. Although a non-smoker, he found cigarette butts in the ashtrays. All of these events he interpreted as signs that his enemies in the Federal authorities wanted him to know they had not forgotten him.

Aviv took statements from a number of his clients who claimed to have been visited by FBI and DEA agents claiming to be seeking evidence for Federal grand jury proceedings against Aviv and others. Aviv claims the agents were seeking to discredit him so that the clients would take their business elsewhere.

One such client was a government agency, the Federal Deposit Insurance Corporation (FDIC), which hired Aviv in 1992 to help trace $35 million hidden by imprisoned banker Jacobo Finkielstain. Though he denied having any assets, Aviv discovered that Finkielstain had bank accounts in Liechtenstein. Despite clearly getting the results the FDIC wanted, Aviv claims to have learned that in 1993 an FBI and a DEA agent had visited FDIC management and told them that he was under grand jury investigation because of his activities in the Pan Am 103 case. They added that Aviv was dishonest and unpatriotic, and provided copies of magazine articles critical of his role in the case. In a sworn deposition, Aviv's lawyer, Gerald Shargel, described speaking to one of the FDIC's managers in July 1995. The FDIC man confirmed that he had been visited by purported government agents who had besmirched Aviv's name. According to Shargel, he also said he would be happy to talk more, but would first have to clear it with a supervisor. A few days later, he reported that the supervisor had refused to allow him to speak further.

The FBI then appeared to interfere directly with the Finkielstain case. According to Finkielstain, around June 1993 an FBI agent, Tim Childs, visited him in prison and asked him about Aviv. In a formal deposition interview, Finkielstain said he was shown some information about the case, confirming that the investigation was taking place and alerting the prisoner to the fact that Aviv had tracked down his assets in Liechtenstein. They also confirmed that the FDIC was trying to prevent his release from prison long enough to seize his assets.[2] Childs did not deny that he visited Finkielstain, but denied showing him the information in question.

Lester Coleman, the former Cyprus-based employee of the DIA and DEA, also ended up in trouble after alleging governmental foul play. Coleman had claimed that Khalid Jaafar was utilised by the DEA for controlled deliveries of heroin. He claims that in the wake of his acrimonious departure from the DEA, the inhabitants of the murkier corners of the secret state identified him as a potential whistle-blower and set out to pre-emptively destroy him. He points out that by the end of 1989, Juval Aviv's Interfor Report and ABC TV's *Prime Time* had both identified Khalid Jaafar as the bomb carrier. The spooks would therefore be very worried in case credible witnesses who could link the young man to the DEA or the CIA were to emerge.

Coleman maintains that shortly after Lockerbie his mother received anonymous telephone calls on her unlisted number, threatening his life and that of his wife and children. He claims that in late 1989 the DIA reactivated him for another sensitive Middle Eastern operation, code-named Shakespeare, which involved gathering intelligence on the relationship between Michel Aoun's Lebanese army and Iraq. He maintains the agency instructed him to acquire a passport in a false name.

Coleman made the passport application on 26 March 1990. Five weeks later he was woken by FBI agents who informed him that he was under arrest for attempting to fraudulently obtain a passport. He claims he tried to telephone his DIA contact, but the line was dead. Having been warned never to reveal his DIA employment, he realised it wouldn't be easy to get himself off the hook. He told the FBI that he had worked for the DEA, but when he turned to the DEA field office in Birmingham, Alabama for help, he was given the cold shoulder.

Coleman's court-appointed attorney, Michael Deutsch, filed a discovery motion for documents that might show his client had been acting under orders when he made the passport application. The DIA, the CIA and the DEA all declined to comply with the motion on the grounds of national security, thus denying Coleman an opportunity to clear his name. Shortly after the motion was filed, Coleman was introduced to the attorneys representing Pan Am in London. The airline's Corporate Security Manager,

Jim Berwick, who met him off the plane at Heathrow airport, later recalled: 'I've never seen a man so frightened in my life.'[3]

By now the story appeared to be leaking out from other sources. Both NBC and ABC television were planning exposés of the DEA's alleged role in the disaster, and journalists from each network eventually met with Coleman. He did not wish to appear in either programme, but his hopes of maintaining anonymity were shattered on 21 December 1990, when he was outed by CNN television. Branding him 'a disgruntled former DEA confidential informant who was terminated', reporter Steven Emerson suggested that Coleman had been the main source for the earlier NBC and ABC television reports and suggested that he had hoodwinked those mighty TV corporations in a mischievous act of revenge. The fact that both NBC and ABC had other sources for their stories well before they met Coleman seemed to have been overlooked.

A few months before his attack on Coleman, Emerson's Lockerbie book, *The Fall of Pan Am 103*, co-authored with Brian Duffy, had been published. Not surprisingly it was totally dismissive of the Interfor Report, which, according to the 'intelligence officials and police investigators' who were the book's sources, was 'a classic "spitball", a messy amalgam of known facts, clever suppositions and wholesale fabrications'. Some time later, one of the 'known facts' reported in his book was later dismissed by those self-same 'intelligence officials and police investigators' as another 'wholesale fabrication'. The fact in question was the discovery of a large quantity of heroin in a suitcase which landed in a field belonging to farmer Jim Wilson in Tundergarth. Chapter seven of the book gave a graphic account of how Wilson reported the suitcase to a senior Scottish police officer and then helped a junior officer empty its contents into a plastic bag.

By the time the book was written, the 'official' line on Lockerbie was that the bomb was contained in an unaccompanied bag from Malta. As far as Emerson and Duffy's sources were concerned, however, the Malta link was weak. The book's final chapter reported, 'Investigators believe that an unwitting Khalid Jaafar wound up with the deadly Samsonite.' Here, then, was yet another key element of the NBC and ABC bulletins that Emerson appeared to be supporting, but, as with the drug find, it was not mentioned in his CNN report.

For Lester Coleman, the most serious aspect of the report was that it beamed his name and picture around the world, making him a potential target for the drug runners and terrorists whose activities he had monitored. Believing the odds to be stacked against a fair trial on the passport fraud charges, he decided to cut his losses and flee the US. Stopping over in

Brussels, he met with Pan Am's legal team for five days and swore an affidavit about the DEA's Cyprus operation. This revealed, for the first time, that he was employed by the DIA as well as the DEA. The following month, May 1991, he travelled with his family to Sweden, where he walked immediately into a police station and requested asylum, the first US citizen to do so since the Vietnam War.

In response to Coleman's affidavit his former boss, the DEA Cyprus Country Attaché Michael Hurley, produced a statement of his own, denying that his office was involved in any controlled deliveries of heroin which used Frankfurt as a transit point to Detroit. He also denied that Khalid Jaafar was a DEA cooperating individual and that he was ever used as a drug courier by the DEA, or any other agency. Hurley confirmed that Coleman had been employed by the DEA from 31 January 1986. However, he accused him of a number of misdemeanours, including withholding a payment of $5,500 from a cameraman who had acted as a sub-source gathering pictures of Lebanese narcotics production, as well as selling information belonging to the DEA to *Soldier of Fortune* magazine. In addition, Hurley claimed, the Cypriot police had issued an arrest warrant against Coleman for failure to pay his landlord for an outstanding telephone bill. Hurley alleged that Coleman's 'unsatisfactory behaviour' resulted in his being deactivated by the DEA in May 1988.

Further doubt was cast on Coleman's claims by a second affidavit, this one by Lt Col Terry E. Bathen, Assistant General Counsel to the DIA. It denied Coleman had been on the DIA's payroll when arrested in May 1990, but nevertheless confirmed that he had been employed on 'classified Department of Defense intelligence activity' from December 1985 until November 1986. Bathen claimed the DIA had neither assigned Coleman to work with the DEA, nor ordered him to terminate his relationship with the DEA. But even accepting Bathen's dates, when put together with Hurley's statement they demonstrate that from 31 January 1986 until April 1986 Coleman was working for both agencies simultaneously.

Bathen claimed Coleman initiated the contact between himself and the DIA, volunteering his services by telephone in October 1985. Whilst not denying that Bathen was giving an accurate account of what he knew, every follower of spy stories will be disappointed because they believe that agents generally do not volunteer for service, but are rather actively recruited. Furthermore, Coleman could hardly have looked up the number of the highly secretive agency in the *Yellow Pages*.

All this was true, but even some of those who tended to believe the alternative version of Lockerbie (the authors of this book among them) occasionally found Coleman evasive and capable of mischief-making. He was clearly motivated in part by his dislike of Michael Hurley.

Regardless of this, and even if Coleman was a hoaxer, the US government's reaction to him was extraordinary and inevitably fuelled suspicions that he had touched a raw nerve. On 5 September 1993 he was once again indicted by the US government, this time for perjury. The charges related to the affidavit he had produced for Pan Am's lawyers in April 1991, almost 18 months earlier. The only conceivable reason the government waited so long before issuing the charges was that September 1993 also marked the publication of Coleman's book, *Trail of the Octopus.* Coleman claimed that in order to defend himself against most of the seven-point indictment, he required access to documentation which the authorities had already refused to release.

Coleman would not return to the US to face the courts until 1997. As we will show in chapter eleven, his fears of a forceful legal action were well founded.

The Lockerbie victims' relatives' civil liability suit against Pan Am and their insurers finally reached court in April 1992.[4] The plaintiffs' case relied on the official version of Lockerbie, which insisted that the bomb had been in a bag that had been transferred from Air Malta Flight KM 180 to Flight 103A in Frankfurt. Bags which transfer between airlines in this way are known as interline bags. This particular one was supposedly unaccompanied by any passenger, on either flight. Under the Federal Aviation Authority's Air Carrier Standard Security Programme (ACSSP), airlines were supposed to hand-search all unaccompanied interline bags. The interline bags loaded onto Flight 103 on 21 December were only X-rayed, which, the plaintiffs' lawyers argued, constituted wilful misconduct.

Having been consistently denied access to government documents, the airline's legal team were unable to effectively mount a defence suggesting the bomb could have reached Flight 103 via a CIA-protected drug-running operation.

The only hard evidence of the Malta theory were the two documents from Frankfurt airport which purported to show that a bag from KM180 had been sent through the airport baggage system to Flight 103A. This evidence would be severely undermined by any conflicting evidence that a rogue bag had been introduced into the luggage stream at the airport. Most of the airport's 39,000 employees had airside passes and their bags were not inspected as a matter of routine when they entered restricted areas. Indeed, a Pan Am security officer was ready to testify how he had been able to carry bolt cutters past the security system, using someone else's pass. However, Judge Platt precluded Pan Am's counsel from even mentioning rogue bags in front of the jury.

The employee who X-rayed the interline baggage in Frankfurt, Kurt Maier, testified that he had dealt with 13 interline bags destined for Flight 103. The police were able to positively link 12 of these bags to passengers, so, plaintiffs' counsel argued, the thirteenth bag must have been an unaccompanied bag from Malta containing the bomb. Pan Am's lawyers had evidence that Maier's thirteenth bag may, in fact, have been an unaccompanied Samsonite case belonging to one of the airline's pilots, Captain John Hubbard. If true, this meant there could not have been an unaccompanied bag from Malta on Flight 103, which, in turn, meant the airline's security failings could not be to blame for the bombing. Clearly the evidence concerning Captain Hubbard's case was a vital element of Pan Am's defence, but Judge Platt once again refused to allow the evidence.

Defence attorneys assembled an impressive array of expert witnesses to testify about the inherent unlikelihood of terrorists letting a bomb go unaccompanied on a first flight and then be transferred, still unaccompanied, to another flight, which in itself was only a feeder to the main flight that took off from London. Ariel Merari of Tel Aviv University, one of Israel's leading terrorism experts, and Noel Koch, a former terrorism specialist within the US Department of Defense, could both provide considerable historical background about attacks on airlines by Middle East terrorists. Contrary to what the plaintiffs' expert witnesses claimed, the use of an unwitting dupe to carry the bomb on board was far more likely to achieve success than sending a bag unaccompanied.

A month before the trial opened, lawyers from both sides formally deposed Koch at the Manhattan offices of the defence attorneys Windels Marx Davies & Ives. Apart from the various law firms representing the plaintiffs and Pan Am's own attorneys, a surprising number of representatives from intelligence agencies sat in on this deposition. A CIA lawyer and an officer of the CIA's information directorate, along with a Department of Defense attorney, joined Terry Bathen from the DIA. This was a remarkable number of people from the intelligence community, considering how uninvolved they all claimed to be. Speaking of his deposition, Koch said that some of the questioning effectively represented 'an effort by the government to argue that my knowledge of US security is derived from my experience in government and, on that account, I was prohibited from offering any substantive testimony at all. Or more to the point, any testimony that reflects adversely on the government. That such testimony would jeopardise US national security appeared to have been the argument made in camera to Judge Platt, an argument with which obviously he concurred.'[5]

Two British experts on terrorist bombing and bomb disposal, John Horne and Peter Gurney, were lined up to give evidence for the defence about the importance of X-rays in identifying bombs. Gurney, Britain's most decorated bomb expert – uniquely, the holder of two George Cross medals – was also prepared to testify that terrorists had become so adept at concealing bombs that hand searches of baggage may not be adequate. Furthermore, he did not believe terrorists would risk sending a bomb through Europe's two busiest airports, four days before Christmas, because they would have known that seasonal delays meant the bomb might explode in the airport rather than at altitude. 'Someone who has gone through the trouble of making a bomb of the sophistication necessary to get it on to the airplane and working out the routes would not choose such a slipshod way of doing things,' Gurney observed in a statement for Pan Am's lawyers.

But such views were not to be aired in front of the jury, as Judge Platt refused to allow any of the four terrorism and bomb experts to take the witness stand. He initially made the extraordinary suggestion that Merari's and Koch's testimonies could be excluded on the grounds that the Malta theory had been upheld in indictments issued the previous year against two Libyans accused of the Lockerbie bombing, despite the fact that the indictments had not been tested in court (these indictments will be explored in later chapters). He then justified the decision on the barely less odd grounds that any testimony they might give as to other means by which the bomb might have got on the plane would be 'nothing but speculation and . . . conjecture' and that there was 'nothing in this record', other than the Malta theory, to show how the bomb got on the plane. The Malta theory was just that – a theory. Furthermore, one of the reasons there was nothing in the record other than the Malta theory was that the Judge had specifically ruled against Pan Am's attorneys from introducing any such evidence.

To make matters worse, the judge allowed the plaintiffs' experts, Rodney Wallis, former Director of Security for the International Air Transport Association, and Billie Vincent, former director of the FAA's Office of Civil Aviation Security, to respectively opine that the Malta theory was correct and that unaccompanied bags provided a higher security risk than passengers who had been unwittingly duped into carrying a bomb. When pressed by Pan Am's counsel on whether or not he had any independent way of evaluating the forensic analysis carried out on the bomb, he fell back on the fact that indictments had been issued against two Libyans on the basis of the same evidence.

Platt also allowed the deposition testimony of Detective Constable Derek Henderson, the Scottish police officer who had been assigned the vital task of matching the baggage that could have been in container AVE 4041, where the bomb had exploded, with passengers on Flight 103. This he had done by comparing information gleaned through interviews with relatives and friends of the deceased passengers with records of the baggage recovered from the crash site. It had been calculated that a total of 65 bags which might have ended up in the container were checked in by passengers. Since none of these were apparently the type of bronze Samsonite case which contained the bomb, Henderson concluded that the Samsonite had been unaccompanied.

There was reason to challenge Henderson's testimony. A junior detective from a rural police force, whilst undoubtedly conscientious and thorough, he had no prior expertise in this type of complex passenger and baggage reconciliation exercise. The only check made on his work was by another detective constable. Furthermore, he was relying on information logged into the police's computer, without having done the primary investigation to link bags and passengers himself. In fact, nine of the bags had been linked to passengers by descriptions provided by someone other than the passenger's spouse. Moreover, Henderson's schedule demonstrated that a further nine of the bags, which could have been in AVE 4041, had never been recovered from the crash site. More importantly, even if there was an unaccompanied bag from Malta in the container that held the bomb, why should it be the Samsonite containing the bomb? If nine bags could go missing, why not this extra one?

Judge Platt allowed the jury to hear evidence of shortcomings in Pan Am's security which was completely unrelated to Lockerbie. One such instance, from 1986, involved a public demonstration at New York's JFK airport of dogs supposedly trained to sniff out explosives. The airline had claimed the initiative was part of a dramatically enhanced security programme, but the dogs were in fact untrained and had merely been leased from kennels on Long Island. It was an unpleasant incident, which showed the airline was prepared to put its public image before everything, but it had nothing whatsoever to do with how a bomb got onto Flight 103. By introducing such evidence, the plaintiffs' counsel was able to argue, in the words of one of their submissions, that the airline's 'entire operation was so mindless, so permeated with fault, that however that bag got on the airplane, Pan Am was responsible'. This was an incredible argument to make in a court of law; the advocates' equivalent of having their cake and eating it.

The defence hoped to argue that Pan Am's X-ray system at Frankfurt airport was a more effective means of detecting bombs than the hand searches of interline baggage required by the ACSSP. Barred from calling Peter Gurney as a witness, the evidence of Kurt Maier, the Frankfurt X-ray machine operator, became all the more important. Maier testified that he had been told to look out for radio-cassette players and would have recognised one had it shown up in any of the 13 bags he'd examined, but he was sure that none of them had contained such a device. The plaintiffs' counsel argued that Maier had never been properly trained as an X-ray operator and that he had not been wearing his spectacles at the time in question. Maier told the court that he only needed his spectacles for reading. The defence hoped to show that, even to untrained eyes, a radio-cassette player would show up clearly on the screen of the particular type of machine that Maier had been using. They arranged for a machine to be set up in the courtroom, which would be demonstrated by Professor Lee Grodzins, a nuclear physicist from the Massachusetts Institute of Technology. Judge Platt refused to allow the demonstration.

Even if the plaintiffs' contention was correct and the bomb had come in a bag from Malta which slipped through the Frankfurt X-ray machine unnoticed by Maier, if Pan Am could demonstrate that it was acting in good faith in X-raying rather than hand-searching interline baggage, then it clearly had an extremely strong case for denying the accusation of wilful misconduct. The airline's key witness on this issue was its security chief Daniel Sonesen, who claimed that as a result of consultations with the FAA's Office of Civil Aviation Security, he believed he had obtained an agreement that X-ray inspection of interline baggage complied with the relevant provision within the ACSSP. Once again, this vital testimony was barred by Judge Platt.

The defence were also prohibited from introducing any testimony about an FAA inspection of Pan Am's Heathrow operations in September 1988, just three months before the Lockerbie disaster. The same procedures had been in place at Heathrow as in Frankfurt, yet the FAA did not on that occasion claim that X-raying interline baggage constituted a violation of the ACSSP.

The extraordinary array of impediments placed in the way of Pan Am's defence prompted their lead counsel, Clinton Coddington, to tell Judge Platt towards the end of the trial:

On a scale of one to ten, doing what I want in this courtroom, I
have been about a minus two, or maybe imaginary numbers would
be a better way to describe the level to which I have gone.

Despite the defence's difficulties, the jury took three days to reach their
verdict, during which time they notified Judge Platt they were unable to
reach a decision. Nevertheless, it was hardly a surprise when they eventually
delivered the verdict that Pan Am was guilty of wilful misconduct.

Pan Am's legal team immediately launched an appeal. In response, the
government filed the long-threatened motion to punish both James
Shaugnessy and his law firm for daring to launch their third-party
complaint against the government. The motion alleged that the lawyers had
based their case on claims which to the best of their knowledge, information
and belief were not well grounded in fact. It was also claimed that they had
relied on the 'false allegations in the Aviv report' as a basis for subpoenas and
Freedom of Information requests, which resulted in government officials
wasting thousands of manhours pursuing non-existent evidence. The
motion demanded a punitive sanction of $6 million.

Shaugnessy responded with a blistering 73-page affidavit rebutting the
allegations made against him. Judge Platt accepted the arguments and
denied the motion, but shortly afterwards the Department of Justice
impanelled a grand jury in Alexandria, Virginia, to consider criminal
charges against Pan Am, its insurers, their legal team and Juval Aviv, over
the conduct of the airline's defence. The spectre of the grand jury
investigation would be raised time and again, but the threatened
indictments never materialised.

Despite such legal threats, Pan Am's legal team were confident their
appeal would succeed. The case was heard in May 1993, with a decision
expected the following autumn. Autumn 1993 passed without news, then
rumours began to circulate that the panel of three judges were split, with
one in favour of the appellants, one upholding the original decision and the
third undecided. Finally, on 31 January 1994, the judges issued their
verdict. To the astonishment of Pan Am's lawyers they had decided, two
against one, to reject the appeal.

Their amazement appeared to be shared by the panel's dissenting voice,
Judge Van Graafeiland. Concurring with Clinton Coddington's 'on a scale
of one to ten' analysis, his written judgment stated: 'I have read the record
dispassionately, and I completely agree with this observation.' Quoting at
length from some of the expert testimony barred by Judge Platt, he added:
'I am convinced that, had the jury been permitted to hear this evidence,

there is a strong likelihood it would have rejected the plaintiffs' contention that the bomb which exploded began its deadly journey in Malta.'

The Observer's 1989 attack on the Interfor Report and Steven Emerson's 'exposé' of Lester Coleman were early blows in a long-running media war. Whenever stories appeared implicating US government agencies in the disaster, there soon followed a 'de-bunking' story. Besides Emerson and The Observer's John Merritt, the transatlantic cast of de-bunkers grew to include, among others, US journalist Christopher Byron and the Sunday Times's David Leppard.

Roy Rowan's April 1992 article for Time magazine, which, like the Interfor Report, suggested the bombers had exploited a CIA-protected drug-running operation, prompted scathing articles by Merritt in The Observer, Emerson in the Washington Journalism Review and Byron in New York magazine. All suggested it was a tissue of falsehoods peddled by Pan Am's lawyers and Juval Aviv. As Time's management and Rowan freely conceded, the article made a major mistake in naming a former friend of Lester Coleman, called Michael Schafer, as David Lovejoy, an American double agent who allegedly tipped off the Iranian embassy in Beirut about the movements of Charles McKee's intelligence team.

Emerson's piece made great play of this mistake before going on to attack Juval Aviv and Lester Coleman. Aviv, he claimed, had lied about his background in Israeli intelligence and was sacked as junior security officer for the El Al airline for being unreliable and dishonest. 'None of his allegations have any basis in fact. He is a fabricator and a scam artist,' the former head of the CIA's Lockerbie investigation, Vincent Cannistraro, told Emerson. Cannistraro had retired from the agency in September 1990 and, as we will describe in later chapters, subsequently became a regular media commentator about the bombing, often dismissing allegations of CIA involvement in the bombing.

Turning to Coleman, Emerson claimed he had been 'hired by Pan Am in mid-1990 to assist in the Pan Am 103 investigation' and had profited to the tune of 'tens of thousands of dollars'. In fact, Coleman never met Pan Am's legal representatives until 1 November 1990, and it was only in April 1991 that he provided them with an affidavit. The airline paid expenses amounting to $15,000, plus a further $3,000 to reimburse him for lost time. The implication of the article was that Coleman's testimony would help Pan Am defend the civil action that was being brought by the Lockerbie relatives. It was never intended that this would be the case and Coleman was only ever to be used in Pan Am's attempted third-party liability action against the government, which, by the time the *Time* article appeared, was dead in the water. For good measure, Emerson quoted a passage from Coleman's DEA file, which stated that Coleman had been 'caught up in the quagmire of fabrications with DEA, the Cyprus police force and [his] sub-sources and other associates in Cyprus'. Quite how Emerson had gained access to Coleman's file was not clear.

Unlike Emerson, Christopher Byron had not investigated the Lockerbie bombing, but this did not prevent him launching into a series of articles in *New York* magazine in a similar vein. In attacking the *Time* article, he suggested that Roy Rowan's colleagues at the magazine were unsure of the story, but didn't name any of them. The following month *Time*'s managing editor, Henry Muller, issued a statement which read: 'Roy Rowan is a journalist of extraordinary skill and unimpeachable integrity . . . We emphatically reject the accusation that Rowan or *Time* were "conned" in their investigation, and we question the motives of those making such claims.'

Byron also quoted Vincent Cannistraro, who described Rowan's effort as 'wrong in every particular' and 'the worst piece of reportage I have seen in many years'. The bulk of Byron's piece concentrated on Lester Coleman, branded a fabricator by a number of quoted sources. In concluding his assault on *Time*, Byron declared that Rowan's article 'reveals something about the impulse to self-destruction that seems to be eating away at America's faith in itself and its institutions'.

Time printed a correction the following month, saying it regretted Schafer's picture was used in error, but Schafer, who was by then working as a commercial floor cleaner in Austell, Georgia, sued the magazine for libel. He claimed the paper had recklessly printed the story in the face of overwhelming evidence that it was wrong.

The case came to court in Atlanta, Georgia, in April 1996. Among the witnesses called by the plaintiff was Lee Kreindler, who told the court that he had warned Rowan the story was 'phoney'. Vincent Cannistraro testified that a reporter from *Time*'s Washington Bureau had called him the week before publication asking for information that would help 'kill the story'.[6] In their defence, Rowan and senior *Time* executives pointed out that Rowan had independently checked all the details of the story with a number of sources and had conducted nearly 200 interviews.[7]

The eight-member jury took less than four hours to find in *Time*'s favour.[8]

A few weeks after his assault on *Time*, Byron was once again crusading on behalf of America's institutions in the pages of *New York* magazine. In another lengthy article, entitled 'Pan Am Games', he sought to demonstrate that the various reports of US involvement in the bombing were merely a ploy dreamed up by Pan Am's insurers, the US Aviation Underwriters Inc, to avoid paying compensation to the Lockerbie relatives. The article played on the fact that the head of the underwriter's claims department, Robert Alpert, had resigned, allegedly after a disagreement with company chairman John Brennan, over the strategy that should be adopted for defending the case. According to Byron, Brennan wished to base the defence on Juval Aviv's Interfor Report. Alpert disagreed and was quoted as saying, 'I strongly disagree with the philosophy of the chairman on defending the cases. There is simply no rationalisation . . . to take the position that a US carrier could not be responsible for its security.' With Brennan holding sway, Byron suggested, the insurers and their lawyers embarked on an elaborate strategy of leaks and media manipulation designed to sway the civil damages case in their favour.

Byron had failed to point out that the Interfor Report left Pan Am with no defence whatsoever. Not only was it based entirely on intelligence and therefore completely lacking in hard evidence, but it had also suggested the airline's own baggage-handlers were involved in the illicit movement of drugs and that they had been instrumental in getting the bomb on the plane. Furthermore, if the CIA was protecting the drug-running operation, it was possible that someone within the airline had sanctioned the use of its planes in the operation. This hardly constituted a lack of responsibility for the bomb getting on the plane.

On 20 December 1992, a day before the fourth anniversary of Lockerbie, CBS Television's *60 Minutes* programme pursued the course that had been so well trodden by Byron, Emerson and the others. Juval Aviv was invited to appear on the programme. In 1991 Aviv had been hired by the presenter Mike Wallace and a producer, Barry Lando, to work as a consultant on various assignments for the programme. He naturally assumed the Lockerbie feature would be balanced, but as soon as he heard Wallace's introductory lines he knew that he had walked into a trap. Having reminded viewers that Pan Am and its insurers intended to appeal the guilty verdict in the civil damages case, Wallace went on:

> It is not surprising that Pan Am and its lead insurer, US Aviation Underwriters, would appeal that verdict. What is surprising, perhaps, is that they would hire a private detective like Juval Aviv to help them avoid paying huge damage claims.

It was only much later in the programme that Wallace mentioned that Aviv had actually resigned from the Lockerbie case two years prior to the guilty verdict. And, like Christopher Byron and Steve Emerson before him, he ignored the fact that the Interfor Report reflected badly on Pan Am. Predictably, the programme included recorded interviews with Lee Kreindler and Vincent Cannistraro, both of whom rammed home the message that Aviv was a cruel con man.

The item further claimed that some of the law firms for whom Aviv had worked 'had charged him with everything from ripping off clients for tens of thousands of dollars for spurious investigations, to originally trying to sell his services to the families of those who were killed in the plane bombing'. It was a very serious allegation, yet not a single shred of evidence was offered to demonstrate that Aviv was a con man. Not one disgruntled former client could be found who would testify on the programme.

Wallace announced 'Vince – come on in', and Cannistraro came on set to confront Aviv in the flesh. Cannistraro told him: 'Almost everything you said is completely fabricated. It's invented', and not 'supported by one scintilla of material evidence'. No one pointed out that potentially crucial material evidence, such as the heroin finds at Lockerbie, had been covered up, and that requests to the American government to release documentary evidence had been quashed on the grounds of national security.

After the Cannistraro ambush, Wallace got on to the subject of Lester Coleman. He confronted Pan Am chairman Thomas Plaskett about why he was allowing Coleman and Aviv to be the 'lead investigators' for the airline. Coleman was never an investigator for the airline, 'lead' or otherwise. Furthermore, Aviv had resigned that position two-and-a-half years earlier. Plaskett conceded that he would probably not hire Aviv again; hardly surprising, given that the Interfor Report had been a constant source of grief for Pan Am. Both Steven Emerson and Christopher Byron had a hand in the *60 Minutes* report. Wallace quoted Emerson as saying: 'They knew they were being conned, but they went along because they had a constellation of the same interests.' In rounding up the item, he thanked Byron.

The publication of Lester Coleman's book *Trail of the Octopus* in September 1993 prompted a further *New York* magazine article from Byron. Headlined 'THE GREAT PRETENDER', it trumpeted the charges in the perjury indictment issued against Coleman just days before the book's publication.

The backlash against the book was surpassed by the campaign waged against the documentary film *The Maltese Double Cross*. Made in London by American director Allan Francovich, whose previous investigations of the nastier side of America's covert foreign policy had won international acclaim, it suggested the official story of Lockerbie was a sham and presented new evidence to support the alternative version.

The film attracted considerable controversy, not least because it was initially funded by the British multinational company Lonrho plc, via its subsidiary company Metropole Hotels, which was one-third owned by the Libyan Arab Finance Company, the Libyan government's investment arm. Francovich had a longstanding interest in Lockerbie and was keen to make a film on the subject. He was already known to Lonrho because he had made a number of successful television documentaries for the Observer Film Company, a subsidiary of the Lonrho-owned *Observer* newspaper. Lonrho pulled out of the project after its involvement was revealed by the *Financial Times* in November 1993. Some of its board of directors had always been unhappy about the project, but its renowned joint chief executive 'Tiny' Rowland was determined that it should go ahead. Quite apart from his business interests, Rowland had a close relationship with Colonel Gadafy, who, not surprisingly, had assured him that he was not involved in the bombing. Rowland arranged for nominal ownership of the film's production company Hemar Enterprises to be transferred to an Egyptian, Ibraheem El Marbrouk, who was a director of an Egyptian investment company part-owned by the Libyan Arab Finance Company. Rowland continued to discreetly fund the film via one of his Swiss bank accounts.

Francovich only agreed to be involved in the project on condition that there was no interference from Rowland or Libya, but was inevitably branded a Gadafy apologist by those who accepted Libyan complicity in the bombing. Others, including Dr Jim Swire, the spokesman of UK Families – Flight 103, kept a more open mind about the film. In doing so he found himself under pressure from Linda Mack, who had remained close to the group. Shortly after beginning work on the film Francovich had himself been contacted by Mack, who introduced herself as someone who had not only lost a loved one at Lockerbie, but who also knew a good deal about the subject. She offered her assistance and at the same time said that she was keen to find out more about the production. Relations between the two rapidly deteriorated.

The *Financial Times* story increased the campaign of pressure on Jim Swire to stop cooperating with Francovich. Linda Mack continued to make emotional appeals to him in a series of lengthy telephone calls and, having failed to sway him, she tried a similar approach with his wife, Jane. Furious at her tactics, he resolved to sever all contact with Mack.[9] Further pressure was applied to the Swires by Mack's friends Daniel and Susan Cohen, who sent a stream of angry faxes. Among the most vociferous of the American relatives, although not affiliated to any of the main relatives' groups, the Cohens had lost their only child, 20-year-old daughter Theodora, on Flight 103.

A few days after Lonrho's decision to drop the film, Francovich received a call from Christopher Byron. Hot on the heels of his recent attacks on Lester Coleman and Pan Am's insurers, Byron was predictably keen to ask about the film. Francovich explained how Lonrho had set up the company and that he had only agreed to make the film after he had been given a guarantee there would be no editorial interference. He told Byron, 'If Libya, if Lonrho, if Tiny Rowland, interfere at any stage of this I will have a press conference and I will announce what has happened.' Byron replied: 'I have no interest one way or another in Allan Francovich, or your film company. My sole interest here is in Lester Coleman.' Coleman had recently issued a press release which had inaccurately claimed that Francovich's film would be based on his book. Francovich assured Byron, 'There might be a film based on his book, but it's not this one . . . this film is based on an independent investigation, in which we are pursuing all leads.'

A few days later, *New York* magazine carried an article by Byron entitled 'MOVIE MOGUL MUAMMAR'. It expounded the thesis that the film was part of Gadafy's 'desperate "I didn't do it" campaign'. Byron was unable to produce hard evidence that the film had been instigated by the Libyan government and the only facts he could muster were those already reported by the *Financial Times*. Much of the article was not about the alleged Libyan influence-peddling in Washington, but by mentioning the film alongside these activities it was implied that it too had been dreamed up in Tripoli. The article failed to mention Francovich's control over the contents of the film, and only in the final few paragraphs did he report the director's rejection of any Lonrho or Libyan interference.

Over the following 18 months further articles would appear in Britain and the US, pursuing a similar thesis and peppered with quotes from Lee Kreindler, Vincent Cannistraro and Daniel and Susan Cohen.

Before completing the film, Allan Francovich approached Channel 4 to discuss broadcasting it. The commissioning editor for documentaries, Peter Moore, and his deputy Alan Hayling, were very interested, but shortly afterwards were besieged by faxes and phone calls from the Cohens which variously accused Francovich's team of being 'scum', 'bastards' and 'whoring for Gadafy'.

A year in the making and two-and-a-half hours long, *The Maltese Double Cross*, like the Interfor Report, *Time* magazine and others before it, concluded that the Lockerbie terrorists had exploited an officially protected drug-running operation and that the official account of the bombing was plain wrong. The film was due to be premièred at the 1994 London Film Festival, but for the first time in its 38-year history, the festival pulled out at the last minute, following a legitimate and understandable legal threat from Michael Hurley. Labour MP Tam Dalyell arranged for the première to take place at the House of Commons on 16 November 1994. The following day, *The Scotsman* newspaper organised a public screening in Glasgow.

Further screenings were organised by an anti-censorship centre in Birmingham called the Angle Gallery. The day after the first screening, both the gallery and the home of the organiser were burgled. Nothing of value was taken, but office files had been rifled. A few weeks later the gallery organised a further screening. This time it suffered an arson attack.

In March 1995, Channel 4 agreed to broadcast a 90-minute version of the film. Within days, one of the film's interviewees, Juval Aviv, was arrested on suspicion of fraud in a case ostensibly unrelated to Pan Am 103.

The Channel 4 broadcast was set for 11 May. Shortly after the announcement, stories appeared in the press on both sides of the Atlantic that the US Federal authorities had launched an investigation into allegations that Pan Am's lawyers, insurers and investigators had conspired to deflect blame for the bombing away from the airline.[10] Such stories had, of course, been circulating for years, with the long-threatened indictments against James Shaugnessy, Juval Aviv *et al* never materialising. Nevertheless, with *The Maltese Double Cross* about to be broadcast, the Federal authorities perhaps calculated that the public would infer that the film was merely rehashing lies dreamed up by Pan Am and its associates.

On 26 April, another of the film's interviewees, Tam Dalyell MP, was invited to the US Embassy in London to meet with Todd Leventhal, an employee of the US Information Agency with the Orwellian title of 'Program Officer for Countering Disinformation and Misinformation'. Leventhal did his best to convince Dalyell that the film's sources were tricksters and con men.[11] He followed up with a four-page letter reiterating his previous attacks on the film's 'known fabricators', including Juval Aviv and Lester Coleman. Great play was made of Aviv's recent arrest.[12]

One of the film's contributors was indeed a known fabricator. Former CIA agent Oswald Lewinter was a highly sophisticated disinformation specialist who openly admitted being responsible for a number of scams, some of which were perpetrated against the media. In 1985 he was convicted in the US for his part in an amphetamine importation, but despite the huge amount of drugs involved he only received a six-year sentence, of which he served less than half. In the film, he described how he had posed as a Libyan called Mr Wamma and created a false trail leading back to the Libyan government. He claimed to have been given such a lenient sentence because the judge in the case was secretly informed that he had been engaged in a sensitive operation on behalf of the US government. Francovich handled all information provided by Lewinter with great care, and did not include any of it in the film without independent corroboration.

In 1998 Lewinter was again imprisoned, this time in Austria, for attempting to defraud Mohammed Al-Fayed by selling him documents purporting to show that Princess Diana and Dodi Al-Fayed were killed by MI6. Lewinter continues to insist he was the victim of an elaborate sting.

The weekend before the Channel 4 broadcast, Todd Leventhal's allegations resurfaced in a *Sunday Times* article by David Leppard and Ian Burrell, headed 'FBI EXPOSES DOCUMENTARY ON LOCKERBIE AS A SHAM'. Leppard's involvement in the article was no surprise, since *The Maltese Double Cross* suggested that the official version of Lockerbie, described in his book *On the Trail of Terror*, was erroneous.

Ironically Leppard himself was, at that point, at the heart of one of the most notorious journalistic shams of recent times. Three months earlier his by-line appeared on a front-page story headlined 'MICHAEL FOOT "WAS SPY"', which alleged that the former Labour Party leader had been regarded as an agent of influence by the Soviet KGB. The story was nonsense and resulted in the newspaper making a substantial out-of-court payment to Foot.

Todd Leventhal's approach to Tam Dalyell was merely the prelude to an extraordinary joint assault on *The Maltese Double Cross* by the British and American governments. On the eve of the Channel 4 broadcast, the Scottish Crown Office and the US Embassy in London simultaneously sent every British and Scottish national newspaper a 'press pack', which largely rehashed the now familiar allegations against some of the film's interviewees.[13] The British and American governments repeated the exercise when the film was shown on Australian television the following week.[14] Many felt that these crude tactics backfired. As an editorial in *The Guardian* commented, the 'clumsy attempt . . . to discredit [the film] in advance only invites us to pay more attention'.[15]

The threatened indictments against Pan Am insurers US Aviation Underwriters and their lawyers, insurers and Juval Aviv for fabricating a defence in the Lockerbie case never materialised. Nevertheless, within days of *The Maltese Double Cross* being broadcast, both Juval Aviv and the head of US Aviation Underwriters, John Brennan, were indicted on separate fraud charges. Both were adamant that the charges had been trumped up and, as we will describe later, both were eventually proved correct.

9. A PICTURE BUILDS

The US and British authorities maintained that the alternative version of Lockerbie suggested by Juval Aviv's Interfor Report, NBC and ABC television, *Time* magazine and others was an outrageous fiction. They suggested the whole scenario was originally dreamed up by Pan Am, their lawyers, insurers, Aviv and Lester Coleman in order to get the airline off the hook for its security failures. Then, after two of its citizens were indicted for the bombing, that the Gadafy regime had also promoted the myth via stooges like Allan Francovich in his film *The Maltese Double Cross*. Events at the Lockerbie crash site, such as the discovery of drugs, cash and details of hostage locations in Beirut, and the presence of mysterious Americans, were all officially denied.

Nevertheless, over the years a steady stream of evidence emerged to lend weight to the alternative version.

In the early months of 1989 the FBI got wind of a new and potentially important lead in the Lockerbie case. The tip-off came from Steven Donahue, a former drug dealer who had spent much of the '70s and early '80s exporting hashish from Lebanon to the US. While in Lebanon he had become friendly with various members of the Jaafar clan, in particular one whom we will call Jamil, who made his living through rearing chickens and growing hashish. Some weeks after the Lockerbie disaster Donahue received frantic phone calls from Jamil, who told him that one of his close relatives had been the innocent dupe who had taken the bomb on the plane and that he wanted to convey this information to the American authorities.[1]

Donahue's relationship with those authorities was somewhat strained. After being apprehended in 1983, he struck a secret plea agreement in which he agreed to work undercover for the DEA. The arrangement had been short-lived. His first major assignment was the attempted entrapment of an alleged major Lebanese heroin dealer. He claims that due to faulty security arrangements his cover was immediately blown and that he, his wife and son were held hostage for eighteen months, during which time he was tortured. The DEA denied his claim, maintaining that the fateful trip to Lebanon was undertaken entirely at his own volition and that he concocted the kidnapping story to cover the fact that he had double-crossed the DEA. At the time of Jamil's call he was in the middle of an ultimately unsuccessful civil action against the US government.[2]

Jamil proposed a deal. In return for providing the US authorities with information about how the terrorists had used his relative Khalid, he wanted them to allow him to import a consignment of hashish to the US. On receiving the information, Donahue sought the advice of a private detective friend in New York who agreed to act as intermediary between Jamil and the FBI. Donahue also informed his congressman, Larry Smith.[3]

At a local level, the FBI took the information very seriously, obtaining special permission to record Donahue's telephone conversations with Jamil. Ultimately, though, nothing came of the offer, perhaps because the FBI figured the proposed deal compromised the integrity of Jamil's information.

Five years on, Jamil finally went public with his information and this time there were no strings attached. In an interview for Allan Francovich's documentary *The Maltese Double Cross*, he gave a detailed account of how Khalid had been duped into carrying the bomb. Around 20 years younger than Jamil, Khalid had grown up only a few yards away and was a regular playmate of Jamil's younger brother.

By the time of the bombing the Jaafar clan was split between more traditional secular Shi'ites, such as Jamil, and born-again Moslem followers of Hizbullah, whose influence had spread rapidly throughout the Bekaa Valley during the '80s. In Jamil's view the Hizbullah Jaafars were not devout Moslems at all, but bandits and opportunists who saw the group as a means of extending their power and influence. The rift within the family had frequently been bloody and Jamil made no secret of the fact that this was his primary motivation in going public. 'We are at permanent war with them,' he explained.

According to Jamil, in the months before he died Khalid became captivated by a cousin who was the sister of a Hizbullah captain. Khalid was besotted, but Jamil said the relationship was deliberately engineered as part of a Hizbullah plot. Khalid was promised her hand in marriage on condition that he first go to Germany to earn some money. He was told friends there would sort him out with work, but Jamil claimed these associates were part of a joint PFLP-GC/Hizbullah network. Before Khalid left for Germany, he was given, by a person posing as a friend, a gift of a radio-cassette player. The player was put in a suitcase along with two kilograms of heroin. Khalid was escorted to the airport and seen off on his flight. On arrival Khalid was met by Jibril's people, who took the suitcase and its contents from him. Prior to his eventual departure to the US, unbeknown to him the radio-cassette player was installed with a bomb.

Jamil insisted, 'Khalid didn't know anything about drugs, nor did he work with drugs. They fooled him.'[4] There is nothing to suggest that his fiancée had any knowledge of the drugs or that she and Khalid had been used in the bomb plot.

Jamil conspicuously avoided blaming Syria for the Lockerbie bombing. According to the 1992 US congressional report 'Syria, President Bush and Drugs – the Administration's next Iraqgate', the Jaafar clan was connected to the head of Syrian military intelligence, General Ali Dubbah. Even though many family members may have resented Syria's control, they could not afford to alienate Dubbah and his military enforcers.

Jamil's account of Hizbullah involvement in the bombing nevertheless shed light on an unusual find at the crash site. On 29 December 1988 David Clark, a member of the Teesdale Mountain Rescue team who was helping search for debris in the Kielder Forest, found a white T-shirt stuck in a tree at a location called Forking Syke, at grid reference 610 875. On close inspection he saw that it had green Arabic writing and a logo depicting a hand holding aloft a machine-gun. He handed the T-shirt to the police and a month later was visited by an officer from the Cleveland force, who took a statement from him confirming the find. The officer had spoken to the Scottish police, who viewed the T-shirt as potentially important because the writing and logo were the insignia of Hizbullah.[5]

There were only four or five people on Flight 103 who had been in Lebanon prior to the bombing and who could therefore have been in contact with the group. These were Khalid Jaafar, Major Charles McKee, his colleagues Matthew Gannon, Ron Lariviere and possibly also the Cyprus-based Daniel O'Connor. McKee's team were supposedly on a top-secret mission, and were therefore unlikely to have been in direct contact with the organisation. The more likely explanation was that the T-shirt had been given to Khalid Jaafar.

Jamil claimed ignorance of any connection between Khalid and the DEA in Cyprus. He said Khalid had told his family in the Bekaa that he sometimes visited a journalist friend on the island.[6] Khalid's father Nazir, who lived in the US, denied that Khalid had ever visited Cyprus.[7]

Documents obtained from the DEA under the US Freedom of Information Act showed that Khalid's details had been logged into the DEA's EPIC computer system. Short for El Paso Intelligence Center, EPIC is located at Fort Bliss, El Paso, Texas. Its original mission was to assist in the monitoring of the southern border with Mexico to aid interdiction activities, but it is now responsible for a wide variety of drug intelligence-gathering. (The DEA's main computer system is called

NADDIS: Narcotics and Dangerous Drugs Information System. EPIC's system could be accessed by member agencies while NADDIS is proprietary – open to only DEA. Thus the military, for example, had direct access to the EPIC database but not NADDIS.) The documents, which were partially blacked out, were neither proof that Khalid was a DEA asset nor that he was involved with drug-dealing. Since he made regular trips to Lebanon, it was perhaps inevitable that the DEA would take an interest in him.

It was implicit in Jamil's account that he had a source deep within Hizbullah. Some months later he gave Francovich a handwritten report, detailing exactly how Khalid had been duped and giving names and addresses of members of the PFLP-GC/Hizbullah network whom he had met in Germany. One of these people, the report alleged, had paid a policeman at Frankfurt airport to see Khalid safely in and out of the country. The report read:

> When Khalid got to the German airport, a policeman helped him straight away to stamp his passport without even searching his luggage. This same policeman helped to stamp Khalid's passport on his departure to the United States. Again the policeman didn't show Khalid's luggage to the customs officers. This policeman had received a sum of money he would never have dreamed of earning, even if he spent 50 years in the police.

A crooked policeman acting on his own was, of course, no guarantee of safe passage in and out of the country, unless he was also acting under orders from an official agency.

Suspicions that Jamil had a mole within the enemy camp were confirmed when he produced a videotape filmed at an underground Hizbullah meeting. It showed scores of recruits sitting cross-legged on the floor as a speaker intoned against the West. 'Dear brothers,' he declared, 'facing the campaign of the powerful alliance of the oppressive Jews and the crusaders against our nation, armed struggle is the only way to confront this campaign, and to continue the struggle of the Jihad.'

Much of the sermon urged the audience to work with Palestinians against their common enemies in the West and Israel. The speaker was no doubt pursuing this theme because the audience included a prominent radical Palestinian leader. Clearly visible among the Hizbullah dignitaries was none other than Ahmed Jibril. Although it was known that Jibril had been an active supporter of Hizbullah ever since its inception, his presence at the meeting vividly underlined Jamil's claim that his group worked hand in hand with Hizbullah in their war against the West.

Also on the tape was an interview with an old man, who Jamil claimed was Khalid's grandfather. Sitting with his wife under a picture of Khalid, he appeared choked as he remembered the boy: 'It was too painful . . . even if he was just my grandson he was like my son.' The old man did not talk about Hizbullah and its role in Khalid's death, perhaps because to have done so would have put both him and the cameraman at serious risk if the tape fell into the wrong hands. Briefly alluding to events surrounding Khalid's death, he said people involved in the plot, whom he referred to only as 'they', arranged a visa for him to enter the United States. This was an odd detail, given that Khalid had been a resident of the United States for some time and had a US passport.

The DEA's EPIC computer stated that Khalid's US passport, numbered 022807773, 'was not among items recovered at Lockerbie'. If Khalid did not have his American passport with him there would have been all the more reason to organise a visa for him. His Lebanese passport found at Lockerbie contained a US multiple-entry visa issued at the US Embassy in Beirut on 18 July 1988. Curiously, some of the pages had been partially torn out.[8]

Khalid became a naturalised US citizen on 29 February 1988 and his US passport was issued on 24 June 1988. It seemed strange that he would later need a US visa on his Lebanese passport, particularly given that it is illegal for dual passport holders to enter the US on their foreign passport. Stranger still, according to the US Bureau of Consular Affairs, in July 1988 the US Embassy in Lebanon only issued visas to Lebanese government officials with an official request and US Embassy employees.[9]

In November 2000 the authors e-mailed the Bureau of Consular Affairs, asking how it was that Khalid came to be issued with the visa and why it was necessary for him to have one when he already held a US passport. Despite being sent a number of reminders the Bureau failed to respond.

This curiosity inevitably increased suspicion that Khalid was working undercover, and the missing US passport and the pages torn out of the Lebanese passport perhaps suggested that someone was anxious to conceal details of his movements over recent months.

Among those who maintained that Khalid was working for the DEA and, by extension, the CIA, was former DEA and DIA agent Lester Coleman. In 1996 his claims were dealt a major blow when the publisher of his book *Trail of the Octopus* made a large out-of-court payment to settle a libel case brought by his former DEA boss, Michael Hurley. In a statement read out in court, the counsel for the publisher, Bloomsbury, 'sincerely apologised to the plaintiff for all the distress and embarrassment caused to him by the book' and the counsel for Penguin, which published the paperback edition, added 'there was no truth in the allegations complained of by the plaintiff and they should not have published the book'.

The book alleged that Hurley had a reckless disregard for the security of controlled drug delivery operations and implied that he was, in large measure, personally responsible for the disaster. It was a foolish claim, not only because there was no supporting evidence but also because Coleman had left Cyprus seven months before Lockerbie and had no first-hand knowledge of the events surrounding the bombing. Furthermore, since Khalid Jaafar left Lebanon for Germany six weeks before Lockerbie and flew direct, rather than via Cyprus, he could not have been involved in the type of controlled delivery that Coleman alleged was operated via the DEA's Nicosia office.

Hurley's solicitor, Richard Howard, issued a triumphant press release, declaring that his client's victory 'debunks the wholly unsubstantiated conspiracy theories about US and UK government complicity and cover-up in connection with the Lockerbie bombing'. In an accompanying 'briefing note' he went further, suggesting not only that there was no question of US and UK government involvement in the bombing but also implying that claims of Syrian, Iranian and Palestinian involvement were similarly baseless. The note sketched out the evidence against the Libyans and, for good measure, added Parliamentary quotes from the then Foreign Secretary Douglas Hurd and Prime Minister John Major, to the effect that there was no evidence against anyone except the Libyans.

Following his victory, Michael Hurley issued a libel writ against Channel 4 over its broadcast of the edited version of *The Maltese Double Cross*. Once again there was an out-of-court settlement. Neither film-maker Allan Francovich, nor the channel, intended that the film should – like *Trail of the Octopus* – give the impression that the disaster was due to a lax attitude to security on the part of Hurley. However, in paying costs and 'suitable damages' to Hurley, the broadcaster recognised that some viewers might, nevertheless, have been left with that impression. The film's central claims – that Syrian and Iranian-sponsored PFLP-GC and Hizbullah terrorists had exploited a CIA sanctioned drug-running operation to plant the bomb on Khalid Jaafar – were not withdrawn and remained unaffected by the settlement.[10]

Well before the publication of *Trail of the Octopus* and *The Maltese Double Cross*, Khalid Jaafar's unwitting role in the bombing had been confirmed by another Middle Eastern source. And it was no ordinary source. The Palestinian, named Tunayb, claimed to have been a member of the PFLP-GC for 17 years. Rising to the rank of major and the position of intelligence chief and member of the group's executive committee, he subsequently became the highest-ranking member to defect and live to tell the tale. According to the former head of the CIA's Lockerbie investigation, Vincent Cannistraro, Tunayb was at a key meeting in 1988 between the PFLP-GC and the Islamic Revolutionary Guard Core, a group of Iranian radicals intent on avenging the American shoot-down of Iran Air 655.

Tunayb's Lockerbie revelations were provided to American reporter Morgan Strong, who verified his bona fides with a high-level intelligence agent familiar with the PFLP-GC's operations in Lebanon. Strong met him under conditions of 'extreme secrecy' in a Middle Eastern country. Tunayb was vague, perhaps deliberately so, when asked who sponsored the bombing, saying only that the money came from the Middle East. He said he didn't believe that his erstwhile commander, Ahmed Jibril, knew the bomb was going to be placed on Flight 103. When asked about matters of less immediate sensitivity to his ex-comrades, he was more forthcoming. He claimed the bomb was planted on Khalid Jaafar after he had been picked by contacts in the US who were closely connected to his fundamentalist associates in Lebanon. They were aware that he worked for the CIA and therefore that his bags were not checked when he passed through airports. When he left the Bekaa Valley his case contained drugs and documents concerning Hizbullah, and at some point, according to Tunayb, the bomb was planted on him. He admitted that he was unsure exactly how this was done and who made the bomb.[11]

Tunayb and Jamil Jaafar's assertion that Khalid was involved with Islamic radicals explained one of the oddities in the account of the mysterious Mr Goldberg, who claimed to have met the young man on an evening train from Gothenburg to Stockholm on 19 December 1988. Goldberg had told the story to Pan Am's director of passenger services in Oslo, Ingrid Olufsen, on 2 January 1989, before disappearing. Among the curious elements of his account was that Khalid had been reading the Koran and had claimed his parents were Iranian, when in fact his father was Lebanese and his mother Syrian. Press reports after Lockerbie suggested Khalid had been more interested in fast cars and body-building than the Koran, but if, as Jamil claimed, he was in love with his fiancée, he had perhaps begun to steep himself in Islam in order to please her relatives and, like many Hizbullah supporters, started to view Iran as his spiritual home.

What of the remainder of Goldberg's account? Was there any evidence to support his claim that the young man had been in Sweden shortly before his death? Although his information was passed on to Pan Am's London office, it never reached the company's lawyers in New York and it was not until 1994 that the story was further investigated.

Goldberg had noted that his travelling companion had been staying at '3b Storegatan, 41669, Gothenburg' and was heading to 'Room 4516, Hotel Hem, Norra stationsgatan, Stockholm'. Hotel Hem was a short-stay hostel for immigrants and the homeless. Given the rapid turnover of residents, it was impossible to trace someone who might have stayed there for one night five years earlier. There is no Storegatan in Gothenburg, but there is a Storkgatan, which has the same 41669 postcode noted by Goldberg. Number 3B Storkgatan consists of three apartments, one of which was occupied in 1994 by an Arab man. Contacted by the authors in 2000, the man said he had moved to Sweden from his native Iraq in 1993 and took over the Storkgatan apartment from his brother in 1994. He would not say when his brother had moved into the apartment and said he had never heard of Khalid Jaafar.

If Khalid Jaafar was in Sweden during the two days before his death, what could he have been doing there? And how did he fit into what was already known about Mohammed Abu Talb and his associates in Uppsala? The role they had played in Lockerbie, if any, was unclear. All that was certain was that in October 1988 Abu Talb had visited Cyprus at the same time as the PFLP-GC's Hafez Dalkamoni and then flown on to Malta. He had returned from Malta with clothes, which his wife Jamilla Mograbi told the Swedish Security Police, SAPO, were samples manufactured by Hashim Salem, whose bother Abdel Salem owned a bakery on the island.[12]

In the same month, some of his associates, including his brother-in-law Mohammed Mograbi, had visited the Neuss apartment where Marwan Khreesat had assembled aircraft bombs under Dalkamoni's instructions. Of course, the clothes made by Hashim Salem could not have been the bundle purchased from the Mary's House shop and allegedly wrapped around the Lockerbie bomb. Nevertheless, Maltese clothes were a sensitive issue for Abu Talb. Questioned by SAPO he had contradicted his wife, denying having any other than a pair of black jeans and some shirts.[13] Furthermore, when monitoring her phone calls prior to raiding her house, SAPO reportedly heard the frantic Jamilla urge a friend to 'get rid of the clothes'.[14]

The press had speculated that Mohammed Mograbi had smuggled a bomb back from Germany to Sweden in October 1988 and *The Times*[15] had even reported that Abu Talb had confessed to passing one of the German bombs on to someone else. Could the unwitting Jaafar have been sent to

Sweden to collect a bomb? This scenario was unlikely, for the same reason it was unlikely that one of Khreesat's bombs had started its journey in Malta; trained terrorists would be most unlikely to run the risk of taking a device across international borders.

A more likely explanation was that Khalid Jaafar was sent to pick up the Maltese clothes, which the terrorists had decided to put in the bomb suitcase in order to lay a false trail to the island. This suspicion was strengthened by a close female relative of Khalid, who told Allan Francovich that a few days before the bombing Khalid was driven to Kiel in Northern Germany, from where he had caught the ferry to Gothenburg. More importantly, she said that during his stay in Sweden he had been given clothes, which he had told her were a gift.

Exactly who had bought the clothes and how they got to Sweden was a mystery and, as with Goldberg, the woman could offer no proof to back up her claim. Nevertheless her information was volunteered, unprompted, at a time when Goldberg's story was not in the public domain.

Claims that Jaafar had been in Sweden clashed with the account of Hassan El-Salheli, an unemployed Lebanese barber living in Dortmund, who had seen him off on the train to Frankfurt airport on 21 December. He insisted that Jaafar had spent the entire time since his arrival from Lebanon with him, his brother Souhail and a Lebanese associate, Naim Ali Ghannam. None of the three were implicated in the report passed on by Jamil Jaafar, but their accounts nevertheless proved interesting. In a statement given to BKA in April 1989, Hassan El-Salheli, who was then 24, said he had never met Jaafar before Jaafar arrived in Germany on 8 November 1988. He explained that Jaafar had been told he could stay with him by another of his brothers, Bilal, whom Jaafar knew from Lebanon. Jaafar flew into Frankfurt airport and took the train to Dortmund, where El-Salheli and Ghannam picked him up in a borrowed car. El-Salheli told the police he had at that point only known Ghannam for a month, having met him by chance in the street. Shortly after their meeting Ghannam had travelled to Lebanon for his brother's funeral, before returning to Dortmund just prior to Jaafar's arrival. El-Salheli said Ghannam had told him his brother had drowned, but according to a statement Ghannam gave to the BKA, he died fighting for Hizbullah.

On 14 December Ghannam took Jaafar to a travel agency in nearby Iserlohn. The agency, Alireisebureau, was run by an acquaintance, Ali Jadallah. There, Jaafar bought an airline ticket to the US. The ticket was for a direct flight from Düsseldorf to Detroit on 19 December, but the booking was changed to Flight 103 from Frankfurt on 21 December. The reasons for the change were unclear. El-Salheli claimed Jadallah informed them that the 19 December flight was fully booked, but according to Jadallah, Ghannam returned to Alireisebureau with El-Salheli but not Jaafar, and asked if Jaafar's ticket could be changed or cancelled. Jadallah claimed the new ticket for 21 December was passed by him to Ghannam, rather than Jaafar.

El-Salheli claimed that he, his brother and Ghannam saw Jaafar off on the train from Dortmund to Frankfurt airport on 21 December, but Ghannam told the German police he was away visiting a polystyrene works in Kamen that day. El-Salheli took a photograph of Jaafar at the station, which he subsequently gave to the BKA. El-Salheli's brother Souhail was also in the picture, but according to El-Salheli, a BKA officer cut the picture in two and took only the part showing Jaafar. El-Salheli said he subsequently threw the negative away. El-Salheli denied he was assigned to be Jaafar's minder[16] and that either of them were involved with Hizbullah, but he did confirm Jamil Jaafar's story that Khalid had a fiancée about whom he was crazy.[17]

When allegations first surfaced on American television that Jaafar had been utilised for controlled deliveries, the DEA conducted an internal inquiry which found no evidence to support the allegation. Nevertheless, further confirmation that he was duped into carrying the Lockerbie bomb came from a former colleague of Major Charles McKee, the US military intelligence specialist who was returning from a top-secret hostage rescue mission in Lebanon.

In July 1989 the book *Lockerbie – the Real Story*, by Scottish radio reporter David Johnston, had described how CIA agents had removed McKee's case from the crash site. Johnston had earlier produced a news story, based on sources within the official investigation, which suggested the bomb had been planted on McKee's team. Shortly after the book's publication a colleague of McKee's wrote a five-page letter to McKee's mother Beulah, assuring her that her son's presence on Flight 103 was not the reason it was attacked. In an oblique reference to the book he wrote: 'I know that certain newspapermen and authors have tried to make a connection but believe me, it was only a horrible coincidence.' He then added, 'The people who brought down the plane did not know anyone on that plane, save the poor fool who carried the bomb on board not knowing what he carried.'[18]

In 1996, a second US intelligence agent went on the record to challenge the official story of Lockerbie. The CIA officer, who declined to be named but was described as having worked for the previous ten years in Middle East counter-terrorism, made his revelation in an interview for the German magazine *Focus*. He stated that the bomb originated not in Malta but in

Frankfurt, and that it had got on the plane with the help of a crooked Pan Am baggage-handler who was involved in drugs.[19]

Two Pan Am baggage-handlers, Roland O'Neill and Kilnic Aslan Tuzcu, had been under suspicion after they failed polygraph tests conducted in 1990 on behalf of the airline's lawyers by former US Army polygrapher James Keefe. The tests indicated that both had lied when they denied switching a suitcase loaded on to Flight 103. Such tests can be unreliable and both protested their innocence, but ten years on, O'Neill, who was still loading bags at Frankfurt airport, made an interesting revelation.

In an interview published in Scotland's *Sunday Herald* newspaper he insisted that he did not lie in the polygraph test, but described an event at Frankfurt airport in 1987:

> I do recall about a year before the bombing that two suitcases filled with drugs, belonging to two women, were ordered to go on board a Pan Am flight without being interfered with – opened or X-rayed. That was on the orders of US agents – either the DEA or the CIA. I can't remember which.

He continued:

> I could have unwittingly been part of the [Lockerbie] conspiracy. Security at Frankfurt airport was incredibly slack. It is entirely possible that a bag of drugs was switched for a bag containing Semtex. I often think to myself, 'My God, I could have picked up that bag and put it on board flight 103 . . .' It terrifies me.[20]

O'Neill then went further, saying:

> I can't accept that Libya is responsible for this, you know. There has to be another reason behind this – quite possibly the activities of American intelligence agencies may be involved. Remember if you wanted to bring something – drugs or a bomb – into the airport it could be done. There was really no security. If anyone had a security badge, like I did, they could just walk through with a bomb, put a baggage tag on it and put it on a plane. And that would be it – boom.

Within days of his interview appearing in the *Sunday Herald*, O'Neill's wife faxed the newspaper attempting to deny that these things were said, despite being aware that they had been openly taped on two tape machines.

When O'Neill gave evidence as a Crown witness at the Lockerbie trial three months after the *Sunday Herald* article, he appeared to back-peddle. Under cross-examination by Jack Davidson QC, he was asked: 'At one point did you report on controlled drugs transfers being affected through Frankfurt Airport?' He replied, 'No, no. That was nothing to do with me. I didn't have anything to do with that.' Davidson went on: 'Did you not inform a journalist that such activities took place at Frankfurt Airport involving bags being switched for the purposes of affecting controlled drug deliveries to the United States?' O'Neill replied: 'This was incorrectly interpreted by the reporter.'[21]

Despite the denials of the ex-colleague of Major Charles McKee's, who wrote to his mother, suspicions persisted that the bombing of Flight 103 was connected to the presence on the plane of McKee's team. These suspicions were originally fuelled by the official reaction to David Johnston's brief radio story a few weeks after the disaster, which had suggested the bomb was planted on McKee's team. The reporter was threatened with prison unless he revealed his sources and, having refused, was asked to reveal them to Prime Minister Margaret Thatcher.

A former DIA officer who spoke on condition of anonymity told the authors of an internecine war which has raged in the US between the CIA and the DIA. The source, whom we will call 'V', confirmed that the DIA interest in the Pan Am bombing stems from the fact that Charles McKee was a serving DIA officer when he was killed aboard the fated jumbo jet. He maintains that the CIA refused to act on their own intelligence that the PFLP-GC had carried out the attack.

V also confirmed that Charles McKee was involved in a plan to rescue American hostages held captive in Beirut. These plans were at a 'very advanced stage' when the order to abort the mission was received by McKee's team. Vehicles were already in place and complex plans to attack several locations in Beirut simultaneously were imminent. According to V, the order to abort such a mission had to have come from the highest authority. When asked to say how high, V claims that aborting such a mission would usually come from the 'oval office', indicating that the President of the United States could be involved. McKee was making his way back to the USA because he believed that the CIA intervened with the White House, causing his mission to be aborted. V claims that senior sources within the DIA believe McKee's mission was compromised in order to protect the CIA's involvement with narco-terrorists. McKee was reportedly fanatical in his hatred of drugs and had fired an employee in Beirut after he caught him in possession.

If it was true and if Major Charles McKee was returning to Washington to blow the whistle on the CIA, why did he and his party end up on the same plane as Khalid Jaafar and the bomb? An anonymous source featured in Allan Francovich's documentary *The Maltese Double Cross* suggested an answer. The American man, who was based in the Wurtzburg area of Germany, claimed without proof to be from the same CIA unit which Juval Aviv's Interfor Report and others identified as having instigated the drugs-for-hostages deal. He claimed that his men had put Jaafar on the plane at Frankfurt and that McKee's colleague Matthew Gannon was assigned to escort him back to the US. The implication was that Gannon and McKee knew Jaafar was being used as a drugs mule.

In the absence of any corroborating evidence, the assertion that Jaafar had a CIA minder remains hypothetical. Nevertheless, it chimes with a claim by the PFLP-GC's ex-intelligence chief Major Tunayb that the young man was accompanied by US intelligence agents on his last trip to Lebanon.[22]

And the claim that Gannon was the minder on the last leg of the flight tallies with intriguing evidence from the Lockerbie crash site. Gannon was seated in Row 14 of the Boeing 747, towards the front of the plane in Clipper class.[23] At the Scottish fatal accident inquiry in 1990, the police gave details of where each body had come to rest. Almost everyone from the front of the plane landed in Tundergarth, three miles east of Lockerbie, where the nose cone landed. It was clear that this was the first part of the aircraft to become detached, so those seated at the front were the first to be sucked out and were therefore blown the furthest by the strong westerly winds. There were, however, a couple of exceptions who landed far closer to Lockerbie, one of whom was Matthew Gannon, found in a field in the Beechgrove area. Apart from one other clipper class passenger, all the passengers who landed in that area had been seated at the rear of the plane. Among them was Khalid Jaafar, who was only about 100 metres from Gannon.[24] If the anonymous American was right, it seemed likely that Gannon was with Jaafar at the rear of the plane at the time of the explosion.

It is also the case that Gannon, McKee and their colleagues Ronald Lariviere and Daniel O'Connor all made late changes to their bookings so that they could travel on Flight 103. All had originally been booked on different transatlantic flights after 21 December, and all changed their plans after Jaafar's ticket was booked. Leaked records compiled by the Metropolitan Police showed that McKee was originally booked to fly on Pan Am Flight 103 on 22 December. The booking was made at Lutas travel in Beirut on 16 December and reconfirmed on the morning of 19

December, but in the early afternoon of 20 December the flight was brought forward to 21 December.

Matthew Gannon was also originally booked to fly on 22 December, but he planned to travel on Pan Am 107 from London to Washington. This booking was made on 9 December through R.A. Travel Masters in Nicosia, Cyprus. His booking was changed to Pan Am 103 on the afternoon of 20 December by the US Embassy in Nicosia, again through R. A. Travel Masters. It was later claimed that Gannon brought forward his flight simply because he was exhausted by his mission in Lebanon.[25]

McKee, Gannon and Lariviere all flew from Larnaca to Heathrow on Cyprus Airways Flight CY504, which left Larnaca at 9.30 a.m. O'Connor flew on Flight CY1364Y, an extra flight laid on by the airline which left Larnaca at 1.30 p.m. He had originally been due to return to the US on 23 December, but on 19 December he brought his flight forward by two days. His family have reported that he left Cyprus earlier than originally planned in order to visit a sick relative in the US.[26]

McKee's records confirmed that he travelled from Beirut to Cyprus on the *Sunnyboat* ferry on the early morning of 21 December. Gannon and Lariviere flew by helicopter along with the US Ambassador to Beirut, John McCarthy. After Lockerbie the State Department's intelligence chief, Ronald Spiers, told journalists that McCarthy was scheduled to be on the doomed Flight 103 but had 'got held up in Nicosia'.[27] In a subsequent telephone conversation with one of the authors, the ambassador denied this was the case and claimed he always intended to fly on 22 December. He explained that Lariviere had been booked to fly on the twenty-second, but on arriving in Nicosia had 'dug around' and managed to find a seat on the extra flight laid on by Air Cyprus.[28]

This version of events does not fit with the known facts about Lariviere's travel arrangements. The Metropolitan Police records show that Lariviere was originally booked to fly on 22 December, on TWA flight TW783M from London Heathrow to Washington National airport. This booking was made through the Louis Tourist Agency in Nicosia on 6 December. His booking was changed to Flight 103 on the morning of 20 December, again through R.A. Travel Masters of Nicosia. Furthermore, he caught the scheduled flight CY504, not the extra flight CY1364Y. In November 2000 the authors wrote to McCarthy to ask why his account did not fit the documented facts. He replied that he had 'no explanation', adding that in the previous telephone conversation 'I repeated to you what I thought was true, based on something I had been told by a third party just after the bombing.'[29] The authors wrote back asking for the name of that 'third party'. McCarthy replied that he had 'no recollection' of the source, which is not surprising given that the events in question occured 12 years earlier.[30]

Evidence that certain VIPs had been kept off the plane came via businessman Tiny Rowland, who arranged the funding for *The Maltese Double Cross*. Francovich's sources had told him that the South African Bureau of State Security (BOSS) had been warned of the attack on Pan Am 103 and, always paranoid about terrorism, against S.A. dignitaries, therefore kept the country's Foreign Minister, Pik Botha, away from the flight. Rowland had known Botha for many years because of his company Lonrho's southern African mining interests. He decided to check the information for himself with another old acquaintance from Botha's ministry. The source told Rowland that he, Botha and a group of senior government officials, including Defence Minister Magnus Malan and the head of BOSS, General Nils van Tonder, were due to fly to New York on 21 December 1988 for the signing of the Namibia peace agreement. The original party also included two of his deputies.

Arrangements were made to fly on Pan Am 103, but according to Rowland's mole, not long before they were due to leave South Africa the delegation was steered away from Flight 103 as a result of a warning. He was reluctant to say from whom it came, but admitted it came from a source that could not be ignored.[31] The party's itinerary was altered so that they could take the earlier Pan Am Flight 101, which left Heathrow at 11 a.m. According to evidence heard at the Scottish fatal accident inquiry into Lockerbie, Flight 101, unlike Flight 103, was given special security checks at Heathrow.[32] There is no suggestion that any of Botha's party knew that Flight 103 would come to harm.

Rowland claimed to have checked the information with another member of the South African delegation, who told him the same story. When the allegation was made public in *The Maltese Double Cross*, Botha's spokesman categorically denied the minister had been warned off the flight. His Private Secretary, Gerrit Pretorious, confirmed that the South African delegation had originally been booked to fly on Pan Am 103. He told Reuters: 'We . . . got to London an hour early and the embassy got us on an earlier flight. When we got to JFK airport a contemporary of mine said, "Thank God you weren't on 103. It crashed over Lockerbie."'[33]

South African MP Colin Eglin pursued the matter further. He spoke to the person who made the booking for Botha's party; that person insisted that no booking was ever made on Flight 103. He then sought clarification from the country's Minister of Justice, Dullah Omar, who had responsibility for intelligence matters. In a parliamentary reply, the minister revealed:

> Shortly before finalising their booking arrangements for Pan Am
> Flight 103 to New York, they learned of an earlier flight from
> London to New York, namely Pan Am Flight 101. They
> consequently were booked and travelled on that flight to New York.

The answer did not sit easily with Gerrit Pretorious's earlier assertion that
the decision to switch to Flight 101 was made at the last minute, on arrival
in London. In any event Pik Botha was most unlikely to have known about
the booking arrangements.

What of the allegation that at the time of Lockerbie the CIA was
involved in secret hostage deals with Middle Eastern drug dealers and, by
extension, the groups that were holding the hostages? The British and
American authorities consistently poured scorn on this claim, but the earlier
Iran Contra scandal had already demonstrated the extreme lengths to which
some within the American Government were prepared to go to secure the
release of the hostages. Years later evidence emerged that the Iran-Contra
hostage deals were far more widespread and continued for longer than their
participants had admitted. Furthermore the deals also involved the British
Secret Intelligence Service.

The new evidence suggested that one of the central figures in the Iranian
hostage deals was the Syrian arms dealer Monzer Al-Kassar. It was a matter
of public record that in 1985 Al-Kassar was paid by Oliver North to supply
weapons to the Nicaraguan rebels as part of the Iran-Contra operation and
officially that was the extent of his involvement. But it was claimed his
wider role was covered-up, in part because he was also working for MI6.

The plan to supply TOW anti-tank missiles to Iran in return for US
hostages held in Lebanon was hatched in response to the capture of the
CIA's Beirut station chief, William Buckley, in March 1984. The official
account of the scandal, as laid out by North and his co-conspirators during
congressional hearings in 1987, placed the plot's genesis at late 1985, when
weapons were channelled via intermediaries in Israel. This begged a
question: if North's political masters were so desperate to secure the release
of Buckley and the others, why did they wait so long before doing anything
about it? (Buckley was tortured to death by his captors in March 1985.) It
was also curious that the operation appeared to have completely by-passed
America's closest ally, Britain.

Evidence unearthed by authors John Loftus and Mark Aarons in their
1994 book *The Secret War Against the Jews* indicated both that the arms-for-
hostages deals were, in fact, kick-started very shortly after Buckley's capture
and that MI6 was intimately involved. The arms channel that utilised Al-

Kassar, Loftus and Aarons reported, was entirely separate from the one that went via Israel. It went via Britain and involved an old, British arms-dealing associate of Al-Kassar's called Leslie Aspin. A former SAS member, from the late '60s onwards Aspin had developed a reputation as a fearless and highly successful smuggler of arms and contraband. He shipped arms to Syrian-backed terrorists, in particular Black September and also arranged for fellow ex-SAS mercenaries to fight with and train the group, and for IRA members to be trained in Libya. Unbeknown to him, British intelligence had a mole within Black September who began to report back on his activities. MI6 was keen to know as much as possible about Middle East terrorism, and in particular the links which existed with the IRA.

On returning to Britain for a holiday in February 1970, Aspin was apprehended by MI6 officers at Heathrow airport. Holding him for three days, they asked him to become an informant. He refused at first but was eventually told that if he did not cooperate, MI6 would order its other assets to put the word out that he had agreed to become a double agent and therefore should not be trusted. Since this would have effectively signed his death warrant, Aspin agreed.

Al-Kassar was allegedly recruited three years later. As with Aspin, MI6 allegedly used a carrot and a stick; the carrot being the promise of a substantial financial reward, and the stick the threat that if he did not cooperate MI6 would spread the word that he had.

Fearing that he had been betrayed to the IRA, Aspin fled Britain for the US in 1975, where he was soon recruited by CIA Director and future US President George Bush. He was dispatched to Angola to put together a secret mercenary force to fight alongside local insurgents against the Marxist Government. While there, he met and befriended William Buckley.

During the early 1980s Aspin and Buckley teamed up again, this time with disastrous consequences. By then Ronald Reagan was in the White House, with Bush as his deputy. Obsessed by the threat of terrorism, the new CIA director, William Casey, urged his bosses to strike a blow for American pride by taking decisive action. Buckley was one of Casey's most trusted confidants and, according to Loftus and Aarons's sources, persuaded his boss that a mercenary hit-squad was needed to make pre-emptive strikes against the terrorists. Casey liked the idea and took the suggestion to Bush, who allegedly gave it his blessing. Buckley had a number of meetings with Aspin to discuss the initiative, but before it could be put into action Buckley was captured.

In response, Casey used Oliver North and others to help draw up plans to secure his release. North's diaries, released under the US Freedom of Information Act, show that on 19 April 1984 in Washington he met a

British intelligence officer called Derek Thomas. The White House still favoured the strong-arm approach (described in North's notes as 'pre-emptive options'), but Thomas pointed out that these violated international conventions and risked an 'escalating spiral' of kidnapping. He nevertheless reassured the Americans, 'We do want to work with you, but we want to discuss options with you before a final decision is made.'

The preferred option of the British was to ransom Buckley and his fellow hostages by offering arms to Iran. In making the suggestion, they already had a firm precedent. In 1980 the British had arranged for Browning machine guns to be supplied to Iran in return for the release of two British citizens who had been captured by the Iranian Hizbullah. On that occasion the weapons were supplied by Leslie Aspin and his brother Michael, via a London-based front company they had established, Delta Investments. Loftus and Aarons learned that Monzer Al-Kassar was the middle man who had relayed the Iranian offer to the British.

On 10 May 1984, as the joint American-British plans progressed, Oliver North met in Washington with a British Embassy official called Andrew Green. Green was described as an 'intelligence officer whose speciality was arms transfers and anti-terrorist operations'. Details of the meeting were not released, but a note taken the following day by North's secretary Fawn Hall was. It suggests that the two men had discussed another meeting which was due to take place a few days later and also hints at their anxiety in case the meeting became public:

> Ollie, Andrew Green (Brit you met with yesterday) called 745-4239. He said, 'Of course, we certainly intend that the meeting be confidential, but just in case it should leak, the kind of defensive line we should take is as follows:
>
> "We have said in Parliament that we intend to consult our partners on measures to combat terrorism. We have already discussed this in the European community. We keep in regular touch with the US as well."'

The second meeting apparently took place on 15 May. North's notes of the meeting were completely censored on the grounds that it concerned hostage rescue and counter-terrorist planning with a foreign intelligence service. However, Loftus and Aarons' sources told them that the British plan was to resurrect the Al-Kassar/Aspin axis.

In 1995 Labour MP Tam Dalyell asked the Foreign Secretary the following written questions, based on the claims in *The Secret War Against the Jews.* (1) what meetings his officials had with Colonel Oliver North between 12 November and 19 November 1984; (2) for what reasons Andrew Green of his department met with Colonel Oliver North on 24 July 1984 to discuss hostage rescue missions; (3) for what reasons Mr Derek Thomas of his department met Colonel Oliver North in April 1984 in relation to anti-terrorist and hostage rescue activities in the Middle East; (4) for what reasons on 10 May 1984 Mr Andrew Green of his department and the British Embassy in Washington met Colonel North to discuss Monzer Al-Kassar; (5) why Mr Andrew Green of his department on 10 May 1984 discussed with Colonel North the role of the British Parliament in the hostage situation.

Foreign Office Minister Douglas Hogg replied that in the mid-1980s members of the British Embassy in Washington kept in close touch with the US Administration, including the National Security Council, on matters concerning hostages and on matters of terrorism more generally. This was, and remains, he said, a normal part of the embassy's work.

This was not, of course, a full answer, but it was nevertheless very revealing. There was no denial of the 1984 meetings. Furthermore, the answer (which was no doubt prepared in consultation with Andrew Green) was strangely reminiscent of the 'defensive line' suggested by Green in the message noted by Fawn Hall.

Dalyell also asked the Foreign Secretary if it was with his authority that Monzer Al-Kassar was authorised in June 1984 to ship arms to Iran. There was no denial that the shipment took place. Hogg simply answered 'No'.

Given Andrew Green's alleged role in the secret arms-for-hostage deals, any involvement he might have had in the Lockerbie investigation was potentially of the utmost importance. Later in 1995, Tam Dalyell asked the government: 'What has been the role of Mr Andrew Green of the Foreign and Commonwealth Office in relation to investigations into the Lockerbie crime?' Foreign Office Minister Sir Nicholas Bonsor gave the following, stunning reply: 'From 1988 to early 1991, Mr Green was head of the Foreign and Commonwealth Office department responsible for the international aspects of the Lockerbie affair.'

There were other aspects of the Iranian arms for hostages deals of direct relevance to Lockerbie. According to Loftus and Aarons, at Oliver North's second meeting with the British on 15 May 1984 it was agreed that Al-Kassar would set up an arms shipment to Iran in return for a video of Buckley to prove he was still alive. Once that had been secured Al-Kassar and Aspin would deal directly with his captors to negotiate a price for his release. They are reported to have successfully delivered the video in July.

Towards the end of the year, after a good deal of to-ing and fro-ing, a deal was finally put together for 20,000 American TOW missiles. Just before it was due to go ahead, however, the Americans learned that Michael Aspin had betrayed the deal to US Customs. Although Michael was involved in the deal, he feared that the whole operation was a deliberate attempt by the US authorities to entrap them. In February 1985, Oliver North flew to London to try to reassure Michael that the deal was bona fide. According to Loftus and Aarons, Michael pretended to be convinced but in fact was not. Instead, he continued to work with the unwitting US Customs authorities to betray the deal in a sting operation. Leslie soon realised that his brother's activities were in danger of blowing everybody's cover and recommended to North that the 'British channel' should be closed down.

The Americans were not keen for this to happen, since no one was as well placed as Leslie to carry out such deals. They persuaded him to keep the channel going with Al-Kassar and in the meantime, behind his back, set about a joint scheme with MI6 to get rid of the problem of his brother. Michael was encouraged to set up his own channel, but unbeknown to him there was a plan to bust him.

In January 1986 Michael was arrested, along with fellow arms dealer Eric Matson, international trader John Taylor and Lloyds underwriter William Harper. They were charged with attempting to defraud banks by setting up a bogus weapons deal. The men insisted the arms deal was genuine and had been sanctioned by Western intelligence. When first arrested, Michael gave the police a telephone number to call in Washington DC. That number turned out to be the private line of the then unknown Oliver North.

When the four men faced trial in 1988 the chief defence witness was Leslie Aspin, who by then had become very disillusioned with North. He told the court about the secret arms deal with Iran which had been hatched in order to secure the release of his old friend Buckley. He claimed to have had a number of meetings with Oliver North, one of them in Paris in November 1984, when the pair of them had opened a number of accounts to launder money for the transaction at the Bank of Credit and Commerce International (BCCI). Leslie claimed that there were more deals, all sanctioned by Casey, North and MI6. The one in which his brother and his co-defendants were involved, he said, was part of this sequence.

The prosecution condemned Leslie Aspin's evidence as an elaborate fiction and advised the jury to ignore it. Michael Aspin, Matson and Harper were all convicted and were respectively given six-, three- and two-year sentences. John Taylor was acquitted after a strong steer by the judge.

In January 1989 Leslie staggered into his mother's house in Norwich and collapsed on the floor. Within minutes he was dead. He had a weak heart and in recent months had been under a lot of stress. He insisted to the end that his story was true. Evidence uncovered by Loftus and Aarons suggested he was right.

In 1990, after a protracted legal struggle, Oliver North's office diaries were finally released under the US Freedom of Information Act. Loftus compared their contents with what Leslie Aspin had claimed, and with Leslie's personal papers (which Leslie had ordered to be destroyed on his death, but his family had kept). Loftus discovered that many details of Leslie's story tallied with North's notes, despite the fact that Aspin could not have known what North had written. Among the most heavily censored passages in the diaries were the periods when Leslie alleged North had been in Paris. Loftus obtained North's expenses vouchers for that time, overlooked by the censors, and discovered he was in the French capital on exactly the days Leslie had claimed.

The censors missed something else, something stunning – a note in the margin of North's notebook referring to someone called 'Bringold'. Among Leslie's papers were a number of letters sent between banks and a person called Willi Bringold. The signatures and handwriting of Mr Bringold made it clear that the name was a pseudonym used by Leslie. Moreover, the financial transactions undertaken by Bringold exactly matched transactions uncovered by the congressional inquiry into Iran-Contra, which Oliver North had carried out using another pseudonym. It appeared as if Bringold/Aspin had helped launder $42 million for North's covert arms supply operation.

Years after the trial came another bombshell. John Taylor revealed that throughout the deal he had been reporting back to MI6. Rather than informing him that the deal was bogus and encouraging him to go to the police, his MI6 handler told him to stay involved. It was further evidence to support the Aspin brother's claim that the deal had been sanctioned all along by Western intelligence.

When Taylor was arrested his MI6 contact telephone numbers went dead, but an MI6 lawyer subsequently confirmed the relationship to Taylor's solicitor, Adrian Neale. Taylor and Neale had a series of secret meetings with the head of Customs at the US Embassy in London. Customs agreed to help Taylor by confirming the authenticity of Aspin's TOW missile deal. In return, Taylor and Neale agreed to cooperate with a Customs sting against rogue American arms dealers operating in London. Customs only pulled the plug on the deal after *The Observer* newspaper inadvertently blew the cover on the sting.

There is a further startling reason for the Aspin connection being covered up. Leslie's personal papers record that his last Iranian arms deal was completed on 1 January 1988, which means that the deals continued well after the Irangate scandal broke in November 1986. Numerous intelligence sources told John Loftus that elements within the Reagan administration, particularly George Bush, were desperate to keep a secret arms channel open, even though North had been exposed in November 1986.

If officially sanctioned, secret Iranian arms deals continued up to 1988, was it really so inconceivable that the CIA could have cut its own hostage deals in 1988?

10. THE FINGER POINTS TO LIBYA

At the end of January 1989, the press in London got hold of a letter which appeared to be from the former head of the Libyan mission in London, Saleh Masleam, in which he praised Gadafy for carrying out the attack. Everyone, including the Foreign Office, believed the letter to be a forgery.[1] The story quickly died away and for the first 18 months Libya was hardly mentioned. Juval Aviv's Interfor Report had implicated a Libyan bomb-maker known as the 'Professor' and suggested that Gadafy was supportive of major terrorist strikes against the US, but the report had made it clear that the terrorist masterminds were in Syria, Lebanon and Iran. The only other lead to Libya was Maltese shopkeeper Tony Gauci's description of the mystery clothes buyer as Libyan, along with the fact that Libya was a near neighbour of Malta, where the bomb was believed to have started its journey.

Over the next 18 months, however, Libya would gradually emerge as the prime suspect. The original culprits, Iran, Syria and their PFLP-GC and Hizbullah proxies, would be officially exonerated. The public were told this was the result of a brilliant international investigation led by the canny officers of the Dumfries and Galloway Constabulary. In reality, the momentum for the shift in the investigation came from events that were unfolding thousands of miles away.

Until the autumn of 1989 few people in Britain and the US knew much about Iraq, other than that it had emerged from a long war with its neighbour Iran. Most would have been pushed to name its leader. Within a few months, however, Iraq was on everyone's lips and President Saddam Hussein had become the West's number one pariah. In September 1989, *The Observer* journalist Farzad Bazoft was arrested following a visit to a secret military-industrial complex at al-Hillel in Iraq. Charged with spying for Israel and Britain and made to sign a confession, he was sentenced to death by a revolutionary court and executed on 15 March 1990.

Prime Minister Margaret Thatcher condemned the execution as 'an act of barbarism', but many observers felt that Thatcher could have done more to save the unfortunate journalist. It soon became clear why she had not. A few days after the execution, Customs and Excise inspectors at Teesport seized a number of huge steel tubes destined for Iraq. The manufacturers claimed they were intended for the petrochemical industry, but they were, in fact, parts for the so-called Supergun, a massive artillery cannon capable of delivering shells hundreds of miles. Following the outbreak of the Iran-Iraq war in 1980, it had been official government policy to ban the export of lethal equipment to either side in the conflict. The government denied all knowledge of the lethal purposes of the equipment, but the tail of a very large and politically dangerous cat was out of the bag. Over the next few years it would become apparent that Britain and American manufacturers, with the complicity of their respective governments, had armed Iraq on a massive scale throughout the war.

Against this background, it was small wonder that the British public heard hardly a squeak of protest from the government about the appalling human rights abuses of Saddam's regime. But while the pockets of the international arms trade were being lined, the Western powers were storing up a huge problem for themselves in Iraq. Following his gains in the war with Iran, Saddam was not content to sit back and allow his well-equipped forces to do nothing. He had his eyes on another prize to the South: Saddam regarded the small, oil-rich Gulf state of Kuwait as part of Iraq and in 1990 he decided he wanted it back.

During the summer, tension grew between the two states. Still in debt after the massive expenditure of the war with Iran, Iraq hoped to persuade the OPEC oil-producing countries to raise the price of crude oil, but Kuwait refused. In late July Saddam amassed his forces on the border between the two countries, and on 2 August they stormed into Kuwait, reaching the capital, Kuwait City, within six hours.

Overnight, Western strategy in the Middle East was thrown into turmoil. Iraq had previously been a bulwark against the militant Islamic regime in Tehran, but it now had a dangerous stranglehold over a key Gulf state. For that reason alone Saddam had to be defeated.

The Western powers needed allies among Iraq's Middle Eastern neighbours. To the North, Turkey was a staunch member of NATO. To the South, Saudi Arabia was a reliable ally, which had much to fear from Iraqi expansionism. To the East, Iran had been at war with Iraq for eight years, up to the end of 1988, so while a military alliance with the US was out of the question, Tehran would certainly not side with its old enemy in Baghdad. Jordan, to the West, was in a difficult position. Having been a conduit for illicit British and American arms sales to Iraq during the '80s, it was a friend of both the US and Saddam and would therefore remain neutral in the developing conflict.

The most dramatic shift in relations would be with Syria. Washington and Damascus had been mutually hostile throughout the '80s, but Hafez Al Assad's regime had other enemies and chief among them, besides Israel, was Iraq. Working on the principal that my enemy's enemy is my friend, the USA immediately set about courting Assad. It was inevitable that the policy would have a profound influence on the Lockerbie saga. Now that Syria was needed as an ally in the upcoming war against Iraq, something had to give; the US could not be seen to be making friends with a regime that had helped slaughter scores of American citizens.

What might 'give', the Bush administration hoped, was Syria's support for the PFLP-GC. In September 1990 the US Secretary of State, James Baker, visited Syria as part of the rapidly developing *rapprochement* between the two nations. Baker indicated to his hosts that there was irrefutable evidence to show that the PFLP-GC was behind the bombing and urged them to expel the group from Syria. Unfortunately for Baker, Assad was too wily a politician to agree to his request. Syria's regional power was based, in large measure, on his support for hard-line Palestinians such as Ahmed Jibril. Had he started to dance to America's tune, his status as a champion of the Arab people against Zionism would be severely diminished. Rather than agreeing to Baker's request, the Syrians chose to call his bluff. If the US had hard evidence against the Jibril group, they told him, it should be presented to the Syrian government, which would then bring the group to trial. Baker did not push the point further.[2]

Within weeks of the meeting, the public was given its first concrete indication of Libyan involvement in the bombing. In October 1990 the French news magazine *L'Express* reported that a fragment of the bomb's timing mechanism found at Lockerbie was identical to a number of timers that had been seized from two Libyan agents arrested by police in Senegal, ten months prior to Lockerbie. The two, who were on a stop-over on a flight to the Ivory Coast, were named as Mohammed Al-Naydi and Mansour Omran Saber.

The story was repeated in the *New York Times* on 10 October. The article stressed that the devices found in Senegal differed significantly from those used by the PFLP-GC, who were known to favour a timer allied to a barometric switch. In case readers thought that this was all too convenient at a time when the US was forming an alliance with Syria, unnamed US officials stated that the new finding did not clear Iran, Syria and the PFLP-GC. The latest theory was that Ahmed Jibril had subcontracted the job to Libya after his German cell had been compromised in October 1988. He had provided the blueprint for the bombing, but Libya had supplied its own bomb components and used its own agents.

A follow up article in *L'Express* reported that it was now believed that the mystery clothes buyer in Mary's House was an associate of Al-Naydi. So much for David Leppard's earlier *Sunday Times* report that the Palestinian terrorist Abu Talb had been the clothes buyer. In fact, Leppard himself had quietly dropped this claim. In a huge article for the paper on 30 September 1990, he revealed that Tony Gauci had seen the mystery customer twice more since the fateful purchase, in June or July 1989 and again in September 1989. Though Leppard did not spell it out, this automatically ruled out Abu Talb, who had been held by the Swedish authorities since 18 May 1989.

On 14 December 1990, *The Independent*'s main headline ran: 'LIBYA BLAMED FOR LOCKERBIE'. The accompanying story repeated the allegations in the *L'Express* articles and revealed that the timers seized in Senegal were unique to one Swiss manufacturer. It pointed out: 'Confirmation of Libyan involvement effectively blows apart the favourite theory to date – that the bombing was the work of a German-based cell of the radical Damascus-based Popular Front for the Liberation of Palestine – General Command,' and quoted an anonymous source as saying, 'you can forget Autumn Leaves'.

A month later the US and her allies began the military campaign to free Kuwait from Iraqi control. By the end of February, Operation Desert Storm had successfully vanquished the Iraqis and President George Bush set about constructing his New World Order in which, among other changes, Syria was now regarded as a friend of the US.

As Bush's project began to take shape, the now familiar anonymous sources continued to peddle the 'Libyan sub-contract' theory to the media. In July 1991, the definitive account of the official investigation thus far appeared in David Leppard's *On the Trail of Terror*. The book went along fully with the theory that Jibril had handed the job over to the Libyans. CIA sources told him that Ahmed Jibril had travelled to Tripoli in November 1988 to meet with Colonel Gadafy at the headquarters of the Libyan intelligence service. Allegedly present at the meeting were Gadafy's right-hand man, Major Abdel Salem Jalloud, the deputy head of Libyan intelligence Abdullah Sanussi, and a number of other senior intelligence agents. It was decided that Libyan agents would carry out the attack and Flight 103 was then officially targeted.

Buried in the detail of Leppard's account was the extraordinary claim that British intelligence was warned about the meeting which Major Jalloud held to plan the bombing of Flight 103. The book explains away the fact that nothing was done on the grounds that the mole within Libyan intelligence who supplied the information was regarded as unreliable, and was one of dozens of intelligence tip-offs to pass the desk of MI6's Libya analysts every week.

The mysterious clothes buyer at Mary's House was now confirmed to be a junior Libyan intelligence agent who was under orders from Mohammed Al-Naydi, one of the Libyan agents arrested in Senegal in February 1988. Furthermore, Tony Gauci had made a positive identification of the person and signed an affidavit to this effect. Al-Naydi and his fellow agent arrested in Senegal, Mansour Omran Saber, were seen as central to the plot and had used junior operatives, like the clothes buyer, to carry it out.

According to Leppard, the only major aspect of the conspiracy that had yet to be solved was how the bomb got onto the feeder flight at Malta's Luqa airport. At the time of writing, he reported, investigators seemed fairly sure that the Libyans had someone on the inside at the airport who helped the bomb bag to evade Air Malta's security.

Other details remained unclear. The most important was whether or not the Lockerbie bomb had been one of those prepared by the PFLP-GC in Germany. The earlier *New York Times* report had suggested it was not, but Leppard implied that it was, claiming that Al-Naydi and Saber had decided that a bomb should be smuggled into Malta. An earlier Leppard article had suggested that the PFLP-GC's Ramzi Diab (whose real name was Salah Kwikas but who also went under the name of Ali Nasri Assaf) took the bomb from Germany to Malta, but the book reported that Diab's destination was, in fact, Damascus. The CIA confirmed to Leppard that Diab was killed on the orders of Ahmed Jibril, who believed him to be a mole for Western intelligence.

Had the Lockerbie bomb been one of the PFLP-GC's, it would almost certainly have had the dual trigger mechanism of a barometric switch and a timer of the type Marwan Khreesat had fitted in the Toshiba radio-cassette bomb seized in the Autumn Leaves raids. However, the implication of the Libyan timer story, reported elsewhere, was that the bomb had used those timers alone. Leppard's book speculated that one of Khreesat's barometric bombs may have been modified by the Libyans, using their own timers. The suggestion was bolstered by the British forensic expert, Dr Thomas Hayes of the Ministry of Defence's Royal Armaments Research and Development Establishment, who, according to Leppard, privately believed the bomb contained such a dual mechanism.

Leppard's book glossed over one outstanding problem. In his *Sunday Times* article of 24 December 1989, he had reported that investigators had found plastic among the bomb debris which matched that in the clocks purchased by Dalkamoni and Khreesat in Neuss. If this were the case, and if the Libyan timer story was true, the bomb must have had two timing mechanisms and possibly also a barometric switch, which seemed most unlikely.

Leppard was more precise in his account of the discovery of the Libyan timing mechanism. In this respect he had been fortunate enough to be granted an interview with Dr Hayes, a favour not apparently extended to anyone else in Fleet Street. In June 1990, Hayes had retired from the Royal Armaments Research and Development Establishment's (RARDE) explosive forensic laboratory but was still retained as a consultant to the investigation. He explained that he was able to identify a tiny piece of electronic circuit board as being part of the bomb's trigger mechanism. It appeared to be part of a timing device manufactured by a Swiss company.

Once this had been established, CIA analysts prepared an assessment of the likely source of the board. The preliminary finding was that it might match the batch seized in Senegal. Once this was known, Stuart Henderson, the recently appointed senior investigating officer for the Scottish police, dispatched men to Senegal to retrieve photographs and control samples of the timers. When these were handed over to Hayes it only took him a short time to make the comparison, after which, according to Leppard, he 'looked up from his microscope, elated'. Reporting to the inquiry's head, Chief Superintendent John Orr, Hayes confirmed that the circuit board had been made by the same Swiss company which made the timers seized in Senegal. Leppard described this moment as, 'the crowning glory of RARDE's forensic inquiry'.

As Leppard's book was being prepared for publication, the official line on Lockerbie appeared to be taking a further shift towards exonerating Syria. On 3 June 1991, Reuters reported the head of the CIA's Lockerbie investigation, Vincent Cannistraro, as saying that investigators believed Iran had originally hired the PFLP-GC to do the job, but had handed it on to the Libyans after the October 1988 arrests of the PFLP-GC's West German cell. He added, 'I don't think you can blame the Syrians for what Libya did.' *The Guardian* picked up on the story on 5 June and went so far as to report that Syria had been cleared of involvement in the bombing.

Despite such stories, no one outside of official circles who had followed the Lockerbie story could have been prepared for the bombshell that would be dropped five months later. On 14 November 1991 the Scottish Crown Office and the US State Department issued parallel indictments against two Libyans, Abdel Basset Ali Al-Megrahi and Lamin Khalifa Fhimah, who they alleged had planted the bomb. In view of all the information that had been leaked to the press over the previous year, it was hardly surprising that the Libyans were in the frame. What was surprising, or rather shocking, was that, in announcing the indictments, the US government publicly exonerated Syria. When asked about the allegations that Damascus had played a role in the bombing, President George Bush told the press, in characteristically elegant language, 'The Syrians took a bum rap on this.'[3]

Iran was apparently no longer a suspect either. At the press conference which announced the indictments, a senior State Department spokesman, Richard Boucher, made it clear that Lockerbie was a 'Libyan government operation from start to finish'.[4] The same day Foreign Secretary Douglas Hurd told the House of Commons, 'I understand the investigation has revealed no evidence to support suggestion of involvement by other countries.'[5]

Few believed what they were being told. Lockerbie relatives and editorial writers alike protested that the exoneration of Syria was more to do with post-Gulf War diplomacy than the brilliant investigation of the Dumfries and Galloway police. Embarrassed officials back-tracked, pointing out that the wording of the indictment did not close the door on possible Syrian and Iranian involvement. Neither country had been eliminated from the police inquiries, they claimed. It was simply that there was no hard evidence against them, but the public could rest assured that the investigators on both sides of the Atlantic would continue in their hunt for that evidence.

To aid its spin-doctoring, the State Department issued a 'fact sheet' entitled 'The Iranians and the PFLP-GC: Early Suspects in the Pan Am 103 Bombing'. It was a preposterous distortion to describe Iran and the PFLP-GC as 'early suspects'. Even in the version of events touted by anonymous official sources, both had remained suspects until just a few months before the issuing of the indictments. It was only in the last few months that there had been any hint that the PFLP-GC had not been involved.

The fact sheet summarised the circumstantial evidence which had originally implicated the PFLP-GC in the bombing, then listed the main pieces of evidence which had led the investigation in other directions. The first of these was the fact that the Toshiba recorder that housed the Lockerbie bomb differed markedly in appearance to the one found in the boot of Dalkamoni's car during the Autumn Leaves raids. So what? This had never been raised as an issue before, not least because Marwan Khreesat was known to have built bombs into a variety of different electronic devices. The fact that the Lockerbie bomb was inside a Toshiba recorder had previously been reported as an indication that it *was* the work of the PFLP-GC.

The sheet also claimed the Frankfurt airport records and the clothes from the bomb suitcase indicated that the case had come unaccompanied from Malta. The implication was that, since the PFLP-GC cell had been active in Germany, it could have not have had a hand in the bombing. The fact sheet's authors perhaps worked on the assumption that its readers had short memories and had forgotten that an earlier incarnation of the official story, vigorously peddled at the time by the *Sunday Times*'s David Leppard, had Dalkamoni and Abu Talb visit Malta, where they planned the bombing with the help of a local PFLP-GC cell.

The other main piece of evidence cited was the forensic determination that the Lockerbie bomb had been activated by a single timing device rather than by a dual barometric switch and timer, which was characteristic of the PFLP-GC's bombs. So, what of the possibility that the Libyans had added their own timer to a barometric bomb given them by the PFLP-GC? The fact sheet lamely added that no evidence had surfaced at the Lockerbie crash site to indicate that the terrorists had used an altimeter switch. This was far from being proof that the bomb had not contained such a switch.

At the end of the fact sheet was a section headed 'Collusion by Multiple State Sponsors?' Having conceded that the PFLP-GC had probably been planning a revenge attack on behalf of Iran and that Syria was the group's 'primary political sponsor', it repeated that there was no hard evidence to link Iran, Syria and the PFLP-GC to the Libyan attack on Flight 103.

For those scratching their heads trying to work out how the State Department could possibly dismiss such a connection, a hint of an explanation was offered:

> We believe that Libya . . . was probably aware of Dalkamoni's earlier plans to bomb aircraft. The activities in Fall 1988 by those Libyans directly responsible for the December 1988 Pan Am bombing indicate that Libya was planning an aircraft bombing at the same time as the PFLP-GC cell was building its bombs in Germany. Tripoli was also aware of the PFLP-GC's relationship with Iran.

The following day's *Times* got the gist, reporting, once again with the help of anonymous 'investigators', that the use of a Toshiba bomb was an attempt by the Libyans 'to leave "fingerprints" to implicate other groups, such as the Damascus-based Popular Front for the Liberation of Palestine'. So, the Libyans had seen their chance to hit the US and walk away scot-free, by making sure that Ahmed Jibril and Iran got the blame. Was there no limit to the evil cunning of Gadafy and his henchmen?

The next day, *The Times*'s sister Sunday paper carried an exclusive story headlined 'LOCKERBIE SUSPECTS BOASTED THEY COULD "DESTROY AMERICA"'. It was written by three reporters, including David Leppard and Washington correspondent James Adams who, like Leppard, was renowned in Fleet Street for his intelligence contacts. They revealed that a British businessman, who asked not to be named but was described as a 'former military policeman', had met the two Libyans accused in Malta, just days before the Lockerbie bombing. He claimed to have been introduced to them by businessman Mustafa Housini, who, the article alleged, ran Libyan intelligence in Malta. The two men, whom the anonymous source claimed were 'religious fanatics', allegedly described former President Ronald Reagan as a 'stupid cowboy with no brains' and said they would 'turn against the Americans and destroy them'. The article did not speculate on the reasons why cunning terrorists would boast of their plans to a complete stranger from America's staunchest Western ally.[6]

The indictment issued by the Scottish and American authorities went into great detail on how the Libyans had carried out the attack. The plot went as follows. The two accused, Megrahi and Fhimah, were members of the Libyan intelligence service, the Jamahirya Security Organisation (JSO), working undercover for Libyan Arab Airlines (LAA). Megrahi was the chief of the Airline Security Section for the JSO and, as such, was familiar with international security procedures. Fhimah worked for LAA in Malta and had been its station manager at Luqa airport.

Together with unnamed co-conspirators, the two were alleged to have constructed the bomb using one of the electronic timers and plastic explosive stored by Fhimah at the LAA office at Luqa airport. The timers were of a prototype model known as MST-13, 20 of which had been purchased from a Swiss company called Meister and Bollier – Mebo for short – in 1985, on the orders of two senior JSO operatives, Said Rashid Kisha and Izz al-Din al-Hinshiri. The JSO had a front company called ABH, which rented office space from Mebo at Mebo's Zurich headquarters. Megrahi and another Libyan called Badri Hasan were both involved with ABH.

On 7 December, Megrahi travelled from Libya to Malta and registered at the Holiday Inn in Sliema under the name of Abdel Basset A. Mohmed, a 'flight dispatcher' (sic) for LAA. The same day, he bought the selection of clothes which were to end up in the bomb bag from the nearby Mary's House shop. Two days later Megrahi flew to Zurich, returning to Tripoli, via Malta on 17 December. The following day Fhimah travelled to Tripoli to meet him. On 20 December they both flew back to Malta, Megrahi using the false identity of Ahmed Khalifa Abdusamad. They brought with them a brown, hard-sided Samsonite suitcase, which would be used to carry the bomb. Megrahi once again checked into the Holiday Inn in Sliema, this time using the false identity of Ahmed Khalifa Abdusamad.

Between 8.15 a.m. and 9.15 a.m., local time, on 21 December, the two accused and their co-conspirators managed to place the Samsonite case, packed with the bomb and the clothes from Mary's House, into the stream of luggage destined for Air Malta flight KM180 to Frankfurt. The bag had been fitted with tags stolen by Fhimah from Air Malta, which were marked so that the bag would be placed aboard Pan Am Flight 103 to New York. The timer in the bomb had been set to activate at around 7 p.m. GMT. That same morning, still travelling under his assumed name, Megrahi flew back to Tripoli on LAA flight LN147.

The US State Department supported the indictments with another fact sheet, entitled 'Additional Information on the Bombing of Pan Am Flight 103'. It laid out the evidence against the two accused, beginning with the insertion of the bag into the stream of luggage destined for Pan Am 103. As expected, the two documents from Frankfurt airport were crucial to the case. Without detailing exactly how, the fact sheet stated that these records showed that:

> An unaccompanied bag was routed from Air Malta flight 180 . . . to Frankfurt, where it was loaded onto the Pan Am 103 feeder flight to London. In addition to this Fhimah's diary contained a reminder for 15 December to take tags from Air Malta. Other entries in the diary suggested that he had done this.

Precise details of how the two managed to get the bomb on to KM180 were not given, but the sheet stated that Megrahi's flight back to Tripoli checked in at the same counter as KM180 and that the check-in times overlapped. The implication was that Megrahi checked in the bomb bag, as if for his flight back to Libya, and that the two men then somehow managed to insert it on to Flight KM180.

The fact sheet also elaborated on the timer evidence. The MST-13s provided a definite link to Libya, it stated, because Mebo was the sole manufacturer. Moreover, the company had only ever produced 20 of the devices and all of those had been sold to the JSO. As for the clothes wrapped around the bomb, the sheet stated that in February 1991 Megrahi 'was described as resembling the Libyan who had purchased the clothes'. The most likely date of the purchase was 7 December 1988, a date on which airport arrival cards demonstrated Megrahi to have been in Malta.

To the casual reader the barrage of information contained in the indictments and fact sheets was very convincing, but to those familiar with the subject it raised as many questions as it answered. According to earlier reports, the clothes were purchased on 23 November, a full two weeks earlier than was now being claimed. Furthermore, Tony Gauci had said the mystery purchaser was about 50 years old and around six feet in height. Details released by the State Department showed that Megrahi was only 36 at the time he was alleged to have bought the clothes, and was only five feet eight tall.

Aside from this, there was the question of logistics. If the Libyans were cunning enough to build a bomb into a Toshiba recorder in order to leave traces which would implicate the PFLP-GC's German cell, surely they would make sure that they had cut the labels out of the clothes to avoid a trail leading back to the island. And surely Megrahi would not be so stupid as to stay at the same hotel twice within a fortnight, using two false names. If, as was alleged, there was a substantial Libyan intelligence presence on the island, it could have easily arranged more sensible accommodation, perhaps in one of the many hotels on the island that were actually owned by the Libyan Government. As for the time setting on the bomb, if Megrahi was as knowledgeable about the airline industry as alleged, then he must have known that during a period so close to Christmas long delays were possible. Why then would he have allowed the bomb to be set for just one hour after the scheduled Heathrow take-off time of 6 p.m.? To have done so would have been to run a considerable risk of the device exploding while the plane was still on the tarmac. It would have been far better to have set it for around 10 p.m. GMT, when it was almost guaranteed to have been over the Atlantic.

The most suspicious aspect of the story concerned the crucial discovery of the fragment of circuit board alleged to have been part of the bomb's MST-13 timing device. Speaking to the press when the indictments were announced, US Attorney General William Barr explained that it had been found in a piece of a shirt which had been in the bomb suitcase. But when a reporter asked about the timing and location of the find, the head of the FBI's Criminal Investigation Division, Bill Baker, replied that he could not go into detail.[7]

Baker's reticence was interesting, given that details of the discovery of the other key piece of forensic evidence – the fragment of circuit board that identified the bomb as having been built into a Toshiba – were made public at the Scottish Fatal Accident Inquiry into the bombing. British forensic expert Allen Feraday had also told the FAI that numerous fragments of the

Toshiba radio-cassette player were recovered amongst the debris of the luggage pallet which had contained the bomb suitcase.[8] It seemed strange, therefore, that only one fragment of the timing device had been found. At the press conference, the audience was shown a blown-up photograph of a piece of circuit board, on which the letters M-E-B-O, though partially obliterated, were clearly visible.

The day after the press conference, one of these forensic experts appeared on US prime-time television to explain how this crucial part of the case had been cracked. Sitting at his desk, ABC's 'Man of the Week', Thomas Thurman of the FBI, explained, '15 June 1990 was the day that I made the identification. And I knew at that point what it meant. And because, if you will, I'm an investigator as well as a forensic examiner I knew where that would go . . . I knew that we had it.' Thurman had perhaps not read David Leppard's *On the Trail of Terror*. If he had, he would have known that the vital June discovery that the tiny piece of circuit board was from the bomb's timing mechanism had in fact been made by Dr Thomas Hayes of RARDE. Surely both accounts could not be correct?

Three years later, two books were published on the FBI. Both supported Thurman's version of events. *The FBI* by Ronald Kessler[9] and *The Bureau – Inside Today's FBI* by Diarmuid Jeffreys[10] also stated that it was Thurman who had linked the fragment both to the timers seized from the Libyan agents in Senegal and to the manufacturers, Mebo. But the two books gave conflicting accounts of who actually found the fragment and when. Kessler quoted John W. Hicks, assistant director of the FBI's forensic lab, who said that the British had found the circuit board but were not able to identify its significance. He claimed it was a full year before it was passed on to Thurman, which, given that Thurman claimed to have made the identification in June 1990, would date the find at around June 1989. Jeffreys, by contrast, reported that Thurman himself found the fragment in a piece of shirt. Assuming that it would not have taken him a full year to identify it as being part of the timing mechanism, it must have been found far later than Hicks claimed.

By the time these two books had appeared, another account had been published, adding further confusion. *Eclipse – The Last Days of the CIA* by Mark Perry[11] gave a detailed account of how the Lockerbie case was cracked. In the section of the book relating to the discovery of the fragment, Perry acknowledged the 'extraordinary amount of guidance' that was provided by, among others, the CIA's Vincent Cannistraro. According to this version of events, the crucial fragment was found by a 'Scottish worker' in a field outside Lockerbie in 1990, 'on a misty morning in early April'. This was around ten months after the date suggested by John W. Hicks, obviously inconsistent with the claim that it was found by Thurman. Furthermore, the fields around Lockerbie had all been thoroughly searched within weeks of the disaster. Anything as large as a piece of shirt would have been found by April 1990.

Perry also contradicted the other accounts of who identified the fragment as part of the bomb's timing mechanism. According to him it was a 'veteran CIA analyst', which appeared to rule out both Hayes and Thurman. As for making the link to Senegal, Perry attributed this to 'a young forensic expert from the Scottish police' who, 'acting on a hunch', asked to see specifications for the timers. He may have been confused with Thomas Hayes, who was around 40 at the time and, although not a Scottish police employee, was working indirectly for them. David Leppard's *On the Trail of Terror* attributed the discovery to Hayes, but claimed it was made on the basis of a CIA intelligence assessment, rather than 'a hunch'. Perry and Leppard also differed on the timing of this discovery. Perry suggested it was around October 1990, whereas Leppard stated that it was almost as soon as the Scottish investigators returned from Senegal with photographs of the timers in August 1990.

For good measure, there was further confusion in the account of who made the link to the timers' manufacturer, Mebo. Perry claimed it was 'American investigators', which contradicted Leppard's assertion that it was Thomas Hayes. Inevitably, there were again inconsistencies on the timing of the discovery. Both Leppard and Ronald Kessler implied that it occurred before the end of June 1990, but Perry suggested it did not take place until around November 1990, after the fragment had been linked to the Senegal timers.

Perry and Leppard were also at variance on another key point. According to Leppard, Dr Thomas Hayes was able to make the link to the Dakar timers by comparing the fragment found at Lockerbie with photographs and control samples retrieved from Dakar by the Scottish police. The FBI's John W. Hicks, quoted in Ronald Kessler's book, had also referred to 'devices that had been recovered'. But if Perry's sources were to be believed, there were no timers to be had in Dakar. His book reported that when the alleged Libyan agents were released by the Senegalese authorities in June 1988, all the terrorist accessories that had been seized at the time of their arrests were returned to them. 'Fortunately,' it went on, 'a French magistrate in Dakar obtained permission from Senegalese police officials to photograph the contents of the Libyans' suitcases before they were released.'

The photographs, which Perry claimed were black and white, not colour, were then passed to the French intelligence service, which in turn 'very quietly' slipped them to the CIA. If this account is to be believed, whichever forensic expert made the key breakthrough in the Lockerbie investigation did so on the basis of black-and-white photographs taken not by an intelligence agent skilled in such work, but by a magistrate.

No one who went through these various accounts with a fine toothcomb could help but be suspicious. Even before the books by Ronald Kessler, Diarmuid Jeffreys and Mark Perry appeared, there was enough in the official material released with the indictments to raise very serious doubts. Sadly, apart from the general protests that Syria, Iran and the PFLP-GC had been exonerated out of political expediency, no one in the media chose to tackle these issues.

On 18 November 1991 the last of the Western hostages were released from captivity in Lebanon, including the best known of all, the Archbishop of Canterbury's special envoy Terry Waite. There is no doubt that the release was intimately bound up with George Bush's public exoneration of Syria four days earlier. Everyone knew the militias that held the hostages in Lebanon's Bekaa Valley were ultimately controlled by Damascus. While the finger still pointed to the PFLP-GC and its Syrian sponsors, Syria could keep a spanner in the works of Bush's 'New World Order' by making sure the hostages continued to be held. Now it was official that Syria had taken a 'bum rap' over Flight 103, the last obstacle to a new era of cooperation between the Washington–London axis and Damascus had been removed. The British ambassador to Syria at the time was none other than Andrew Green, the veteran of the secret arms-for-hostages deals of the 1980s who had gone on to handle what Foreign Office Minister Nicholas Bonsor described as 'the international aspects of the Lockerbie affair'.

In September 1992, ten months after the two Libyans were indicted, it was revealed that the US authorities had further evidence against the accused. This time it was someone who claimed to be a first-hand witness of the bomb plot. Once again the news was broken by the French magazine *L'Express*, who named the informant as Majid Giaka, a former colleague of Lamin Khalifa Fhimah at the Libyan Arab Airlines office in Malta. According to the magazine, Giaka had seen Fhimah and Megrahi stockpile explosives at the LAA office, buy clothes to go in the Samsonite case and steal luggage tags from Air Malta. After the bombing Giaka was alleged to have had violent arguments with Fhimah, which had driven him to contact US officials. Eventually he sought asylum in the US, where he was shielded under the Federal witness protection programme.

Years later, a further piece of evidence was reported. The CIA claimed that a Libyan code clerk, stationed at a Libyan People's Bureau in an unnamed European country, cabled a cryptic message claiming the Libyans were behind the bombing and offering a detailed account of how the decision had been made within Libya. The message was allegedly on a frequency readily accessible to the CIA and, according to an anonymous official within the agency's Counter Terrorism Centre, appeared to be a deliberate attempt to contact the agency.[12]

As we will see, in the years prior to Lockerbie, alleged interceptions of Libyan government messages were frequently touted by US intelligence as 'irrefutable evidence' of Gadafy's role in terrorism. As with Lockerbie, on closer inspection that evidence would crumble to dust.

11. USA VERSUS GADAFY

When the indictments were issued against the two Libyans in November 1991, there was a sense of *déjà vu*. Time and again over the previous decade Gadafy had been accused of masterminding shocking acts of terrorism against the West, and now his fingerprints seemed to be all over the worst attack of all. With such a list of atrocities to its name, Libya was undoubtedly the world's number one terrorist pariah.

Or was it? The truth is more complex. There is no doubt that Gadafy was a ruthless dictator who funded and harboured terrorists, but neither is there any doubt that the US exaggerated Libya's role in terrorism for political ends. As with Lockerbie, there was a tendency to trumpet 'irrefutable evidence' of Libyan involvement in terrorism, which, on closer inspection, would evaporate. And, as with Lockerbie, there was a tendency to turn a blind eye to the real culprits.

Gadafy had not always been an enemy. He came to power in 1969, in a CIA-backed coup against the corrupt King Idris. During his early days in power Gadafy bought weapons from the US and was given Western intelligence support against his internal enemies. The young colonel nevertheless refused to be America's puppet and instead fostered a radical Arab nationalism, modelled on that of his hero, President Nasser of Egypt. The entire oil industry was nationalised, he openly expressed his support for various armed struggles, and was prepared to arm and fund a variety of terrorist groups worldwide. Although there was obviously concern in the West that Gadafy's brand of revolutionary politics might spread to Libya's oil-producing neighbours, he was never able to build the necessary alliances and remained isolated. Furthermore, his open hostility towards communism and the Soviet Union meant that he retained many supporters in Washington.

By the end of the 1970s, relations with the US were beginning to sour. In 1977 US intelligence claimed to have conclusive evidence that Libya was supporting a plot to assassinate the US ambassador to Egypt, Herman Elits. In December 1979, the US embassy in Tripoli was set alight as a protest against US policy towards the new Islamic regime in Iran. A few months later, the US expelled employees of the Libyan People's Bureau in

Washington on the grounds that they had been intimidating Libyan dissidents based in America. In late 1980, US fighter planes were twice involved in stand-offs with Libyan jets over the Gulf of Sirte, prompting President Jimmy Carter to declare: 'There are few governments in the world with which we have more sharp and frequent policy differences than Libya.' Yet for all his defiance of the US, Gadafy's global influence remained minimal and his isolation within the Arab world was underlined by the fact that Libya maintained diplomatic relations only with Syria and South Yemen.[1]

The Carter administration's hostility towards Gadafy was as nothing compared to its successor's. Ronald Reagan's ascension to the White House in 1981 heralded a dramatic regeneration of the Cold War, which was accompanied by a new obsession with terrorism. On 27 January 1981, less than a week after Reagan took office, his Secretary of State, Alexander Haig, declared that the Soviet Union had a deliberate strategy to foster and support 'rampant international terrorism' which he described as 'the greatest problem in the human rights area today'.[2]

Haig's assertion came as something of a shock to analysts in the State Department's intelligence branch, who lacked any supporting evidence. Haig was briefed to this effect by the branch's head, Ronald Spiers, but neither he nor Reagan's new CIA director, William Casey, were having any of it.[3] The most rabidly right-wing of Reagan's appointees, Casey ordered his staff to produce a special national intelligence estimate (SNIE) on Soviet involvement in terrorism. The first draft reinforced the State Department's earlier position and, even when re-drafted by someone more sympathetic to Casey's position, it still failed to conclude that terrorism was a Soviet-inspired plot to spread global revolution. Casey was unconvinced; as far as he was concerned, the Soviets supported terrorism. If his analysts could find no evidence to support this theory, they were simply not looking hard enough.[4]

Casey and Haig turned to a bestselling book to justify their bluster. Published just after Reagan came to office, *The Terror Network* by Claire Sterling confirmed all their prejudices, fingering the 'conclusive' evidence of the Soviet role in international terrorism. The book's influence was enormous. Haig had read the advance galley proofs before making his speech of 27 January,[5] and in rejecting the original SNIE on Soviet support for terrorism, Casey allegedly snapped: 'Read Claire Sterling's book and forget this mush . . . I paid $13.95 for [the book] and it told me more than you bastards, whom I pay $50,000 a year.'[6]

A senior CIA staff member pointed out to Casey that the book was actually recycled disinformation, but Casey refused to accept it.[7] In the foreign policy he spearheaded, reality was subordinated to neo-Conservative ideology and political opportunism. America's status as the world's leading superpower was perceived to be on the wane: the humiliation of Vietnam had left deep scars, the Soviet Union was seen as getting away with the invasion of Afghanistan, and the revolution in Iran not only threatened US oil supplies but had resulted in the humiliation of the 444-day seizure of the US embassy staff in Tehran. Reagan's fellow travellers staked their electoral future on boosting America's confidence again, and an aggressive foreign policy was central to their plans.

Given this background, it was perhaps unsurprising that Libya should be catapulted from relative obscurity to international Public Enemy Number One. A third-rate military power with a population of under four million, the country offered no real threat to the US. Moreover, there was precious little evidence of Libya actually instigating terrorist attacks, as there was in the case of Syria, Iraq and the new regime in Iran. Neither was there any evidence to suggest Libya was a Soviet client state, actively involved in a global communist conspiracy. While Gadafy had bought military hardware from the Soviet Union, he remained fiercely independent and suspicious of all foreign powers, particularly non-Arab ones.[8] Since the Iranian revolution, Islamic fundamentalism was a far more potent force in the Middle East than Gadafy's old-style Arab nationalism and although he applauded the Iranian revolution and the Lebanon's burgeoning Hizbullah movement, he would not tolerate Islamic fundamentalism at home.

Libya was neither a critical player in the Arab-Israeli conflict nor a crucial supplier of oil to the US. By picking on Gadafy, Ronald Reagan could make himself appear a decisive leader who stood firm against the twin threats of terrorism and the Soviet Union, while simultaneously avoiding a genuine conflict with the Soviets or the rest of the Arab world. With his fierce anti-Western rhetoric and his open support for Middle Eastern terrorist groups, Gadafy played straight into Reagan's hands. Howard Teicher, a senior director in Reagan's National Security Council (NSC) from 1985 to 1987, later acknowledged that Libya was an easy target:

> The Syrians were much more capable of concealing their direct role
> [in terrorism]. The Iraqis had been taken off the list of countries that
> supported terrorism at the direction of CIA Director Casey in early
> 1982, in order to facilitate the US tilt towards Iraq. The Iranians,
> because of their geographic proximity while clearly an
> acknowledged sponsor of terrorism, were . . . also hard for the

United States to reach . . . What emerged in US policy was the tendency to be able to most directly deal with Libya, because of Libya's geographic proximity to Europe and the United States as opposed to Iraq, Iran or Syria. [It] was much more difficult to deal with the other countries.[9]

Put more bluntly by State Department intelligence analyst Lillian Harris: 'Gadafy presented this marvellous target, because you could fight the Soviets, you could fight terrorism, and you could fight the evil Arabs.'[10]

Despite the absurd imbalance in power between the US and Libya, the Reagan Administration unleashed a CIA programme against Gadafy that was to be one of the most extensive in the Agency's history.[11] Even before Reagan's inauguration, Alexander Haig had called a meeting of the State Department's top intelligence officials to discuss what action could be taken against Libya. Haig was convinced by Claire Sterling's assertion that Gadafy was 'the Daddy Warbucks of terrorism' and believed Gadafy's Soviet arms purchases provided a cover for the creation of Soviet military bases in North Africa. When Lillian Harris pointed out that the arms were of secondary quality and not of the calibre the Soviet Union would itself use, a disbelieving Haig wrote in the margin of her memo, 'Oh come on, they've got 'em in droves.' In background briefings with reporters, he began to refer to Gadafy as 'a cancer that has to be cut out'.[12]

In the early '80s, a stream of intelligence information suggested Gadafy was planning a terrorist war against the US. In November 1981, a Libyan claiming to be a terrorist walked into a US embassy in Africa and told officials he had been at a terrorist training camp in Libya, where he had witnessed Gadafy, at a meeting there, personally approve plans to send assassination squads to the US to kill Reagan, Vice-President George Bush and Haig. The fact that the whistle-blower failed a CIA polygraph test did not diminish the impact of his story. Washington was gripped by paranoia. Ronald Reagan was driven around in unmarked cars and decoy limousines were put onto the capital's streets in order to confuse would-be attackers. Plans to have the President switch on the Christmas lights on Pennsylvania Avenue were cancelled, and even the daughter of Reagan's Deputy Chief of Staff, Michael Deaver, was escorted to school by a secret service car.[13]

While there was little doubt that Gadafy had sent hit squads to the US and elsewhere to eliminate political enemies, neither the FBI nor the CIA could produce any evidence that assassins had been dispatched to kill Reagan and his team. Lillian Harris described the official reaction as 'hysterical' and suggested that the scare might have been a 'third country disinformation scheme'.[14] It subsequently emerged that much of the information came from Iranian arms dealer Manucher Ghorbanifar, who was suspected of working for the Israeli intelligence service, Mossad. Despite having failed a string of CIA polygraph tests and being branded a fabricator by the agency, he later became a key middleman in the Iran-Contra affair.[15] Since CIA Director William Casey had earlier issued a global directive to CIA station chiefs to initiate a disinformation campaign against Libya, some of the so-called intelligence about Gadafy's terrorist aspirations could simply have been recycled CIA lies.[16] One of the most active participants in the disinformation campaign was Lt Col Oliver North, who, according to erstwhile colleagues, had no compunction about spreading false stories.[17]

A propaganda war was not enough for the hawks in Reagan's government. Fuelled by outrage at their own side's misleading yarns, they wanted military action. The 'hit squads' story prompted Alexander Haig, William Casey and Secretary of Defense Caspar Weinberger to order that contingency plans be drawn up 'to carry out military action against Libya in self-defense, following a further Libyan provocation'. Every option was to be considered, short of a full-scale military invasion.[18]

Despite the administration's willingness to believe unsubstantiated intelligence, the White House was denied a pretext to execute the plans. During the whole of 1982 and 1983, the State Department could not find a single terrorist incident in which there was any evidence of Libyan involvement. Nevertheless, in early 1983 a top-secret plan code-named Early Call began to take shape with help from Egypt and Sudan. Early Call aimed to lure Gadafy into making a strike on Sudan so that his forces might be ambushed. To lay the bait, a bogus revolutionary cell was established in Sudan, which appealed to Gadafy for help. US AWACS radar planes were secretly sent to Egypt to assist the Egyptian Air Force in carrying out the attack. A military build-up near Libya's border with Sudan suggested Gadafy was taking the bait. The operation was poised to begin when a sandstorm forced three of the AWACS planes to land at Cairo's main civilian airport and news of the plans were leaked to ABC Television. No doubt realising that he was in danger of walking into a trap, Gadafy appeared to abandon his plans. The US claimed the débâcle as a victory against Libyan aggression.[19]

In May 1984, a CIA-sponsored coup attempt by Libyan exiles resulted in the bloody purge of 75 military officers whom Gadafy suspected of treason. By this time the hardliners within the NSC and the CIA were becoming increasingly frustrated by what they viewed as the failure to deal decisively with Libya.[20] The NSC directed the CIA to draft a presidential finding, authorising the agency to provide lethal aid to the Libyan armed opposition groups. To lay the groundwork the NSC's director of politico-military affairs, Donald Fortier, turned to CIA officer Vincent Cannistraro, who was drafted onto the NSC to head its Libya task force, among other things.[21] He and Fortier proposed two new policy approaches to keep the heat on Gadafy; one characterised as 'broad', the other as 'bold'. The former involved increasing pressure on US citizens and businesses to leave Libya, coupled with measures which would make it appear that the US was taking a more activist approach to Libya. Among the suggested measures was the revival of US naval freedom-of-navigation exercises off Libya, along with provocative ship movements in the Gulf of Sidra immediately to the north of Libya.

The bold approach envisaged 'a number of visible and covert actions designed to bring significant pressure to bear upon Gadafy and possibly to cause his removal from power'. Specifically the paper suggested the US should encourage Egypt and Algeria 'to seek a casus belli for military action against Tripoli', and that the US should supply arms and intelligence to opposition groups that would enable them to carry out sabotage within Libya.[22]

In 1985, top secret concrete plans to get rid of Gadafy took shape under the code-name Flower/Rose. Largely the work of Robert Gates, who later became the Director of the CIA under President Bush, it involved planning a pre-emptive military strike with America's allies, which Gates promised would 'redraw the map of North Africa'. In such military strikes the US would supply air support, with a target being Gadafy's barracks.[23] When he came to office Ronald Reagan signed Executive Order 12333, directing that 'No person employed by or acting on behalf of the United States government shall engage in, or conspire to engage in, assassination.' In discussing Gate's plan, Reagan made it clear he would personally take the flak if Gadafy was killed.[24]

As 1985 wore on, the NSC continued to push the plan, but objections from Secretary of State George Schultz and a cooling of relations with the crucial ally, Egypt, caused its eventual abandonment. This did not abate the NSC's preparations for an attack on Libya, nor its desire to undertake one.[25] This desire was raised to fever-pitch by a series of high-profile terrorist incidents later in the year. In June 1985, two Lebanese men hijacked TWA Flight 847 as it took off from Athens to Rome. Forty Americans were among the passengers forced to endure a 17-day ordeal, initially in Beirut and then in Algiers. One of them, US Navy diver Robert Stethem, was killed. There was no evidence to link Gadafy to the hijacking, which was undoubtedly the work of Hizbullah.[26] The US could not hit back at Hizbullah and its sponsors in Iran and Syria, because they held Americans hostage and there was no wish to repeat the 1980 Tehran Embassy crisis.

In October 1985, four terrorists of Abu Abbas's Palestine Liberation Front hijacked the Italian cruise ship the *Achille Lauro* after it had left the port of Alexandria in Egypt. An elderly and wheelchair-bound American passenger, Leon Klinghoffer, was shot dead and his body dumped over the side. Once again, there was no link to Gadafy.[27]

The next month there was another bloody hijacking as three members of the Abu Nidal organisation seized control of an Air Egypt flight from Athens to Cairo. Following a gunfight on board which caused the cabin to depressurise, the plane made an emergency landing at Luqa airport on Malta. A botched raid by Egyptian commandos, egged on by the US, resulted in 57 deaths.

This time the US announced it had evidence of Gadafy's involvement. Not only was Abu Nidal based in Libya, but the NSC also claimed to have intercepts of communication between the Libyan People's Bureau in Malta and the government in Tripoli. These messages, the NSC alleged, showed Tripoli was a partner in the hijacking and had relayed messages to the three terrorists.[28] None of the intercepts were ever released for independent scrutiny and, according to Watergate journalist Bob Woodward, other intelligence intercepts of Gadafy's conversations at the time of the hijacking suggested there was no Libyan involvement. Woodward reported that Oliver North was actively seeking such connections, and speculated that when none appeared he simply made them up.[29] The Egyptian intelligence service and the then Prime Minister of Malta, Mifsud Bonnici, each confirmed the hijacking had in fact been masterminded in Damascus.[30]

Two days after Christmas 1985, the Abu Nidal gunmen simultaneously opened fire on ticket desks at Rome and Vienna airports, killing 19 people, including five Americans. President Reagan spoke of 'irrefutable evidence' linking Gadafy to the attack. The terrorists were carrying Tunisian passports, which the Tunisian government said had been confiscated from Tunisians working in Libya. Gadafy did little to allay suspicions when he described the double massacres as 'heroic actions',[31] but when the evidence was analysed there was nothing to implicate Libya in the attacks. The best US intelligence could come up with was a report showing that Libyan agents had transferred $1 million to an Abu Nidal bank account in Bulgaria a few years previously.[32] The month after the incidents, the State Department's anti-terrorist chief, Robert Oakley, admitted there was 'little or no evidence to link Gadafy'. The sole terrorist to survive the Rome attack told the Italian authorities that he had been trained by Syrian agents at a camp in Lebanon's Bekaa Valley and that they had escorted him from Damascus to Rome.[33] After a year-long investigation, Italian Prosecutor Domenico Sica concluded that both attacks had indeed been planned in Damascus.[34]

Reagan's hardliners did not trouble their minds with such minor considerations. Within days of the Rome and Vienna massacres, US Air Force officers at the Lakenheath air base in England had been ordered to draw up plans for air strikes against Libya's two main air bases. As the spring of 1986 approached, the momentum to launch an attack against Libya had become unstoppable.[35]

Donald Fortier, by then Reagan's deputy national security adviser, proposed there should be 'disproportionate' responses to Libyan provocation, but in the event the provocation would come from his own side. In January, the US 6th Fleet began a series of exercises with the official title 'Operations in the Vicinity of Libya'. The Commander of the US 6th Fleet, Vice Admiral Frank Kelso, subsequently revealed: 'Our directions were to operate US Navy Forces in the Gulf of Sidra. You can put any context you want on it, but those were the directions.'

Over the next few months, the penetrations into the gulf became deeper and deeper. The operation echoed Vincent Cannistraro's earlier proposals, only this time the aim was not so much to destabilise Gadafy as to lure him into an attack which would provide an excuse for the 'disproportionate' response.

In March the third phase of the operation began, code-named Prairie Fire. Sixty billion dollars' worth of military hardware was assembled, including three aircraft carriers, but still Gadafy would not rise to the bait. Desperate for action, the US government ordered a dramatic change to the rules of engagement. Under normal circumstances naval commanders were only allowed to retaliate against a hostile act, but this action was now permitted against anyone deemed to have 'hostile intent'. Since hostile intent was defined as being in a position to launch an attack, a whole range of Libyan ships, planes and military positions had, with the stroke of a pen, become fair game.

On 24 March, after US Navy F-14 fighters had flown to within 60 miles of the Libyan coast, the Libyan forces were finally provoked into reacting, launching two surface-to-air missiles. Possibly reflecting the competence of the Libyan military, both fell harmlessly into the sea. To the consternation of Reagan's hawks the Fleet Commander, Vice Admiral Frank Kelso, opted not to retaliate. Shortly afterwards, however, US Navy planes sank two Libyan patrol boats.

As the stand-off continued, the US was finally handed the pretext it needed. At 1.49 a.m. on 5 April 1986 a bomb exploded in La Belle Disco, a Berlin nightspot packed with US servicemen, killing two people including a US Army sergeant. US intelligence claimed to have intercepted incriminating messages to and from the Libyan Peoples' Bureau in Berlin.[36]

Nine days later, on 14 April, the US finally unleashed its military might on Libya. In an operation code-named El Dorado Canyon, Air Force and Navy bombers launched simultaneous attacks on Tripoli and Benghazi, killing 41 people. Appearing on American television that night to justify the attack, President Reagan once again claimed that there was 'irrefutable evidence' to show that Libya was behind the Berlin bombing.

Although the White House denied it, the bombing was almost certainly an attempt to assassinate Gadafy.[37] Pilots involved in the raids subsequently claimed they had orders to hit the air-conditioning unit on the roof of Gadafy's house , within the huge El Aziziya barracks.[38] Laser-guided missiles were launched against the barracks, but the house was the only building to be hit. Although the Libyan leader was lucky to escape with his life, his 15-month-old adopted daughter Hana was killed. On the evening of the attack Ronald Reagan appeared on coast-to-coast television to justify the raid. In researching his book *To the Ends of the Earth*, author David Yallop established that the President's autocue was originally primed with a speech which justified the killing of Gadafy, but since this had not occurred it was changed.[39]

After the dust had settled in Tripoli and Benghazi, Reagan's 'irrefutable evidence' was once again shown to be wanting. Experts consulted by Yallop were categorical that the La Belle Disco bombing was the work of Syria. A Syrian agent, Ahmed Hasi, was originally arrested for the La Belle bombing and when police raided his apartment they found a drawing which closely resembled the floor space of that nightclub. He was also responsible for another bombing in Berlin shortly before the disco bomb. His brother, Nezar Hindawi, was arrested a few weeks later over the Syrian-inspired plot to blow up an El Al flight from Heathrow to Israel.

As for the intelligence intercepts of the Libyan People's Bureau, the original tape recordings were never handed over for independent scrutiny. The German intelligence service, the BND, was provided with a copy, but was left unconvinced. BND officials and agents of the Italian, French and Israeli intelligence services told Yallop the tapes were phoney and may well have been concocted by the NSC.[40]

Another explanation was offered by former Israel agent Victor Ostrovsky. In his book *The Other Side of Deception*, he claimed the messages between Tripoli and Berlin were not from Libyan intelligence but from a Mossad disinformation unit engaged in an operation called Trojan. He claimed Israeli commandos secretly landed on the Libyan coast in February 1986 with special communications equipment, which Mossad agents then set up in an apartment near Gadafy's headquarters. Shortly afterwards, Ostrovsky alleged, Mossad began relaying messages which made it appear as if a series of terrorist orders were being transmitted to various Libyan People's Bureaux.[41]

The raids of 14 April were by no means the end of the Reagan administration's efforts to get rid of Gadafy. Almost as soon as the raids had finished, planning began for a second raid. The NSC's head, Admiral John Poindexter, ordered Vincent Cannistraro and his NSC colleagues James Stark and Howard Teicher to produce a report for the President outlining the available options. Cannistraro concentrated on intelligence and Stark on the military options, but, much to their chagrin, the memos were re-written by the ultra hardline Oliver North, who sought to encourage Reagan to take decisive action.[42]

When Gadafy failed to provide a pretext for any further military action, the emphasis of US policy shifted to psychological warfare. In October 1986 Bob Woodward was leaked a State Department working paper which declared:

> The goal of our near-term strategy should be to continue Gadafy's paranoia so that he remains preoccupied, off balance . . . [and] believes that the army and other elements are plotting against him . . . Believing that, he may increase the pressure on the [Libyan] army, which may in turn prompt a coup or assassination attempt.

The embarrassing references to assassination and disinformation did not appear in the subsequent National Security Decision Directive (NSDD) signed by Reagan, but the directive nevertheless ordered 'covert, diplomatic and economic steps designed to . . . bring about a change of leadership in Libya'.[43]

Vincent Cannistraro and Howard Teicher were named by Woodward in the *Washington Post* as supporters of the deception and disinformation strategy. In fact, both were actively involved in trying to ensure that the policy eventually laid out in Reagan's NSSD was not watered down. Teicher was asked to produce a distillation of the State Department paper for a meeting of Reagan's cabinet. At the same time Elaine Morton, a former State Department North Africa officer who had been assigned to the NSC, produced a separate distillation for the President himself. Even though they were based on the same report, the two versions differed sharply. Teicher's, in effect, called on administration officials to spread the same false stories about Gadafy's imminent demise that the CIA had been spreading.

Elaine Morton was reportedly appalled by the idea, and with some of the other suggestions that had been floated. Making her feelings clear on the NSC's office computer, she described most of the schemes which had been outlined as 'Wizard of Oz'. She had what was described as a 'sharp disagreement' with Cannistraro over the suggestion that the US should seek to increase Gadafy's paranoia by flying reconnaissance planes over Tripoli to create sonic booms. For Morton, this was as ludicrous as anything that the supposedly mad Gadafy could have dreamed up. In his reply Cannistraro wrote: 'Elaine, I have profound disagreements with the substance of your position . . . we have established, I think, that pressure against Gadafy does indeed work and can serve to condition/moderate his behaviour . . . . There is a psychological momentum among those opposed to Gadafy that needs to be sustained. Sonic booms are indications that Gadafy is not out of the woods, thus encouraging his opposition and affecting his equilibrium. Not to say this is effective in and of itself, but as part of, albeit [an] important part, of a broader campaign, it is necessary. We should sustain pressure, not release it, and not blindly hope his economy will collapse and save our strategy.'[44]

The fact that a mid-ranking US intelligence officer should actively promote dirty tricks designed to effect a change of leadership in another sovereign nation might be shocking if it were not so commonplace. Vincent Cannistraro has never sought to hide his role in the anti-Gadafy programme, and why should he; after all, the programme had received presidential sanction. His role would not be of particular interest were it not for the fact that he would go on to lead the CIA's investigation of the Lockerbie bombing.

Urbane and slow-talking, Cannistraro is the antithesis of the wild-eyed ideologue of the Oliver North and William Casey mould, yet during the mid-1980s he worked with North on both the anti-Gadafy programme and the Iran-Contra operation.[45] CIA director William Casey liked North's rule-bending, can-do approach, but had the political nous to realise that North could be dangerous. It was speculated that level-headed and much respected CIA veterans such as Cannistraro were drafted onto the NSC as a counterbalance.

Cannistraro retired from the CIA in September 1990, having spent the previous two years as head of operations and analysis for the agency's counter-terrorism centre. His retirement coincided with a spate of media reports which claimed, for the first time, that Libya had been conclusively linked to the Lockerbie bombing. The first of these came in *L'Express*, which revealed that the fragment of the circuit board found at Lockerbie was part of a timer identical to those allegedly seized from Libyan agents in Senegal in February 1988.

A few weeks later Cannistraro came out into the open for the first time. Speaking at a luncheon sponsored by the conservative think tank, the National Strategy Information Center, he told reporters that Iran had ordered the Lockerbie bombing as revenge for the downing of its airbus by the USS *Vincennes*. The *Washington Times* gave the story front-page billing under the headline, 'EX-CIA MAN SAYS IRAN ORDERED FLIGHT 103 BOMBING AS REVENGE'. The newspaper noted that Cannistraro's revelations were 'the most explicit to date by current or former officials close to the investigation', and were 'highly unusual, coming as they did from a senior intelligence officer so soon after retirement'. Cannistraro didn't mention Libya at the meeting, but hinted that Iran may not have acted alone. 'I'm persuaded that the Iranian government commissioned it,' he said, adding, 'That's not to say that the Iranian government actually implemented it. That may have been a different step, and that part I don't want to get into.'[46]

Other newspapers failed to pick up on his remarks about Flight 103, choosing instead to concentrate on outspoken criticisms that Cannistraro had made in his speech about US anti-terrorism policy. He complained that the State Department had 'constantly undercut' the CIA account of Iraq's support for terrorism and described the removal of Iraq from the official list of countries sponsoring terrorism in the early '80s as a 'terrible mistake'. Iraq was, of course, at the forefront of everyone's mind at the time he made the speech, since it was less than four months after the invasion of Kuwait. Cannistraro nevertheless warned that America's attempted *rapprochement* with Iraq's great enemy Syria could be equally disastrous, as Syria had itself been behind some 'really horrible' acts of terrorism.[47]

Over the coming years Cannistraro would be quoted time and time again, in the media, on the CIA, on terrorism and, most importantly, on Lockerbie. In particular, he would pour cold water on allegations that US government agencies were complicit in the disaster. Reporters might not have been prepared to accept the government's assurances on this matter, but when those assurances came from Vincent Cannistraro, a man not afraid to voice dissident views, they were far more likely to be believed.

Within a month of the luncheon speech, Cannistraro had begun to discuss the emerging Libyan angle to the bombing. On 14 December *The Independent* ran its main front-page article under the banner 'LIBYA BLAMED FOR LOCKERBIE'. The article cited a claim by anonymous 'high-level sources' that there was now 'conclusive proof' that Gadafy was behind the bombing. It again concentrated on the evidence of the timer fragment, and revealed for the first time that it had been linked, along with those found in Dakar, 'to one Swiss manufacturer', who was not named. On 19 December the paper ran a follow-up article headed 'LOCKERBIE BOMB BORE LIBYAN SIGNATURE', in which Cannistraro revealed that Libyan involvement had been suspected for several months and that concrete evidence had come from a British forensic examination of the fragment of circuit board. The article reported that Cannistraro had emphasised that these developments had occurred since he left the investigation and that he had no direct knowledge of the Libyan link.

This claim was at odds with David Leppard's book *On the Trail of Terror*, which was written at around the same time. A largely uncritical account of the official investigation, based on generous inside sources, its final chapter described how the Libyan connection was finally made in the summer of 1990. It reported that an analysis of the fragment of circuit board by British forensic expert Dr Thomas Hayes linked it to the Swiss manufacturer, Mebo. According to Leppard, Cannistraro told the Scottish police that an assessment by his analysts had indicated possible similarities with timers seized in Senegal. Furthermore, Leppard reported that Cannistraro made a preliminary assessment that the two people caught with the timers were Libyan agents. If this were true, why did *The Independent* report that he had no direct knowledge of the Libyan link?

No one in the media spotted these contradictions and reporters continued to accept Cannistraro's word uncritically. As we have seen, in June 1991 he announced that Lockerbie investigators believed that, following the October 1988 Autumn Leaves raids, Iran had handed responsibility for the bombing from the Syrian backed PFLP-GC to the Libyans. He was reported as saying, 'I don't think you can blame the Syrians for what Libya did.'

A few months later, indictments were issued against two Libyans, George Bush uttered his notorious comment that Syria had taken 'a bum rap' and the State Department made it clear that Lockerbie was a 'Libyan government operation from start to finish'. Within a week the last remaining Western hostages were released by their Syrian-controlled captors, fuelling suspicions that a deal had been done to exonerate Syria and clear the last remaining obstacles to Bush's New World Order. A few days later some of the American Lockerbie family members met with State Department officials in Washington, in part to push for sanctions against Libya but also to press for the full story of Flight 103 to be exposed. Press reports suggested that many were angry at the blatant way in which Syria had been exonerated. At least one of them had called Bush a liar.[48]

The next day Cannistraro again spoke up against his government, describing the official exoneration of Syria and Iran as 'outrageous'.[49] Although somewhat at odds with his reported earlier statement that Syria could not be blamed for what Libya did, his comment showed that he was on the side of the anguished American relatives.

Cannistraro certainly impressed Daniel and Susan Cohen, who lost their daughter Theodora in the bombing. The couple were the most outspoken of all the US families in their criticism of the official cover-up of Syria's and Iran's involvement. As described in Chapter 6, like Cannistraro, they were equally vocal in their condemnation of those who suggested the Libyans were innocent and that the bombers had exploited a CIA-protected drug smuggling operation. The Cohens got to know and like Cannistraro, with Daniel calling him affectionately 'Vinnie the Spy'. 'He is not the image of a man who keeps secrets,' Daniel wrote. 'He is humorous, affable, chatty, indeed downright garrulous, though after a while you realise that he is saying a lot less than you think he is.' In assuring them that the Libyan sub-contract theory was correct, Cannistraro told the Cohens the CIA had learned that, soon after the bombing, Jibril held a champagne party at his Damascus offices at which he declared jubilantly, 'The Americans will never, ever find out how we did it.' Cannistraro told them, 'We didn't know what he meant by that at the time. Now we do.'[50]

Despite his frequent denunciations of the CIA drugs-and-hostages story, Cannistraro was startlingly unaware of an aspect of the most notorious of the previous covert deals, Iran-Contra. The book *The Secret War Against the Jews* by John Loftus and Mark Aarons revealed that involvement of Syrian arms dealer Monzer Al Kassar in Iran-Contra was much deeper than had been revealed by the congressional hearings into the scandal. Moreover, it made the remarkable claim that he was an MI6 agent throughout the '80s.

The book claims Cannistraro confirmed that he was well aware of the Syrian, but he was stunned when Loftus told him that Al-Kassar was involved in the Iran-Contra deals and that congressional investigators had uncovered payments made to him by Oliver North.[51]

Cannistraro worked with North on a day-to-day basis; indeed, from the end of 1985 he worked in the next-door office.[52] The payments to Al-Kassar were revealed in congressional hearings in 1987 and reported in the media.[53] If Cannistraro was unaware of such events, why should the American public believe his assurances that the CIA was not up to its neck in the Lockerbie bombing?

In the course of researching this book the authors sent Cannistraro a list of questions about his role in the US Government's anti-Gadafy programme of the 1980s and his subsequent involvement in the Lockerbie case. Among the questions we posed were:

(1) It is a matter of public record that you had a hand in the formulation of polices designed to weaken and overthrow Gadafy. That being the case, do you consider that you were an appropriate person to head the CIA's (supposedly impartial) investigation into a major act of terrorism in which Libya would inevitably be among the list of suspects?

(2) You told *The Independent* newspaper [19th December 1990] that the concrete forensic evidence that linked Libya to the attack (ie the fragment of circuit board) had been made after you left the CIA. You have also stated that the major breakthroughs in the case were made by the criminal investigators. How do you square these claims with:

(a) the fact that Tom Thurman says he linked the fragment to Libya in June 1990, three months before you stood down from the investigation;

(b) that according to David Leppard's *On the Trail of Terror* (a book with which you co-operated) from mid-1990 onwards the Lockerbie investigation was, in effect, run by the CIA and that you personally told the Scottish police in the Summer of 1990 that an assessment by your analysts had indicated possible similarities between the fragment and the timers seized in Senegal.

(3) The book *Secret War Against the Jews* by John Loftus and Mark Aarons reports that you were stunned when they told you in 1992 that Monzer Al-Kassar had been involved in the Iran-Contra deals and had been paid by Oliver North. Why were you ignorant of this fact given that:

(a) you worked closely with North during the relevant period in the mid-'80s;

(b) it had been revealed during the 1987 congressional investigations into Iran-Contra and reported in the media at the time?

Given that on the account you gave to Loftus and Aarons you were unaware of Al-Kassar's involvement with US intelligence, which was taking place under your nose, how can you be so sure that covert CIA hostage deals were not central to the Lockerbie bombing?'

Cannistraro responded: 'Most of what you state in your e-mail has a false basis. It shows the dangers of taking various published media stories at face value, accepting them as historical record. *The Independent* story is incorrect. The forensic identification was made by the criminal investigators before I retired from CIA in November 1990. David Leppard's work is fundamentally flawed. I didn't "cooperate" with Leppard, I answered a few of his questions and, not for the first time, David got the answers skewed. I had experience with you skewing some of my responses as well, so I am familiar with the phenomenon.'

He added some defamatory comments about John Loftus then went on: 'I was at the NSC from 1984 to 1986 and I contributed to the NSC policy that identified Gadafy as a danger to US interests. I was a staff director for intelligence policies at the National Security Council and was not operationally involved with the CIA's covert program designed to weaken the Gadafy regime. As you should be aware, it was Richard Clark, currently the USG's "Czar" for counter-terrorism, who was the patron saint of that program. Clark, who is based now at the NSC, was deputy chief of State's Intelligence and Research (INR) in 1986 and wrote the famous proposals for a "disinformation" and covert action program directed against Libya. That said, I was certainly in favor of the bombing of Tripoli in 1986, and the policies I helped to formulate contributed to the President's decision to bomb Tripoli.

'When the intelligence investigation of Pan Am 103 began, and for a period thereafter of at least 18 months, there was no indication that Libya was a suspect in the bombing. Do you think I should have been prescient enough to know the future before hand, and take myself out of the initial investigation? As you know, the criminal indictments of the two Libyan intelligence officers was handed down by the Department of Justice one year after I left government service. The indictments were made on the basis of criminal investigation carried out by the FBI, the law enforcement branch of the US Government. CIA, of course, has no law enforcement authority. Criminal investigation and decisions to indict are Department of Justice decisions.'

The authors wrote back, challenging Cannistraro to state exactly what in their previous e-mail had a 'false basis'. We added a list of supplementary questions, including:

(1) A number of published accounts describe the Reagan administration's anti-Gadafy strategies in the mid-eighties and refer to your role within them. One of those is Mark Perry's book *Eclipse*. In one of his chapters on Lockerbie Perry reports: 'By the end of 1984 the Reagan administration's top intelligence officers had become obsessed with the problem of getting rid of Gadafy, and a senior intelligence group, headed by Libya task force chief Vince Cannistraro and NSC staff officer Donald Fortier, drew up a paper that proposed a two-part strategy to deal with him that included arming Libyan dissident groups in Egypt and Algeria.' I note that Perry acknowledges the 'extraordinary amount of guidance' you provided him on Lockerbie and I therefore take it that you concur with his account of the bombing. Can I also take it that his account of your role in the anti-Gadafy programme is accurate? If so, given that you were involved in formulating policy designed to get rid of the leader of a sovereign Middle East nation, do you think you were you an appropriate person to lead a supposedly impartial investigation into a major act of Middle East terrorism?

(2) *The Independent* article of 19th December 1990, by Leonard Doyle, reported on an interview with you about the newly revealed forensic evidence linking Libya to the bombing. It read, 'Mr Cannistraro emphasised that the developments [ie; the linking of the circuit board fragment to Libya] occurred since he left the investigation and that he had no direct knowledge of the Libyan link.' How do you account for this sentence?

(3) What exactly did David Leppard get wrong? Do you deny that you told the Scottish police in the Summer of 1990 that an assessment by your analysts had indicated possible similarities between the fragment and the timers seized in Senegal?

(4) And what exactly did John Loftus get wrong? You state that Al-Kassar did not work with US intelligence. Are you therefore denying that Oliver North made million dollar payments to Al-Kassar from his Swiss bank account to fund Contra arms shipments (a fact uncovered by the congressional investigation of Iran-Contra)? Do you deny being 'stunned' when Loftus told you of this?

Cannistraro replied: 'I'd like to help you out, Ian, but you have to realise that we are in a competitive situation here, with my work for ABC World News and my own writings. So I can't give you much beyond general comments. If you look closely at all the media accounts you cite in your query, you will recognize some fundamental contradictions.

'Re Perry's book, I already told you about writing the policy paper in 1986 while at the NSC. What I principally told Perry was an account of the Abu Nidal operations, and even there he didn't get it right, although he was very kind to me. His accounts of Lockerbie are not, in my view, terribly accurate and that, I believe, is not my fault. He consulted many other sources, as indeed, you are doing.'

12. 'AN OLD-FASHIONED POLICE INVESTIGATION'

'The greatest investigative team effort of our time.' So proclaimed the *Daily Mail*, the day after indictments were issued against Abdel Basset Ali Al-Megrahi and Lamin Khalifa Fhimah. Like the rest of the media, the paper had taken its cue from officialdom. The governments on both sides of the Atlantic went out of their way to praise the investigating authorities. US Attorney General William Barr said they had conducted a 'brilliant and unrelenting operation', while the Scottish Lord Advocate, Lord Fraser of Carmyllie, paid tribute to the 'outstanding work' by the 'many police officers and agencies . . . throughout the world'. Particular praise was reserved for the police, especially the Dumfries and Galloway Constabulary, whose 'painstaking and skilled work' was, according to Scottish Secretary Ian Laing, 'simply breathtaking'.[1]

The message was that for all its international complexities, Lockerbie was just like any other police investigation. All leads had been pursued and all the evidence rigorously assessed. And it had been controlled by the tiny Dumfries and Galloway force throughout. But while there was no doubt that much diligent and dedicated thoroughly professional work was done in difficult circumstances by investigators on both sides of the Atlantic, it was equally obvious that this was no straightforward police investigation.

Amid the media fanfare, virtually nothing was heard of the CIA. This was rather curious because the CIA had provided the vital intelligence linking the fragment of circuit board to the Swiss manufacturer Mebo, and to Libya. Indeed, according to David Leppard's *On the Trail of Terror*, which trumpeted itself as *The Inside Story of the Lockerbie Investigation*, by mid-1990 the investigation was, in effect, being run by the CIA rather than the Scottish police. Vincent Cannistraro, who headed the Agency's investigation, was nevertheless reluctant to take credit. He was quoted as saying that the Libyan connection had been established after his retirement in September 1990 and emphasised that all the major developments in the case were provided by the criminal investigators, rather than the CIA.

Yet there was evidence that Western intelligence agencies, especially Cannistraro's colleagues from the CIA, interfered with the investigation from day one. Within an hour of the crash, the agency had dispatched agents to the crash site and Americans in cream-coloured trench-coats were spotted in Lockerbie within two hours. As many sources have independently testified, it was plainclothed Americans, rather than the Scottish police, who appeared to be running the show in the days after the crash. The discreet retrieval of the bags belonging to Major Charles McKee and his colleagues, as well as the other sensitive items, like drugs, flew in the face of the strict rules of evidence-gathering that should apply to murder inquiries.

And there is evidence that the CIA intervened to prevent the Scottish police from interviewing one of the key witnesses regarding the original suspects. The PFLP-GC's master bomb-maker Marwan Khreesat was an undercover agent of the Jordanian intelligence service. He had been mysteriously released from custody after the BKA's October 1988 Autumn Leaves raids, and allowed to return to his native Jordan. The Jordanian service had been set up with extensive CIA assistance, and was known to have retained close ties to the CIA and other Western intelligence services. The FBI was informed by the CIA of the fact that Khreesat was working for Jordanian intelligence. Such were the close ties between Jordanian intelligence and the CIA that it is inconceivable the CIA were not made aware of Khreesat's activities in Germany from Jordanian intelligence sources. The CIA, independently of the BKA and the FBI, kept the PFLP-GC cell under surveillance, at one point noting that the group had 'cased' the Pan Am terminal at Frankfurt airport. Informed sources have confirmed to the authors that it is likely that Khreesat would have been given operational support by CIA agents in Germany and was also an asset of German intelligence.

During the spring of 1989, Detective Chief Superintendent John Orr sent his deputy, Detective Superintendent Stuart Henderson, to the Jordanian capital of Amman to meet with government officials, to discuss interviewing Khreesat. According to David Leppard, who had access to Scottish police reports, the meeting was mysteriously cancelled. Leppard reported that in May 1989 a Special Branch officer, Detective Superintendent Ian Armstrong, travelled to Washington DC for a meeting with Khreesat's Jordanian intelligence handler. On arrival, FBI agents informed him that the CIA had arranged the meeting for the next day, but according to Leppard's Scottish police sources, the meeting was blocked by the CIA.

Khreesat was eventually interviewed in 1989, at least twice – once in June and once in November – by the FBI and the CIA, but never by the Scottish police. Among those taking part in the November 1989 interview in Jordan was an FBI explosives forensic specialist, Supervisory Special Agent James T. Thurman, known to all as Tom. According to a formerly very senior Scottish legal officer, with intimate knowledge of the Lockerbie case, interviewed by the authors, the reports of these meetings were not made available to the Crown at the time.

As well as being obstructed by American agencies, the investigation had, of course, apparently not rigorously followed up a number of potentially vital leads. The drug find at Tundergarth Mains Farm, for example, was brought to the authorities' attention by Rev John Mosey at the Lockerbie fatal accident inquiry in 1990. Detective Chief Superintendent John Orr assured Mosey that Farmer Jim Wilson would be visited by a senior police officer, but that visit never took place. The British government would later deny that there were any significant drug finds at the crash site (see Chapter Five).

Neither the Scottish police nor the FBI attempted to interview Pan Am's investigator Juval Aviv about the findings of his Interfor Report and instead, the FBI smeared him. Lester Coleman, like Aviv, the former spy claimed no direct knowledge of Lockerbie, but he did have first-hand knowledge of Syrian and Lebanese drug smuggling. Moreover, he claimed that Khalid Jaafar had been used in DEA-controlled drug deliveries. The Scottish police nevertheless seemed content to believe the US government's claims that Coleman was a con man and not to be trusted. Evidence unearthed by Pan Am's lead attorney James Shaugnessy in the wake of the Interfor Report was also disregarded. Instead, Shaugnessy, like Aviv and Coleman, found himself under FBI investigation.

The official investigation also appeared to ignore vital evidence that Khalid Jaafar was in Sweden immediately before the bombing. The lead had come from Ingrid Olufsen, Pan Am's director of passenger services in Oslo, who informed her colleagues in London about her encounter with the enigmatic Mr Goldberg. Pan Am's Heathrow-based security manager, Mike Jones, notified Bob Mahoney at the US Embassy in London. Jones then heard nothing until early July 1989, when Mahoney called and asked for copies of Goldberg's and Olufsen's notes to be sent to him. Jones faxed the documents on 7 July, but neither he nor Olufsen were contacted by any of the investigating authorities.[2]

The British and American governments emphasised that the indictments against the two Libyans rested on solid evidence, of the kind that cannot be influenced by backroom manoeuvring by the intelligence services. 'The investigation has been driven by the collection of forensic evidence, not intelligence,' Vincent Cannistraro emphasised. 'Almost all of the major developments have come from laboratory analyses which do not lend themselves to politicking.'[3]

Yet at a reception on the evening of Thursday, 14 November 1991, within hours of the indictments being announced, the outgoing head of the FBI's criminal investigative division, William M. Baker, praised the CIA and other espionage services for what he called 'their unheralded work in the Pan Am inquiry'. Informed sources told reporters that Baker was referring in part to a previously undisclosed intelligence operation in the autumn of 1990, which had produced a key element of the case: the diary of Lamin Khalifa Fhimah, containing references to the Pan Am plot. The *New York Times* on 16 November 1991 carried a description of what Baker was referring to:

> Mr Lamin's indictment charges that he used his access to the airport to steal luggage tags for Air Malta flights, one of which was placed on the suitcase that held the bomb. That evidence came from Mr Lamin's private diary. In an entry dated 15 December 1988, a week before the bombing, he wrote, 'Abdel Basset is coming from Zurich with Salvu,' and added, 'bring the taggs [*sic*] from the airport.' Abdel Basset [*sic*] is one of the two Libyan agents indicted in the case.

In fact, there was a further entry written entirely in Arabic in the notes section at the back of the diary which, properly translated, read 'collect the tags from the airport'.[4] The entry of 15 December actually read, 'collect taggs from Air Malta' with the misspelled word 'taggs' written in English and the remainder in Arabic.

It subsequently emerged that the diary had been seized on 18 April 1991, not in August 1990. It was taken from the Mosta offices of Medtours, a travel company that Fhimah had established with a Maltese friend, Vincent Vassallo, in 1989. Present at the time were Detective Chief Inspector Harry Bell of the Scottish police, his colleague, Sergeant Peter Avent, FBI Special Agent Philip Reid and Maltese police officer Sergeant Albert Galea. According to the police, they went to the office to conduct an interview and look around, during which time they spotted a diary belonging to Fhimah and another belonging to Vassallo. They claim they asked if they could take them and Vassallo agreed.

Vassallo was unsure whether or not the police had a search warrant. In fact, they did not. His feeling was that they knew exactly where to go to locate the diaries, and found it difficult to understand why they kept opening drawers and rifling through papers. On finding Fhimah's diary, most of which was in Arabic, according to Sergeant Galea, they mentioned that they had found a reference to airline tags, which was curious given that the word 'taggs' was the only part of the phrase 'collect taggs from the Air Malta' written in English. How did they know the reference was not to some other type of tag?

FBI Agent Reid claimed they did not conduct a search, as they were just looking around and found Fhimah's diary on top of the desk. Vassallo said he did not know his rights regarding whether or not he could object to this. He also stated that he felt 'cornered'. Later the diaries were removed, but Vassallo insisted that in doing so they did not seek his permission.

According to Vassallo, a few days before the police visit there was a break-in at the Medtours office. Despite the fact that the office contained petty cash, a TV and a VCR as well as normal office equipment, nothing was stolen. Perhaps this was just a coincidence, but on the same day an office in Prague, associated with Medtours, also suffered a break-in. Again, nothing was taken. Could someone with prior knowledge of the location and possible contents of Fhimah's diary have tipped off the FBI, or the Scottish police?

Both of these organisations had already felt the wrath of the Maltese government in 1989, when Maltese security police discovered that telephones in the office and homes of the owners of the Miska Bakery had been subject to illegal phone-tapping. Representatives of the Scottish police, FBI and BKA were summoned to a meeting with Maltese government officials who demanded to know who was responsible for the taps. All denied involvement, but the Maltese government was so infuriated that it withdrew its cooperation from the investigation. This meant the entire inquiry had to be suspended. Malta made strong complaints to the US, UK and German governments, and forced all three to give undertakings about their future conduct while on the island.

So who was carrying out the wire-taps? Sources within the FBI let it be known in off-the-record discussions that they believed it to be the CIA. Prior to any Pan Am investigation in Malta, the CIA had been monitoring the movements of the Miska Bakery personnel. So the Agency must have been aware of Mohammed Abu Talb, who had visited bakery owner Abdel Salem and his brother, Hashim Salem, during his stay on the island two months before Lockerbie.

A senior Maltese police officer told the authors that the CIA was also believed to have carried out the burglary at the Medtours office, but they had no 'hard' evidence to prove it. Could this have been the previously undisclosed intelligence operation to which William Baker was referring?

The Scottish police did not rely only on the CIA and the FBI. As would be confirmed at the subsequent trial of the two Libyans, a key role was played by British forensic investigators from the explosives forensic laboratory of the Royal Armament Research and Development Establishment (RARDE), a Ministry of Defence organisation concerned with the research and development of hi-tech weaponry. The British government has had a facility to deal with the forensic investigation of terrorist incidents ever since the Gunpowder Plot. The RARDE lab is its direct descendent.

Originally based at Woolwich in south-east London, the lab shifted to Fort Halstead in Kent.[5] An MoD reorganisation in 1991 saw RARDE replaced by the Defence Research Establishment and a further reorganisation in 1995 created a new umbrella organisation, the Defence Evaluation and Research Agency (DERA). Outside Northern Ireland, the lab has been the only centre capable of handling the full range of explosive forensic work. Most terrorist incidents on the mainland have therefore been automatically allocated to it, rather than the Home Office's Forensic Science Service.

RARDE's forensic team was presented as the best in the business. 'We're very good on the forensics,' an anonymous FBI investigator told reporters investigating Lockerbie, 'but the Brits are very, very good.'[6] As so often in the Lockerbie case, however, the truth was rather more complex.

In 1974, RARDE scientists gave evidence in the case of Judith Ward, who was convicted of three IRA bombings, including the M62 coach attack which claimed the lives of 12 British soldiers and their relatives. The RARDE team maintained their tests had established, beyond any doubt, the presence of nitro-glycerine on Ward's hands and in the caravan she had been living in. Douglas Higgs, who had been in charge of the forensic lab since November 1973, told the court that the tests were absolutely specific for nitro-glycerine; there was no possibility of innocent contamination.

In 1991 Judith Ward successfully appealed against her conviction, and in doing so completely demolished the credibility of the forensic tests. More worryingly, the RARDE team's own notebook, which had been concealed from the defence at the time of the trial and not disclosed until the appeal was being prepared, showed they were in possession of evidence which demonstrated the opposite of what they had claimed in court. For example, they knew that the forensic tests on the supposedly incriminating samples produced results outside the range which they themselves had determined was conclusive for nitro-glycerine. Tests they had carried out the previous year demonstrated that a chemical present in a range of commodities, such as shoe polish, could produce similar results to nitro-glycerine, yet this was also kept from the defence. So too was the fact that during the trial itself they had conducted tests which demonstrated the possibility of innocent nitro-glycerine contamination among people who had come into contact with debris from an explosion. Given that Ward had been present at the aftermath of one of the three bombings, this was a vital omission.

Summing up their failure to disclose this evidence, the Appeal Court judges said that Higgs and his senior colleagues 'took the law into their own hands' and 'knowingly placed a false and distorted scientific picture before the jury'. The judges concluded: 'Forensic scientists employed by the government may come to see their function as helping the police. They may lose their objectivity. That is what must have happened in this case.'[7]

RARDE's role in the Lockerbie investigation was first described in detail by David Leppard in *On the Trail of Terror*. Dr Thomas Hayes, in charge of the Lockerbie investigation until his retirement in 1990, was described by Leppard as 'probably one of the best forensic explosives experts in the world'. Having joined RARDE in 1975, by 1985 he had become the head of the forensic explosives laboratory, known as EC3. His deputy in the Lockerbie investigation was Allen Feraday, who had 34 years' experience in forensic explosives. After Hayes retirement, Feraday took over the top spot in the forensic lab division, which had been renamed EC5. Neither Hayes nor Feraday were involved in the Judith Ward case, but neither were they strangers to miscarriages of justice.

Hayes had joined RARDE shortly before the Judith Ward case and, although only 27 at the time, was more qualified than his senior colleagues. Such an injection of expertise should have helped safeguard against a repeat of the Judith Ward case, but within a few months the lab contributed to a similar fiasco.

In December 1974, seven Irish people living in London were arrested on suspicion of having been involved in bomb-making for the IRA. Most of the seven were members of the Maguire family, whose relative Gerard Conlon was one of the so-called Guildford Four, who were later wrongly convicted for the Guildford and Woolwich pub bombings a few weeks earlier. The police fingered the Maguire Seven after false confessions by Conlon and another of the Guildford Four, Paul Hill. Bewildered and intimidated, both implicated Conlon's aunt Annie Maguire in the bombing.[8]

Despite intense police pressure, the Maguires never confessed to the crime. The police were unable to find the bombs they had allegedly prepared, or components used in their manufacture. Sniffer dogs failed to detect explosives and 45 swabs taken from various surfaces around the house tested negative for explosive residues. The only evidence against the seven were the results of tests, carried out by a RARDE team led by Douglas Higgs and including Dr Hayes, on swabs taken from their hands and fingernails. According to the scientists, these tests demonstrated that the accused had knowingly handled nitro-glycerine. Under cross-examination, they were adamant that the tests could not confuse any other substance with nitro-glycerine and that innocent contamination was impossible.

Following the successful appeal of the Guildford Four, the government ordered an inquiry into the two cases, to be headed by Sir John May. Over the course of the inquiry, the Maguires' legal team were able to expose a catalogue of failures to disclose evidence which would have helped the defence at the original trial. The evidence included a second set of tests on the hand and fingernail swabs which were negative, and experiments which demonstrated that the tests used on the swabs were not specific to nitro-glycerine. RARDE also acknowledged that the forensic explosives lab was contaminated with nitro-glycerine – a fact which could have accounted for the Maguire's positive results. As with the Judith Ward case, the team had conducted tests which showed that innocent contamination was feasible, but these too were kept from the defence.

David Leppard's *On the Trail of Terror* describes Hayes's colleague Allen Feraday as 'the archetype of the secret scientist'. Leppard adds:

> He travels to work in a hire car which he changes each week. Even some of his closest colleagues do not know where he lives; just that he has a wife and family and that they live somewhere in the south of England.

Such secrecy, Leppard explains, was necessitated by Feraday's involvement in high-profile IRA cases, including the 1982 Hyde Park bombing which killed four Household Cavalrymen and the SAS shooting of three IRA members in Gibraltar, in 1988. Leppard's readers were no doubt left with the impression that Feraday had brought a great forensic talent to bear on these cases. In fact, in these and other cases, his evidence was later exposed as fundamentally flawed. Although he was at the forensic lab for much longer than Hayes, Feraday has no academic qualifications. Indeed, his only formal qualification is a Higher National Certificate in Applied Physics and Electronics – essentially a technician's qualification – obtained in 1962.[9]

Irishman Gilbert 'Danny' MacNamee was convicted for the Hyde Park bombing in 1987, after the court was told he was the master bomb-maker behind the attack. The conviction rested on prosecution evidence that his fingerprints were found on masking tape in two IRA arms caches and on a battery in an unexploded bomb. MacNamee had worked in an electrical store in Dundalk, the co-owner of which had been convicted of an IRA offence in France. The defence argued that tape or batteries innocently handled by MacNamee could subsequently have been used by terrorists.

In order to link him to the bombing, the prosecution relied on three assertions by Feraday. The first was that an electronic fragment found in Hyde Park was from a circuit board which had been designed specifically, and solely, for use as an amplifying circuit for a radio-controlled bomb. In other words, whoever made the circuit board could not have designed it for any other purpose. The second was that the 'artwork' on the Hyde Park circuit board matched a circuit board found in one of the arms caches. The third was that the same person had made both boards.[10]

Experts who subsequently scrutinised Feraday's evidence described all three claims as nonsense. They pointed out that the pattern on the circuit boards in the arms cache showed that they were of quite a general type and could therefore be utilised for a number of different functions. Even if MacNamee had built both circuit boards, there was nothing to say that it was him who subsequently either fitted the circuit to the board or built the bomb. The makers of the board, the circuit and the bomb could very easily have been three different people. To claim the similarities in the circuit board meant they were made by the same person was the equivalent of claiming that two knitted garments were made by the same person because they were based on the same pattern. The quality and design of the boards found in the arms caches varied considerably, with the soldering by and large of a quality to be expected of a complete novice rather than a master bomb-maker. Since he had a degree in electrical engineering, MacNamee would have been capable of a much tidier job.

Much of the ground for Feraday's evidence was laid by Thomas Hayes, who testified that two pieces of circuit board recovered from the scene of the Hyde Park bombing were from the same circuit board and that this circuit board was part of the bomb's detonation mechanism. The first fragment was found on the day of the explosion; the second a few days later, and further away. The defence argued that the board was of a type found in numerous household items and pointed out that no tests were conducted on the fragments for the presence of explosive.

The court was told that analysis of the fragments was carried out by Hayes's late RARDE colleague Walter Elliott and that Hayes was simply testifying to the accuracy of his findings. During cross-examination by Richard Ferguson QC, the following exchange took place.

> Q. You assume that it is an amplifier circuit board?
> A: I do.
> Q. Why do you assume that?
> A: Because in all respects, by comparison with a known amplifier circuit board, it matches.
> Q. Yes, but it could also match a number of other boards performing different functions?
> A: If you say it can I will accept that. I am not an expert in electronics.[11]

Presumably over the next three years Hayes attained expertise in electronics, because he told David Leppard he had been able, in a matter of minutes, to accurately match the fragment of the timer found at Lockerbie to the MST-13 timer found in Dakar. [12]

After 11 years of wrongful imprisonment, Danny MacNamee's conviction was finally overturned in December 1998.

The Gibraltar shootings was one of the most controversial episodes in the history of the Northern Ireland troubles. It was alleged that, at the time of the killings, the three IRA members were planning the imminent detonation of a huge car bomb. It soon emerged that the trio were unarmed and that no car bomb had been brought onto Gibraltar. When a Thames TV programme, *Death on the Rock*, produced witnesses who suggested that the three had actually been trying to surrender when they were shot, Margaret Thatcher's government was faced with a major scandal.

On 1 May 1988 the official account of the shootings took a significant twist, when an article by David Leppard's *Sunday Times* colleague James Adams revealed that the SAS team believed their targets were carrying 'sophisticated remote control devices' capable of detonating a bomb in Gibraltar from Spain. In fact, the unit were carrying no remote control devices, but the story provided the SAS with a justification for the shooting. At the inquest into the killings, Feraday confidently asserted that the type of remote control devices used by the IRA would be capable of triggering the non-existent bomb. On a split decision, the jury eventually found that the killings were lawful, thus saving the government a major embarrassment.

Dr Michael Scott of Dublin City University was called to give evidence by the lawyer representing the families of the IRA team. Having gained a BSc in electrical engineering, an MSc in electronic engineering and a PhD in control engineering, he was vastly more qualified than Feraday. He was surprised by the RARDE man's evidence. Tests had shown that it was possible to transmit a weak voice signal between the two places where the shootings occurred and where the suspect car was parked. Feraday claimed it was therefore also possible to transmit a much stronger encoded tone signal, of the type used by the IRA for the remote detonation of bombs. In Scott's view, anyone with an elementary knowledge of radio communications would know this to be nonsense. The only means by which the non-existent car bomb could have been activated was via the vehicle's aerial, a bent piece of wire 30 inches long. Feraday told the inquest that the aerial could receive a clear enough signal from a remote control device if the frequencies were matched up. In fact, Scott pointed out, the orientation and mounting of the aerial would not be optimal at any frequency.

Feraday asserted that it would have been easy for the IRA unit to have activated a remote control device if they had been arrested, rather than killed, by the SAS. In fact, to use the type of device in question, they would have had to switch on the transmitter and a tone encoder, set the correct frequency using three thumb switches, put three other switches in the correct position and finally press the transmit button. It would have been possible to set up the device in advance so that only the transmit button need be pressed, but in these circumstances a slight jolt of the handset could have activated the bomb, in which case it would be irresponsible to shoot the suspects down.[13]

It was not only in high-profile IRA cases that Feraday had given dubious evidence. In two unrelated but remarkably similar cases in 1982 and 1985, he helped to convict two businessmen, John Berry and Hasan Assali, on terrorist conspiracy charges. Both men had successful businesses manufacturing electronic equipment, including components for the defence industry. In each instance the prosecution centred on electronic timing devices, which the two men had offered to supply to Middle Eastern customers. In both cases, Feraday asserted categorically that the timers in question were designed specifically for terrorist purposes, and that there was no conceivable innocent use to which they could be put. Berry was sentenced to eight years in prison and Assali to nine.

In September 1993, John Berry took his case to the Court of Appeal. His legal team lined up four expert witnesses to demolish the credibility of Feraday's testimony. Upholding the appeal, Lord Justice Taylor singled out Feraday for special criticism, saying that his evidence had been expressed in terms that were 'extremely dogmatic . . . uncompromising and incriminating'.

Hasan Assali was born in Libya but has lived in the United Kingdom since 1965. He was charged under the 1883 Explosives Substances Act, namely making electronic timers, and convicted in 1985. In seeking to have the conviction overturned, his legal team lined up an equally impressive team of experts, who made a devastating critique of Feraday's evidence. Berry and Assali met in prison and Assali went on to help Berry's successful appeal.

One of the forensic experts used by both men was former British Army electronic warfare officer, Owen Lewis. In a report on the Assali case, Owen Lewis stated:

> It is my view that Mr Feraday's firm and unwavering assertion that the timing devices in the Assali case were made for and could have no other purpose than the triggering of IEDs is most seriously flawed, to the point that a conviction which relied on such testimony must be open to grave doubt.

A number of other scientists, all vastly more qualified than Feraday, concurred with Lewis. A report by Michael Moyes, a highly qualified electronics engineer and former Squadron Leader in the RAF, concluded: 'There is no evidence that we are aware of that timers of this type have ever been found to be used for terrorist purposes. Moreover, the design is not suited to that application.' Moyes was also struck by the similarities in the Berry and Assali cases, in terms of the Feraday evidence.

Assali's case is currently before the Criminal Cases Review Commission (CCRC), the body entrusted with reviewing alleged miscarriages of justice. It has been there since 1997. Assali believes that his case might have been delayed deliberately, as he stated to the Home Secretary, Jack Straw, in a fax in February 1999: 'I feel that my case is being neglected or put on the back burner for political reasons.' Assali believed that if his case was overturned on appeal during the Lockerbie trial, it would have been a further huge blow to Feraday's credibility and ultimately the Crown's case against the Libyans.

Feraday and Hayes have not been corrupt and they have undoubtedly helped convict guilty people as well as innocent. The same can be said of Tom Thurman, the main FBI forensic expert involved in Lockerbie, but, as with Feraday and Hayes, his work has also come in for criticism. In an interview with the authors in 1999, Oliver 'Buck' Revell described Thurman as 'Currently one of the most capable bomb explosives experts in the world.'

Thurman came fully to the public's attention when he was named

'Person of the Week' on 15 November 1991, on the American TV network ABC. During the programme, Thurman described his feelings at identifying the circuit board fragment: 'When that identification was made of the timer, I knew that we had it. Absolutely positive euphoria, just euphoric. I can't describe it any better than that. I was on cloud nine.' From photographs shown on the programme, Thurman's task must have been made easier by the fact that the letters M-E-B-O, though partially erased, were legible on the circuit board. The programme stated that the fragment was found 18 months after the explosion. It sang the praises of Thurman, describing him as 'a man with an eye for the smallest detail'.

Others, more familiar with Thurman's work, have a different opinion of him. Frederick Whitehurst, a former chemist with the FBI, had so many doubts about the handling of evidence in the FBI's laboratory that he took the matter up with the Department of Justice. In an interview with the authors, Whitehurst expressed grave doubts about Thurman. According to Whitehurst, a PhD chemist and lawyer, 'I was writing very in-depth technical reports and he [Thurman] took it upon himself to alter my reports. He changed the meaning significantly in a number of these reports.'

The Inspector General's report backs up Whitehurst's view. It states that it found that 'he [Thurman] had been routinely altering the reports of scientists working in the FBI Explosives Unit' – the unit where he made the Lockerbie match in 1990. Fifty-two of the reports, which he supervised between 1987 and 1992, were reviewed by the investigation. Only 20 had not been altered by Thurman, and in 13 of the reports he had changed the meaning of what had been written, resulting, albeit unintentionally, in a bias to the prosecution case.

Whitehurst went further, saying: 'A colleague of mine testified before the Senate that over 90 per cent of the reports that were altered were altered in such a way that it would make a prosecutor's case stronger.' Confidential memos, discovered during the making of the BBC Scotland documentary *Silence Over Lockerbie*, contained disturbing comments on Thurman.

> It is clear that SSA Thurman does not understand the scientific issues involved with the interpretation and significance of explosives and explosives residue composition. He therefore should realise this deficiency and differentiate between his personal opinions and scientific fact. An expert's opinion should be based upon objective, scientific findings and be separated from personal predilections and biases.

The memo concluded with the following comment:

> SSA Thurman acted irresponsibly. He should be held accountable.
> He should be disciplined accordingly.

Despite his 'Person of the Week' status, Thurman left the FBI and presently teaches courses at Eastern Kentucky University, lecturing police officers on procedures at bomb and explosion scenes.

13. VENDETTAS

If the official story of Lockerbie was correct and the tales of CIA-protected drug-running were nonsense, why were so many people claiming the contrary? Ever since the bombing, journalists and Pan Am's lawyers, as well as their investigator Juval Aviv, claimed to have found evidence that gave the lie to the official story. The US authorities could dismiss the journalists as incompetent, misguided or Libyan stooges, but the lawyers and Aviv were a different matter; so too were their sources, such as Lester Coleman and Joe Miano. If the official version was correct, they were either wicked pranksters or had conspired, along with US Aviation Underwriters (USAU) – which managed the airline's insurance – to concoct a story to get the airline off the hook for its faulty security. The US DoJ initiated a grand jury investigation of this allegation, led by the US Attorney's office in the Eastern District of New York, but this failed to find the evidence necessary to bring charges. Nevertheless, in May 1995 separate and unrelated charges were brought against both Aviv and USAU's president, John Brennan.

But were the charges unrelated? Well, not exactly. In fact, both sets of charges closely mirrored the allegations levelled against Aviv and Brennan in the Lockerbie case. Aviv was accused of fabricating an investigative report for a client in order to secure further business for himself, and Brennan was accused of fraudulently shifting insurance liability for an air disaster away from one of USAU's clients. Equally tellingly, both indictments concerned alleged offences that had occurred years earlier, and both were issued within days of the broadcast of Allan Francovich's high-profile Lockerbie documentary *The Maltese Double Cross*, which rejected the official version and presented new evidence to support the story posited by Aviv and others.

As they unfolded, the various criminal cases only served to strengthen suspicions that the US government was desperate to conceal the truth about Flight 103 and was engaged in a coordinated and well-resourced effort to discredit those who challenged the official version of the disaster.

The case against Aviv centred on a security survey he had carried out for the General Electric company in 1991.[1] The company intended to take senior executives on a cruise around four of the US Virgin Islands, and hired Aviv to assess the possible dangers of the trip and provide a security plan. The company decided not to implement Aviv's security plan, but seemed happy with his report and paid him $20,000. The FBI received no complaint from General Electric about Aviv's work, but four years after the event its agent, David Edward, claimed to have gathered evidence that he had acted fraudulently. Edward was assigned to the FBI's Melville, Long Island office in the Eastern District of New York, but Aviv's company, Interfor, was based in Manhattan, in the Southern District of New York and General Electric was based in another state entirely, Connecticut. Edward alleged in an affidavit that Aviv's report had lied in claiming that he had met with five Virgin Islands officials, and an FBI agent, whilst conducting the survey, and that he had falsely ascribed statements to two of those people. The purpose of Aviv's report, the indictment claimed, was to:

> Defraud [General Electric] into believing that Aviv had done substantial work to support both his fee and the conclusion since the report, and thereby to induce [General Electric] to retain Aviv and Interfor to implement a costly security plan outlined by Aviv in the report.

The relevant passage of Aviv's report read:

> I met with Governor Alexander Farrelly, Lt Governor Derek Hodge, Administrator Harold Robinson, Police Commissioner Milton Frett, Police Lt Noel Martin, and local FBI agent Kevin Dooley. Lt Martin reports that [St Thomas's 200 police officers] are demoralised, due to a recent new concept which takes them out of their patrol cars and has them walking their beats.

Edward said that all six men had been shown a videotape of Aviv, and that each stated they did not recognise him and had never met or spoken to him. He added that according to Israeli government documents, Aviv 'never worked for the intelligence community of Israel, nor was he ever connected to it'. Since the videotape had obviously been shown to the six men well after the event, it was hardly surprising that they would not remember a brief meeting. Aviv was adamant that the meeting had taken place. Moreover, in the case of Lt Martin he had documentary proof: not only did he still have a copy of Martin's business card, but he also had telephone records showing that some 15 calls had been made to Martin's office prior to Aviv's visit to the island. Aviv presented notes of the meeting with the officials, which were subsequently tested at an FBI laboratory and found to be genuine.

As for the statements attributed to Martin, Aviv had never claimed that they had been made to him personally. He could easily have read Martin's comments in the local press, or heard them from hotel staff.

Even if Aviv had lied, and had never had conversations with either of the two officers, it was the substance of the report, rather than its sources, that General Electric had bargained for. Had Aviv falsely claimed that Martin and Dooley had told him the island was perfectly safe, then the company would have had legitimate grounds for complaint. But instead the report had been cautious and responsible in its recommendations. Furthermore, Aviv had surveyed four islands, but the six officers named were all based on just one of these islands, St Thomas.

On 5 September 1995, Aviv's attorney, Gerald Shargel, filed a motion for the government's case to be dismissed on the grounds that the prosecution was vindictive. In a supporting affidavit, Shargel did not mince his words:

> I have been practising criminal defense work in the federal and state courts in New York for more than 25 years. In all my years of practice, I have never seen the resources of the FBI and the US Attorney's office devoted to such an insignificant, inconsequential, isolated four-year-old contract matter – a matter that, as discussed below, does not even amount to mail or wire fraud – as the indictment in this case represents.

He added:

> What in the world is the government doing sending FBI agents to the Caribbean to interview individuals as having met with Mr Aviv four years ago for a client who paid $20,000 for the work, never complained, [and] did not challenge Mr Aviv's conclusions? . . . We believe that the evidence points to a clear relationship between Mr Aviv's authoring of the Pan Am report and this mail fraud prosecution.

Shergal suggested it was no coincidence that the indictment was issued around the time of the British broadcast of *The Maltese Double Cross* and that it coincided with charges brought by the US Attorney's office in the Eastern District of New York against John Brennan. For Edward then to be involved in Aviv's prosecution, Shargal's motion claimed, was 'very unusual'.

It was clear that the Israeli government would never publicly acknowledge that Aviv worked for Mossad, but Shargel's motion nevertheless contained a startling revelation. Aviv had secretly been employed, it declared, by two US Federal government agencies, the Internal Revenue Service (IRS) and, ironically, the DoJ. Attached to the motion to dismiss was a copy of the agreement made with the FBI and the very same US Attorney's office in the Southern District of New York that was now prosecuting Aviv. The documents demonstrated that Aviv had agreed to provide information about terrorist threats to the president and other national security matters, on condition that his anonymity be guaranteed and that he would not be called upon to give evidence in any court case. The agreement was contingent upon his passing a lie detector test and that:

> No information will be sought from Aviv as to the details of his prior military and intelligence service for the State of Israel . . . and no information will be sought which may tend to incriminate Aviv under the security laws and regulations of the State of Israel.

It was clear from this passage that the FBI had little doubt about Aviv's background in Israeli intelligence. Indeed, it was clear that the FBI had only agreed to employ him after it had satisfied itself that he was no longer working on behalf of Israel. Shargel included pages from the report of the FBI's investigation, obtained under the Freedom of Information Act. Although heavily censored, it stated that the investigation 'has failed to reveal that Juval Aviv . . . is involved in any type of intelligence or espionage activities'. Also included was a page from another report which had obviously been prepared at around the same time. Under the heading 'Observations of Interviewing Agent', it stated: 'Subject impresses one as being knowledgeable in the area of international terrorism . . . Aviv was professional in his manner and did not appear to be trying to impress the interviewing agents.'

The revelations were sensational. For years Aviv had been portrayed as a con man who had fabricated his Israeli intelligence credentials, but here were documents which showed that two government agencies, including the one which was now pursuing the prosecution, accepted those credentials were genuine.

Forced onto the back foot, the prosecution played for time, but only succeeded in digging a bigger hole for themselves. A subsequent submission by Assistant US Attorney Christine H. Chung was condemned by Judge Louis Stanton as 'dishonest and not helpful'. By contrast, the judge described the defence's previous presentations on the issue of selective prosecution as 'unusually strong'.

On 18 December 1995 the *Wall Street Journal* ran a story about his case headed 'HE FORESAW DANGER IN CARIBBEAN JUNKET, AND A QUICK $20,000 – SECURITY CONSULTANT CHARGED GE TO CHECK TRIP'S SAFETY: NOW HE'S THE ONE CHARGED'. Most of the article was a faithful report of the government's case and implied that Aviv's report for General Electric had exaggerated the dangers of the trip in order to persuade the company to purchase additional security measures from him. Only at the end did the article mention Aviv's role in investigating Flight 103 and report Gerald Shargel's claim that the prosecution was part of a vendetta. The fact that General Electric had never complained about Aviv's work and that the FBI had dredged up a four-year-old case was never mentioned. Aviv maintains that since they were unable to beat him in the courts, his opponents hoped to do as much damage as possible to his reputation by having their case reproduced in a newspaper likely to be read by the majority of Aviv's corporate clients.

The newspaper article was not the only assault on Aviv's business. Early in 1996 he set up a Bermuda-registered asset search-and-recovery company called Interclaim Ltd with two partners, including New York-based international lawyer Martin Kenney, who specialised in serious financial crime. The plan was to utilise Kenney's legal skills and Aviv's investigative knowhow. A handful of distinguished legal and commercial figures from Britain and the US were lined up to become investors and members of the company's board of directors. They also approached an investment banking firm from the City of London and three major accountancy firms, all of whom were enthusiastic about Interclaim. Aviv was completely open with Kenney about the outstanding fraud charges, and Kenney conducted his own investigations into the allegations and into Aviv's background. In an affidavit produced for Aviv's case, he stated: 'I found the incongruity between the fact of the indictment and the quality and content of Mr Aviv's professional background, standing, and professional and client references to be remarkable.'

Suddenly, in May 1996, Kenney regretfully asked Aviv to step down from the company. According to Kenney's affidavit, the bankers, accountants, and at least one of the directors, had suddenly got cold feet and there was a danger that they would abandon the venture. The reason, he claimed, was that most of them had been warned by unnamed US government officials that Aviv was a man who was not to be touched.

When the fraud case finally came to trial in December 1996, Judge Louis Stanton told the court:

> The chronology of the investigation, the fact that it is resulting from
> no external complaint whatsoever, but simply internally within the

PFLP-GC leader Ahmed Jibril.
© PA

The apartment block in Neuss, Germany, where PFLP-GC members
Hafez Dalkamoni and Marwan Khreesat stayed in October 1988.
© American RadioWorks/MPR

Kalid Jaafar.
© Popper Foto

Investigator Juval Aviv.
© Interfor Inc.

Mary's House shop, Sliema, Malta, where the clothes that ended up
in the bomb suitcase were allegedly purchased.
© American RadioWorks/MPR

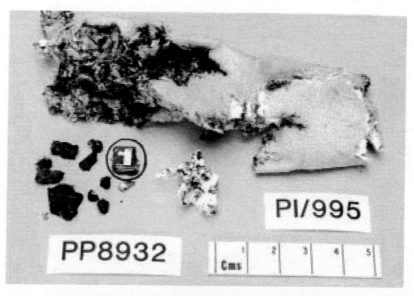

Handwritten worksheet from Frankfurt airport, one of the documents which, according to the Lockerbie prosecutors, showed that a bag was transferred on to Flight 103 from Air Malta flight KM 180.
Crown copyright

The charred fragment of a grey Slalom brand shirt (numbered PI/995) from which the crucial fragment of Mebo circuit board (cirded) was recovered.
Crown copyright

A sample Mebo MST-13 timer, the type allegedly used in the Lockerbie bomb.
Crown copyright

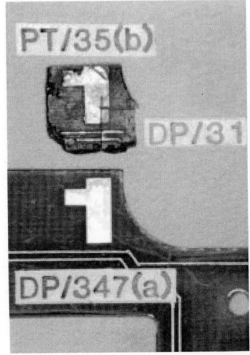

The fragment of circuit board (numbered PT/35(b)) next to a complete circuit board.
Crown copyright

Toshiba RT-SF16 radio-cassette recorder of the type that allegedly contained the Lockerbie bomb.
Crown copyright

A mock-up of the Lockerbie bomb built into a Toshiba RT-SF16.
Crown copyright

An artist's impression of the customer who allegedly bought the clothes from Mary's House that ended up in the bomb suitcase.
Crown copyright

9/13/89

Photograph of Abdel Basset Al-Megrahi, which shopkeeper Tony Gauci described as resembling the clothes purchaser.
Crown copyright

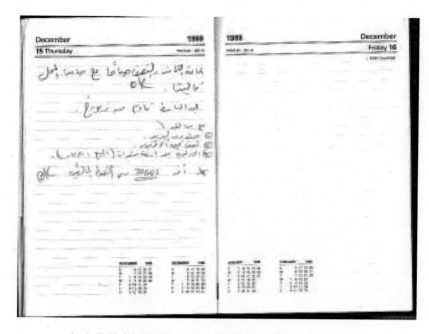

Lamin Khalifa Fhimahi's diary entry for 15 December 1988 referring to 'taggs'.
Crown copyright

The Libyan informant Majid Giaka,
prior to having cosmetic surgery.

Vincent Cannistraro, head of the CIA's intelligence investigation of Lockerbie, 1988 to 1990.

In
Remembrance
of
all victims of
Lockerbie Air Disaster
who died on
21st December 1988

Lockerbie memorial stone.
© American RadioWorks/MPR

FBI as far as any witness has testified, leads to an inference that it was generated from some other source . . .

The jury took no time in acquitting Aviv on all charges. Predictably, Aviv's acquittal was completely ignored by his detractors.

The case against John Brennan also concerned an incident which had occurred years earlier and was again generated by an FBI inquiry, rather than a complaint from an aggrieved party. In December 1987 43 people died after a former employee of the airline, USAir, smuggled a gun on board a Pacific Southwest Airlines flight from Los Angeles to San Francisco and shot the two pilots. USAir were in the process of acquiring Pacific Southwest at the time. Relatives of the dead brought negligence claims against USAir, Los Angeles Airport and Ogden Allied Corporation, the security company responsible for pre-boarding screening at the airport.

Brennan's company, USAU, managed the insurance for United States Aircraft Insurance Group (USAIG), a consortium of insurance companies which pooled their resources to insure aviation-related risks. USAU did not itself provide insurance, but rather wrote insurance policies, collected premiums, arranged reinsurance, investigated losses and managed litigation.

At the time of the disaster, USAIG was the lead insurer for USAir and the sole insurer for Ogden Allied. USAir's risk had been fully reinsured, leaving no financial exposure for USAIG, but Ogden's risk was only partially reinsured, which left USAIG with a potential payout of $7.5 million. All of the cases were settled out of court, with USAU having responsibility for evaluating relative liability and apportioning the settlements among the various parties. USAU concluded that USAir bore 100 per cent of the liability and all the parties accepted this assessment.

The indictment alleged that Brennan had fraudulently attempted to shift full responsibility for the crash from the security company onto the airline, in order to save its client, USAIG, from paying out.[2] The core of the government's case was that USAU had a conflict of interest, which it had illegally failed to disclose to USAir, its co-insurer and one of its reinsurers. As co-defendants, Brennan and USAU argued that they were under no legal obligation to make the disclosure. Each side was able to cite New York insurance industry case law to support their case.

The case finally came to court in May 1997 and after a seven-week trial which largely revolved around complex legal interpretations, Brennan and USAU were each found guilty on all 43 counts of mail fraud. Brennan was sentenced to 57 months' imprisonment and a $100,000 fine, and USAU was fined $20.6 million.

The defence successfully argued that the sentences should be stayed pending an appeal. The main thrust of that appeal was that the so-called rule of lenity should apply. This rule in effect gives defendants the benefit of the doubt in cases such as this, in which the relevant law was ambiguous. The appellants also argued on the issue of the trial's venue, pointing out that the Sixth Amendment to the US Constitution protects a defendant's right to be tried in the 'district wherein the crime shall have been committed'. USAU was based in the Southern District of New York and the air crash had occurred in California. Not a single piece of the allegedly fraudulent mail was sent from, or received in, the Eastern District of New York where the case was tried, yet the trial judge had instructed the jury that the government need only prove that the mailings had passed through the Eastern District to prove its case. The fact that the indictment emanated from that district, John Brennan believes, was a clear indication it was a selective and vindictive prosecution designed to discredit him and, by extension, the allegations that the government had covered up the truth about Flight 103.

In hearing the appeal in November 1999, the circuit court chose not to rule on the rule-of-lenity point (perhaps recognising that to have done so would have involved sorting out over a century's worth of inconsistent case law) and concentrated instead on the issue of venue. It accepted the appellant's claim that the trial was unconstitutional and duly overturned the conviction.

Many considered that Brennan and USAU had got off on a technicality, but a senior lawyer commented in the *New York Law Journal* that the venue issue 'rarely commands sufficient interest in the Court of Appeals to lead to the reversal of criminal convictions'. Indeed, in delivering its judgment the court revealed serious misgivings about the government's case, which, it said, appeared in a number of respects to be 'seriously problematic'.

Brennan avoided prison, but Lester Coleman was not so fortunate. In October 1996, after almost six years on the run, the former DIA and DEA agent finally returned to the US to face the outstanding passport fraud and perjury charges. On arrival he was arrested and remanded by Judge Thomas Platt to New York's Metropolitan Detention Centre (MDC). The same judge had presided over the Pan Am litigation, in which Coleman had provided the 1991 affidavit that was the subject of the perjury charges.

While in prison, Coleman developed a cancerous tumour on his collarbone. He claims he repeatedly requested medical treatment, which was not forthcoming. His case was taken up by attorney Vivian Shevitz, who agreed to work without a fee. On 12 January 1997 she visited Coleman and witnessed the oozing growth and his T-shirt, covered in blood.[3] He was eventually operated on nine days later, but was returned to jail the next day and claimed not to have been visited by the MDC's medical staff for the next 16 days. On 6 February, he was taken to hospital accompanied by two US marshals. Shevitz subsequently spoke to both marshals who, she reported, were disturbed by what they had witnessed. One described a foul odour emanating from behind a dirty bandage, which, when removed, revealed a suppurating wound resembling a piece of meat.[4]

In March 1997, after five months in the MDC, Coleman was released and placed under house arrest. The following September, suffering from post-traumatic stress disorder, and with the threat of a lengthy prison sentence hanging over him, Coleman was offered and accepted a plea bargain agreement. In return for the promise that he would not return to prison, he agreed to plead guilty to the perjury charges and admit that he had concocted the claims in his 1991 affidavit, in the Pan Am civil action. On 11 September 1997, he appeared before Judge Platt at the Federal court in Uniondale, Long Island and pleaded guilty to five counts of perjury. Sentencing was delayed, but he was allowed to walk free.

After a month spent recuperating with his family, Coleman landed a job on a talk radio station in Lexington, Kentucky, presenting a programme that focused on exposing government misconduct and corruption. He interviewed many guests, most of whom had something critical to say about the Federal or local governments.

The sentencing hearing took place on 15 May 1998. Judge Platt sentenced him to the amount of time already served, plus three years' supervised release and a fine of $30,000. One of the conditions of release was that he did not speak about his case on the radio. Protesting that his constitutional right to free speech had been violated, Coleman filed an appeal, demanding that the sentence be quashed. In May 1999 the appeal court ruled that Judge Platt had indeed violated Coleman's civil rights.

The New York perjury case was, of course, not the only indictment hanging over Coleman on his return to the US. There were also the Chicago federal passport fraud charges which had originally caused him to flee the country. As with the perjury charges, he opted to enter a plea agreement, resulting in a similar prison sentence as the New York case, to run concurrently. The deal allowed him to go free on supervised release.

A few months into Coleman's stint as talk show host, he and all the other on-air personalities were let go of to make way for nationally syndicated programmes. Following that, Coleman had odd jobs, including an associate professorship in the Journalism Department of Fugazzi College, and started doing some investigative work for a man named James Cormney regarding his son's criminal case. His investigation revealed that some of the witnesses had exaggerated their credentials. Coleman's investigation forced the police department to release some of the relevant documents, after appealing to the state attorney general. These events were played up in the media, and Coleman was interviewed on local television shows regarding his investigation. None of it was favourable to the police.

Around this time a website was set up which, among other things, appealed for financial donations to help support Coleman and his family. He claims that in mid-1999 he was visited by an individual who told him he had several cheques he wished to deposit into Coleman's bank account. They were all endorsed by this individual rather than by Coleman, but were deposited into Coleman's account. In addition, two cheques drawn on foreign banks, which Coleman claimed were sent via the website, were deposited into his landlord's account and a further cheque, which he received in an envelope from Europe. All of these cheques turned out to be fraudulent.

Coleman was once again arrested. Searches of his briefcase and home revealed a number of forged cheques from banks throughout the world along with other allegedly forged documents, including a passport and birth certificate. He was charged with 42 counts of Criminal Possession of a Forged Document, second degree. During the course of the trial, the charges were reduced to 36. He was convicted on all counts and sentenced to ten years in prison, suspended pending five years' probation.

Since it was a condition of his earlier supervised release from Chicago that he be detained if arrested for another crime, in the wake of the Kentucky conviction Coleman was re-arrested and transferred from state to Federal custody. A judge in Fayette County Federal Court released him without bond on the promise that he appear in Chicago Federal Court at a future date, but the following day Judge Thomas Platt issued a no-bail warrant for him and he was arrested and transported to New York to appear before him. Platt ruled that he had violated the supervised release and sentenced him to ten months in prison. He was then transferred on to Chicago, where the judge also sentenced him for ten months to run concurrent with the New York sentence.

Coleman was originally due to be released on 17 September 2000, but according to Federal Board of Prisons documents, good behaviour and other accumulated credits meant his release should have been brought forward to July 2000. But July came and went and on 16 September 2000 he began to be transferred around the country. He was in Oklahoma for a few days and on 22 September he was in Atlanta, Georgia. According to his Kentucky lawyer, he was kept in solitary confinement and was only allowed to make two telephone calls a week, and only allowed out of his cell for around two hours a week. Coleman was finally released on 7 December 2000, vowing to appeal his conviction and threatening a $100 million civil action against Lexington police and various federal agents.

Coleman's fellow former DEA employee Joe Miano also found himself facing criminal charges. Miano had kept in contact with Juval Aviv, to whom he had first spoken in 1989 following the leak of the Interfor Report. In June 1992, Aviv offered him a job. Miano declined, but on 15 September that year he learned that his bank records had been requested by a federal grand jury.

> It took me a week to find out what was going on.

He later recalled:

> I contacted a prosecutor's office and arranged a meeting to discuss the matter. On 22 September, I walked into an office in the US Customs Services where I was confronted by two FBI agents, two DEA agents and two agents of the US Treasury.

Miano believes the investigation was started when a colleague reported the job offer from Aviv. Using his friendship with Aviv, the colleague secretly taped conversations with Miano asking him if he was afraid of getting into trouble for giving Aviv information.

> I was not afraid of getting into trouble, because I had not given Aviv anything.

Miano insists:

> When he asked me why I was not afraid, I spoke correctly but probably too exactly for the investigators to understand what they heard on the tape. I told him that there was nothing to be afraid of since I had not given him anything written that could be used as proof. This was misunderstood and taken as an admission that I had given Aviv information verbally.

Miano agreed to help the government go after Aviv. He wore a microphone during a meeting with Aviv and made several phone calls, which were monitored. Finally he attempted to send Aviv sensitive documents, which, had Aviv accepted, would have landed him in trouble. In the event Aviv refused and severed all contact with Miano, but according to Miano, this merely convinced the investigators that he had tipped off Aviv about the investigation. He says:

> They were almost schizophrenic about the whole thing. First it was a case against me. Then they would say it was all about Pan Am 103. I recall very vividly a Federal Government official telling me: 'Joe, this is not about you. It is about Pan Am 103.' I was shocked.

Miano cooperated with the government throughout the investigation into Aviv, reasoning that his innocence would become apparent once the facts were known. He admits today that he was naïve: 'I was trying to do my job – to go the extra mile and work on the Pan Am case to help find the truth.'

By the autumn of 1993, the pressure of the investigation had begun to tell on Miano. He was reassigned to duties in the Financial Crimes Enforcement Network (FinCEN) training office, where he was subjected to the humiliation of having to sign in to enter his office every day. Depressed and certain that his government career was in ruins, in January 1994 he found a position with a humanitarian organisation doing relief work in the Balkans, and went to work in Belgrade. 'The relief was immediate,' he says. 'I was working and living in a police state, but I felt safer and freer than I had in over a year.'

In June 1994, Miano was summoned back to the US for questioning. He contacted Kenneth Mundy, a high-profile defence lawyer, best known for having represented Washington DC mayor Marion Barry in his drug trial a few years earlier. Mundy had the ear of the press and, according to Miano, his involvement in the case caused the government to rethink its strategy. He was questioned twice by a team of government agents, then told he could return to his job in Serbia.

Miano's relief was short-lived. He learned soon after that Mundy had dropped dead from a heart attack. His contract in Serbia expired, and he returned once again to the United States to find himself accused of a variety of felonies. The government reasoned that when he had continued working on the Pan Am case without explicit authorisation, it amounted to personal business. Thus, each time he signed his time card for pay, the government reasoned that he had acted fraudulently by claiming for hours that he had worked while not on government business.

Miano admits:

> I was scared. My job description had said I could work
> independently, pursue leads and gather intelligence. Some people at
> FinCEN were interested in what I was finding. I thought I was
> doing my job. But all they had to do was say that I was not
> authorised to do what I did and it would be a gamble with a jury.

In November 1995, he accepted a plea bargain deal which involved him
pleading guilty to two misdemeanours: the unlawful disclosure of sensitive
law enforcement information (talking to Aviv) and theft of government
property (the theft being the act of looking at information on the computer
terminal he used to make his enquiries). The government promised to
mention his cooperation in the investigation and to ask the judge to make
a downward departure from the sentencing guidelines, which called for a
three- to six-month prison sentence. In the event he was given a 30-day jail
sentence and agreed to pay $100,000 over five years, plus a further $11,567
in fines, his incarceration and electronic monitoring costs, and legal fees of
around $70,000.

Miano has since left the US to live in Europe. He remains bitter about
his experience:

> I was trying to be the best intelligence analyst I could be. I kept
> seeing things that disturbed me about the government's case and
> would not quit. I had taken an oath to defend the United States
> against all enemies – foreign and domestic – and it seemed to me
> that someone was subverting or attempting to subvert justice in the
> Pan Am 103 case.

Another to suffer a government vendetta was Dr William Chasey, a highly
successful Washington DC lobbyist.[5] Unlike Juval Aviv, John Brennan, Lester
Coleman and Joe Miano, he had no reason to doubt his government's account
of the Lockerbie bombing. The ultimate establishment figure, the former
Marine Corps officer was a conservative Republican by instinct. After 22 years
in the game, he had many influential contacts in the government and his
clients included some of America's largest corporations. In 1992 he took on
what, for him, was a slightly unusual contract, with an American company
called International Communications Management (ICM). ICM had been
hired by the government of Libya to help normalise relations with the US in
the wake of the Lockerbie indictments and the resulting UN sanctions.

When he was first approached about the assignment Chasey felt uneasy, but, on reflection, decided that the assignment needn't necessarily involve acceptance of Libya's innocence. In any case, the US did business with plenty of the world's more unsavoury regimes. Chasey agreed, on condition that everything be played by the book. Under US law, anyone representing a foreign government in this way must register as a foreign agent. If the assignment was in breach of the UN sanctions, he assumed that the DoJ would deny his registration. It did not, and he became registered as foreign agent number 4221.

Over the coming weeks Chasey met with representatives of the Libyan regime, who assured him that the American government had deliberately covered up the truth about Lockerbie. He didn't believe them, but accepted that they deserved a fair hearing on Capitol Hill. Before he was able to make any headway, his world fell apart.

On 3 December 1992, the US government's Office of Foreign Assets Control (OFAC) issued him with a formal order to stop work on the contract. He was told that it was in breach of UN sanctions and that he would be liable to criminal charges. Chasey was bemused; if the contract was illegal, why had he been allowed to register as a foreign agent? Nevertheless, he agreed to cooperate with OFAC and felt sure that everything could be sorted out amicably.

Two weeks later, as he was about to leave for a Christmas skiing vacation, his wife Virginia phoned, panicking, to tell him that their bank account had been frozen. He immediately called OFAC, where an agent explained that the action had been taken because he had breached sanctions by accepting Libyan money. Chasey again pointed out that the money had come from an American company, ICM, but to no avail. OFAC refused to budge and the account remained frozen.

Chasey became convinced that he was under surveillance. 'Whenever I arrived in Washington, the FBI would greet me at the airport,' he later recalled. 'How could they have known my travel plans without monitoring my calls?' He also claims to have received anonymous phone calls in which a man with an Arab accent warned him: 'There are a lot of people who don't want this case reopened. If you want to stay alive, stay away from Pan Am 103.'

Eventually, in May 1994, OFAC fined Chasey $50,000. He was never allowed a hearing to put his case. By that time, his lobbying business had been badly hit. As with Juval Aviv, a number of clients were approached by the FBI and told that he was under investigation for fraud. In 1995 he finally wound down the company and got out of Washington. He lost his homes there and in California, and, at 55 years old, was forced to rebuild his life from scratch. With hindsight, Chasey believes his story demonstrates that the Libyans were right all along: 'They went after me because they were worried that I might stumble upon this almighty cover-up and tell my friends in Congress about it.'

Like Lester Coleman, Chasey was moved to write a book about his experiences. Called *Foreign Agent 4221: The Lockerbie Cover-Up*, it was launched in Washington on 22 April 1995. As he entered the city's airport to return home to California, there was another encounter with the FBI. An agent served him with a grand jury subpoena for all his business records dating back to 1989. He also questioned Chasey about the Oklahoma City bombing three days earlier. He asked if Chasey had any contact with the 'Libyans' and warned that he would be prosecuted if he failed to report any future contact with them. The book opened with a quote from George Washington: 'Government is not eloquence. It is not reason. It is a force. Like fire, a dangerous servant and a fearful master.' Chasey then added his own: 'I love my country, but I fear my government.' The sentiment would be shared by all those who probed the dark secrets of Flight 103.

14. THE CASE CRUMBLES

Innocent until proven guilty. It is the most sacred principle of criminal law, but in the Lockerbie case it was jettisoned from day one. On 14 November 1991 Abdel Basset Ali Al-Megrahi and Lamin Khalifa Fhimah were not only indicted for the bombing, but were also, in effect, tried and convicted. The British and American authorities willingly colluded with the process, letting it be known that they had a cast-iron case – the police had got the right men, end of story. The US State Department even issued 'fact sheets' outlining the evidence against the two men and the media on both sides of the Atlantic were quietly briefed that Lockerbie was Gadafy's revenge for America's 1986 air raids on Libya.

But it wasn't that straightforward. As so often in the past, when the 'irrefutable evidence' of Libyan involvement was held up to the light it was shown to be shot full of holes.

The entire official account hinged on the Maltese connection. The crucial documents from Frankfurt airport supposedly showed that an unaccompanied bag had been transferred from Air Malta flight KM180 to Pan Am 103, and clothes wrapped around the bomb were linked back to Mary's House in Sliema, where shopkeeper Tony Gauci supposedly identified Megrahi as the mystery clothes buyer.

Tony Gauci was one of the prosecution's star witnesses. The Scottish police must have been delighted when he told them he could remember the customer who bought the random assortment of clothes, but with each successive encounter with the shopkeeper their hearts must have gradually sank. Between September 1989 and February 1991 he gave a total of 19 statements and his brother Paul a further four. By the end of that period they were rendered weaker as witnesses against the two Libyans.[1]

Tony's first statement described the various items that had been bought by the mysterious customer. He listed the items as two pairs of trousers in sizes 34 in and 36 in, a 42 in-sized imitation Harris tweed jacket, three pairs of pyjamas, a woollen cardigan, a blue Babygro with a sheep's face design on the front and an umbrella. The order came to Maltese £76.50, which was paid for in cash. Tony said the customer left the clothes in the shop, leaving him to wrap them. He took with him only the umbrella, which he had bought because it had started to rain. A short while later the customer returned to collect the bundles. Gauci offered to take the parcels to his car, but the man declined, saying that he had a taxi waiting up the road. Following him to the door, Tony saw a white Mercedes taxi parked up the street, but he never actually saw the man get into it.

He could not remember the date of the purchase, saying that it was 'one day during the winter of 1988'. The only clue to the date was that it was on a day when his brother Paul had gone home to watch a football match. The time of the purchase he put at around 6.50 p.m., which he could remember because it was just before the shop closed at 7 p.m. Crucially, he was able to provide quite a good description of the customer. He was about six feet, not fat but with a large build, in particular a big chest and a large head. His overall appearance was smart and he was clean-shaven with dark hair, and wearing a dark suit. Tony believed he was a Libyan. He said he could distinguish between Libyans and Tunisians because Tunisians often started to speak French when they had been talking for a while. He was memorable because he seemed not to care about the size and colour of the clothes he bought, and chose things pretty much at random. Tony was clear that the customer 'has not been in the shop before or since'.

On 13 September 1989, Tony made three more statements. The first one followed a session during which he had sat down with Scottish and German police officers in an attempt to come up with a photofit picture of the customer. He said that the final photofit that the police came up with was 'as similar-looking to the man as I think I could get'. The next statement followed a similar session with an artist. Tony stated that with a few minor alterations to the age and hairstyle, the final artist's impression 'was a very close resemblance to the man I saw in the shop'. At the end of the statement he proclaimed, 'I cannot read English. I have had this statement read over to me and am happy with the content.'

In the third statement he described being shown a blue Babygro with a white lamb on the front by Detective Chief Inspector Harry Bell. He said it was exactly the same colour as the one bought by the mystery customer, except that one had just a sheep's head on it. He knew this to be the case because the lamb design only came in to the shop after the manufacturers stopped making the sheep's head design. He then stated that he remembered seeing the customer again just three months previously, on a road called the Strand in Sliema, sitting outside a bar called Tony's Bar. He was with three other people, all of whom Tony believed to be Libyans. He said that they ranged from about 55 to 60 years of age, and had slightly lighter skin than the customer. He did not explain why he had omitted this important detail from his earlier statements.

The following day, Tony gave another brief statement describing how the police showed him photographs and asked him to identify anyone who might resemble the customer. He said that one of the photographs showed someone similar, but about 20 years younger than the customer.

On 19 and 26 September he made two further statements about a cardigan bought by the customer, which was strange because the earlier statements hadn't mentioned a cardigan. In the 19 September statement he also recalled that the purchase was made midweek and added that it was before he had put up the Christmas decorations, which he generally did around 15 days before Christmas.

In another statement given on 26 September, Tony reported a dramatic development to the police. At 11.30 a.m. the previous day the mystery customer had returned to the shop while he was in there alone, this time buying dresses to fit a four-year-old child. With the memory fresh in his head, Tony still described the customer as around 50 years old, well built but not fat, and around six feet tall; in other words, considerably older and bigger than Abdel Basset Ali Al-Megrahi. He explained that he did not inform the police straight away because to have done so would have alerted his brother and father, both of whom were frightened and had urged him not to have anything to do with the police.

On 2 October the police showed Tony freeze-frame pictures of a man on a videotape. He told them the man was similar, but not identical, to the customer. Whereas the man on the tape was thin with a receding hairline, the customer had a fuller head of hair. Once again this suggested that Megrahi could not have been the customer, since he too had a receding hairline.

On 4 October Tony and his brother Paul were visited at the shop by Inspector Harry Bell. Paul gave Bell a pink Babygro and a child's dress similar to the one the mystery customer had bought on 25 September. The Babygro had a full lamb's body design on the front and was from the original order from the manufacturers. Tony therefore changed his story from his earlier statement, saying, 'I accept that the lamb motif on the front was probably the same style.' This was a curious turnaround from his earlier, very precise, statement that the lamb motif had superceded the sheep's head motif.

There was a gap of almost three months until Tony made his next statement. Dated 5 January, it was just a few lines long and followed a visit by the police to his shop, in which they purchased a few items of clothes, including two white shirts and a Slalom sweatshirt. The Slalom brand was to loom large in the case against the two Libyans. Tony demonstrated how he had wrapped up the clothes for the mystery customer and gave further details of the taxi which he assumed had picked up the customer. The taxi sign on the Mercedes was, he said, on the right above the windscreen, not inside the car, as he had previously reported. No explanation was offered as to why he could remember such a small detail, and why he should change his story. Curiously, the last line of the statement read: 'I don't want to sign anything.'

On 30 January 1990, the police again showed Tony fragments of bomb-damaged clothes. The statement, which was taken concurrently, indicated that he was able to identify some as having been sold by him, but most as not. Tony also reported that he believed he was being watched by a man from the Libyan Cultural Attaché's building, which was situated on the same street as the shop. It was hardly surprising that Libyan officials were taking an interest in the shop. The British press had, a few weeks earlier, revealed that a shopkeeper in Tower Road had identified the clothes purchaser as a Libyan and that investigators believed that person had been in direct contact with the bomb plotters.[2] Tony also said that three weeks previously he had spoken to a Libyan he had known for ten years, who told him he had seen his picture in a German newspaper. Tony believed that this man was one of the people in the photos he was asked to look at.

On 21 February Tony was shown yet more fragments of clothes, but although he believed he could identify them, he once again refused to sign anything. And there was another significant shift in his account. He now believed the man who bought the clothes had also bought some blankets from the shop in May 1987. On that occasion the customer had no transport, so Tony delivered them to him at the Hilton Hotel. Remarkably, Tony could remember his room number: 113. The statement also described how the police showed him a number of items of clothing. He was adamant he had never sold these clothes and that they were of a type he had never seen on the island. The clothes were, in fact, among those seized from Mohammed Abu Talb in Sweden.

Tony once again changed his story on 5 March 1990. This time he stated that when the mystery customer had returned to the shop to pick up his parcels of clothes he was in a taxi. Furthermore, having previously told the police that he did not see the customer get into the waiting taxi when he left with the two bundles, Tony now remembered seeing him get into the taxi and drive off. Asked why he did not mention this before, he could only offer the lame explanation that he thought he had been asked already.

Tony also recalled further details of the delivery of blankets to the Hilton Hotel. When he arrived at the hotel's reception, a member of staff rang the customer, who appeared shortly afterwards to collect the blankets. He now believed the incident may have taken place in June, rather than May, 1987.

More importantly, Tony recalled how six to eight weeks prior to giving the statement, his bother Paul had showed him an article from the British *Sunday Times* newspaper, which he believed to have been dated 5 November 1989. The article carried a picture of Mohammed Abu Talb and Paul had asked him if he believed that was the person who bought the clothes. Tony said he told his brother that he was not sure, but he told the police, 'I think the man looks like the same man as the one who bought the clothing.' If Abu Talb had been positively identified as the clothes buyer, it was hugely significant, but, like Al-Megrahi, Abu Talb was in his mid-thirties at the time of the purchase, and therefore around 15 years younger than the person described by Tony. Furthermore, he is not as well built as the person in Tony's description and, unbeknown to Tony, he had a pronounced limp. If the customer had, as Tony claimed, returned to the shop on 25 September 1989, Abu Talb was automatically ruled out, because he had been in custody in Sweden since the previous May.

It was almost six months later, on 31 August 1990, that Tony gave his next statement. The police had shown him a number of photographs, but he was unable to identify any of them as the clothes buyer. He maintained that although it was almost two years since the incident, he still felt he would be able to recognise the person in question. Tony again reported that he believed he was under surveillance by officials from the nearby Libyan Cultural Attache's building.

On 10 September 1990, Tony attended police headquarters to go over his previous statements and look at more photographs. In the statement, Tony confirmed his change of story about the motif on the Babygro. He also confirmed that it had been raining when the customer left the shop, which accounted for him buying the umbrella.

The police once again asked Tony to describe the customer. He did not go into the same detail as previously, saying only that he was a Libyan of about 50 years of age. He was still unable to pinpoint the date of purchase, but believed it to be at the end of November 1988. And Tony was now less sure that it was the same person who had bought the blankets in 1987. All he would say was that the person was 'similar'.

Yet again, Tony added crucial new details to his account. He now believed the mystery customer had bought two shirts as well as the clothes described previously. One was beige and the other blue-and-white striped, and both were made by Slalom. He had remembered this a couple of weeks before, when clearing out boxes that had contained Slalom shirts. He never explained why this should have jogged his memory, when an earlier purchase of Slalom shirts by the police did not.

Shown a freeze-frame picture of Mohammed Abu Talb, Tony again would only say that he was 'similar' to the man who bought the clothing. He also picked out three other photographs of people who resembled the clothes buyer, listed in his statement as Salem Mohd Adbel Hadytaha, whose nationality was not indicated but whose date of birth was given as 2 April 1958; a Mr Khalil, whose other names were not given, but who was born in 1957 and held a Sudanese passport; and Ayad Salama Hussein Mustafa Abueweiner, a Palestinian passport holder, born on 10 July 1970. It was clear that none of them were the clothes buyer. Tony said that Hadytaha had similar facial features, but was otherwise not old enough; Khalil had similar hair, but not as bushy; and Abueweiner only had a similar hair style. He added, 'I have been shown many photographs over the last year, but I have never seen a photograph of the man who bought the clothing.' Tony had more luck recognising the Libyan officials who had been coming into the shop. Shown photographs, he was able to positively identify four of them.

Tony's final statement was given five months later, on 15 February 1991. Once again he was shown photographs, and once again he failed to positively identify the clothes buyer. One of the photographs, numbered eight, he described as 'similar' to the customer, but he said, 'The man . . . is in my opinion in his 30 years [sic]. He would perhaps have to look about ten years or more older and he would look like the man who bought the clothes.'

When the indictments were issued against the two Libyans, the accompanying US State Department 'fact sheet' claimed that, 'In February 1991, Al-Maqrahi [sic] was described as resembling the Libyan who had purchased the clothes.' Photograph number eight was obviously of Al-Megrahi, but, equally obviously, Tony had not identified him as the clothes buyer. The use of the words 'described as resembling' rather than 'positively identified' suggests that whoever drafted the fact sheet was aware of this shortfall in the evidence. Sadly, press reporting of the indictments did not pick up on the subtleties of the State Department's language. As far as the media were concerned, the British and American authorities were claiming that Al-Megrahi had been identified as the clothes buyer and no one within the authorities tried to dissuade them from that view. At the very least, this was disingenuous. At worst it was deliberate deceit.

Greater honesty on the part of the authorities would have led to an admission that their supposed star witness, Tony Gauci, was hardly the most consistent witness in a number of other important areas. He had changed his story on key points of evidence, often months after originally being approached by the police. The consistent elements of his account were that a smart, clean-shaven Arab man, approximately six feet tall and 50 years of age, had bought a random bundle of clothing at about 6.50 p.m. during the middle of a week sometime in November or December 1988. The only other things he could say with certainty were that it was raining when the customer left the shop and that he appeared to be travelling in a white Mercedes taxi. None of this could be of much use to a prosecutor trying to convict the two Libyans.

The statements by Tony's brother Paul also gave the police a major headache. In his first statement, dated 1 September 1989, he confirmed that on the day in question he had left the shop early in order to watch a football match on television. He was not sure which match it was, but was fairly certain that it involved an Italian club playing in a European competition. On 19 October, Inspector Harry Bell of the Scottish police visited him with a list of European football matches that had been played that particular season.

The matches involving Italian clubs which were played that day were listed as Dynamo Dresden vs AS Roma, Girondins de Bordeaux vs Napoli and Bayern München vs Internazionale. Such ties are played over two legs, a fortnight apart. Paul stated that he watched the return leg of the first of these games, Roma vs Dresden on 7 December. He remembered that it was played at 3 p.m. in the afternoon, and was followed by FC Liegeois vs Juventus. Perhaps, after all, the indictment was correct and the day in question had been when Paul was watching the return leg. However, he went on to state that he had only seen the early stages of the first half of that game. Instead of watching the rest, he walked along Tower Road, possibly intending to drop in on some of his fellow shopkeepers. But he remembered seeing the whole of the first leg, which had been played in Dresden. The statement rounded off by saying, 'On the basis that there were two games played during the afternoon of 23 November 1988 and only one game on the afternoon of 7 December 1988, I would say that 23 November 1988 was the date in question.' It is understood that Megrahi had an alibi for 23 November, so Paul had dealt another very important blow to the official version, which insisted that Megrahi had bought the clothes on, or around, 7 December.

Meteorological data for Malta is recorded at Luqa airport just a few miles from Mary's House. The records for 23 November 1988 show that there were heavy showers at 4 p.m. and more rain between 7 p.m. and 10 p.m. Tony Gauci recalled the customer leaving the shop just before it closed at 7 p.m. and buying an umbrella because it had started to rain. The only rain on 7 December fell between midnight and 12 noon, and even this was only classed as a light shower. The next rain did not occur until 0600 on 8 December. This made it most unlikely that any rain fell outside Mary's House on 7 December.

The Gauci brothers' statements and the meteorological evidence were major blows to the official story of Lockerbie. However, the indictments against the Libyans also relied on the ostensibly much firmer evidence that an unaccompanied bag had been transferred at Frankfurt airport from Air Malta Flight KM180 to Flight 103A. The main evidence in support of this claim were the two documents from Frankfurt airport – the computer printout and the handwritten worksheet – which had emerged some time after the bombing. Since all the other bags on Flight 103 had supposedly been matched to passengers and found not to have contained the bomb, it was deduced that the bomb must have been in the bag transferred from KM180.

Despite the strange circumstances surrounding the documents' emergence, they nonetheless appeared to provide conclusive proof that a bag had been transferred at Frankfurt from Flight KM180 to Flight 103A. On closer inspection, however, the documents were far from conclusive.

One of the first people to express doubts was FBI agent Lawrence Whittaker. It was he who had visited Frankfurt airport in October with Scottish police officer Detective Inspector Watson McAteer. As *Time* magazine reported, he informed FBI headquarters by telex that they had witnessed someone introduce luggage to the computerised baggage system without making a note on a worksheet. This showed that rogue bags could easily get into the system without anyone being the wiser.[3] Having studied the crucial computer printout, Whittaker further pointed out that it showed 'only that a bag of unknown origin was sent to coding station 206 at 1.07 p.m. to a position from which it was supposed to be loaded on to Pan Am 103.' As for the handwritten worksheet, his telex reported that it indicated 'only that the luggage was unloaded from Air Malta 180. There is no indication how much baggage was unloaded or where the luggage was sent.' He concluded: 'There remains a possibility that no luggage was transferred from Air Malta 180 to Pan Am 103.'[4]

Another US agency appeared to share Whittaker's doubts about the Malta connection. In a December 1989 briefing document on the bombing, not declassified until 2000, the DIA wrote: 'DIA believes the device was placed aboard Pan Am 103 in Frankfurt, West Germany.' The Frankfurt airport documents had at that stage been known about for months, yet the document made no mention of them or of an unaccompanied suitcase from Malta.[5]

A more seismic blow to the official case was dealt by Air Malta. In 1990, a Granada Television drama-documentary production, *Why Lockerbie?*, showed terrorists taking a suitcase containing a primed bomb to Luqa airport. Air Malta objected to the film's implicit criticism of its security arrangements and sued Granada.

In contrast to Pan Am and Frankfurt airport, the airline still had complete records from the day of the bombing. These showed that there were only 55 pieces of luggage checked onto Flight KM180 and that all of these were accompanied by one or other of the flight's 39 passengers. Of the 55, only 12 were interlined to other airlines at Frankfurt and each of these continued to be accompanied by their owners.

The airline's documents did not, of course, prove that Libyans at Luqa airport had not added the rogue bronze Samsonite to the stream of luggage destined for KM180. However, at the time of Lockerbie, Air Malta was one of the few carriers that required their head baggage-loader to count all the bags going into the hold to ensure that the number tallied with a list of all the checked baggage.

For expert assistance Air Malta hired two of Britain's top airline security experts from the independent consultancy Asgard Security Management Services. Denis Phipps spent 26 years in the Royal Military Police, rising to the rank of Lieutenant Colonel. In 1974 he became head of security for the BOAC airline, and remained in that position when it merged to become British Airways, during which time he was Chairman of the International Air Transport Association's (IATA) Security Advisory Committee. He was also a member of the UK National Aviation Security Committee and founder chairman of the security group of the Association of European Airlines. His colleague Nan McCreadie also worked for BOAC and British Airways, and represented British Airways at IATA.

Phipps and McCreadie travelled to Malta to study the airline's records and interview its baggage-handlers. Together, Phipps said, these provided 'a very complete chain of evidence'. Recognising that in such situations there is no guarantee that everyone will tell the truth, they were nevertheless unable to spot any unexplained discrepancies in the handlers' accounts.[6]

In defending its programme, Granada relied on the computer printout and the handwritten worksheet from Frankfurt airport. The printout documented all the baggage transactions relating to Flight 103A which took place within the airport's automated baggage system. All the bags it listed had supposedly been accounted for, except for one, which had been put into the system in a tray which the computer had numbered 8849. The printout indicated that the tray had been entered into the system at coding station 206 at 1.07 p.m. on the day of the disaster. The handwritten worksheet had been filled in by the operators of coding station 206. It showed that between 1.04 p.m. and 1.10 p.m. they were dealing with a batch of bags from KM180. It therefore followed, according to the official case upon which Granada were relying, that the mysterious bag in tray number 8849 had been transferred from KM180.

Phipps and McCreadies' findings at Frankfurt Airport dealt a devastating blow to this thesis.[7] They pointed out that the computer list only tracked the movement of bag number 8849 between coding station 206 and gate B-44, where Flight 103A was loaded. There was no documentation which demonstrated that the bag had been unloaded from KM180 in the first place, or that it had eventually been loaded onto Flight 103A. Furthermore, there was no record of the following: 1) how many bags had been unloaded from KM180; 2) who had done that unloading; 3) who had driven the bags to coding station 206; 4) whether or not all the bags taken off KM180 actually reached coding station 206; 5) the extent to which they were supervised between being unloaded and entered into the system at the coding station; and 6) who might have carried out that supervision.

An added problem, highlighted by Phipps and McCreadie, was that no computer printouts were saved which related to the other flights departing from Frankfurt airport that day. These would have showed the destination of the other bags after they were coded in at station 206. In their absence, it was impossible to cross-check whether the bags from KM180 had been sent elsewhere than gate B-44. As for the handwritten worksheet, Phipps and McCreadie pointed out that it was compiled only for the purposes of charging airlines for handling their baggage. These charges were always worked out by the number of wagonloads of bags dealt with, as opposed to the total number of individual bags. So, although it was vital that the coding station operators knew exactly where each bag was to be sent, they did not need to know, or record, exactly where each one came from. Since each wagon could carry around 40 bags, and since there were only 12 or – if Granada and the indictments against the Libyans were correct – 13 interline bags from KM180 that required taking to coding station 206, there was clearly plenty of room for bags from other flights to be added to the wagon.

By observing coding station operators, Phipps and McCreadie calculated that it took around seven seconds to process each bag. It should therefore have taken only about one-and-a-half minutes for the two men who were operating the coding station at that crucial time, Mr Koca and Mr Candar, to enter all 12 bags from KM180 through station 206. However, the entry on the handwritten worksheet records the bags from KM180 as having been entered between 1304 and 1310 – a full six minutes. It could well be that the extra four-and-a-half minutes was due to the fact that they were having to deal with bags from other flights which were in the same wagon. Koca had filled in the worksheet, while Candar actually put the bags onto the conveyor belt system. Based in the coding booth, Koca would not have had a clear view of Candar and therefore could not have known for sure that the bags he was coding in were definitely from KM180.

Since the deadly suitcase supposedly entered the system at 1.07 p.m., the accuracy of all the timings recorded was all-important. A margin of error of more than three minutes either side would mean it could not have been transferred from KM180. When they investigated this matter, Phipps and McCreadie discovered that there was good reason to doubt the accuracy of the times indicated on both the key documents. The time on the Frankfurt Airline Company (FAG) computer, from which the printout was derived, was entered each morning by employees who would use their wrist watches or a wall-mounted clock as their reference. Furthermore, the time recorded on the computer was prone to deviate by a few minutes whenever the electrical circuit frequency fluctuated. As for the worksheet, the timings listed were not derived from the FAG computer, but from Koca's watch or a wall-mounted clock, so there was no reason to believe that the timings given on his sheet synchronised with those on the computer printout. There is no suggestion that Mr Koca and Mr Candar were other than diligent, trustworthy and skilled employees.

When Phipps and McCreadie studied the other handwritten entries that Koca and Candar had made during the same shift, they found a number of possible inaccuracies. One entry, for example, indicated that a wagonload of bags from flight PA072 had been entered at station 206 between 8.49 a.m. and 8.54 a.m. It was normal practice to send bags to the nearest baggage coding station, but PA072 was parked at gate B-46, which was far closer to another coding station than it was to station 206. The worksheet recorded that immediately before dealing with the bags from KM180, the men at station 206 were handling luggage from Lufthansa flight LH1498 – but no such flight existed.

Phipps and McCreadie checked the worksheets from the other coding stations that had despatched bags to Flight 103A. In doing so, they found that the worksheets did not tally with what the police had established about the bags and passengers on that flight. For example, the computer printout showed that bag tray number 5620, which supposedly contained a bag destined for Flight 103, was entered into the system at coding station HM3 at 3.44 p.m. The sheet from station HM3 indicated that luggage from Lufthansa Flight LH1071 was being dealt with at that time. However, there is no record of a passenger or a bag transferring from LH1071 to Flight 103A.

Elsewhere on the printout it was listed that Flight 103A had been loaded with bags from tray numbers 3148 and 4573, both of which had been entered into the system at coding station HM2 at 11.31 a.m. The worksheet for HM2 stated at that time they were dealing with bags from a non-existent Air India flight, numbered AI465. There was a flight AI 165 but, as with LH1071, there was no record of any bags or passengers having transferred from that flight to Flight 103A. The computer printout indicated that 11 bag trays were sent to Flight 103A from coding station HM4 between 11.59 a.m. and 12 noon. However, the worksheet for HM4 showed that no bags were being entered into the system between those times.

Taken together, the worksheets from the various coding stations indicated that not one, but 14 unaccompanied pieces of luggage were sent by the computerised system to Flight 103A, any one of which could, in theory, have been the bronze Samsonite which contained the bomb. The police, of course, never found 14 such items, because it was almost certain that many of the worksheets were inaccurate. There could be no guarantee that the vital worksheet from station 206 was not among them.

Granada had an admirable reputation for defending the integrity of its journalism. To fight the case, it hired one of Britain's most formidable defence barristers, Anthony Scrivener QC. But having received Air Malta's submissions based on Phipps and McCreadie's investigation, Granada decided to throw in the towel. On 13 August 1993 the company paid £15,005 in court to satisfy Air Malta's claim, without admission of liability. Air Malta opted to accept the payment. On 1 November 1993, counsel for Air Malta read out a statement in the High Court in London which was approved by the judge, saying that 'Air Malta regards this result as achieving, in substance, its purpose in bringing the action.' The airline's victory dealt a stunning blow to the official account of Lockerbie, yet went almost completely unreported.

The US Federal Aviation Authority (FAA) appeared to share Air Malta's conviction that Luqa was a relatively safe airport. The authors have learned independently from sources within the FAA and from a European government minister that FAA inspectors carried out an inspection at Luqa airport, Malta, in 1987 and gave the airport a clean bill of health. It commented on the fact that armed soldiers from the Maltese Armed Forces guarded the secure airport areas and made only a minor administrative recommendation to the Maltese government. The same could not be said for the FAA assessments of Frankfurt and Heathrow during that period.

Less than 48 hours after Pan Am 103 blew up, FAA inspectors breached Pan Am's security at Heathrow, spending almost three hours in the Pan Am baggage area, during which time they went unchallenged.[8] A senior source within the FAA told the authors that if these three airports had, at that time scored according to their respective levels of security, been given points out of ten, which they were not, the result would have been that Malta would have come out well above both Frankfurt and Heathrow. These assessments might have been used at the subsequent Lockerbie trial, but the original reports were routinely shredded in 1993/4.

A further element to the Malta connection, potentially the most damaging to the two Libyan suspects, was the evidence of their former workmate Magid Giaka. Giaka had worked as Fhimah's deputy in the Libyan Arab Airlines office at Luqa airport. During their time in Malta, Giaka and Fhimah were regular visitors to the Libyan government-owned Jerma Palace Hotel in Marsascala, which was often used by crew and passengers of Libyan Arab Airlines. The hotel's public relations manager, Guima Nasser, later recalled that Giaka would be at the hotel two or three times a week, often in the company of different women, whom he tried to impress by exaggerating his status with the airline and spending a lot of money. Nasser and others reported that he had a reputation for owing money. The hotel had an arrangement with LAA whereby it would supply money for the airline's crews when they stayed the night. Nasser claimed Giaka misled hotel staff into believing he had been authorised to sign for the money, which he then failed to pass on to LAA employees.

Given that Nasser and his colleagues at the hotel were Libyan government employees, the impartiality of their account was open to question. Nevertheless, they did not exaggerate Giaka's flaws. They made it clear that, as far as they knew, he never made any sexual advances to the women he brought to the hotel and he never touched drink.[9] In a move which was to anger the Maltese authorities, Giaka was 'removed' from Malta by the CIA and DoJ personnel on 14 July 1991. He was taken by speedboat from the island's M'sida yacht marina, close by the US Embassy, to rendezvous with the USS *Butte*, an American warship lying 27 miles off the Maltese coast. His departure was shrouded in secrecy and it was some time before the Maltese authorities knew anything of it. A senior minister in the Maltese government described the attitude of the Americans, not for the last time in this case, as 'treating us as some kind of banana republic'.

Giaka's first statement, taken later that same day aboard the USS *Butte*, started off with his reason for fleeing Malta, given as wishing to assist the US investigate terrorism sponsored by Gadafy. On board the *Butte* were several FBI agents, Hal Hendershot, Philip Reid and Nicholas Hreiz, who would now assume responsibility from the CIA. Hendershot and Reid would do the questioning and Hreiz would translate from Arabic.

Giaka's wife, Cynthia Mifsud, left Malta to join him in the Witness Protection Programme on 5 September 1991, flying to London by Air Malta flight KM120. On this leg of the journey her mother and uncle accompanied her. They were all given club-class seats, numbers 2 a, c and d. A man calling himself Mr Wakefield paid for these tickets in cash at a travel agent in Putney. He gave an address in Scarsdale Villas, Kensington, and a telephone number, 071-938-1478, but subsequent enquiries at this address proved fruitless.

According to the US State Department's fact-sheets, one of the most important pieces of evidence implicating Fhimah in the plot was the diary entry from 15 December 1988 reminding him to take tags from Air Malta. Of course, the relevant entry in fact read: 'collect taggs [*sic*] from the Air Malta'. Also written was: 'Abdel Basset is coming from Zurich with Salvu.' Whatever the peculiarities surrounding the discovery of the diary, it seemed odd that a devious terrorist would record his practical preparations for mass murder in a diary. Stranger still that he would leave the diary behind in Malta for two-and-a-half years, especially as the last 18 months had seen the island regularly visited by Lockerbie investigators.

What of the diary entry itself? Was it really as damning as the State Department had implied? Fhimah's explanation for the 'taggs' entry is that he wanted to secure a contract for printing Libyan Arab Airlines' luggage tags in Malta. The printer, he said, had simply asked for a sample. Several other entries seem to support this story. On the page for 10 December, for example, the Arabic translated as 'Go to the printer' and in the notes in the back of the diary was written, 'Contact the printer'.

The only physical evidence to implicate the two Libyans in the bombing was the fragment of circuit board, which allegedly came from the bomb's timing mechanism. Edwin Bollier, owner of Mebo, the company that manufactured the timing device, had supposedly identified the fragment as being from a prototype timer of a model called the MST-13. He said only 20 such timers were made, including the five prototypes, and that all 20 were sold to Libya. Mebo also rented part of its Zurich office space to a Libyan company called ABH, for whom Al-Megrahi worked. The indictment against the two Libyans alleged that ABH was a front for the Libyan intelligence service, the JSO.

Despite peculiarities and inconsistencies in the many media accounts of the discovery and identification of the fragment, Bollier's account appeared to provide a cast-iron link between the timing device and the two accused. Shortly before the fifth anniversary of the bombing, however, he threw a large spanner in the works. Interviewed on BBC Radio 4's *File on Four* programme, Bollier revealed that in addition to the five prototype MST-13s sold to Libya, he had supplied a further two or three to the East German government. The revelation was hugely significant, because it was well known that the East German secret service, the Stasi, maintained very close ties with a number of radical Palestinian groups, among them Ahmed Jibril's PFLP-GC. Indeed, Hafez Dalkamoni was known to have made regular trips to East Berlin, ostensibly to receive treatment for his damaged leg.

Bollier refused to name the person who had bought the timers in East Germany, saying only that he was from the purchasing department of the army. He said that he had delivered the devices to East Berlin personally in 1985, at roughly the same time that the five other devices were delivered to Libya. Bollier had been reminded of this by his engineer, Ulrich Lumpert.

The British Foreign Office reacted to the *File on Four* programme by leaking a Scottish police document to *The Guardian*.[10] The following day, the paper ran a front-page story headlined 'LOCKERBIE CLUES "POINT TO LIBYA".' Based around 'previously unpublished' details, the article suggested that, despite Bollier's revelations, investigators on both sides of the Atlantic were confident of the case against Libya. The leaked document revealed that on 18 December 1988, a Mebo representative travelled to Tripoli to meet with JSO officials. He was carrying a batch of 40 commercially purchased, seven-day capacity Olympus timers which he had arranged to deliver to a senior JSO official called Izz al-Din al-Hinshiri. The following day, the Mebo representative met with Hinshiri at the JSO's offices, but Hinshiri refused to purchase the timers. Later that day another meeting was arranged, this one at the house of Abdel Basset Ali Al-Megrahi. The following day, the Mebo representative took the Olympus timers from Hinshiri's office and returned to Zurich. When he later checked the timers, he discovered that one of them had been set for a Wednesday at 1930, uncanny given that the Lockerbie bomb exploded at 1903 on the Wednesday of that particular week.[11]

The document was later obtained by the British Lockerbie relatives' spokesman Dr Jim Swire, who discovered that it included far more details than *The Guardian* had reported. For example, it stated that while at Megrahi's house, the Mebo representative had caught sight of a group of six to ten men in a room, including two senior members of the Libyan intelligence services, Abdallah Senussi, Director of Operations Administration at the JSO and a man called Shur. The Mebo representative remembered that Shur had supervised the test explosions in the desert in 1986, which had used the MST-13 timers. He was not allowed into the room and left without meeting Hinshiri and Megrahi.

Perhaps the most curious detail in the document was that a month after Lockerbie, on 22 January 1989, the Mebo representative was approached in East Berlin by a Libyan official to whom he had delivered the five timers in 1985. This person asked him if he had noticed anything unusual about the timers he had taken back to Zurich on 20 December.

The most logical interpretation of these supposed facts was that the Libyans had originally intended to use one of the Olympus timers in the Lockerbie bomb. At the meeting in Hinshiri's office on the nineteenth, one of them had tested out the timer by programming it for the approximate time that they wanted the explosion to take place two days later. Then, at some point that same day, it was decided not to bother with the Olympus timers and instead to use one of the MST-13s already in their possession. As for the mysterious tip-off in Berlin, this was probably from someone within Libyan intelligence who did not approve of the bombing.

Edwin Bollier subsequently confirmed that he was the source on which the document was based, and added some more intriguing details. He said it was not until he had returned to the office after Christmas 1988 that he noticed one of the Olympus timers had been set. By that time they had been left in the office, unguarded, for five or six days. Shortly after the *File on Four* programme, he demanded an independent analysis of the vital fragment of circuit board. Having studied photographs, he claimed to be '70 per cent certain' that his timer was not used in the Lockerbie bomb. More importantly, Bollier now revealed that the fragment may have been part of a circuit board intended for inclusion in a batch of 17 timers which had remained incomplete and in storage at the company's Zurich factory. He claimed that after stocktaking, following an approach from the Lockerbie inquiry team, he had discovered that one or two blank circuit boards were missing. Furthermore, between October 1988 and February 1989, he had alerted the Swiss police to a number of break-ins at the factory. The person responsible seemed to have used duplicate keys, as there was no sign of force having been used. Nothing of value had been taken, and all that appeared to be missing were empty circuit board prints, of the type used in MST-13 timers, and some circuit diagrams. If someone had entered the office during that time, they could surely have set the timer as well.

Apparently convinced that had happened, Bollier declared: 'The first question is, is this [fragment of circuit] board from a timer or an empty board? The second question is, was this in the explosion, or prepared and brought by somebody to the place?'[12] The implication was that the Lockerbie fragment may have been planted. He claimed the FBI had told him that three of its men had found the fragment in a piece of coat, but was later told that the Scottish police found it in a piece of shirt.

Despite repeated requests, the Scottish police and the FBI refused to allow Bollier to see the crucial fragment. At one point he even spent a week with the Scottish police, but all they would allow him to see was a photographic enlargement.[13]

It later emerged that a photographic enlargement, rather than the fragment itself, was the basis upon which the FBI's forensic expert Tom Thurman made the 'identification' of the MST-13. Thurman claimed that the enlargement was 'much better than the actual item because . . . you can see the detail with the naked eye in that photograph that you can't see on the actual item without a microscope.' However, when pressed, he admitted that it would have been better to have viewed the item under a microscope. He said the Lockerbie fragment and circuit boards from the MST-13 seized from the Libyans in Africa were 'as alike as two thumbprints'.

Edwin Bollier did not agree. Having studied the photographic enlargement, he became convinced that it was part of a handmade circuit board from a prototype MST-13 timer. This was significant, he said, because the prototypes were not supplied to Libya. He was sure it was handmade because the curved edge of the fragment was rough. The boards in the timers supplied to Libya were stamped out mechanically, but he claimed the prototypes were cut by hand with a hacksaw.

In 1998, Bollier's claim was put to the test by Channel 4's *Dispatches* programme. The photograph was given to Owen Lewis, the former military explosives forensic expert who had also been involved in Hasan Assali's case (see Chapter 12), along with a photograph of one of the complete machine-made boards. Lewis was in no doubt that the two items did not match. He agreed with Bollier that the curved edge of the Lockerbie fragment was different to the machine-made board. Furthermore, the T-shaped foil strip known as the touch pad was of different proportions and in a different position in relation to the edge of the board. Lewis concluded: 'They are similar – same design – but they are not the same. You would not get those differences if they came from the same manufacturing run.'[14]

Such issues aside, there was a large question mark over the suitability of the MST-13 timer for the radio-cassette bomb. As Bollier pointed out, since it measured about 9 x 7 x 7 cm, it was too large to fit into the twin-speaker Toshiba player utilised by the Lockerbie bombers, unless removed from its fibreglass casing. He insisted that the timer was also impractical. Designed for controlled military detonations, it operated on a 10,000-hour, rather than a 24-hour, setting. This meant that the Lockerbie terrorists could only have set it by calculating how many hours in advance they wanted it to activate the bomb. All in all, it would have been far easier to use a cheap, and much smaller, 24-hour timer switch that could easily be bought from any electrical catalogue.[15]

Bollier's steady stream of revelations coincided with the further revelation that his legal expenses were being paid by the lawyers of the two accused Libyans.[16] Sources within the official investigation let it be known that Bollier could no longer be trusted and that the amendments to his story were tailored to suit his paymasters in Tripoli. The fact remained, however, that he was a linchpin of the case against the Libyans and any damage to his credibility was, first and foremost, damage to the credibility of that case.

According to Vincent Cannistraro, whose CIA department produced the crucial intelligence that linked the timer evidence to Libya, the timers sent to East Germany were irrelevant because they contained brown circuit boards, whereas the Libyan ones had green circuit boards which matched the fragment found at Lockerbie.[17] Cannistraro's claim was based on Bollier's recollections, but Ulrich Lumpert, who actually made the timers, recalled that the Libyan and Stasi timers all incorporated green circuit boards.

In May 1994, the German magazine *Der Spiegel* added a further important twist to Bollier's story. The magazine had obtained a copy of a recent interrogation by Lockerbie investigators of a former Stasi agent named Joachim Wenzel, who had worked as a technician in the so-called Section Three. His primary purpose was to develop the organisation's electronic spying capacity. Wenzel said he had personally taken delivery of Bollier's MST-13 timers and claimed that Bollier had supplied Section Three since its formation in the late 1960s. At the time, the Stasi had been desperate to get hold of electronic equipment and Bollier was capable of getting much of what they needed. Among other things, he provided cipher equipment and polygraph machines. Bollier's importance to the organisation was such that he would dine with the head of Section Three, Horst Maennchen, at an expensive hotel. The Stasi considered him to be one of its unofficial members and gave him the code-name Rubin, with Wenzel himself acting as his handler from 1983 onwards.

Wenzel claimed the MST-13s were stored in the same building as the Stasi's Section 22, which was ostensibly responsible for terrorist defence but in fact maintained close ties with a number of terrorist organisations, including radical Palestinian groups. *Spiegel* reported that the timers had subsequently disappeared, with no one being certain whether they were destroyed before the Stasi was disbanded or whether they had found their way into the hands of terrorists.

Bollier's close relationship with the Stasi came as no great surprise, given his earlier revelation about the sale of the timers to East Germany, but there was a further twist to the tale. Wenzel said the Stasi was concerned that Bollier was selling directly to other terrorist groups, such as the Basque separatists ETA, the Red Army Faction, the IRA, and also to Libya. Moreover, he was strongly suspected of being a CIA double agent. This was the view of, among others, Colonel Gerhard Hoeferer, Maennchen's deputy at Section Three. *Spiegel* reported that another former Stasi officer had told the BKA, 'a man like Bollier had protectors hidden in the West'. Suspicions had been aroused by the fact that Bollier seemed able to get hold of very sensitive Western spy equipment without difficulty. When a *Spiegel* reporter put the double agent allegation to Bollier, he refused to comment.[18] As the subsequent Lockerbie trial would reveal, Bollier's contacts with both the Stasi and the CIA raised yet more questions about his value as a witness against the two Libyans.

The evidence against Megrahi and Fhimah certainly looked shaky, but what of the case against Gadafy? In the years following the issuing of the indictments, a steady stream of evidence was to emerge which shifted the finger of guilt away from Tripoli and back towards the original suspects. One of the sources was Abolhassan Bani-Sadr, who was president of Iran during the two years immediately after the 1979 Islamic revolution, until being forced out of office. Although living in Paris, he maintained high-level contacts in his home country. Interviewed for Allan Francovich's documentary *The Maltese Double Cross*, he confirmed that Iran had ordered the attack and that it was carried out by the PFLP-GC. He said that Hafez Dalkamoni in particular was close to the Iranian regime, spending much of his time in Tehran. On 22 January 1995, the *Sunday Telegraph* reported that the PFLP-GC member Abdel Fattah Ghadanfar had been released from prison in Germany as part of a secret deal negotiated with Iran. Ghadanfar was one of the 16 suspects arrested in the Autumn Leaves raids two months before Lockerbie, and was eventually charged, along with Hafez Dalkamoni, of the troop-train bombings near the German town of Hedemünden. Not convicted until 1991, he and Dalkamoni were respectively given 12- and 15-year prison sentences.

The newspaper revealed that Ghadanfar was released in total secrecy two months earlier and deported to Syria. A few months later, Dalkamoni was also released. If Germany had released both men to Syria, why was a third country, Iran, involved? As far as Germany was concerned, there was a very obvious answer; nurturing links with Tehran was good for business. Towards the end of 1994, Germany had agreed to construct two nuclear reactors near the Iranian port of Bushire. The plan was only called off after intense pressure from the US government. In Germany, intelligence chief Bernd Schmidbauer received his Iranian opposite number, Ali Fallihian, and gave him a guided tour of the service's headquarters in Wiesbaden. It was later revealed that Germany had struck a deal to supply hi-tech spying equipment to Iran, and that Iran had been allowed to set up an intelligence centre in Bonn which would allow it to monitor Iranian dissidents. The *Sunday Telegraph* alleged that in 1991 Germany had discussed another secret deal with Iran, in order to secure the release of two German businessmen held in Lebanon. Once again, the Germans' part of the bargain was the release of Ghadanfar and Dalkamoni. Tehran's motivation was, perhaps, more obvious: the two men had been planning to avenge the downing of Iran Air Flight 655.

Dalkamoni and Ghadanfar were, of course, stopped in their tracks by the Autumn Leaves Raids, two months before Lockerbie. In the official version of the bombing, the raids put paid to the entire Iranian/PFLP-GC revenge mission, but other information was to leak from official sources which appeared to give the lie to this claim. One such was the internal bulletin issued by the US State Department's Office of Diplomatic Security on 2 December 1988, described in Chapter 2. More than a month after the Autumn Leaves Raids, the bulletin warned that a team of Palestinian radicals were planning a strike against US targets in Europe, including Pan Am.

When this warning was finally revealed in 1995, it caused outrage among the British Lockerbie victims' relatives, whose government had assured them that no credible, specific warnings were received prior to the bombing. UK Families Flight 103 wrote to Prime Minister John Major to ask if, in the light of the newly uncovered warning, he stood by those assurances. In a masterpiece of Whitehall obfuscation, Major's private secretary Edward Oakden replied that the analyst who produced the document 'assessed the threat as circular reporting, possibly versions of two Counter-Intelligence Daily Summaries'. He went on:

> These earlier summaries remain classified, but the US authorities have assured us that neither made mention of Pan Am, nor of any other specified suspected target, but rather referred to a threat to US-suspected targets generally. It appears that some with whom the original non-specific intelligence reports were shared jumped to conclusions about possible specific targets based on their own conjecture and that the 2 December report recycled this feedback. The US document was thus not the specific warning that it might first appear.

In other words, an intelligence officer, reading reports of a general risk to US targets, decided to hazard a guess at a possible target and by pure fluke chose Pan Am.

The warning tallied with information leaked by a senior Tehran source to Iranian journalist Dr Ali Nuri Zadeh, which – as we described in chapter four – provided the basis for a highly detailed account of the bombing which appeared in the *Al-Dustur* newspaper on 22 May 1989. The article reported that on 7 December 1988 Jibril informed the head of Iranian intelligence, Moshen Armen, 'that the "setback" the operation suffered as a result of the arrest of some supporters in Germany had been compensated for. This occurred through the arrival of three new persons in Frankfurt.'

In July 1997, there came still further evidence of Iranian involvement and this time the source could not be easily dismissed. Abolghasem Mesbahi was a co-founder of the Iranian secret service, Vevak. He had defected to Germany in 1996 and became a key witness in the trial of five people (one Iranian and four Lebanese) accused of the killing in 1992 of four Kurds in a Berlin restaurant called Mykonos. All five were convicted and the court found that the assassinations were ordered in Tehran.

Mesbahi reportedly told Frankfurt prosecutor Volker Rath that the late Ayatollah Khomeni had personally ordered the bombing, in retaliation for the shoot-down of Iran Air 655. He also said that a Government Minister had conducted negotiations with Libya and Abu Nidal aides on how to carry it out. He claimed an Iranian Intelligence agent smuggled the bomb parts on to a plane to London, where they were assembled before being loaded onto Flight 103. He insisted that the US must have known the truth, but preferred to keep it quiet for fear that a dispute might lead to the murder of US hostages held by pro-Iranian kidnappers in Lebanon.

Mesbahi denied having any part in the planning or implementation of the alleged attack, and made it clear that he had only heard about it from senior contacts in Tehran. In explicitly ruling out the possibility that an intact and primed bomb had been loaded in Frankfurt, he was perhaps aware of the sensitivities of his German protectors. This was perhaps further reflected in the fact that there was, apparently, little or nothing in his account to implicate the German-based Autumn Leaves gang. It surely remained an acute embarrassment to German intelligence and the BKA that all but one of the group's bombs had been evaded prior to Lockerbie. The reaction of the Scottish Crown Office to Mesbahi was somewhat bureaucratic. When informed that a high-level Iranian had disclosed details pertinent to the Pan Am bombing, the Crown Office responded to the authors by stating 'he [Mesbahi] should present himself to a police station in Dumfries'.

It seemed inherently unlikely that bomb components would be smuggled to Heathrow and assembled there, but could a bomb originating in Germany have been primed at Heathrow? Pan Am's Heathrow terminal was adjacent to that of Iran Air and the two airlines shared tarmac space. Furthermore, as the BKA's analysis had revealed, the Autumn Leaves gang's barometric bombs were set to explode after they had been in the air for between 35 and 45 minutes. Flight 103 had, of course, been destroyed around 38 minutes after take-off. In the absence of any further corroborative evidence, however, the theory remained speculative.

What if the Lockerbie bomb had incorporated one of the MST-13 timers supplied to Libya in 1985? If true, it was by no means proof that Libya was behind the bombing. It was well known that during the mid-'80s the country harboured and funded a number of radical Palestinian groups, including the PFLP-GC and the Abu Nidal organisation. Furthermore, Libya was a willing quartermaster for terrorist groups throughout the Middle East and beyond. Colonel Gadafy's government would probably never admit it, but it was quite possible that they had supplied the timers to Ahmed Jibril's group or its allies.

Iran obviously had a strong motive to launch the Lockerbie bomb, but so too, surely, had Libya. As the Lockerbie indictments were issued, unattributable briefings by British and American government officials let it be known that Lockerbie was Gadafy's revenge for the 1986 bombing raids on Libya. If that was the case, it must have come as quite a shock to Margaret Thatcher, who was British Prime Minister at the time of those raids and of Lockerbie. In seeking to justify her active support for the raids, she later declared in her memoirs: 'The much vaunted Libyan counter-attack did not and could not take place.'[19]

15. STALEMATE AND BREAKTHROUGH

From the day that the indictments were handed down against the Libyans Megrahi and Fhimah, questions still remained about the US response to the charges. Should it be economic sanctions or military strikes, or a combination of both? The US had broken nearly all its economic relations with Libya more than five years earlier over Libya's alleged involvement in acts of terrorism. One official at the time said the administration was discussing the possible embargo with 20 to 25 nations, most of them countries which regularly bought Libya's high-quality crude oil. Opinion was divided, but in the United States politics is business. Could pressure be brought to bear on Gadafy, forcing him to hand over the two men? Would a pre-emptive strike similar to that carried out by US bombers on the cities of Tripoli and Benghazi be enough to force the issue? In the end, the United States did everything and nothing.

The issue of military strikes was considered but discounted, primarily because the United States could not carry its European partners along that road. Many Arab states had also expressed their opposition to any form of military response. It would also probably have triggered an increase in world oil prices, a consequence the White House almost certainly needed to avoid in an election year already plagued by economic troubles.

Gadafy's offer to have his men stand trial at the world court was dismissed out of hand. State Department spokesman Richard Boucher accused Libya of stalling. 'We reject the idea,' he said. 'It's not a matter for international arbitration. The murder of US citizens is properly a matter for investigation and adjudication by US courts.'[1] The accusation that Gadafy was stalling was one which was to be repeated ad nauseam for the next several years. Any request made by Gadafy to have the trial in any country other than the UK or the US was met with contempt and instantly dismissed.

Although publicly the United States felt that they had to stand tall against Gadafy, privately President Reagan made huge concessions to his friends and supporters in corporate America. Quietly and without any fanfare, on 20 January 1989, just hours before leaving office, Reagan signed an executive order permitting US firms to resume dealings with Libya through wholly owned foreign subsidiaries. This hypocrisy, especially regarding Libya, was synonymous with the Reagan–Bush administration and continued throughout the Bush–Quayle White House. Consumed with a passion that was described at times as 'Islamaphobia', the new Bush administration continued to talk tough on Libya and yet secretly allowed US business to trade with Libya through subsidiaries in, amongst other places, Seoul, South Korea. For many US companies it was 'business as usual', despite the sanctions.

On 27 November 1991 the governments of the United Kingdom and the United States each issued a statement calling upon the Libyan government to hand over the two accused to either the Scottish or the American authorities for trial. Requests for their extradition were transmitted to the Libyan government through diplomatic channels. No extradition treaties were, or are, in force between Libya on the one hand and the United Kingdom and United States on the other.

Professor Robert Black QC, who was later to design the legal and administrative framework for the trial in the Netherlands, explained in a legal paper:

> Libyan internal law, in common with the laws of many countries in the world, does not permit the extradition of its own nationals for trial overseas. The government of Libya accordingly contended that the affair should be resolved through the application of the provisions of a 1971 civil aviation convention concluded in Montreal, to which all three relevant governments are signatories. That convention provides that a state in whose territory persons accused of terrorist offences against aircraft are resident has a choice, *aut dedere aut judicare*, either to hand over the accused for trial in the courts of the state bringing the accusation or to take the necessary steps to have the accused brought to trial in its own domestic courts. In purported compliance with the second of these options, the Libyan authorities arrested the two accused and appointed a Supreme Court judge as examining magistrate to consider the evidence and prepare the case against them.

Professor Black commented,

> Not surprisingly, perhaps, the UK and US governments refused to make available to the examining magistrate the evidence that they claimed to have amassed against the accused, who remained under

house arrest until they were eventually handed over in April 1999 for trial at Kamp van Zeist.

Although charges had been brought against the Libyans, many relatives of those who died were still uneasy about what they saw as an exoneration of Iran and Syria by the UK and the US. Many of the victims' relatives have protested that the exoneration of Syria and Iran, the original suspects in the incident, was politically motivated. Syria, they say, was promised vindication as an enticement to join the anti-Saddam Hussein coalition and the peace process. And Iran was being courted to facilitate the release of the hostages in Lebanon, held by Iranian-sponsored Hizbullah terrorists.

But the victims' families are not the only ones uneasy about the British–American conclusions. Experts who have thoroughly investigated the case are convinced that the real culprits are the Iranian regime, which had threatened to retaliate for the American downing of an Iranian passenger flight in the last weeks of the Iran-Iraq war, and its Syrian allies. As Robert Kupperman, senior adviser at the Washington Center for Strategic and International Studies, has put it in a *New York Times* article, they believe that 'compelling evidence still suggests that Iran commissioned the bombing and, with Syria's help, paid Ahmed Jibril's PFLP-GC to carry it out'.

As time passed from the announcement of the indictments against the Libyans, the press reports which insisted on an Iranian and Syrian involvement in the bombing diminished. Those who had previously reported and written about the events in that vein gradually succumbed to 'Libyacreep'. Some, like Vincent Cannistraro, continued to state that the original suspects, Ahmed Jibril's PFLP-GC, were still involved in the planning and manufacture of the bomb, but that 'it was a hand-off to the Libyans'.

Until it became clear that a trial was going to take place in the Netherlands, the seesaw approach of the UK and US governments persisted throughout the mid-'90s. Several UN resolutions attempted unsuccessfully to persuade or force Gadafy to hand over Megrahi and Fhimah for trial in the US or Scotland. No amount of pressure, it seemed, was ever going to persuade the Libyan leader to hand over Libyan citizens for trial in Britain or the United States. Gadafy's reasoning was that no jury could be found that would be able to deliberate impartially, considering the media attention the bombing had attracted. Whatever overtures Gadafy made regarding a trial in a neutral country were met with the unified US–UK response of 'No'.

The Montreal Convention route was exhausted and it appeared that a trial would never take place. Many relatives of the victims and observers at the time believed that neither the US nor the UK governments had any appetite for a trial which might put US intelligence operations under scrutiny. In the civil trial, Pan Am's attorneys had experienced first-hand the lengths to which the US government would go to deny access to any intelligence files. The overwhelming sense from a government perspective was that if they waited long enough, it would all go away.

In the run-up to the UN sanctions deadline of October 1993, Libya was exploring again the options of a trial in a neutral corner. In September 1993, Ibrahim Legwell, the Libyan legal representative for Megrahi and Fhimah, was having serious talks for the first time with lawyers from Scotland. Alistair Duff, a very able 39-year-old solicitor-advocate from the Edinburgh firm McCourts, agreed to a meeting with Legwell. Duff was ultimately destined to stay part of the defence team and represent the first accused, Abdel Basset Ali Al-Megrahi, at the trial. Duff called on the services of a British Labour Party peer, Lord Macaulay QC, a leading criminal defence advocate. Together they flew to Tripoli for their first meeting with Megrahi and Fhimah.

Following their consultations with the two accused, the Libyan Foreign Ministry reported, through JANA, the official Libyan News Agency, 'We do not oppose their standing trial under the Scottish legal system, and we urge them to accept that.'[2] But the statement added that before the problem was resolved, the suspects, their families and their lawyers must 'be persuaded to stand trial under the Scottish legal system'. In the same article, Duff was quoted as saying: 'They [Megrahi and Fhimah] have to make up their own minds as to whether they wish to stand trial in Scotland or any other place, or whether to stand trial at all.' Commenting on the statement by the Libyan government, Duff said: 'In that sense, the remarks by the Libyan government do not change anything at all.' The following month saw increased sanctions being imposed against Libya, and claims by the US State Department and UK Foreign Office that Gadafy was simply using different legal propositions in order to stall the sanctions.

Following a meeting with Legwell in Tripoli on 12 October, Professor Robert Black QC set out his own proposal for a trial in the Netherlands, in a letter dated 10 January 1994. Professor Black's proposals suggested a tribunal sitting in the Netherlands, with no jury and presided over by a panel of judges, the president of which would be a Scottish judge proposed by the UK government. He went on to explain:

> I put this idea forward as a means of resolving the impasse which
> had been created by the strict insistence of Britain and the United
> States that the terms of the United Nations resolution [must be
> adhered to].

Black, a native of Lockerbie, worked tirelessly to have the trial take place.

'The Libyan suspects were not satisfied that they could receive a fair trial before any Scottish jury, given the amount of pre-trial publicity there had been in Scotland over the Lockerbie affair.' This could hardly have been a surprise to either the UK or the US governments, since both had been involved in attacking those who dared challenge the official line. Professor Black went on:

> Pre-trial publicity always took it as given that the prosecution's
> version of events was correct – that the allegations which were made
> in the charges against the Libyans were in fact what had happened,
> rather then simply allegations which would then have to be proved
> in a judicial process. The Scottish press had treated it as if what the
> prosecution said must be correct.

Not only the Scottish press but almost the entire world's media had condemned the two Libyans named on the indictment, and the entire Libyan nation.

Importantly, the Libyan government accepted Black's proposal. 'I put forward the idea of a non-jury court sitting in the Netherlands. That proposal was accepted in writing by the Libyan defence team . . . [and] by the Libyan government.'

It took Ibrahim Legwell, the Libyan lawyer of the accused, only two days to write back to Professor Black stating: 'I am able to confirm that my two clients do not object to appearing before the court as explained in your proposals.' This was the very first indication from the suspects that they were prepared to stand trial in a neutral country.

If the Libyans were disappointed at the lack of resolve by the US and the UK to remove the legal impasse, they would have to live with that disappointment for more than four years. Despite the suggestions of the mainstream media that Libya was intransigent, the record shows that it was the attitude of the US and UK governments which prevented a trial from taking place four years earlier. Senior officials on both sides of the Atlantic completely misread the situation on two fronts.

The victims' relatives, who had fought long and hard to see the judicial process prevail, were not prepared to let the issue drop and lobbied hard for a change in the Clinton administration's policy of trial in Scotland or the US only. In the UK, Jim Swire, who lost his daughter Flora on Pan Am 103, went to Libya and pressed Gadafy to personally intervene. His trip drew an angry response from American relatives, in particular Bert Ammerman who lost his brother Tom on the flight. Ammerman said:

> Dr Swire no doubt acted from sincerity, but it is the first time he left his brain at home. It was particularly counter-productive, just when we have raised the issue from a criminal matter on to the political stage. The Libyans have been trying to muddy the waters and win a propaganda coup, and have manipulated a private individual who is hardly astute in the ways of the world.[3]

Although they shared a common bond in the deaths of their loved ones, Swire's trip to Libya widened the rift between some of the relatives, with more of the Americans favouring military action against Libya.

Anniversaries of the bombing came and went accompanied by 'hearts and flowers' coverage by the US media in particular. The US media is so controlled by relatively few large corporations that it became a monumental task for investigative journalists to air any views other than those enshrined in the indictments. In the years between indictment and trial, little of substance was aired in the US.

Pan Am fatigue had set in and little changed until murmurings started, in July 1998, about a possible breakthrough. In the House of Lords on 30 July, Scotland's top law officer, Lord Advocate Andrew Hardie QC, a 1997 appointee to Tony Blair's New Labour government, confirmed that alternative ways of bringing the accused to justice were under consideration. He told peers at Question Time, 'Although I remain committed to a trial in Scotland, I can confirm that I have considered alternative ways of securing my objective of bringing the accused to justice.'[4]

The news quickly spread that Libya had relented and finally agreed to hand over the accused. The truth was that Libya had been prepared in principle since 1994 to hand over the two men for trial in a neutral country. On the same day Andrew Hardie was making his statement in the House of Lords, the United States and Britain refused to grant permission for a flight from Cairo to Tripoli by Arab League chief Esmat Abdel Meguid. Diplomatic sources said that the two countries blocked the request in the UN sanctions committee. A British diplomat said that the decision to reject the flight was taken because the journey could not be justified on humanitarian grounds. Abdel Meguid had informed the sanctions committee that he wished to travel to Tripoli on a four-day trip with a delegation to hold talks on the Lockerbie issue,[5] but family members remained sceptical, saying 'we will believe it when we see it'.

Gadafy's acceptance of the plan was announced on 26 August, but was the plan a new initiative worked out by senior diplomats? To the shock of many, it was not. The *Washington Post* reported:

> Indications last night were that the Libyans are prepared to go ahead. The US-British plan is almost identical to one that the Libyans themselves offered in 1994, and has been endorsed by the Arab League and other international organizations. Arab League Secretary General Esmat Abdel Meguid said on Tuesday that he expects Libya to accept.[6]

The plan was therefore essentially the same plan submitted by Professor Robert Black to Libya on 10 October 1993, and accepted by Libya in January 1994.

There had been over four wasted years while the United States and Britain prevaricated and blamed Libya at every opportunity. The trial, soon to be dubbed 'the trial of the century', was beginning to look as if it might take place. There were eight months from the time of the submission of the 'new' plan to the handover of the two accused into Scottish custody, a mere moment in diplomatic terms, compared to the years squandered by the UK and the US. With support from the Arab League, UN Secretary Kofi Anan and not least Nelson Mandela, Gadafy was reassured of the security arrangements necessary for the trial to proceed.

Along the way, as was to be expected, there were some minor hiccups. The day after he agreed to the trial, Gadafy announced he was concerned about the Americans 'playing tricks' and demanded further assurances. Ibrahim Legwell said that any sentences should be served in Libya, not Britain. Legwell went on to say that he needed guarantees of unfettered access to his clients and demanded that no access to the accused should be given to foreign agencies, and that there should be no lengthy delays to find witnesses. By 5 September, Gadafy had completely changed his mind and rejected the trial plan, accusing the United States and Britain of trying to use the Netherlands as a 'transit point' to get suspects extradited from there to Britain.

Meanwhile, Camp Zeist, a former US airforce base in the Netherlands, was chosen as the site for the trial. The Lord Advocate Andrew Hardie announced that he would lead the Crown's case with a team of six leading Advocates Depute. In Tripoli, Gadafy responded by replacing the Libyan lawyer who had handled the Libyans' defence. Out went Ibrahim Legwell and in came the astute Kamal Mahgoub, Libya's former foreign minister.

The next few weeks saw diplomatic letters flying fast and furiously between Tripoli, London and Washington. Libya was said to be unhappy with the choice of Camp Zeist and was concerned that if it belonged to the US, the Americans might kidnap the suspects. The Foreign Office in London told Libyan diplomats they would not change the condition in the agreement that the Libyans would serve their sentences, if convicted, in a British prison. One week before Christmas, it was announced that Libya's parliament endorsed the agreement to try the suspects in the Netherlands.

The new year heralded the start of some shuttle diplomacy by Prince Bandar, Saudi's ambassador to the USA. Accompanied by Jakes Gerwel, a senior aide to South African president Nelson Mandela, the prince met with Gadafy in Tripoli and attempted to address the Libyan leader's remaining concerns. Speculation from informed sources at the meeting suggested that a handover of the men could come about within weeks.

February proved to be a winter of discontent, from Tripoli to London. Gadafy was still insisting on the International Court at the Hague as the venue for the trial and appeared to be pulling back from the plan. The Foreign Office, in an effort to keep the plans on track, agreed to allow UN monitoring of Barlinnie Prison in Glasgow, the Scottish jail where the Libyans would serve their time, if convicted. Prison officers at Barlinnie had already dubbed the area set aside within the prison the 'Gadafy café'.

Following a lengthy meeting with Nelson Mandela, Gadafy announced on 2 March that the verbal assurances given by the South African leader were enough to break the deadlock. After further meetings with Hosni Mubarak, and with Mandela at his side, Gadafy told the assembled media that Libya would hand over the suspects by 6 April. In a press release on 23 March, the United Nations indicated that UN sanctions against Libya would be lifted on the handover. It now looked clearer than ever that the years of diplomatic stalling and intransigence were almost over. Less than two weeks later, on 5 April, accompanied by UN Counsel Hans Corel, Abdelbaset Ali Mohmed Al Megrahi and Al Amin Khalifa Fhimah walked down the steps of the plane at Camp Ziest and were immediately arrested on an International Warrant by the Dutch police.

With their suspects safely in custody within the confines of Camp Zeist, it soon became clear that the Scottish Crown, having had almost eight years to prepare for this trial, were in fact not yet ready. The accused spent part of the time hooded and when they eventually arrived at the prison the unfinished building had no beds. Under Scots law, accused persons held in custody must be brought to trial within 110 days. Sources close to the Libyan defence team indicated that if the '110-day rule' had been applied, it was doubtful that the prosecution would have been able to proceed against Megrahi and Fhimah.

Since Scots law requires co-accused individuals to be represented separately in court, by May 1999 Alistair Duff, while continuing to represent Megrahi, had handed on the representation of Fhimah to Edward MacKechnie, a partner in the Glasgow firm McGrigor Donald. The choice was a surprise to many in the legal establishment, as neither MacKechnie nor his firm had a reputation for criminal work.

The defence had what must have seemed a mammoth task ahead of them. They had been handed a Crown witness list containing nearly 1,200 names, from as far east as Tokyo and as far west as Montevideo. The list was sprinkled with obvious witnesses from the FBI and the Scottish police, along with officers from Germany's BKA. Alongside these names were others not so obvious for the Crown's case: Steven Greene, Michael Hurley, Fred Ganem and Bohdan Mizak were all either serving or retired DEA agents. Two FBI agents, Dave Edward and Chris Murray, whose role in the Pan Am investigation had respectively spilled over into separate prosecutions of Juval Aviv and Lester Coleman, appeared alongside convicted terrorist Mohammed Abu Talb.

While the inclusion of some of these witnesses was surprising, those whom many believed had close knowledge of the investigation were ominously missing from the Crown list. These included the former head of the Lockerbie Task Force and later chief constable of Strathclyde Police, Sir John Orr. He consented to a defence lawyer's request to provide a precognition statement, during which he was accompanied by a police lawyer. Another major omission from the witness list was the CIA's former head of counter-terrorism, Vincent Cannistraro. Considering his central role in the Agency's Lockerbie-related efforts in the first two years after the bombing, during which time the Agency provided vital intelligence concerning Libyan timing devices, it would have been logical and almost elementary police procedure to call him as a witness. Not only was his name removed from the original witness list, but Cannistraro also claimed that he was never interviewed by Scottish police or the prosecution. Cannistraro told the authors: 'Given that my views on the subject are somewhat at variance with the government's position, I imagine it was the Department of Justice that removed my name from the list of potential witnesses.' He added:

As far as the Crown is concerned, I never had any dealings with them. In fact, no one in any official capacity, either in the US or the UK, has contacted me on this matter, with the single exception of the invitation to a meeting with the defence team visiting Washington DC.[7]

Cannistraro refused to meet with the defence team and insists he would have testified had he been asked. In an earlier interview, however, he stated that he would not attend the trial as a witness for two reasons: firstly that his life would be endangered, and secondly, that there was nothing admissible to which he could testify.[8]

It might have been expected that the Scottish police and Crown would be relaxed about an investigation, which had been all but completed prior to the 1991 indictments. There would of course be a certain amount of tidying up to be done, but all the evidence must have been in place when the Lord Advocate, Lord Peter Fraser, announced the indictments. Or was it?

Behind the scenes, what really happened on that day in April 1999 when the two Libyans surrendered themselves to the Scottish police was described by a senior source within the Crown Office as 'panic'. 'After all,' the source went on, 'no one ever expected that Gadafy would allow the men to stand trial.' This source, who for obvious reasons cannot be named, was to talk constantly of a 'concern' over what some prosecutors saw as a weak case. Scotland's top two law officers had responsibility for the prosecution. The Solicitor General for Scotland, Colin Boyd QC, was, like Lord Advocate Andrew Hardie QC, an appointee to Tony Blair's New Labour government. Hardie was regarded by legal and political insiders as a shrewd and intelligent operator.

The imminent trial revived media interest in the Lockerbie story. One of the authors of this book was commissioned to produce a US radio documentary on the case. While researching the programme in Germany during the autumn of 1999, he came close to literally bumping into Scottish police officers scouring the country for potential witnesses to interview. One of these witnesses was Gunther Kasteleiner, a Frankfurt Airport employee who was on duty dealing with the airport's baggage on 21 December 1988, at the time of the departure of the Pan Am feeder Flight 103A to London. Interviewed for the radio documentary, Kasteleiner said he had been interviewed several months after the Lockerbie bombing by the BKA, but was not interviewed by the Scottish police until August 1999. When Kasteleiner gave evidence in the Pan Am civil compensation trial in

1992 he was on the witness stand for five days, yet his inteview with the Scottish police lasted only an hour.

A former CIA agent, who spoke to the authors on condition of anonymity in 1999 and again in 2000, described the original investigation into the bombing of Pan Am 103 as 'more of a stall than a proper investigation'. One of the many disturbing aspects of the police and Crown Office investigations was how much they would rely on the work of the FBI and the CIA. For years the public had heard of painstaking detective work, but now, with the trial imminent, it was clear that much of the detective work had been overlooked. With hindsight, had defence teams insisted on their clients being tried within the 110 days the case would probably have collapsed.

Correctly working on the principal that the prosecution might be in possession of a 'smoking gun' – a piece of evidence so powerful that it would take much painstaking work to undermine – both defence teams set about the huge task of taking precognition statements from the army of Crown witnesses. The vast geographical spread of the witnesses made this exercise a logistical nightmare. More than half of the witnesses were outside the UK, with the list of countries to be visited including Australia, Canada, Cyprus, the Czech Republic, Denmark, France, Germany, Italy, Ireland, Japan, Libya, Malta, Senegal, Sweden, South Africa, Switzerland and the USA. With the huge task of interviewing witnesses set to take many months, the defence teams would be spending a lot of time in the air. Mindful of the difficulties faced by both sides, the presiding judge Lord Sutherland twice agreed 110-day extensions, delaying the opening of the trial until May 2000.

Would all of the nearly 1,300 witnesses be called? Probably not. Nevertheless, it was reasonable to assume that all would, in some way, be relevant to the case. But as the defence lawyers blazed a trail through the United States, it became clear that many of those on the Crown list had no idea why they were there. The reality was that many of those listed, as former and serving agents of the FBI, had absolutely no connection with the Lockerbie investigation. Lawyers travelled thousands of miles to interview FBI agents who would recount stories of their part in the Oklahoma bombing but knew nothing of the Lockerbie investigation.

What was going on? Why would the Crown list witnesses whom they had never even interviewed? The Crown Office declined to answer any questions on this matter. Could it be that the Crown needed the time to prepare their own case? Sources at the Crown Office, who spoke on condition of anonymity, claimed a less sinister motive, saying the Crown

Office had simply accepted a list provided by the US Department of Justice (DoJ). This begged the question, did the Crown check those witness with whom it was not familiar?

The two lead defence solicitors, Alistair Duff and Edward MacKechnie, had to appoint Senior Counsel. Duff chose the ebullient William Taylor QC as lead counsel, assisted by David Burns QC and John Beckett. Taylor was one of those rare QCs who by qualification could appear in both English and Scottish courts. If the odd eyebrow had been raised in Edinburgh's New Club at MacKechnie's appointment, jaws must have dropped at his choice of lead counsel. Richard Keen QC was a civil law specialist and had never before appeared in any criminal trial. He had earned the nickname of 'The Rottweiller' for his no-nonsense advocacy, commanding court presence and outstanding attention to detail. MacKechnie balanced his team with two advocates with considerable criminal experience, Jack Davidson QC and Murdo MacLeod.

The prosecution team was to be led by Andrew Hardie QC, assisted by Senior Counsel Alistair Campbell QC, Alan Turnbull QC and juniors Jonathan Lake and Morag Armstrong. That, at least, was the plan. But on 16 February 2000, Andrew Hardie resigned his position in order to become a High Court judge.

The news came as a bolt from the blue to many of the relatives who had been receiving assurances about the trial from the Crown Office, but others were less surprised. Hardie denied his decision was anything to do with Lockerbie, describing claims that he had accepted the appointment because the successful prosecution of the two Libyan suspects was in doubt as 'outrageous'. Nevertheless Hardie had, in the past, made no secret of his opposition to the Lockerbie trial taking place anywhere but Scotland. *The Scotsman* observed: 'The case against the two Libyan suspects of the Lockerbie bombing has looked increasingly rocky over the past few months, leaving the task of leading the prosecution a potentially poisoned chalice.'[9] The *Sunday Herald* was more blunt, commenting: 'Hardie's explanations for why he resigned were at best ambiguous. He muttered about it being time to move on, but that was about it as far as reasons were concerned.'[10]

Hardie's predecessor as Lord Advocate joined in the criticism. Writing in the *Mail on Sunday*, Lord Peter Fraser of Carmyllie remarked:

> He played a tireless and distinguished part in laying out the evidence before the Fatal Accident Inquiry in Dumfries. He must have heard the sound of silence as the relatives of those killed saw that instant of irreversible horror. Yet he has chosen to leave his

office as Lord Advocate only weeks before the trial begins . . . This should have been the time to demonstrate to the world the robust, straightforward fairness of Scottish criminal justice. Instead, we have the American relatives of those slain above Lockerbie reeling in disbelief that Scotland's most senior law officer has, without warning or explanation, elevated himself to the bench of our Supreme Courts.[11]

A week after Hardie's resignation, his deputy and former Solicitor General, Colin Boyd QC, was installed as Lord Advocate. The new boy would now have to do the rounds of the US DoJ and meet the US relatives to assure them that the case was still on course.

As the trial date approached, Boyd applied to the court for a further postponement, on the grounds that the prosecution needed time to interview the people who appeared on the defence's witness list, but the application was rejected by Lord Sutherland. The Crown subsequently suggested, wrongly, that the defence list was submitted late. When the claim was successfully refuted, the Crown's spin was that although not submitted late, neither was it submitted early.

It would not be the last time that the Crown was economical with the truth.

16. NO SMOKING GUN

Eleven years, four months and thirteen days after the Lockerbie bombing, the case finally reached the criminal court. On 3 May 2000, in an atmosphere described by one relative as 'saturated with emotion', the trial of Abdel Basset Ali Al-Megrahi and Lamin Khalifa Fhimah opened at Camp Zeist in the Netherlands.

The public gallery was packed with relatives of victims and a number of journalists lucky enough to get a seat in the courtroom. The rest of the assembled media had to watch the proceedings from the Press Centre, formerly the gymnasium of the camp in its military days. In the newly completed high-tech courtroom the stage was set, at last, for the day many had thought would never come. The assembled gathering waited. For many, it would be their first glimpse of the accused Libyans.

This was Scotland's High Court of Justiciary. The huge seal of the court hung on the wall above the bench, at which the four Law Lords would sit and hear the case. The courtroom itself resembled no other Scottish High Court. Television and computer monitors dominated the desks in the well of the court. Each lawyer had access to a Live Note transcription of the proceedings, which flowed to their screens from the terminal of the court reporter who was seated alongside and to the right of the judges.

A huge floor-to-ceiling bulletproof, soundproof glass wall had been installed to separate the public and press from the lawyers and judges, as well as the accused. Advocates in traditional black robes and grey wigs milled around silently behind the glass, talking with their instructing lawyers and court officials. Headsets enabled onlookers and members of the media to hear what was being said in court. Translators, hidden behind a smoked-glass balcony, provided instant Arabic translation of the events for the accused and their families. Witnesses would later testify in German, Japanese and Maltese. Closed-circuit TV monitors were installed to allow the public unprecedented close-up views of documents and pieces of evidence as they were presented to the court.

The accused were seated very close to the glass wall on the left of the court. Flanked by two police officers, they were led into the dock at the start of each day in court, Megrahi always followed by Fhimah. Megrahi's seating left him almost within touching distance of his family members at the other side of the glass. Immediately in front of the accused sat Megrahi's legal team, with his solicitor, Alistair Duff, taking the back row behind William Taylor QC, David Burns QC and John Beckett, the advocates. Fhimah's legal team, headed by Eddie MacKechnie, were seated nearer the judges' bench, with their front row of advocates, Richard Keen QC, Jack Davidson QC and Murdo MacLeod.

Closest to the glass and in the middle sat the witnesses, with their backs to the public. Immediately to the right of the witness box were two figures whose very presence in the court caused some eyebrows to be raised. Their behaviour would later give rise to comment. Brian Murtaugh and Dana Biehl were attorneys representing the United States Department of Justice (DoJ). Murtaugh was one of the attorneys who drew up the US indictment against the two Libyans.

Richard Keen QC is said to have been incandescent with rage at the presence of the DoJ attorneys, and was prepared to raise the matter with the court. Eddie MacKechnie, though, mindful of his ongoing precognitions of US witnesses and the need for the cooperation of the DoJ, persuaded Keen to calm down. To the right of the US attorneys sat the Crown legal team, led by Colin Boyd, Scotland's Lord Advocate. Scotland's top law officer Boyd would play little part in the actual trial in the courtroom. This task would fall to his Advocates Depute, Campbell and Turnbull, assisted by Lake and Armstrong.

Scotland's legal system has its own peculiar idiosyncrasies and one of these is the Macer. This court official walks ahead of the judges as they enter the courtroom, solemnly carrying the mace which is hung on the wall below the Royal Arms of Scotland, emblazoned with the Latin inscription *Nemo Me Impune Lacessit*, which roughly translates to 'No one attacks me and gets away with it'.

At the start of each court day the judges, Lords Sutherland, MacLean and Coulsfield entered from the left, bowed deferentially to the standing gallery and court and took their seats. They were accompanied by a fourth judge, Lord Abernethy, who was sitting in case one of the other three were to become indisposed. The Clerk of the Court seated immediately below and in front of the judges then uttered the phrase he would say every day the court was sitting: 'Call the diet, Her Majesty's Advocate against Abdel Basset Ali Mohmed Al-Megrahi and Al-Lamin Khalifa Fhimah.'

Many of the US relatives who attended the trial were soon to discover that Scottish trials bear little resemblance to legal procedures in their own country. This trial would have no opening statements by either Crown or defence. Many journalists, who had done little research on the case, relying instead on an opening statement by the prosecution to outline the charges, would be disappointed.

The first few hours of the trial's opening day were taken up by reading the entire indictment into the record. Many relatives carried photographs of their loved ones, lest any one should forget why they were there. Eager reporters shouted questions outside the court and some family members, who had become something akin to media celebrities, gratefully gave interviews. Other relatives preferred to savour a quiet moment of reflection.

The defence gave an indication of their tactics when they lodged notice of a 'special defence' with the court. This made it clear that the defence were going to implicate other people in the Pan Am bombing. The Clerk read into the record:

> My Lord, there is lodged by each of the accused a notice which in each case reads in the following terms: that the accused state that they plead not guilty, and further, especially and without prejudice to said plea, give notice at their trial that they may lead evidence calculated to exculpate themselves which evidence may tend to incriminate the persons listed in the schedule attached to this notice and the commission of the crimes libelled in the indictment, either singly or in concert with others in the schedule or in concert with other persons.
>
> And the schedule, My Lord, reads as follows:
>
> (1) Members of the PPSF, which may include Mohammed Abu Talb, Crown Witness Number 963, Talal Chabaan, present whereabouts unknown, Mohammed Ghaloom Khalil Hassan, present whereabouts unknown, Hashem Salem, also known as Hashem Abu Nada, present whereabouts unknown, Mohamed Abu Faja, present whereabouts unknown, Abd El Salam Arif Abu Nada, Magdy Moussa, Jamal Haider, all present whereabouts unknown, but all formerly directors of the Miska Bakery, Malta and Imad Adel Hazzouri, Gawrha, 42 Triq Patri, Guzi Delia Street, Balzan. (2) Members of the Popular Front for the Liberation of Palestinian – General Command. (3) Parviz Taheri, Crown Witness 996.¹

The first witness to be called by the Crown was Richard Ellis Dawson, an air traffic controller from Taplow in Buckinghamshire. The Crown's intention was to track, for the benefit of the court, the Pam Am flight from

Heathrow to that fateful portion of the dark skies over Lockerbie. Dawson told the court he was the flight departure controller who handled the departure of Flight 103 from Heathrow. He was one of the very few witnesses to be examined by the Lord Advocate himself. He described how he cleared the Pan Am flight for take-off with the words, 'Clipper 103's cleared for take-off, 27 right, surface wind 240 at 12 knots.' He recounted that he noted the flight was airborne at 1825.

The new high-tech facilities in the courtroom, in particular the sound system, were acting up, causing Lord Sutherland to call an adjournment – the first of many, although not all for technical reasons.

Further evidence was heard from other air traffic controllers, including Alan Topp who described losing contact with the jumbo jet. He talked the court through videotape of the radar screen, explaining at one stage: 'Well, I've lost secondary response, and the single primary response has now developed into . . . here are three primary responses. And there's a further two appeared.'[2] These five pieces were pieces of Pan Am 103 in the moments after the bomb detonated, blowing the plane apart.

Airline pilot Robin Chamberlain, a captain with British Airways flying the shuttle from Heathrow to Glasgow that evening, described what he saw from his cockpit window:

> We were at our cruising altitude of 35,000 feet, approximately 15 miles to the south of Carlisle. And out of my left-hand side, at what we would call our 1100 position, just slightly left of the nose, I caught a glimpse of a flashing orange light. I hadn't been doing shuttle flights for very long, and I wasn't aware that we had any oilfields, or whatever, out to that side of the country. But it looked just like a gas flare burning off, as they do from the oilfields in the Middle East and places like that.
>
> I saw something else, approximately 30 seconds later, in the same relative position to us, which my co-pilot also saw. It was a very large explosion, which was obviously on the ground . . . it looked very much to me as if something like an oil storage – sorry, a petrol storage tank – had blown up. That's what it looked like from where I was. If you imagine things that you see in films, it looked just like that, or, you know, a huge explosion, a bomb, or something of that nature.

At the time he could not possibly know it, but what Captain Chamberlain and his co-pilot were seeing on the ground below was the fuel-laden tanks of Pan Am's *Maid of the Seas* exploding on a quiet Lockerbie street, bringing death by inferno to all in its path.

The first day ended as quietly as it had begun. The assembled media rushed for the first day's comments from relatives, from friends, from anyone who seemed likely to be involved. Relatives ran a gauntlet of the world's media as they departed the court building. As the trial progressed the media presence would diminish to a mere sprinkling, comprising of less than a handful of reporters and one stalwart freelance photographer, Paul O'Driscoll, who attended the trial every day.

As this trial was being heard without a jury, it was thought that the Crown would not necessarily call local residents to attest to the fact that something very dramatic had happened in Lockerbie on that fateful day of 21 December. The Crown, though, in part understandibly to satisfy the clamour from US relatives, decided to relive the night of horrors by bringing a succession of local Lockerbie residents into the witness box. These witnesses went unchallenged by either of the defence teams and, as a consequence, on the second day of the trial the Crown ran out of witnesses and the trial adjourned early.

During Friday, 5 May, day three of the trial, the names of all those who perished aboard Pan Am 103 and on the ground in Lockerbie were read into the record. This was, perhaps, the most sombre and poignant moment for all those in court, but especially for those who had lost loved ones and friends; 270 names in all.

Day three also brought about the confirmation that agents of the US Central Intelligence Agency were on the ground in Lockerbie very quickly. Chief Inspector Alexander McLean admitted under cross-examination by Richard Keen QC, for Fhimah, that CIA agents were involved in the recovery of items:

> *Q.* And I infer from your answer that you are aware that items were being recovered from the site by members of the Central Intelligence Agency?
> *A:* I understand at one point there may have been, sir, yes. It was a necessity for a liaison officer like myself to be appointed, to ensure that the procedures, as far as the productions in the criminal inquiry, were carried out to its extent.
> *Q.* It would be unusual, in the course of most criminal inquiries, to find members of a foreign intelligence agency recovering evidence at the site, would it not?
> *A:* Well, yes. It would be, sir, yes. It wouldn't be allowed,

particularly. It would be under the control of the Scottish police.

Q: Do I take it that this was not something that you'd encountered in the past?

A: I hadn't personally encountered this.

One police witness inadvertently, or perhaps with a Freudian slip, described the CIA as the Criminal Intelligence Agency.

Week two began with mostly repetitious police testimony concerning the labelling of items of debris and property found at Lockerbie and beyond. During the course of the examination of Detective Constable Thomas Gilchrist, the court would hear about the 'discovery' of what was one of the prosecution's main items of forensic evidence, the fragment of circuit board allegedly from a Mebo MST-13 timer sold to Libya. Although not identified in detail as such, it was referred to as 'PI/995'.

From the cross-examination of Gilchrist by Richard Keen QC, it was clear that this piece of evidence had been originally labelled 'cloth', because it was supposedly tucked away inside a grey piece of 'Slalom 2' shirt. But the word 'cloth' was later written over with the word 'debris'. Gilchrist admitted that he had replaced his original 'cloth' description with 'debris'. He denied that he had been asked to do this, but could not account for the change in description. Neither could he account for the whereabouts of this piece of evidence from 13 January 1989, the date it was found, to 17 January 1989, the date it was logged into the police property log.

This was a rather innocuous introduction into the court record of one of the most hotly disputed pieces of evidence, and was pounced upon by Keen. The Mebo fragment would later resurface under its designated evidence label of 'PT/35B', but for the moment its significance was lost on all but the most avid Lockerbie observers.

On 10 May Gwendoline Horton, a pensioner from Morpeth, Northumberland, testified about the discovery of an instruction manual for a Toshiba radio-cassette player. She had found it on the morning after the bombing among the debris in a field near to her house. The exhibit, labelled 'PK/689', which was shown to the court, was a torn and charred page, containing the final letters 'IBA' of Toshiba, and the incomplete words:

Cassette recorder
SF-16
BomBeat SF16

She said she recognised the item, but remarked, 'I'm sure when I handed it in, it was in one piece.'

The week would prove to be short. The Crown had intended to call over 240 witnesses to speak of the collection of debris from Lockerbie. The defence teams did not challenge most of these witnesses, and it was obvious to observers at the trial that the constant trail of witnesses into the box with no defence challenge did not sit well with their Lordships. Subsequently, Advocate Depute Campbell for the Crown told the court that both sides had been in consultation and agreement was close on a joint minute, which would eliminate a large number of witnesses and therefore speed up the entire process. It was also clear that the Crown needed time to take precognition statements from four defence witnesses.

The Crown Office had been intimating that the defence had not been timely in the notification of its witness list, but in reality the defence had complied with the rules governing the notification of witnesses. The Crown were assisted in this by the US Department of Justice, who were always willing to suggest that almost every adjournment was the fault of the defence.

During this period, one of the Crown's own witnesses, Edwin Bollier of Mebo, was informing the world's media that he had commissioned a forensic report, the results of which were at odds with the Crown's own theory of the bombing.

On 11 May, after only seven days of trial and six days of testimony, the court was adjourned until 23 May. This adjournment, one of many, would leave family members who had travelled to Camp Zeist from the USA kicking their heels as tourists in the Netherlands.

Monday, 23 May came and went, with no witnesses called and a further adjournment. The High Court's new high-tech system had failed. The following morning saw the reappearance in court of Colin Boyd, the Lord Advocate. The reason for his attendance had little to do with the trial, and more to do with an article in the Scottish *Sunday Herald.* The article had so infuriated the Lord Advocate that he had decided to use the privilege of the court to attack the newspaper and the two journalists, Neil MacKay and Ian Ferguson:

> *The Lord Advocate.* My Lords, the evidence this morning will be led by the learned Advocate Depute, Mr Campbell; but before starting hearing this evidence, there is a matter of concern to me which I wish to bring to the court's attention. It concerns an article which appeared in the *Sunday Herald* on 14 May. As My Lords will be aware, the *Sunday Herald* is a newspaper which is published and

circulates in Scotland. My Lords, I have copies of the article for the court, in case My Lords have not seen it. My Lords will see that the article is entitled 'LOCKERBIE REPORT LEAVES TRIAL IN CHAOS', and appears under the by-line of Neil Mackay, the home affairs editor, and Ian Ferguson in New York.

My Lords, the article is largely inaccurate and misleading. However, it is not for that reason that I bring it to the court's attention; it is because it makes allegations about the Crown's conduct, which impinge on our relationship with the court. My Lords will see that the article starts off: 'The two Libyans accused of downing Pan Am 103 could not have planted the bomb, according to a devastating scientific report submitted by one of the Crown's star witnesses. The report threw the prosecution into disarray and forced the adjournment of the Lockerbie trial for 12 days.'

The article goes on to say that the Crown witness sent me a report claiming the Crown's version of the bombing was scientifically impossible. My Lords, I can confirm that I did receive a document from this witness. It was in German. It was sent for translation, and the English version was received last week. I understand that the Defence have a copy.

He continued:

My Lords will see, in the first column, that the article quotes an unnamed senior legal expert who alleges that the Crown will drag the case out for as long as possible so that they can say they tried their best. That is, of course, nonsense. In the fourth paragraph, immediately after that, the article then says: 'Senior Crown Office sources have admitted to the *Sunday Herald* that the report submitted to the Lord Advocate just days before the trial started provided such startling new evidence that the prosecution had no alternative but to seek an adjournment to consider the future of the trial.'

My Lords, there is no truth in that allegation. The article quotes further from alleged unnamed Crown sources. In the first paragraph of the third column, My Lords will see a direct quote attributed to a Crown source. Then, in the second full paragraph in column 4, we see the following: 'On Thursday the prosecution successfully asked for the case, being heard at a Scottish court sitting in the Netherlands, to be adjourned for 12 days. Alistair Campbell QC said that the Crown needed more time to interview witnesses over technical and scientific matters relating to the destruction of Pan Am 103' . . . My Lords, there is no Crown Office source. No member of the Lockerbie team spoke to the *Sunday Herald*. And nobody with any knowledge of the Crown case or of the Lockerbie team could have spoken those words.

My Lords, the clear implication of the article is that the Crown misled the court. According to the article, it was the appearance of this document that was the reason for the adjournment. My Lords, the reasons for the adjournment were quite clearly stated in open court by the Advocate Depute. He stated that it was to enable the four Defence experts, whom he named, to be seen and precognosced for the Crown, and for the Crown experts to be seen so that they could respond to whatever Defence evidence could be anticipated.

My Lords, the article makes numerous references to the evidence, which would be quite unacceptable if this were a jury trial. I gave consideration as to whether or not it might amount to a contempt of court. However, standing the reasoning in the case raised by the two accused against the *Sunday Times*, I do not intend to make a submission to that effect. I appreciate that this is a case which arouses considerable media interest, and from time to time much speculation and comment . . . I hope that I have now set the record straight.

My Lords, I should perhaps add that from what I have seen of the reporting of the trial itself, it is generally excellent. It is fair, accurate and balanced, and it performs a vital service in informing the public, both in Scotland and elsewhere, of what is happening in the trial. We must not forget, of course, that justice must not only be done, but be seen to be done, and journalists must be free to report and comment on the proceedings. And I commend the press for the high quality of service in covering the trial itself.

I hope, however, that journalists will remember that it is the evidence in court which matters, and not what is downloaded from the internet. It is a trial process, which tests the evidence and decides ultimately on the guilt or innocence of the accused according to our law. It is in nobody's interests that we try and prejudge the issue and usurp the function of this Court.

Lord Sutherland: Thank you, Lord Advocate. I am sure the court accepts entirely what you say . . . accordingly, the court would have no difficulty in accepting entirely what you say and regretting this fairly lamintable article. It is entirely clear to us that if this had been a jury trial, then of course an article of this nature would have been a gross contempt of court. We understand your reasons for not wishing to treat it as a contempt of court in the present circumstances, but, like you, we very much regret that idle speculation of this kind should be bandied about in the press, which is entirely contrary to the responsible reporting to which you have referred.[3]

The *Herald* reporters had more than one senior source in the Crown Office connected with the Lockerbie team. It was perhaps the thought that his own department may have been leaking to the press that partly precipitated the Lord Advocate's fury. It was also known that the Crown was taking Bollier's report very seriously, and were able to have it checked out during the adjournment under cover of the legitimate reason given to the judges by Alistair Campbell. The *Sunday Herald* vigorously defended its story and was one of the few British, and the only Scottish, newspapers with the courage to report on the issues at Lockerbie, with other exclusives 'CIA GAGS WITNESS'[4] and 'PAN AM LAWYER HOLDS EVIDENCE TO RANSOM'.[5]

By this time, day ten of the trial, only a handful of the victims' relatives were to be found in the public gallery. Two of the British ones, Jim Swire and Rev John Mosey, were almost permanent fixtures, listening attentively and from time to time taking copious notes. They were about to witness a highly technical chapter in the trial, that of the piecing together of the elements of the Air Accident Investigation Board, along with scientific officers from the Defence Evaluation and Research Agency, formerly RARDE.

The court, once again, had to be adjourned early in order to rebuild what was left of the luggage container AVE 4041, said to have contained the bomb suitcase. This chapter of evidence was to be a battle of wits and intellect between various witnesses and Richard Keen QC, who single-handedly carried out the cross-examination of the Crown's technical and scientific witnesses.

While the drama in the courtroom revolved around the reconstructed baggage container, the defence team was busy exploring numerous lines of investigation. Before the end of the trial, Fhimah's lawyer, Eddie MacKechnie, would instruct the Washington DC law firm of Butera & Andrews to raise three legal actions in the United States. MacKechnie was clearly not leaving anything to chance in the defence of his client.

The first of these legal moves was a subpoena served upon James Shaughnessy, the New York lawyer who had represented Pan Am and their insurers in the aftermath of the disaster. Shaughnessy claimed to one of the authors that he had retained evidence from the civil compensation case, which Pan Am lost, evidence which Shaughnessy maintained would lead to the acquittal of the Libyans if presented at the criminal trial. Shaughnessy was not prepared to hand over this evidence, even when it was put to him that this very evidence might prevent a miscarriage of justice. When pressed further, he declared the 'evidence' did not belong to him but to the airline's insurers and Pan Am itself, which was still a legal entity.

Despite humanitarian pleas and questions of wrongful conviction, Shaughnessy made it clear that access to his 'evidence' would cost a quarter of a million dollars.

Within weeks of this story breaking in the *Sunday Herald*, Shaughnessy had instructed an Edinburgh law firm to sue the newspaper for libel. His appetite for a court battle diminished when he was informed that both meetings with the author had been secretly recorded. MacKechnie's team successfully retrieved at least part of Shaughnessy's 'evidence' and, although some of it was thought to be useful, it in no way matched Shaughnessy's own opinion of the material. In the run up to the trial, Shaughnessy had offered his services, and presumably his material, to the defence team for a much larger sum than the quarter of million he was later to demand, but had been turned down flat.

Back in court, the Crown attempted to establish the exact whereabouts of the bomb suitcase within the luggage container. For the brown Samsonite to have been transferred from the Air Malta flight to the Pan Am feeder flight 103A to Heathrow, it had to have been placed at least one layer off the floor of the container, because the bottom layer comprised luggage loaded at Heathrow. The Crown made a great effort to prove the so-called 'stand-off distance', the distance between the blast and the aircraft's fuselage. Through a succession of technical experts, Peter Claiden, Ian Cullis and Professor Christopher Peel of the Defence Evaluation and Research Agency (DERA, formerly RARDE), and Christopher Protheroe of the Department of Transport's Air Accident Investigation Branch, along with an equally baffling set of statistics and formulae, the Crown spent much of the fifth week of the trial dealing with this issue.

Professor Peel concluded, from examination of the baggage container and the fuselage, that the device had detonated relatively low down in the container near to the outer wall but was not in a bag on the floor of the container. Peel would insist that his calculations showed a stand-off distance of over 20 inches, but under masterful cross-examination by Richard Keen QC he conceded that, using another formula, the distance would be much less than 20 inches and that he may have unconsciously retrospectively altered his view of the facts in order to apply them to his analytical model. The Crown seemed taken aback for the technical expertise that Keen exhibited in his cross-examination. The defence would subsequently make much of this during their closing arguments.

In June, as the trial moved painstakingly slowly on to further technical evidence, Alistair Duff and Eddie MacKechnie, lead lawyers for both the accused, flew to Amman, the capital of Jordan, to meet with the Autumn Leaves bomb-maker Marwan Khreesat. The meeting would be a formal precognition of a wanted terrorist who had escaped trial in Germany in 1988, when he had informed German police that he was a double agent for Jordanian intelligence. He had spent the remaining years in protective custody in Jordan, agreeing only to briefings with the CIA and the FBI.

As anticipated, Khreesat denied that he had anything to do with the bombing of Pan Am 103. Astonishingly, he went on to say that he had carefully designed bombs that would not explode, but he could not explain how one of his devices went off, killing a German police bomb technician. When asked about the other members of the PFLP-GC's Autumn Leaves gang, Khreesat made the extremely odd claim that gang members Martin Kadorah and Abdel Fattah Ghadanfar were one and the same person. Ghadanfar served a prison sentence along with Hafez Dalkamoni, while Martin Kadorah remained free and was living in a Stuttgart suburb when contacted by the authors in 1999. Ghadanfar is believed to have returned to Syria on his release from prison.

In the Scottish legal system, the contents of a precognition cannot be used as evidence. Khreesat could not be summoned as a witness, but the defence hoped he might testify over a video link from Jordan. Later in the trial, the Crown advised that this video link would not take place.

One of the most significant facts to come from the Khreesat meeting was his confirmation that when making his bombs in Germany he used both mono and stereo models. This important fact was also given to the CIA, who debriefed Khreesat in 1989, months before the FBI gained access to him.[1]

Throughout the years from the indictment till the trial itself, spin doctors for both the Scottish Crown and the US Department of Justice maintained that the case against the Libyans was strong. As the trial itself progressed, however, doubts grew that the prosecution had a 'smoking gun'.

Tension mounted at the trial as the manufacturer of the timer alleged to have brought down Pan Am 103, Edwin Bollier, was tipped to give evidence soon. But before Bollier was to fly in from Zurich, the trial would hear lengthy evidence from two more witnesses, Dr Thomas Hayes and Allen Feraday, whose testimony was fraught with problems and issues of credibility.

Dr Hayes, formerly head of the Forensics Explosives laboratory at RARDE, with 16 years' experience, was a highly trained scientist but had since become a chiropodist. He testified to many of the items of clothing and debris, which the Crown alleged were associated with the suitcase containing the bomb. His testimony was crucial to the Crown and yet when the time for cross-examination began, his credibility was put immediately under scrutiny. Richard Keen QC's opening questions set the tone for what was to come.

> Q. Dr. Hayes, you told us in your evidence in chief that you were head of the Forensic Explosives Laboratory at RARDE until 1989?
> A: Yes, sir.
> Q. And your change of career from forensic scientist to chiropodist would appear to coincide in point of time with the decision of the Home Secretary to appoint Sir John May to inquire into the trial of those known as the Maguire Seven. Is that true?
> A: I believe so. I don't recall clearly.
> Q. Well, don't you recall that on two occasions you were called to give evidence to that inquiry?
> A: Yes.[6]

The May Inquiry had concluded that the RARDE scientists' notebooks, including that of Hayes, had not been fully disclosed. The inquiry also discovered that a second set of tests had been carried out, but the results were not disclosed.

Keen read out loud the most damning indictment of Hayes's RARDE colleagues:

> In the appellant's case, the disclosure of scientific evidence was woefully deficient. Three senior RARDE scientists took the law into their own hands and concealed from the prosecution, the defence, and the court, matters which might have changed the course of the trial . . . [they] knowingly placed a false and distorted scientific picture before the jury. It is, in our judgement, also a necessary

inference that the three senior RARDE forensic scientists acted in concert in withholding material evidence.'

Whatever the opinions of the result of the testimony of Hayes, Keen had firmly and very adroitly highlighted the issue over the credibility and competence of the RARDE witnesses.

Under cross-examination, Hayes was unable to account for a number of occurrences. The Crown contended that Hayes discovered the crucial fragment of circuit board from the Mebo MST-13 timer, later to be labelled, on 12 May 1989. The pagination in the notebook, in which Hayes claimed to have made contemporaneous notes, was distinctly out of synch and had been renumbered. Pages 51–55 were reset as 52–56. When pressed on this, Hayes described it as 'an unfathomable mystery'. Under cross-examination, Hayes also stated that he had no clear recollection of finding the circuit board designated PT/35B. He now relied on his notes and yet was unable to explain why a designation of PT/30 would appear after the entry for PT/35B. Keen asked Hayes about the memo sent by his colleague Allen Feraday to Detective Inspector William Williamson. The memo dated 15 September 1989 read: 'Willy, enclosed are some Polaroid photographs of the green circuit board. Sorry about the quality, but it is the best I can do in such a short time. The diameter of the curvature of the edge is 0.6 inches IE.'

Hayes was unable to explain why an article that had been discovered in May and photographed by the forensic photographer would require poor quality Polaroids in September. The memo continued, with the following request from Feraday: 'I feel that this fragment could be potentially most important, so any light your lads/lasses can shed upon the problem of identifying it would be most welcome.'

It was not lost on the defence that the lads/lasses could hardly shed any light at all on an item they had not seen, as it had been embedded in a shirt collar and not recorded at the time as a piece of green circuit board. So why did Feraday not send the larger, better-quality photographs to the police? Hayes continued to be lost for an answer and had a problem with his memory, an affliction shared by many of the Crown's key witnesses.

Continuing relentlessly, Keen pressed Dr Hayes on the issue of a grey suitcase that had appeared at RARDE with a rectangular hole cut in it, near to the locking mechanism. The hole, according to Hayes, was neither the result of blast damage, nor of impact damage. Yet his notes had stated 'clear indications of explosives involvement' and had described the case's contents as: 'Assorted clothing which, unlike the suitcase from which it was supposedly taken, showed little evidence of explosives involvement.' Hayes agreed with the suggestion, put to him by Keen, that the case with the absence of any brand-name labels, name tags or other identifying marks, the cut hole and the clothes were consistent with interference by a third party prior to its arrival at RARDE.

The case in question belonged to Major Charles McKee, the intelligence officer returning home from Beirut. Who had tampered with McKee's case might remain a mystery, but whatever the real contents of McKee's case might have been, it was fairly obvious that someone could have in fact removed items[7] and replaced them with clothes from another case. These disturbing admissions once again fuelled the debate over the CIA's involvement at the crash site.

But what of the 'smoking gun'? As the trial stumbled on, it was becoming crystal clear that the only smoke was the variety associated with 'smoke and mirrors'. A trickle of seemingly innocuous testimony had revealed that the celebrated circuit board fragment had been 'discovered' by Thomas Hayes hidden within a piece of shirt, whose police exhibits label had mysteriously changed from 'cloth' to 'debris' sometime between its find in Lockerbie in January 1989 and its examination by Hayes in May 1989. Yet, according to an interview with the *Sunday Times*'s David Leppard in *On the Trail of Terror,* Hayes had made the crucial identification of the fragment in June 1990. The whole circuit board story was looking stranger than ever.

In order to pull some evidential strands together, the Crown would now bring on some protected witnesses from the United States. Their arrival at court in vehicles with blacked-out windows gave the appearance of dramatic testimony to come. As we shall see, what was crucial about this testimony was not what was revealed in court, but what was kept hidden.

The first to testify about the timer was Richard Louis Sherrow, a US Army veteran with over 20 years' service who, on retirement from the army in 1984, joined the US Bureau of Alcohol, Tobacco and Firearms (ATF). Sherrow was an expert on ordnance, and in particular explosives ordnance disposal. He testified that in September or October 1986, at the request of the State Department, he travelled to Lome, Togo, accompanied by Edward Owen of the ATF and James Casey of the State Department. During the trip, Sherrow examined a variety of ordnance laid out on a table at a military camp, comprising weapons, explosives and items connected with explosives.

Sherrow said he was most interested in two electronic timers of a type he had never before seen. He stated that one of the timers was taken back to the USA in a diplomatic pouch. On his return to the USA, he took the timer to the ATF's headquarters for bench testing and was then requested to move it to the CIA's HQ in Langley, Virginia. Following a briefing with the CIA, the timer was left in their custody. This timer was identified, according to comparison photographs shown to Sherrow in court, as a Mebo MST-13. So, it was confirmed that two years before Lockerbie the CIA had an MST-13 timer, the type allegedly used by the bombers. The only difference was that the circuit board used in the CIA's timer was double-sided, whereas the Lockerbie fragment was from a single-sided board.

There was, however, an important postscript to Sherrow's story, which may have never been made known to the judges or the defence.

In May of 1993, Sherrow met with investigative journalist Don Devereux and disclosed to him information which, if it had been brought forward at the trial, would have cast further doubt on the prosecution's case. According to Devereux, during the course of a planned meeting in a 'Denny's' restaurant in Scottsdale, Arizona, Sherrow passed him an A4-sized envelope containing a number of colour photographs mounted on a sheet of paper. Some showed a piece of electronic timer, some arms and others the items he had seen in the hut in Lome, Togo. The photographs were undoubtedly the same as those shown to Sherrow during his testimony at the Lockerbie trial.

Devereux says Sherrow told him that, while working for the ATF, when asked to identify the timer in the photograph he was certain that he knew its origin. Far from implicating Mebo, Sherrow said a company in Florida made the timer, and made it exclusively for the CIA. Sherrow also told Devereux that when he brought this information to the attention of senior personnel at the ATF he was reprimanded, immediately removed from active duty and taken off the Lockerbie investigation.

Angry at the reaction of his ATF bosses and concerned that his pension might be threatened, Sherrow sought advice from Arizona Senator John McCain. A McCain aide, Thomas McCanna, met with Sherrow. In explaining the background to his problems, Sherrow had to brief McCanna on the details of his Pan Am investigations. McCanna introduced Sherrow to Chuck Byers, who was also having trouble with the Federal government and the CIA. Byers, a 'special ordnance' manufacturer, had a long-running dispute with the ATF and the CIA and already knew Devereux from another story.

Devereux, a veteran investigative journalist with over 30 years' experience and two Pulitzer Prize nominations, was, at the time of the meeting with Sherrow, researching the mystery surrounding the crash of an Arrow Air DC-8 in Gander, Newfoundland in December 1985. The cause of this crash, which killed 256 people including 248 members of the US Army's 101st Airborne Division, has been shrouded in controversy.

Devereux explained to the authors:

> Rick (Sherrow) wanted to talk about Pan Am 103 and I wanted to talk about Arrow Air and Gander. Byers then facilitated the meeting between myself and Sherrow, as he felt Sherrow had important information. Sherrow had also told Byers that the timer allegedly used in the bombing of Pan Am 103 was made by a Florida company for the CIA. Byers described how in 1994 he took the photographs given to him by Sherrow to an 'invitation only' trade show for 'Special Operations' held at Fort Bragg North Carolina. At the show he showed the photographs to another exhibitor, Dan Perrault, the owner of a Florida Electronics Company called Mathews and Associates. Byers claims that he asked Perrault if he could make such an item and again, according to Byers, Perrault said that his company did make the device. Byers asked him for whom they were made and, according to Byers, Perrault said, 'the same people you make your stuff for, the CIA.'

The timing of these events meant though that if, indeed, Mathews and Associates had made a timer identical to the Mebo one, supplied it to the CIA, and for whatever reason one of these timers was used on Pan Am 103, it would have to have been made prior to December 1988. At that time Mathews and Associates was owned by the founder, Herman Mathews, with Perrault taking over in 1993. Perrault has no recollection of speaking to Byers at the trade show but does not deny that the encounter took place, especially as Byers had retained his business card. When asked if he remembered anyone showing him a photograph of a timing device, he said lots of people show him photographs of samples and it would not have been unusual. Perrault said it is possible that, when asked by Byers if he knew who made the devices, he may have replied, 'Yes we did.' He explained that he would often respond in that way as many normal business people would, on the basis that he may be able to subsequently figure out how he could make such a device. The authors sent Perrault the photographs Byers claimed to have shown him. Perrault said he did not make anything similar.

When Herman Mathews was contacted, he claimed that he never did any circuit board work, or any other work, for any branch of the US military. Although he did not wish to comment on Mathew's statement, Perrault said that Mathews and Associates, under Herman Mathews, did in fact work with circuit boards and that the majority of this work was done for the Defense Department. Perrault went on to explain it was possible that circuit boards could have been ordered without either he, or Mathews, knowing anything about the end user. There is no suggestion that either Dan Perrault or Herman Mathews were in any way dishonest in their responses, or that they ran anything other than an entirely legitimate business.

The story took a further twist when Byers contacted the Scottish Crown Office regarding this information. He was interviewed, along with Don Devereux, by two Procurators Fiscal, Miriam Watson and Douglas Hardie. At the start of this meeting in Arizona, Byers asked for and received an assurance that any information he or Devereux imparted to the Crown would be shared with the defence. But according to the defence they were never informed by the Crown. Considering the gravity of this information, one might have expected the Crown to have carried out a thorough investigation of the claims. The Crown, though, didn't pull out all the stops in their efforts to investigate the matter.

In a letter to Dan Perrault, dated 4 April 2000, Procurator Fiscal Depute Lindsey Anderson stated: 'It would be helpful if you could have available for the purpose of our meeting any negatives, circuit diagrams, component invoices, componentry, or indeed complete devices which relate to the photograph of the electronic device which was shown to you by Mr Byers or any similar devices. Subsequent to receiving the letter Perrault spoke to a member of the prosecution team by telephone. He said that he would be agreeable to meeting with them, but would not be available on the date they suggested. He recalled that the conversation lasted maybe five or six minutes. He heard nothing more from the Crown, and that was the end of the matter – hardly a ringing endorsement for professional investigators involved in the 'trial of the century'.

The authors wrote to the Lord Advocate with some questions about the way the Crown had handled the evidence of Chuck Byers, Don Devereux and Dan Perrault. Responding on the Lord Advocate's behalf, Principal Depute John Logue wrote: 'In any criminal case, communications between the Crown and the defence are confidential. I am therefore not prepared to disclose the detail of those communications. Nonetheless, I can tell you that both defence teams in the Lockerbie trial were advised of the identity of Mr Byers and a summary of his evidence. By that stage, at least one of the Scottish solicitors representing the second accused [Fhimah] had already interviewed Mr Byers. Mr Byers therefore had the opportunity to impart to the defence any information that he felt was relevant. Furthermore, both defence teams were provided with copies of the material received from Mr Byers. In relation to Mr Perrault, I can confirm that the Crown wrote to him to arrange a meeting. During a subsequent conversation with a member of the prosecution team, it became abundantly clear from what he had to say that a meeting would be unnecessary because he had nothing to contribute to the case. As a result of the assistance given by the Crown to the defence, there was nothing to prevent the defence calling Mr Byers or Mr Perrault as witnesses in the trial.'

On receiving Logue's letter, the authors made further contact with Byers, Devereux and Perrault. Byers and Devereux both confirmed that Fhimah's Scottish solicitors did not speak to either of them, either in person, or by 'phone, in any way that might be construed to be an interview. Byers corresponded with a US firm of attorneys instructed by the Scottish solicitors, but only with regard to arranging a meeting with the Scottish solicitors, which, in the event, never took place. The authors put it to Perrault that the Crown Office had stated that, during that conversation 'it became abundantly clear from what he [Perrault] had to say that a meeting would be unnecessary because he had nothing to contribute to the case.' He said he could not comment on this because, to the best of his recollection, the prosecution team member did not say to him in the course of their conversation that a meeting would be unnecessary. He did not get the impression from the call that the Crown was finished with the matter, not least because the person he spoke to had asked him to put his account in writing. Perrault also confirmed that no one from either the Crown Office, or the US Department of Justice, visited him to view his negatives, circuit diagrams, component invoices, componentry and complete devices.

Having made these checks, the authors wrote back to Logue, pointing out that his previous letter was contradicted by the three American witnesses. The authors asked:

1. Who was it that 'advised' both defence teams 'of the identity of Mr Byers and a summary of his evidence'? More specifically, was it the Crown? If so, did they formally notify the defence?
2. What is the source of your claim 'at least one of the Scottish solicitors representing the second accused had already [ie; by the time they were advised of his identity and a summary of his evidence] interviewed Mr Byers' ?
3. Are you aware that both Mr Byers and Mr Devereux are adamant that they were not interviewed by Mr Fhimah's Scottish solicitors?
4. What was the nature of 'the material received from Mr Byers'?

5. Was this material received by the Crown?
6. Who provided that material to the defence? The Crown?
7. Were the precognition statements taken from Mr Byers and Mr Devereux by Procurators Fiscal Watson and Hardie given to the defence? If not, why not?
8. Your letter failed to address the question of the evidence supplied to Watson and Hardie by Mr Devereux. Could you explain why that was?
9. Given that the Crown Office had previously asked Mr Perrault if it might view his circuit boards and diagrams, why did it not go ahead with that viewing?
10. Why did the prosecution team member, who spoke to Mr Perrault by telephone, reach the conclusion that it was 'abundantly clear' that 'he had nothing to contribute to the case', given that Mr Perrault did not come to the same conclusion?
11. On what basis did the prosecution team member reach that conclusion when no one from the prosecution team had viewed Mr Perrault's negatives, circuit diagrams, component invoices, componentry, or complete devices?
12. Given the potential importance of Mr Byers' claims in respect of Mr Perrault (referred to in my previous letter) to the entire Lockerbie prosecution, should not a Crown official have visited Mr Perrault, regardless of the conclusion reached by the prosecution team member who spoke to him by 'phone?
13. Did the Crown Office notify the defence of its contact with Mr Perrault and of the content of the telephone conversation between him and the prosecution team member? And, if not, why not?

In response Logue wrote: 'As I stated in my previous letter of 28 February, communications between the Crown and the defence in any criminal case are confidential. At the risk of repeating myself, it would be improper of me to deal with the issues raised in your most recent letter because this would involve disclosing the detail of those communications. I am therefore not prepared to answer the 13 questions which you list in your letter or comment on the other issues raised by you. Finally, it is worth repeating the point that there was nothing to prevent either defence team calling Mr Byers, Mr Devereux or Mr Perrault as witnesses at the trial.'

Back at the trial, serious questions were being raised regarding the Lord Advocate's having permitted a contract with the translation company which allowed the translators to interpret the evidence being given rather than providing a verbatim record. It was a matter of comment among legal observers that the Crown did not seem to anticipate a potential problem with interpretative rather than verbatim translation. The defence had raised the issue of these translation problems several times before the Crown was forced to acknowledge the problem.

The first of the anonymous CIA witnesses to testify was given the pseudonym 'Kenneth Steiner'. He described being in Dakar, the capital of Senegal, West Africa, in February 1988 when he was summoned to the airport. He subsequently learned that two men, plus a local religious leader, Ahmed Khalifa Niasse, were detained at the airport and that a number of items, including an electronic timer, had been confiscated. Steiner informed CIA HQ in Langley about the items, which also included Semtex-H, detonators and a pistol with silencer. He stated that his office wanted to send someone else to check out the timer.

Under cross-examination, it was suggested that two FBI agents visited Steiner in Senegal in the summer of 1989. Steiner said that he remembered them coming but could not recall the month. Advocate Depute Turnbull asked on re-examination if it could have been July 1990, and again the CIA agent could not recall the date. Steiner's CIA colleague Warren Clemens, also a pseudonym, testified to examination of the timer and described it as bearing the mark MST-13.

Scottish detective William Williamson described how he and other detectives, along with Allen Feraday, visited the FBI's office in Washington and were shown firstly photographs and then an actual MST-13 timer, which FBI forensic examiner Tom Thurman claimed was from Togo. Williamson then related how they first went to meet Edwin Bollier of Mebo on 15 November 1990, in the company of Thurman and two other FBI agents, Hal Hendershot and Robert Fanning. During these trips, both the Scottish police and the FBI took items from Bollier's office, including two MST-13 timers and numerous circuit boards.[8]

Williamson was asked, under cross-examination by Richard Keen QC for Fhimah, about his visit to Switzerland. He agreed that as he arrived there two FBI agents, Marshman and Bolcar, were leaving. He initially said that Thurman was present, but later corrected this to Marshman.[9] Keen continued with his inferences regarding the FBI and the CIA:

> *Q.* I'd like to refer you to an account of certain matters in respect of your visit to Switzerland and then to ask you certain questions as to your state of knowledge.
> *A*: Yes, sir.

Q. And if I can just quote this following account: 'In early September 1990, members of the Scottish Lockerbie inquiry team, together with officers of the British Security Service, were making arrangements to travel to Switzerland. Their intention was to meet members of the Swiss police and intelligence service. The purpose of the meeting was to take forward a line of inquiry suggesting that the company Mebo might have been the manufacturers of the MST-13 timing device. Such a device had already been identified as forming part of the improvised explosive device responsible for the destruction of Pan Am 103. Prior to the departure of these officers, a request was made by the CIA to the British Security Service to deter or delay' – I'll read that again – 'to deter or delay the members of the Scottish Lockerbie inquiry team from making the visit. This request was refused, and the visit proceeded as planned. Separately, officers of the CIA met with the Swiss police and intelligence service on the day before the visit made by the Scottish Lockerbie inquiry team and the British Security Service.' Now, Mr Williamson, were you made aware of these steps to deter or delay the members of the Scottish Lockerbie inquiry team from making the visit to Switzerland?

A: Absolutely not, sir.

Q. These were never disclosed to you?

A: I have no knowledge of that information you've just read out whatsoever.

Q. Was it disclosed to you that the day before you met with the Swiss police and intelligence services on the first visit, the CIA had already met with them?

Before Williamson could answer Advocate Depute Turnbull objected, but Keen had made his point and made it well.[10]

Tension at the trial mounted as the media speculated about the arrival of Edwin Bollier, the partner in Mebo. Bollier was expected to be controversial. Although it would be a few days before he arrived, those who expected controversy from the Crown's next witness would not be disappointed.

Allen Feraday, Dr Thomas Hayes's successor as the head of the explosives laboratory at DERA, told the court that he had managed to recover and identify tiny fragments from amongst the Pan Am debris and establish eventually that they had once been part of a Toshiba radio-cassette recorder called a 'Bombeat'. Feraday was taken step by step through his report, which described the recovery of tiny fragments from suitcases and clothing. Of prime importance to the Crown, of course, was item PT35B, the minute remnant of green circuit board, allegedly from a Mebo MST-13 timer. Photographs showed the number one and two parallel tracking lines on the less-than-9mm square fragment, under 50 times magnification.

When Richard Keen QC began his cross-examination of Feraday he immediately attacked his credibility by citing remarks made by Lord Chief Justice Taylor, who had described Feraday's testimony in the case of John Berry (see Chapter 12) as 'extremely dogmatic'. Keen put it to Feraday that the remark came about when, at appeal, other expert witnesses cast huge doubts on his original assertions in the case, which also involved electronic timers. Feraday had testified that the timers could only be used for terrorist purposes.

When challenged by Keen, Feraday reached for his copy of Chambers Dictionary to give the definition of dogmatic. The exchange went on:

> The Chief Justice, Lord Taylor, noted that 'Mr Feraday expressed it as his strong and firm conclusion that these timers could only have been designed for use by terrorists to cause explosions'?
> *A:* Yes, sir.
> *Q.* He quotes you as saying: 'As a result of an examination of the timing device, I came to the conclusion that it was specifically designed and constructed for a terrorist purpose; that is to say to be attached to an explosive device. I came to the conclusion that it could only be designed and manufactured for a terrorist operation.'
> *A:* Yes, sir.

The exchange continued:

> *Q:* It is the case, is it not, that at the re-trial you yourself partially conceded that your original extremely dogmatic opinion was open to doubt, at the very least?
> *A:* I didn't conclude that, no, sir. As far as – the reason I was described as 'extremely dogmatic' was because I held the view that it was specifically a terrorist timer.
> *Q.* . . . in the pre-penultimate paragraph, Lord Taylor observed: 'In our judgement, Mr Feraday's conclusions, which he no doubt honestly held, were, as he himself has now partially conceded, open to doubt at the very least.' Is that a correct representation of the position in that case, Mr Feraday?

A: To my knowledge, I don't think it is.

Q. I see.

A: . . . I was a bit surprised to see that written like that in the judgement. But I agree I was dogmatic, and I maintain I was right to be so.

Q. In your evidence in the original trial, Mr Feraday, you had asserted that the item could only be designed and manufactured for a terrorist operation?

A: That's correct, sir.

Q. At the subsequent re-trial, in the face of the further expert evidence that was led, you yourself partially conceded that such a conclusion was open to doubt, at the very least?

A: I never said that was open to doubt, at the very least. In fact, I steadfastly maintained that it was for a terrorist purpose. And I still maintain that.

Q. Yes. But what you had to concede . . . in the face of the further evidence, was the possibility that the item was not for such use?

A: I didn't concede that. It was put to me that it was for other use. And I dogmatically, as you want to put it, and as the Lord Chief Justice puts it, was of settled opinion in that I maintained it was for a terrorist purpose, which it was . . . And I was subsequently proven correct.

Q. You didn't just maintain, Mr Feraday, that it was for a terrorist purpose; you maintained that it could not conceivably be for any other purpose.

A: That's correct.

Q. And it was that which you partially retracted at the second trial?

A: I don't have that degree of recollection. As I maintained, and still do, it was specifically for a terrorist purpose.

So the dogmatic witness Allen Feraday was right, and Lord Chief Justice Taylor was wrong.

Feraday admitted to some apparently inconsistent accounts of examinations of items of evidence. In the first case he claimed that he examined a piece of a black umbrella, alleged to have been in the bomb suitcase. Feraday's contemporaneous notes appeared to show that he examined it on 3 October 1989, but the property log which listed items of evidence showed that the piece of umbrella was only at Feraday's laboratory from 16 January–8 February.[11] Feraday also claimed to have examined a section of a black vinyl suitcase on 21 March 1991, when the evidence log showed that the same piece of evidence was destroyed at Linwood on 24 May 1990.[12] Finally, Feraday was able to examine a black briefcase, with the name of Thomas Walker attached, on 29 March 1990, when in actual fact the briefcase had been returned to the owner's family on 9 November 1989.[13]

The most extraordinary revelation came during cross-examination about a report by Feraday, dated 3 February 1989, which was sent to the then Detective Chief Superintendent, John Orr. In it Feraday stated:

> I have compared some fragments of electronic circuit board recovered at Lockerbie (Longtown) and marked them as item AG/145 with various radio-cassette tape recorders. I am completely satisfied that these fragments originate from a Toshiba-brand radio-cassette recorder, type RT-8016 or RT-8026. These fragments are shattered in a manner consistent with their intimate involvement in a violent explosion, and I therefore conclude that the bomb was concealed in the aforementioned Toshiba portable radio-cassette player. The Toshiba RT-8016 and RT-8026 are visually similar and differ only in that the 8026 has a three-band graphics equaliser on its front panel. Both sets measure 16-and-a-half in by 5-and-a-half in by 4 in. The set used in the bomb possessed a white plastics case. Photograph of RT-8016 enclosed. Colour photographs and other details will be available early next week.

So Feraday was 'completely satisfied' that the bomb was inside a white Toshiba radio-cassette recorder, and had narrowed it down to two models, the RT-8016 or the RT-8026. Of course, by the time he wrote the later report with Dr Hayes, not only did the model change to Toshiba RT-SF16, but it also changed colour, from white to black. Why had Feraday not identified the RT-SF16 from the start? The police had, after all, the remains of the RT-SF16 instruction manual found by Gwendoline Horton in their possession since the day after the bombing.

Before Feraday's testimony ended, Richard Keen QC extracted from him the sum total of his academic qualifications – a Higher National Certificate in Applied Physics and Electronics, obtained in 1962.

In late June the court considered the defendants' passports, including one belonging to Megrahi in the name of Ahmed Khalifa Abdusamad. They were examined for entry and exit stamps, relating to Libya and Switzerland for Megrahi and in Fhimah's case Libya. Andre Klauss, an official in the Swiss Embassy in Libya from the late 1980s until approximately 1992, confirmed a number of visa applications made in the name of Al-Megrahi and the visa and Swiss entry and exit stamps from July and August 1988 on his passport. Visa applications in the names of Nasr Ahmed Salem and Ben Hassan El Badri, and one such application made in the name of Fhimah, were also identified. The trial had at this stage been running for nine weeks, yet Fhimah had hardly been mentioned.

The testimony moved on to former employees of the Holiday Inn at Sliema, in Malta. Both confirmed registration cards for Megrahi under the name of Ahmed Khalifa Abdusamad. Witnesses confirmed that he stayed at the hotel on 2–23 August 1988, 9–10 October 1988, 18–20 October 1988, 7–9 December 1988, and 20–21 December 1988.

After only 30 days of evidence, the trial was once again adjourned for almost two weeks. Already there was a growing sense of impatience amongst some of the victims' relatives. One, who wished to remain anonymous, commented: 'They must be saving the best for last, because we have heard nothing yet.'[14]

On 12 July, a day otherwise taken up with procedural matters relating to the indictment and formal charging of the two Libyans, the remarkable events in Malta surrounding the illegal wire-tapping of telephones quietly found its way into the record, during the cross-examination of Detective Chief Superintendent Harry Bell:

> *Q.* Do you recollect the time, during your inquiries in Malta, when a number of police officers, British, American, and German, were expelled from the island of Malta by the Maltese authorities?
> *A:* We weren't expelled. The inquiry was suspended, yes.
> *Q.* You were asked to leave?
> *A:* The inquiry was suspended, as far as I can recollect, sir. We were never – the Maltese never asked us to leave. They suspended the inquiry at various times.
> *Q.* Was that related to the discovery of unauthorised telephone tapping on the island? And when I say 'unauthorised', I mean unauthorised by the Maltese authorities.
> *A:* That was one occasion, yes.
> *Q.* And did the Maltese authorities take it rather amiss that the policing methods employed by the foreign police forces did not in fact accord with the requirements of Maltese law and the requirements of the Maltese authorities?
> *A:* The Maltese authorities were clearly annoyed that such action had been taken.[15]

On 18 July the court heard from Yoshihiro Miura, who at the time of the bombing was a section manager for the Toshiba Corporation in Japan. He testified that in October 1988 a shipment of 20,000 black RT-SF16 radio-cassette players were shipped to Libya, and that during the six-month period from October 1988 to March 1989 75.94 per cent of the entire worldwide distribution of that particular model went to Libya. Miura had distribution figures dating back to October 1985, but no evidence was adduced concerning the number of black RT-SF16s sold to Libya and elsewhere in the three years leading up to October 1988.

Behind the scenes another row was brewing, this time over the reluctance of some Maltese witnesses to attend the trial. The judges allowed the Crown yet another adjournment. Coming hard on the heels of the previous one, the latest adjournment was bound to increase pressure on the Crown's team, who had known for months that problems might arise regarding a group of witnesses from Malta. Crown Office sources were saying that these witnesses were 'crucial' but also 'not damaging' to their case. Obviously, if they were cited as witnesses and called they must have been relevant to the Crown's case, so their absence can hardly have been anything but damaging. In any event, a number of observers expected that we had not seen the last of Crown applications for adjournments.

Law Professor Robert Black QC commented at the time:

> If the Crown are having difficulty in securing witnesses to appear before the court, and their need to request an adjournment when these Maltese witnesses (whose reluctance to attend has been known for months) balked at appearing seems to suggest that they are, perhaps they should reconsider their apparent decision not to call Chief Constable John Orr, Oliver 'Buck' Revell and Vincent Cannistraro.

The Crown, for reasons best known to themselves and which baffle observers to this day, never called any of these three investigators-in-chief from, respectively, the Scottish Police, FBI and CIA.

By early Friday, 21 July, the Crown had once again run out of witnesses, and while proceedings in court were calm, continued with testimonies from Frankfurt Airport personnel and former Pan Am employees.

On 28 July the trial went into a planned recess for the summer and this provided time for reflection on the case so far. Professor Robert Black commented:

Apart from graphically setting the scene by establishing that Pan Am 103 was destroyed over Lockerbie and that 270 people were killed as a result, how far does the evidence to date go towards establishing the case set out in the indictment against the two accused persons? On the assumption that the witnesses who have so far given evidence which is favourable to the Crown case are accepted by the judges as credible and reliable, it is possible that the following might be held to have been provisionally established, always subject to any later contrary evidence which may be led by the prosecution or the defence:

1. That the seat of the explosion was in a particular Samsonite suitcase (which contained clothing manufactured in Malta and sold both there and elsewhere) at or near the bottom of a particular aluminium luggage container (AVE 4041).

2. That the bomb had been contained in a black Toshiba RT-SF16 cassette recorder.

3. That a fragment of circuit board from an MST-13 timer manufactured by Mebo formed part of the timing mechanism, which detonated the bomb.

4. That Mebo supplied MST-13 timers to the Libyan army, as well as to other customers such as the East German Ministerium fuer Staatssicherheit (Stasi).

5. That the first-named accused, Abdelbaset Ali Mohmed al-Megrahi, was known to the owners of Mebo AG; that he was involved, in an official capacity (possibly as a member of the Libyan intelligence services), in obtaining for Libya electronic equipment (including timers) from Mebo; and that a company of which he was a principal for a time had accommodation in the premises occupied by Mebo in Zurich.

6. That the first-named accused possessed and used Libyan passports in false names.

7. That the first-named accused, on occasion under the false name of Ahmed Khalifa Abdusamad, visited Malta on a number of occasions in 1988, including the night of 20/21 December.

8. That some weeks before 21 December 1988, a person who "resembled a lot" the first-named accused, but who also "resembled a lot" Mohammed Abu Talb (a Crown witness named in the special defence of incrimination lodged by the defence) bought in Malta items of clothing that the Crown claims were in the suitcase that contained the bomb.

9. That the second-named accused, Al Amin Khalifah travelled by air to Malta on 20 December 1988 and departed by air the following day

10. That the second-named accused was then in possession of a permit (obtained when he was station manager for Libyan Arab Airlines) which allowed him access to airside at Luqa Airport.

11. That it would have been theoretically possible for a suitcase to be introduced into the interline baggage system at Luqa, although there is no documentary record of any such piece of baggage on Air Malta flight KM180 to Frankfurt on 21 December 1988.

No evidence has as yet been led which could be held to establish that the Samsonite suitcase containing the bomb was launched on its fatal progress from Malta (as distinct from being directly loaded onto Pan Am 103 at Heathrow, or starting its journey at Frankfurt) *or which links either of the accused with that suitcase.* [Emphasis added.]

Black concluded:

In the light of defence challenges in cross-examination regarding e.g. the accuracy of record-keeping, the provenance of certain crucial items of wreckage (where, when and by whom they were found; through whose hands they thereafter passed), the credentials, competence and neutrality of certain expert witnesses, and the motives that certain witnesses may have had not to tell the whole truth, judicial acceptance of the credibility and reliability of every Crown witness cannot be regarded as a foregone conclusion. Witnesses employed in 1988 at Frankfurt Airport have conceded in cross-examination (a) that the US Federal Aviation Administration reported in early 1989 that, even after the Lockerbie disaster, security there was very lax; and (b) that it would have been possible for a suitcase to enter the interline baggage system there without any record being kept.

The trial reconvened on 22 August and moved on to what the Crown called the 'Heathrow chapter'. Many observers, including former police officers, indicated that the police inquiry at Heathrow was very limited. One reason for this may have been the speed with which the investigators homed in on Frankfurt.

One of the witnesses to be called for the Crown on 24 August was Jim

Berwick, who, at the time of the disaster, was Pan Am's Head of Corporate Security for Europe. During his cross-examination by Bill Taylor QC, it emerged that one of the passengers aboard the 21 December flight Pan Am 107, which left Heathrow at 1.30 pm destined for Los Angles via Washington DC, was a man wanted by the police in connection with the 1985 hijacking in the Mediterranean of a cruise ship, the *Achille Lauro*. His name was Armad Jusiff Saoad Jusif, but he had flown in to Heathrow from Teheran on an Iran Air flight that morning under the name of Ali Nassr Zia.[16]

In 1988, the Iran Air terminal was adjacent to the Pan Am terminal and they shared tarmac space. The Lockerbie Fatal Accident Inquiry in 1990–91 was told of a period of around 40 minutes when the luggage container AVE 4041 lay unsupervised. The lack of security at the baggage hall in Heathrow was brought into question during this chapter of evidence.

During the Heathrow chapter of evidence, a former Pan Am baggage-handler, John Bedford, reviewed with Jack Davidson, QC for Fhimah, a statement he had made to the police on 9 January 1989.

> *Q.* 'I went to see Peter Walker in baggage build-up leaving Kamboj in interline'?
>
> *A*: Yes, sir.
>
> *Q.* 'I returned about 4.40 p.m. Kamboj told me . . . two further suitcases had arrived for PA 103 which he had put in the tin.' All right?
>
> *A*: Yes, sir.
>
> *Q.* Do you remember saying that to the police?
>
> *A*: I don't remember saying it, no, sir.
>
> *Q.* I beg your pardon?
>
> *A*: I don't remember saying it.
>
> *Q.* Right. Do you accept that you did say it?
>
> *A*: Yes, sir.
>
> *Q.* It carries on: 'I looked inside the tin and saw the suitcases that I had put in the tin still in the same position.' Do you see that?
>
> *A*: Yes, sir.
>
> *Q.* 'Lying on their sides in front of the other suitcases, handles pointing towards the back of the tin, were two suitcases.' Do you see that?
>
> *A*: Yes, sir.
>
> *Q.* 'They were hard suitcases, the type Samsonite make.' Do you see that?
>
> *A*: Yes, sir.

Q. 'One was brown in colour, and the other one, if it wasn't the same colour, it was similar'?

A: Yes, sir.

Q. 'In size, they took up the remaining base area of the tin'?

A: Yes, sir.

Q. Now, would you have been telling the police the truth on that occasion, to the best of your recollection, Mr Bedford?

A: Yes, sir.

Q: And if that is the truth, Mr Kamboj had placed two suitcases of that description in the front of the container in your absence?

A: Yes, sir.

Bedford's testimony and statements to the police from as early as 3 January 1989 would figure large in Bill Taylor's closing statements.

One of the most eagerly anticipated of the Crown's witnesses was Mohammed Abu Talb. For five months he had been waiting in his Swedish prison cell for the call to Camp Zeist, and by October it looked as though his time had come. Why exactly a convicted terrorist serving life in Sweden would willingly cooperate with the Scottish Crown and attend Camp Zeist was something of a mystery. True, the defence had named him the special defence of implication, but why would Abu Talb, who could not be compelled to testify, willingly come and put himself under the spotlight at the Lockerbie trial? Did the Crown wish to elicit a simple denial of his involvement? Could they simply be trying to spoil a line the defence might use?

The answer is yes and no. The activities of the Crown and the Scottish police in the run-up to the trial would give some real clues to the reason for Abu Talb's inclusion as a Crown witness. Abu Talb was a major source of danger for the prosecution for a number of reasons, not least that he was originally one of their own prime suspects. They would say, of course, they had ruled him out prior to issuing a petition against Megrahi and Fhimah, but in those early days many senior police officers felt Abu Talb had been dismissed too easily. When it became clear that a trial would indeed take place, the Crown and the police were thrown into something of a panic. They anticipated that the defence would seek to implicate Abu Talb and they knew that they would have to ensure nothing could backfire, giving credence to the Libyans' claim of innocence.

In September 1999, the Crown made the first overtures to the Swedish government for assistance in getting access to Abu Talb. He would need to be re-interviewed and his story checked out, this time thoroughly. A court hearing was held in Stockholm, behind closed doors, in October 1999. The Crown made an application to the Swedish Court setting out their case for assistance in the matter of Abu Talb and the Pan Am case. The Crown denied that this meeting took place, but were embarrassed to discover that Sweden's liberal system meant the lid could not be kept on it for long.

Back in Scotland, a team of Scottish policemen was preparing to travel to Cyprus. The purpose of the visit was to ensure that they could check out Abu Talb's visit to the island in 1988. They could not afford to miss any information that might give the defence an opening. A retired Scottish police detective, who lived in Cyprus at the time and met socially with some of the Lockerbie Task Force during their stay, told the authors that it was 'odd to see cops checking out the alibi of a bomber like Abu Talb'. He explained, 'normally cops are trying to find holes in alibis to expose them', this time they were attempting to shore one up'.

With news reports of the Lockerbie trial circulating throughout Sweden, Abu Talb would have been very aware of the type of reception that lay ahead with Keen and Taylor, so why risk testifying about a crime in which he has always denied any involvement? Presumably because he wanted out of prison and saw an opportunity to help himself. He knew, from meetings, that the Crown wanted him to testify and he extracted a price, namely an early release from his sentence.

Abu Talb had, earlier in 1999, made his second unsuccessful attempt to have a time limit put on his life sentence. Now a golden opportunity was handed to him on a plate. The pressure on the Crown was such that they could not afford for Abu Talb's name as a convicted bomber to be bandied about the court without an actual denial coming from his own lips. He would testify, but only if his conditions were met. Although no concrete promises were made to Abu Talb, he presumably felt there was little doubt that his cooperation with the Scottish authorities would be a very favourable step towards getting his release date.

The authors put the following questions to the Lord Advocate's office:

1. Has the Crown granted immunity from prosecution to Mohammed Abu Talb, Crown witness number 963?

2. If not, does the Crown plan to offer any form of immunity to this witness?

3. If the Crown has formally offered this witness immunity, when was it offered?

4. Is or has immunity from prosecution been offered to any other witnesses, whether Crown or defence?

5. Has any offer or inducement been made directly or indirectly to Mohammed Abu Talb?

6. Has the Crown sought an arrangement with any agency of the government of Sweden in respect of Mohammed Abu Talb's testimony at the trial?

The Lord Advocate's spokesperson replied:

You recently emailed questions relating to Abu Talb. The Crown response is that we say what we have to say about witnesses in court.

The authors wrote:

I am going to take the opportunity to ask that the questions I submitted to the Lord Advocate and that you addressed in your last e-mail to me today be addressed again. In doing so, I wish to emphasise that none of the questions in any way relates to the possible content of any evidence to be given but they do go to the protocol of witnesses cited. May I suggest that we have a conversation before proceeding any further in this matter?

Following this, a telephone discussion took place and as a result of the call, the following statement was sent by the Lord Advocate's spokesperson:

I have consulted with officials of the Crown prosecution team and advised them of the information you have from a source in Sweden re Talb – claims of witness inducement. The Crown has nothing further to add to the short statement provided earlier.

The Lord Advocate studiously avoided answering any of the detailed questions put to his office. He presumably would have gathered from the telephone call with his spokesperson that the information about Talb's inducement came from a very senior unnamed source within the Swedish judicial system, and yet he chose not to answer any of the questions. The source, who had supplied the authors with reliable information over many years and who, for obvious reasons, spoke on condition of anonymity, said:

The Scottish officials, during meetings, made it clear that Abu Talb's testimony was crucial to their case against the two Libyans. Although unwilling to enter into any formal deal with Talb, Swedish

officials sympathetic to their Scottish counterparts' plight agreed
to make certain overtures to Talb.

Abu Talb's progress to the witness box was abruptly halted when on 9 October the Lord Advocate made an unscheduled appearance before the court and made a motion to adjourn, with a dramatic announcement:

> My Lords, on the afternoon of Wednesday, 4 October, the Crown received certain information from a foreign country, not the United States, which is relevant to the evidence in this case. I was shown this information on Thursday and instructed that inquiries be carried out. Certain inquiries were carried out at a very senior level on Friday, and the matter reviewed by me with Crown counsel and others over this weekend. The matters raised by this information are of some complexity and considerable sensitivity. They relate not to the Crown case, but to the defence case.

This startling news was the precursor to an adjournment of over three weeks. Events during those weeks took the defence team to Norway and the USA, and centred around a document which became known as the Goben Memorandum.

Whatever the provenance of the Goben Memorandum, it was clear that the Lord Advocate's office took it very seriously and needed time to investigate it. The Crown knew that the information in the documents could be very damaging to their case and imposed a strict media blackout on their inquiries. For one of the very few times in this trial, the blackout worked – but not for long. A report reached the authors of renewed Scottish police activity in the USA and also in what was first described to us as a 'Scandinavian' country.

Nearly two weeks into the adjournment, the details of the Scandinavian country started to emerge. Sharp investigative work by a Norwegian journalist, Kjetil Stormark, confirmed that the mystery country was Norway. The picture which became clearer over the next few days was both intriguing and on the face of it pretty damaging to the Crown. A group of asylum seekers from Syria, all of whom were formerly connected to the PFLP-GC either directly or by marriage, had passed information to the Norwegian security police, the Politiets Overvaakingstjeneste (POT). After their de-briefing by the POT, their information was passed on to the British Special Branch, who in turn passed it over to the Lord Advocate.

One of the most interesting characters to arrive in Oslo from Damascus was a Serb national called Miroslva Globovitch, the widow of the PFLP-GC terrorist Mobdi Goben, who ran the safe house in Krusevac, Yugoslavia, that was raided shortly after the Autumn Leaves raids. Goben had got away, but among other items the police found Semtex and detonators. Originally from the area of Krusevac, where she lived with Goben and her son and daughter, Globovitch was hiding in Norway, using a new identity supplied by the POT. She had arrived in the country with a document typed in Arabic, the contents of which must have sent a shudder through the police and Procurators Fiscal who first saw it. The memorandum, allegedly dictated by Goben, was a personal history of his time in the PFLP–GC and contained some remarkable claims, many of which, if they could be verified, would seriously jeopardise the Crown case against Megrahi and Fhimah.

Goben claimed that the Lockerbie bomb was planted in the suitcase of an unsuspecting Khalid Jaafar by a terrorist using the *nom de guerre* of Abu Elias. Elias had been named in a number of early media reports, but Goben went further, claiming the man was a relative of Ahmed Jibril. Our investigations have established that this relative knew Hafez Dalkamoni. A Syrian passport holder, he became an American citizen and is known to the FBI (and presumably the CIA). He denies being Abu Elias and all of Goben's other claims.

Goben's allegations were sufficiently serious to cause Megrahi's team to seek a formal letter of request to the Syrian government, seeking its help in securing three missing pages from the Memorandum. The Syrians were not pleased and turned the request down flat, stating: 'PFLP–GC and the Syrian government are not one and the same', which, considering Syria's support for Jibril's group, showed a certain economy with the truth.

The authors attempted to locate Globovitch and the rest of the asylum-seekers during an investigation in Norway, but the POT, sensing their exposure, relocated them on the day of our arrival in Oslo, which told us it had 'no comment'. A senior source in the Swedish police confirmed that he had known of this operation, as one of the PFLP–GC members had sought asylum in Sweden. How many former PFLP–GC members, with information regarding Pan Am, have defected is not known. It would, of course, be contrary to the US standpoint if any such defectors were able to further publicly implicate the PFLP–GC in an atrocity that was officially a 'Libyan government operation from start to finish'.

While the Goben Memorandum saga unfolded, plans were under way in Sweden to have Mohammed Abu Talb transported to Camp Zeist, where he would share prison facilities with the accused. Recent changes in the law of

Sweden meant that Abu Talb was no longer free to decide whether or not he could come to Camp Zeist. Under the European Mutual Assistance Treaty of 1959, to which Sweden was a signatory, Abu Talb could only have been brought to the trial with the consent of the Swedish authorities, and his own consent. However, at the beginning of October 2000, the Swedish Parliament brought into being a law whose terms meant he was obliged to give evidence.

The first obstacle was the Swedish airline, which refused to fly Abu Talb because he had been convicted of a bombing against an airline office. Travel arrangements were eventually made with the military. It was to be more than a week after Abu Talb finally arrived in Camp Zeist before he testified, during which time he had numerous meetings with Crown Office lawyers. Sources among the Scottish prison officers based at Camp Zeist, who spoke on condition of anonymity, said these meetings occurred every evening and sometimes went on until after 10 p.m. Clearly, the preparation of Abu Talb had to be very thorough.

Abu Talb was eventually shown into the witness box late on Friday, 10 November. Shortly before his appearance, Bill Taylor QC for Megrahi made an impassioned appeal to the court, stating a number of reasons why his testimony should be delayed:

> The witness Abu Talb, who is the individual that the Crown now seeks to call as the next witness, is not here to give any evidence in relation to the Crown case. He does not advance the Crown case at all. He has nothing to say, so far as the Crown are concerned, in relation to the destruction of this airliner, and there is no part of his evidence upon which the Crown will found, as I understand matters, at the conclusion of these proceedings to show that the Crown have made out the case of which we have notice in the indictment. The reason why he is called is because his name features in a notice of intention which was lodged both by the first-accused and by the second-accused prior to the commencement of this trial, indicating that he and his gang may have had something to do with the destruction of Pan Am 103. So he is a witness who is being called in order to demolish in advance, if that's possible, the notice of the line of evidence which the Crown anticipate the defence will be taking in the course of the defence case, at a time when the defence case is still under investigation in important matters.[17]

The judges waved aside the plea and Abu Talb was sworn in. Despite what they were saying publicly, the Crown could hardly have been happy about having to conclude their case offering the court the testimony of a convicted bomber whom they were once close to indicting.

Abu Talb was examined by Advocate Depute Campbell, who began by asking him about his current life sentence. Reluctant to admit his guilt, Abu Talb said, 'I was accused of having certain operations against the Jews in Denmark.'[18] Campbell had the unenviable task of taking the witness though his life in the Palestinian armed struggle. The examination was uneventful and gave Abu Talb an opportunity to answer questions he was well prepared for. At no point did he raise objections to Campbell's questions, and the Crown was careful not to treat him with hostility. Much of the examination was reminiscent of a travelogue through Europe: Did you stay at this hotel in Nicosia? And did you travel to Malta?

Less than 90 minutes later, Campbell was finished. The court adjourned for their long weekend, Abu Talb was returned to prison.

Bill Taylor QC had to wait till Tuesday for the start of his cross-examination. An almost surreal picture is conjured up by the Camp Zeist prison that weekend; three prisoners, one former suspect and the two accused, all under the same roof sharing the same level of security. Fhimah, who elected himself cook-in-chief, busily preparing food for Megrahi and himself while along the corridor sat the man originally suspected of the Pan Am bombing. Irony indeed.

Taylor began his cross-examination relatively gently, telling Abu Talb that he was going to be asking him some questions about his associates, Martin Imandi and his brothers-in-law Mustafa and Mahmoud Mograbi, all of whom were convicted with him in connection with the bombings in 1985 and 1986. Taylor put it to Abu Talb that he had undergone commando training in Armenia. Abu Talb denied this and also rejected Taylor's later suggestion that he spent time in the Soviet Union being trained in the use of Sam-3 shoulder-launched rockets. He admitted that he had been in the Soviet Union, but refused to discuss his reasons for being there.

Abu Talb also admitted that, following his desertion from the Egyptian army, he went to Jordan and enlisted in the Popular Palestinian Struggle Front (PPSF). He was subsequently arrested and jailed in Egypt for membership of the organisation, rather than for his earlier army desertion. He admitted escaping prison at the end of 1973 and fleeing to Lebanon, where in 1977 he became the bodyguard for the then leader of the PPSF, Sami Gusha. He claimed to have been based in Lebanon until he left for Sweden in 1983.

Returning to the Soviet Union, Taylor asked:

Q. You were there from August 1980 until October 1981. Am I right?

A: I don't remember the exact dates, but it seems plausible.

Q. And would I be right in thinking that there you were trained in what were called organisation, training and recruitment techniques?

A: I refuse to answer this question.

Taylor complained to the judges and sought them to instruct Abu Talb to answer. Lord Sutherland asked the witness why he was refusing to answer, and he explained that he did not think it was relevant, as the events occurred 30 years ago. It was in fact only 20 years – Abu Talb had clearly not studied arithmetic in the Soviet Union. Taylor dropped the issue, suggesting he may need to return to it.

Abu Talb confirmed that following Israel's 1982 invasion of Lebanon he went to Damascus, Syria, and met Mahmoud Mograbi, at that time a member of the PLO's armed wing, Al Fatah. He claimed that after 1982 he ceased all activities relating to Palestine. Taylor countered with an angry outburst:

> *Q.* Well, I am puzzled by that answer, you see, because you told me at the beginning that the reason you were in prison just now was in respect of bombing attacks which had taken place in Copenhagen, in Stockholm, and in Amsterdam, for which you were responsible in the period of 1985 and 1986.
>
> *A:* That is not correct. The fact that I was charged doesn't mean I was necessarily there or that I committed these acts. I said that I was charged with committing them.
>
> *Q.* Well, you were convicted of them, weren't you, and sentenced to life imprisonment?
>
> *A:* That is correct.
>
> *Q.* And these were in respect of bombings which took place in the years 1985 and 1986, a point which you say was some three years after you had ceased to be a member of any Palestinian organisation.
>
> *A:* I was convicted on one charge only, a bombing in Denmark of a Jewish site, not of anything else. I was convicted even though I was not there, and I did not confess to the crime.[19]

Abu Talb conceded that the PFLP–GC and the PPSF shared similar aims and goals. He denied possessing a number of forged passports, which gave Taylor the opportunity to review all the forged passports seized during the

Swedish police raid. These included a Moroccan one in the name of Belaid Masoud Ben Hadi, an Egyptian one in the name of Ali Awad Hassan Abu Derra and a Yemeni one in the name of Mohamed Abu Talib.

Pressing the witness on his family connections, Taylor suggested that he and Martin Imandi persuaded Mahmoud Mograbi to go to Syria and be trained in bomb-making under Sami Gusha. Taylor said that when Mograbi arrived back in Sweden he had with him several thousand dollars to help finance the bombing campaign for which they were eventually convicted. Abu Talb denied the claims, but said it was possible that Mahmoud had been in Syria. Taylor quizzed him about the handle of the suitcase that Mahmoud brought back from Syria, which Mahmoud had claimed was used to smuggle in detonators. He replied: 'If it's in the file then it is correct, but I have nothing to do with it.'

Taylor led Abu Talb through his various trips to Cyprus and Malta, questioning him about calls he made to Algeria while in Malta. At times his story sounded implausible. As in his police interviews over a decade earlier, he claimed that a complete stranger had lent him money at Rome airport to carry on with his travels. He again claimed to have bought a ticket to Libya from Rome but that the Libyan security staff would not let him board. Anyone familiar with international travel knows that visas must be shown when a ticket is purchased not when the passenger is about to board the aircraft.

Bill Taylor turned to the directors of the Miska Bakery in Malta, whose names were found during the search of Abu Talb's home on 1 November 1988. He denied knowing that any paper had been found with those names.

He was next asked if he could explain the travel details of his wife Jamila Mograbi. She had flown from Sweden for Cyprus, on 1 July 1988, returning on 11 July and immediately flying on to Warsaw, which she left for Algeria on 13 July, returning to Sweden on 8 August. He denied his wife was ever in Cyprus or Warsaw.

In a testy exchange, Taylor asked:

> *Q.* And I wouldn't hold you to being able to remember exact dates. But as part of a closely-knit family, Mr Talb, as you have insisted, you would know that your wife was away from home for a period of about six weeks or so in 1988, wouldn't you? It's the kind of thing you would remember, a man with a young family and a wife away for a period of about six weeks. You would remember that?
> *A*: Yes. As I told you before, my wife does not leave home without

informing me. My wife went to Algeria, I told you that, and I know that, but she did not go to any other country. And you can ask her that question when she comes here.

Q: Well, I am wondering, you see, if you do know anything about this at all, or whether this is something that the Mougrabis kept from you, Mr Talb. We've seen that she's a member of a famous family, in Palestinian Arab terms; that's right, isn't it?

A: No, this is not so. They do not hide anything from me. If my wife leaves home, I am informed. And please do not delve into my private life.

Q: I have no intention of doing that, Mr Talb, I assure you. But I do want to know if you can help me with why someone would undertake a journey from Sweden to Cyprus and Cyprus back to Sweden, the same day travelling from the same airport to Warsaw, to stay there for two days and then to travel from Warsaw to Algeria to visit her sister. Why on earth would your wife undertake such a journey?

A: You can ask her that when she comes here, and you will certainly find the answer to your questions.

Q: If you were to travel – if you were free today and resident in Sweden and were to fly to Algeria to see your sister-in-law, how would you fly? What's the best and most direct way of flying?

A: The exact route does not really matter, but the cheapest possible ticket.

Q: I suggest the cheapest ticket would not be Sweden/Cyprus, Cyprus/Sweden, Sweden/Warsaw, Warsaw/Algiers. That would not be the quickest route.[20]

With that, Taylor was finished and Richard Keen QC was on his feet. He immediately launched into a highly provocative exchange:

Q: Mr Talb, on 30 October 1989 the United States government officials announced: 'Mohamed Abu Talb, a Palestinian being held on terrorism charges in Sweden, has admitted to investigators that between October and December 1988 he retrieved and passed to another person a bomb that had been hidden in a building in West Germany used by members of the Popular Front for the Liberation of Palestine General Command.' Now, Mr Talb, did you make such an admission to investigators in 1989?

A: This is untrue; I did not talk to any American investigator.

Q. The statement did not say that the investigators were American, Mr Talb; it merely said that they were investigators. Now, did you make such an admission to any investigators, whether they be American, Swedish, Scottish, German, or any other nationality?

A: This is not true.

Q. Well, why would United States government officials be reported as saying that, if it was not true, Mr Talb?

A: You should ask them.

Q: But you must surely respect the opinions of United States government officials, do you not, Mr Talb?

A: No.[21]

Without referring to the party involved, who was in fact Special Agent Hendershot of the FBI, Keen put it to Abu Talb that he had spat at an American investigator. He denied it, saying that he had merely refused to say hello. Keen prodded him further:

Q. Mr Talb, you are not only a murderer, you are a liar. Is that not correct?

A: I am not a liar.

Q. You are just a murderer?

A: Nor a murderer.[22]

Like Taylor before him, Keen pressed Abu Talb about his time in the Soviet Union and about SAM missiles. When the witness refused to answer, Keen replied: 'I don't care whether you want to enter into those details or not, Mr Talb. Answer the question.'[23] Keen asked the judges to direct the witness to answer, but Lord Sutherland replied that they would need to be assured that the question was material. With Abu Talb absent from the court during the legal arguments, Keen told the judges:

My Lords, I proceed upon the premise that this man is in fact a professional terrorist. He was trained as a professional terrorist in the 1970s. He operated as a professional terrorist. Then, in 1983, he removed to Sweden, where he would have the court believe that he effectively retired and from time to time accompanied his brother-in-law to a cafe where he helped out. In fact, as will become apparent, the man continued to create false identities for himself after 1983, and then took part in a series of terrorist outrages in 1985 and 1986. He also arranged for friends and relatives to

undergo training for the purposes of such terrorist atrocities, and
latterly he was involved in a series of moves in 1988 which cast
considerable light upon what was going on with regard to the
bombing of Pan Am 103.

So the entirety of his training and background is material to his
ability to wage terrorist activity. This helps to explain why he was
promoted so swiftly within the PPSF . . . [who], along with the
PFLP–GC, was an extreme Marxist-Leninist group . . . bent on
repudiating any political settlement of any kind in the Middle East and
in securing their aims by violence. Both were widely implicated in
terrorist actions in the 1970s and '80s. I intend to explore all of that,
and it is relevant to know that this man is a highly trained terrorist.'[24]

What transpired was very disconcerting. The judges appeared to have no
idea how to deal with a witness who refused to answer questions. Normally,
in a High Court setting, if the judges are happy that the questions are
appropriate they will order the witness to answer. They have the power to
jail those who refuse for contempt of court. Here in this little piece of
Scotland, faced with a witness from another jurisdiction, the judges
appeared to be very indecisive about their legal position. The Crown
submitted that although the judges did have the power to impose sanctions
on Abu Talb, they did not have the timescale available to do so as Abu Talb
was to be returned to Sweden by 18 November, three days away. Having
heard the legal submissions, the judges accepted that they did have power
to cite the witness for contempt. Lord Sutherland warned him:

> We should tell you that it is a matter for this court and not for you
> to decide what is relevant for the purposes of this trial. As a Crown
> witness, you have immunity from prosecution for the offence with
> which this court is currently concerned; namely, the bombing of
> Pan Am 103. And that being so, you are obliged to answer any
> questions which in the court's view are relevant to this inquiry . . .
> Do you understand what we have said?
> A: Yes.[25]

Keen then took Abu Talb through a list of questions about his many forged
passports and international travel documents. He implied that Abu Talb
destroyed or lost documents and obtained replacements, which meant his
previous travels could not be traced. Abu Talb, of course, denied it, but his
answers were not entirely convincing.

Keen again challenged him about his brother-in-law, Mahmoud Mograbi, being ordered to Syria to learn bomb-making. Mahmoud had claimed that his bomb-making instructor, Abnan Abu Sultan, had visited Uppsala and had direct financial dealings with Abu Talb. Abu Talb vehemently denied this, which was strange, because when interviewed by the Swedish police he had admitted to receiving money from Abu Sultan, claiming it was the repayment of a debt.

Questioning him about his current conviction, Keen pointed out that he had claimed to be alibied, but that the alibi had been destroyed twice over. The second instance was of particular interest because Abu Talb had produced a four-year-old ticket for the Kiel–Gothenburg ferry, which he claimed alibied him. The police subsequently discovered that the ticket had never been used. The obvious parallel with the Lockerbie case, Keen implied, was that he had again produced a ticket, this time an unused portion of a ticket to Malta.

Asked again about the Amsterdam and Copenhagen bombings, Abu Talb's answers became somewhat enigmatic. He insisted he 'did not do it' but also said he was 'not innocent'. He refused to tell who had ordered him to carry out the attacks, saying that the person's name 'has been mentioned in this investigation'. When pressed, he would say only that his brother-in-law Mahmoud had named the person as Sultan.

Turning to the police raids in Uppsala in 1989, Keen asked Abu Talb about the items that had been found at his house and that of his brother-in-law Mustafa, where he had been staying. Around 14 watches, some of which had been tampered with, were found under the bed along with a barometer with the barometric device removed. Abu Talb claimed that this belonged to his other brother-in-law, Mahmoud, but Keen pointed out that in his police interview of 3–5 April 1990 he had stated: 'I do remember such an instrument at my house, but I cannot remember anything missing from that instrument. In that case, I cannot know if something is missing. I cannot say where that piece or part is, or who dismantled it.'[26] Some 16,000 Swedish kronor were found in Abu Talb's house, with a further 85,000 kronor in a bank account. Mahmoud Mograbi told the Swedish court that Abu Talb used to go to Cyprus to collect money for the operations of the PPSF. Questioned by Keen, Abu Talb denied it, claiming he had borrowed 45,000 from one bank and deposited it in another, with the aim of obtaining a further loan from the second bank.

Asked about his connections to Malta, Abu Talb said that he had first visited the island in 1984 and that he had been told that Imad Chabaan (aka Martin Imandi) had lived there for a time. Keen put it to him that he and Chabaan had visited East Berlin and East Germany together, but Abu Talb insisted they went to Berlin. Keen then commented that he had attempted to leave Sweden for Cyprus on 1 March 1986, the day after the Swedish prime minister Olaf Palme was assassinated. The airports and seaports were closed but Abu Talb managed to get to Cyprus by 2 March, leaving there six days later. Abu Talb said he had gone from Cyprus to Egypt, which prompted Keen to point out that in his earlier testimony he had said that he could not return to Egypt, as he was a wanted man there. Abu Talb replied:

> Correct. But I want . . . to clarify one thing. On this part before – the name is Mohammed Abu Talb, born in Sabra, Lebanon, and not born in Egypt. This is the first point. The second point is that when I decided to go back to Egypt, I made that decision because I had to see my mother at any cost. And, as I mentioned during the investigation, some of my relatives lived in Egypt. I contacted them by telephone to make sure that they could help me enter Egypt on my arrival.

The exchange went on:

> Q. Your mother seems to feature quite a lot, because you went to Malta in 1988 in the course of making strenuous efforts to cross the desert from Libya to Egypt to see her again, didn't you, Mr Talb?
> A: Yes, this is correct.
> Q. Mr Talb, the passport or travel document before us contains no immigration or passport stamps for Egypt. Accordingly, you did not enter Egypt.
> A: This is true . . . who said that I entered Egypt? I did not say that I entered Egypt. I said I went to Egypt.
> Q. Were you refused entry to Egypt?
> A: Yes. I was in transit.
> Q. And did you then return to Cyprus?
> A: Our relatives in Egypt sent me some money, and when I was unable to enter Egypt, I bought a ticket and went back to Cyprus.
> Q. So would you have been in the transit area of the airport in Cairo for this purpose?
> A: Yes.
> Q. Well, Mr Talb, according to your passport, you didn't re-enter Cyprus until 27 March 1986. Now, are you suggesting to this court

that you spent 19 days – virtually three weeks – in the transit lounge
of Cairo Airport?

A: Yes, and if you don't know, you can ask about this. Palestinians
can spend not just weeks but months in Arab airports. Months.

Q. Where were you in the period from 8–27 March 1986, Mr Talb?

A: I was in the transit lounge at Cairo airport.[27]

During his 19 days in Cairo airport he had obviously been fortunate
enough to avoid the Egyptian security police, who were still seeking him for
army desertion and prison escape.

Moving on to the trip to Malta in 1988, Abu Talb said he'd had no strong
reason to visit the island, but admitted that he did not use his return ticket,
from Cyprus to Sweden, and instead used the last of his money to book a
ticket from Cyprus to Malta, via Athens and Rome. Keen suggested this
demonstrated that he had in fact a very good reason to go to Malta:

> *Q.* Mr Talb. Your destination was Malta, and once you undertook
> the journey, you were without funds and could not even have paid
> for another fare back to Sweden unless or until you received funds
> from Abdul Salem. Is that not the case?
>
> *A*: Let me explain a bit to you. When I booked this ticket from
> Cyprus, my destination was Malta, and my main reason for my
> going to Malta was to try to enter Libya and then Egypt to see my
> mother.
>
> *Q.* Pause there for a moment, Mr Talb, because that has not
> consistently been your explanation for this trip at all. Can I just
> remind you of what you originally said about this trip? First of all,
> in your statement to the Swedish police in April 1990, you were
> asked, and this was ten years ago: 'What was the reason for travelling
> to Malta at this time?' You answered: 'The reason for my going to
> Malta was that I was going to do business with Abdul Salem and his
> brother Hashem Salem.' Now, is that an accurate statement of what
> you told the Swedish police in 1990, Mr Talb?
>
> *A*: I said that. Yes, I said that then, and I said it here as well.
>
> *Q.* And then, on a different date, you were asked: 'What was the
> exact reason for you to visit the Salem family?' You said: 'I wanted
> to visit Magdea Salem, since she had been in Egypt and among
> other things visited my mother there, and I wanted to hear about
> my family.' Is that correct?
>
> *A*: Correct.[28]

The problem with this story is that it was in direct conflict with the one Abu Talb had given when questioned by the prosecution a few days earlier. He had then stated that the purpose of his trip to Malta was to obtain clothing to sell in Sweden, in particular T-shirts. At Keen's request Abu Talb looked at one of the items of clothing he had brought back to Sweden, a T-shirt with 'Malta' printed on the front. Keen then asked: 'Now, Mr Talb, do you seriously expect this court to believe that you thought in 1988 there might be a market in Sweden for T-shirts with the word "Malta" printed on the front?' To which Abu Talb replied: 'Why not?'

Keen suggested that his Maltese host Abdel Salem was not really a friend, but a PPSF contact who had taken deliveries of goods from Lebanon for the group. Abu Talb denied it, but could not explain why Salem had told the Lockerbie investigators that he had only encountered Abu Talb once in Malta, a chance meeting in Valetta in October 1988. Neither could he explain why Salem had given him the details of a PO box in Malta which, though belonging to Salem, was in the name of Bitar. Abu Talb claimed not to remember the discrepancy in the names, prompting Keen to say: 'Can I suggest to you that you are a man with the intelligence to notice detail?' Ever slippery, Abu Talb replied: 'That is not true. Had I been an intelligent man you would not see me here today.'

Keen moved on to Tony Gauci's identification of Abu Talb and his interview by the Swedish police about a possible second trip to Malta in November 1988:

> *Q*. Were you in Malta on about 23 November 1988, Mr Talb?
> *A*: I travelled on the 26th, so of course I was in Malta.
> *Q*. On 23 November 1988, Mr Talb, were you in Malta?
> *A*: No, I was not in Malta on 23 November.
> *Q*. Well, it may be alleged by you that it is merely a slip, but can I remind you of a statement which was taken by the Swedish security police from you on 24 August 1989, between the hours of 1200 and 1430 at the police station in Norkopping, where, having referred you to a plane ticket, they recorded: 'According to Abu Talb, this is the trip he made from Malta to Stockholm, 26 November, 1988.' Now, did you make such a trip, Mr Talb?
> *A*: This is not correct.[29]

It may have been a Freudian slip for Abu Talb to state that he was in Malta on 26 November, but he was not able to explain away the statement of the police other than to say it was incorrect. If he was indeed on the island in the days running up to 26 November it was, of course, of huge significance, because 23 November was the day that Tony Gauci's brother Paul said he went home to watch the football match – the day Tony said the mystery customer had bought the clothes. Although Abu Talb did not match Tony Gauci's description of the clothes buyer any more than the defendant Megrahi, who was to say that the mystery purchaser had not handed the clothes on to him?

Keen was getting very close to the end of his cross-examination, and was leaving no stone unturned. He asked Abu Talb if he had sent anything to the PO box in Malta following a phone call from Abdel Salem on 11 December 1988. Abu Talb said that if he had sent anything it would have been videos. Keen asked him if he had sent a radio-cassette player. Abu Talb denied sending such a device anywhere. Keen then suggested there was something unusual in the fact that Magdy Moussa, a former director of the Miska Bakery in Malta, whose name was found in Abu Talb's apartment in Uppsala, and Martin Imandi's brother Talal Chabaan, had left Denmark for Malta on 13 December 1988 and contrived to remain there until 22 December.[30]

Finally, Keen asked Abu Talb if he considered the destruction of Pan Am 103 by a bomb to be a criminal act. He replied: 'Yes.'

After a few questions of re-examination by Campbell, Abu Talb left the witness box to be transported back to his cell in Sweden.

In the event, the cross-examination of Abu Talb was as close as the court came to hearing evidence of the alternative account of the bombing of Flight 103. But there was another witness, whose name would never crop up during the court proceedings, who might have taken that account much further. Away from Camp Zeist and the media glare an intriguing side-show was to develop, at the centre of which was this witness.

Richard Fuisz seemed an unlikely character to be involved in the Lockerbie saga. A medical doctor described as a brilliant entrepreneur, he held numerous world and US patents on pharmaceutical delivery systems. Yet Fuisz also seemed to have knowledge of the bombing of Flight 103.

According to former US Congressional aide Susan Lindauer, Fuisz told her: 'If the [US] government would let me, I could identify the men behind this attack today. I could do the right thing . . . I could go into any crowded restaurant and pick out these men. I can tell you their home addresses . . . You won't find [them] anywhere in Libya. You will only find [them] in Damascus. I was investigating on the ground and I know.'[31] So concerned was Lindauer by what she heard that she recounted the meeting in a sworn affidavit.

In a telephone call with one of the authors in the spring of 2000, prior to the opening of the Lockerbie trial, Fuisz confirmed that he had knowledge of the bombing. When asked if the two accused Libyans were involved, he said, 'No.' He stated that he could not go into detail and when asked if he could not or would not, said: 'I cannot even tell you why I cannot tell you, as that would get me in trouble'.

In a subsequent interview at his office in Virginia, accompanied by his son Joseph, an attorney, Fuisz handed over a copy of the order from the court, which he said prevented him from talking about the case, but insisted that he would talk if ordered to by a judge.

The Fuisz story broke in Scotland's *Sunday Herald* newspaper on 28 May 2000 with the headline 'LOCKERBIE: CIA WITNESS GAGGED BY US GOVERNMENT'. Enquiries to the CIA and the US DoJ proved fruitless. No one would talk about Fuisz other than to hint that perhaps he was a conspiracy theory fantasist. Yet Fuisz was covered by a gagging order issued under the umbrella of Military and State Secrets Privilege. It transpired that this order was imposed in relation to information he had given to Congress regarding the delivery of military equipment to Iraq by a US company. The link to Lockerbie was unclear at this stage, but events in a Federal courthouse would later show that Fuisz, far from being a fantasist, did indeed hold information that could be crucial to the trial.

Following the *Sunday Herald* story, Fhimah's lawyer Eddie MacKechnie raised the matter with the US DoJ, initially through the department's attorney Brian Murtaugh, who was an observer at the trial. Fuisz had stated to the authors that he would be willing to meet with representatives of the defence if he was granted some form of 'judicial relief'. In his response to MacKechnie, Murtaugh claimed that there was no impediment to any meeting with Fuisz. Behind the scenes at the DoJ, senior officials were alerted to the request to meet with Fuisz. Murtaugh, it seemed, had overstepped his authority in stating that there was no impediment to the Fuisz meeting. A senior DoJ official, Stanley Rothstein, was dispatched to the CIA's headquarters in Langley, Virginia.

The CIA did indeed have an interest in keeping Fuisz quiet. Following a meeting with Fuisz in the USA, MacKechnie instructed their US legal partners, the law firm of Butera and Andrews, to seek to take a deposition from the witness, under oath and before a judge. This legal process did not happen until December and at the first of two hearings, in the presence of three attorneys from the CIA and two from the DoJ, Fuisz was deposed. The CIA attorneys objected about the simplest of questions put to him. Fuisz himself seemed reluctant to give definitive answers. When asked if he had ever been in Damascus, Fuisz replied 'I do not recall.' So numerous were the objections that the judge agreed to adjourn and hear legal argument later.

Within two weeks, despite receiving a letter from the CIA director George Tenet (the contents of which were never disclosed), the judge overruled most of the CIA's objections and Fuisz was forced to admit that he'd had contact with very high-level Syrian and Russian officials and that he had reported the contents of these meetings to the CIA. When asked for the names of these officials, he said that to name them, even in a sealed hearing, might put his life in jeopardy. The judge allowed them to be written down and they were placed under what was described as a 'double seal'. It seemed that Fuisz was indeed part of the CIA's human intelligence, or HUMINT.

If Fuisz's original claims, as recorded by Susan Lindauer, are correct, it is reasonable to assume that these briefings with Syrian officials must have concerned the involvement of Ahmed Jibril, who operated under the wing of the Syrian government. Whatever the exact details of these briefings, it is clear that the US government once again attempted to stop the defence gaining access to material that would assist their 'special defence' of incrimination. Had the deposition of Fuisz taken place earlier than December 2000, as the trial was drawing to a close and after the Crown case rested, we may have seen him called as a defence witness.

In the event, a trio of Crown witnesses were to hog the limelight.

17. 'THE BIG THREE'

Scores of witnesses came and went from the Camp Zeist witness box, very few of whom did much to significantly advance the prosecution case. As time went on it became increasingly clear that no magic rabbit would be pulled from the Crown's hat to guarantee a guilty verdict. As predicted, the prosecution case would rely heavily on three witnesses: Edwin Bollier, the proprietor of Mebo, the company that supplied MST-13 timers to Libya; the Maltese shopkeeper Tony Gauci, who sold the clothes that were supposedly wrapped around the bomb; and the Libyan informant Majid Giaka.

Before Bollier took the stand, the court heard from his business partner, Meister. Although he had founded Mebo with Bollier in the early '70s, it was always clear that Bollier was the more extrovert of the two; the hustler, the mover and shaker who operated on the more secretive side of the communications business.

On more than one occasion during his evidence, Meister referred to his failing memory. Following his examination in English by Advocate Depute Turnbull and having consulted with his lawyer, Dr Neupert, over the weekend recess, he opted to respond to cross-examination in German. At times he was reluctant to be pressed to answer questions from David Burns QC for Megrahi. He had perhaps formed the same opinion as his partner Bollier, that even though they had been called by the Crown, the defence considered them to be friendly. However, he experienced some hostile cross-examination, although nothing compared to the storm that would soon be unleashed on the unsuspecting Bollier.

When asked about Mebo's supply of MST-13 timers and other items to the Stasi in East Germany, Meister played down the extent of his knowledge. He confirmed that when Bollier returned from Libya on 20 December 1988, he brought back with him some Olympus timers which the Libyan intelligence service had ordered and then rejected. Some time after Bollier's return, Meister said, Bollier had showed him one of the Olympus timers and asked him to note that it had been programmed for a Wednesday at 7.30 p.m. Meister claimed that he saw the time and day, but when pressed admitted making a statement on 14 February 1991 in which he claimed to have seen the date 21 December 1988, the time 7.30 and the day Wednesday.[1] He repeated this claim to Scottish police officers in April 1991.[2] Unfortunately for Meister, that particular model of Olympus timer, the TM2, does not display a date.

Could it be, as was later suggested, that Meister and Bollier had decided to try to implicate Libya in the bombing in return for possible reward money? The possible financial motive would not be aired publicly until Bollier's evidence was given.

Under pressure from David Burns QC for Megrahi, Meister also admitted that both he and Bollier had composed a letter, dated 6 February 1991, to the Libyan Minister of Communications, a Mr Ezzadin, informing him of their interview with the Swiss police and the FBI in December 1990. Noting the Lockerbie connection, the letter stated, 'Our timer had been confiscated in Senegal.' It went on to tell Ezzadin: 'I could prove [to] them that in 1985 they [Mebo timers] had been sold to a Mr Khouri in Beirut, Lebanon.'[3]

The implication seemed obvious; Meister and Bollier were trying to put the bite on the Libyans. They went as far as adding a postscript to the letter: 'I heard you are now Minister of Communications. Are there any new projects in which we could participate?'[4] The Mebo directors saw an opening for more business from Libya if they produced evidence that additional timers were supplied to a non-existent customer in Beirut. Libya had never denied ordering MST-13 timers and there was already evidence that the same model of timer had been sold to the Stasi, which was known to have acted as quartermaster for groups including the PFLP-GC.

Meister's more colourful partner was always likely to have been a problem for the Crown. Given that he had spent much of the previous seven years casting doubt on the case against the Libyans, the prosecuting counsel had to tread a fine line between leading evidence that they hoped would implicate the Libyan Intelligence Service and casting doubt on his credibility. The latter proved much easier to do, but that ran the risk of the judges disregarding his entire testimony.

Advocate Depute Turnbull began with a fairly mild examination of Bollier, but before long he began to question him about briefcases he had sold the Stasi, which were fitted with pagers that could be remotely detonated. He asked Bollier if he was aware that a similar device had been found in the flat, in Budapest, of someone known as 'Carlos'.[5] Bollier denied any knowledge of it. The reference was never expanded upon, but the question obviously referred to the notorious terrorist Carlos Ramirez Illych Sanchez, better known to the world as the 'Jackal'.

Bollier attempted to suggest that MST-13 timers were made in the USA for the CIA. When questioned about the source of that information, he struggled to think of a name and then blurted out 'Buyers'. Turnbull suggested that he meant 'Chuck Byers'. In uttering the word 'Chuck', Turnbull let slip that he was aware of the allegations of Chuck Byers and others which had been brought to the attention of the Crown. Turnbull allowed this part of a partial story, with which Bollier was not fully familiar and which Turnbull's own office had seemed to play down.

Translation issues were continually raised during Bollier's testimony, as David Burns QC, William Taylor QC and Richard Keen QC complained on behalf of their clients of various problems. It transpired that the Crown had not felt it necessary to hire translators who could translate from German to Arabic. Instead, they had to relay everything into English and then into Arabic, which meant the accused were often several lines behind what was actually going on in court and were having difficulty following the testimony. Many experienced observers who attended the trial during this phase expressed difficulty in following Turnbull in English, such were the convolutions in his approach.

At the end of Turnbull's examination came one of the trial's most extraordinary revelations. The court was told that on 5 January 1989, only two weeks after the bombing of Flight 103, Bollier had written to the CIA implicating Libya in the Pan Am bombing.

For nine years the British and American governments had insisted that the Lockerbie investigators had fingered Libya as the result of straightforward detective work. They repeatedly said that the crucial fragment of circuit board had been linked to Mebo and Libya through exhaustive forensic analysis, beginning with Thomas Hayes's discovery of the fragment on 12 May 1989. According to other evidence heard at the trial, the Scottish police spent many months making fruitless inquiries within the printed circuit board industry before receiving information from Tom Thurman of the FBI in June 1990, as a result of which Chief Inspector William Williamson and Allen Feraday of RARDE travelled to Washington DC, where they were shown an MST-13 timer. The timer had at that point recently been handed over by the CIA, who had had it since 1986, when Richard Sherrow of the Bureau of Alcohol, Tobacco and Firearms brought it back from Togo. The agency also had photos of the timers allegedly confiscated from Libyan agents in Dakar, Senegal, in February 1988.

So, by early January 1989 the CIA not only had a sample and photos of an MST-13 timer, but also had a letter from the timer's manufacturer tipping them off that Libya may have been behind the bombing of Flight

103. If the Lockerbie investigation was the great international co-operative effort it had always been proclaimed to be, then surely the CIA would have shared this information with the British investigators and the case should have been cracked soon after Hayes discovered the fragment. Unfortunately, neither counsel nor judges sought to establish why this had not happened.

Asked why it was he came to write the letter, Bollier gave an interesting account:

> *Q.* All right. Now, you tell us, then, why you wrote this letter to the CIA, and then we'll have a look at the letter.
> *A:* Okay. On the 30th of January – on the 30th of December, I'm sorry, 1988, around ten in the morning, when I came to the Mebo offices there was a man standing close to the main entrance. When I entered, he asked me: 'Are you Mr Edwin Bollier?' I answered 'Yes.' And then I told him, 'Please come in.' We entered my office and he says to me – well, after a few words, I realised that this must be someone from the security services. You can tell immediately when you deal with people from the intelligence service. He said, 'Mr Bollier, you were in Libya. You delivered 40 MST timers. You returned via Malta to Zurich. And I can tell you that the Libyans are connected with this attack.'
>
> I was very surprised. I wanted to know who he was. He said that was of no importance. He gave me very clear instructions: 'Write a letter to the CIA and send it to the embassy and explain that Colonel Gadafy and Mr Senussi are behind this attack, etc, etc. You are smart enough to write such a letter. And all I can say is do it, otherwise you will have to suffer the consequences. Well, you'll see the consequences in the media, etc.' And then he disappeared the same way he had shown up on the scene.
>
> What struck me right then was that this man had inside knowledge. He knew that I had been to Libya with 40 timers. What was wrong in his account was that he didn't know they were MST-13 timers. Second, he did not know that I had returned directly to Zurich and had not flown via Malta. And this was what, around the New Year . . . There was another important point. He said that I had to type this on a typewriter with a Spanish letter set. I think the 'N' has a little arch on top, and there are other characters that are special. Over New Year, I thought about whether I should do this or not. And then I decided I would do it and was looking for a typewriter with a Spanish letter set in Zurich.

Q. Let's just stop there for a second. So with that explanation, then, Mr Bollier, you are perhaps going to go on and tell us that you managed to obtain an appropriate typewriter, were you? Just yes or no will probably do.

A: Yes.

Q. All right. Can we now, then, have a look at the letter, having understood why it was that you wrote it. Could we scroll down a little further, please. Do we see that the letter suggests that there can be contact between you, using a code name, and sets out how that contact can be initiated? We don't need the details. Just tell me if I'm right about that.

A: That is correct.

Q. All right.

A: I wanted to know what – who was behind the man who had come to visit me.

Q. All right. And then we see paragraph eight. Do you see paragraph eight?

A: Yes.

Q. It says: 'The first short information concerning the Pan Am Flight 103.' That's what it says?

A: That is correct.

Q. And then there is some information. Perhaps we could see the next image. More information is then given on the second page; is that right?

A: Correct.

Q. And reading the matter shortly, does it indicate that Libya and the people mentioned in the letter have an involvement in the bombing of Pan Am 103?

A: That is correct.

Q. All right.

A: This is what he requested.

Q. All right. Were you saying in that letter that Libyans and some of the people mentioned here were to blame for the bombing?

A: That is correct.

Q. All right.

A: This is what this unknown man requested me to do.

For many US relatives attending the trial at this time, Bollier was the first witness they could fixate upon as being one of the villains. They were certainly enjoying Turnbull's attack on the Swiss witness, so much so that in a briefing held in private in the Families' Lounge Turnbull was greeted with a standing ovation. No doubt spurned on by the Crown's chief spin-doctor Norman MacFadyen and those from the DoJ's Office for Victims of Crime, these American relatives thought that attempting to destroy one of the Crown's main witnesses was something worth cheering. These briefings were seen by many as an attempt to influence opinion. Evidence would later emerge of misleading statements being issued to the special website set up for the relatives – statements which sought to attribute the cause of an adjournment to the defence, when in fact it was quite the opposite.

Although Bollier was subjected to continual attacks from Turnbull, it was not until his cross-examination got under way that the fireworks really began. David Burns QC for Megrahi started off quietly and gradually set about laying the foundation for the allegation that Bollier was a long-time Stasi collaborator. He questioned the businessman about his company's dealings with the former East German security service, alleging that he was tasked to find sophisticated electronic eavesdropping and cipher equipment.

Bollier's nightmare began in earnest when Richard Keen QC rose to his feet. In an acidic tone, Keen continually referred to him as a 'legitimate Swiss businessman'. Raising the issue of the now infamous 'Spanish typewriter' letter to the CIA, Keen proceeded to take Bollier step by step through the bizarre chain of events. The letter was written on notepaper from the Al Kabir Hotel in Tripoli, and hand delivered by Bollier to the US Embassy in Vienna. In it, Bollier suggested code names for both him and his CIA contact; he would be 'AGA' and the CIA man 'AGU'.[6] Contact, Bollier suggested, would be made by radio telegraphy and he requested that the CIA give him, under code, fax, telephone and telex numbers, along with a PO box in the USA.[7]

Keen went on to talk of Bollier's interview at the FBI HQ in Quantico, Virginia, between 11 and 15 February 1991. Although conducted by the FBI, three Scottish police officers, Detective Superintendent James Gilchrist, Detective Chief Inspector John McLean and Detective Sergeant Pat Byrne, were present. The transcript of this interview, which Keen read to Bollier, included the following passage: 'The idea to send an anonymous letter to United States officials investigating the Pan Am flight 103 case originated with both Bollier and Meister after an incident on 5 January 1989, involving Mustapha and a Stasi man in Berlin. In January 1989 Bollier travelled to Berlin on business.'[8] During their meeting, Bollier and the Stasi discussed the 40 timers that he had taken to Libya in December 1988. When Keen tackled Bollier on the FBI notes, Bollier claimed that a

Stasi agent called Gerber rather than Mustapha was present. He explained:

> This is false, because it wasn't Mustapha who was there. It was Mr
> Gerber. At the time, I did not give the name of Mr Gerber. But
> today one can say that, because the Stasi doesn't exist any more. But
> at the time, it was Mr Gerber and another man whose identity was
> unknown to me. They came to the hotel and asked for this, yes.[9]

Bollier went on to confirm that around two weeks after he delivered the
letter to the US Embassy in Vienna, he was in radio contact with the CIA.
He said that he had offered to be a CIA operative and sent them high-speed
Morse code that he had taped. The FBI notes, which Bollier acknowledged
at the time to be accurate, stated that 'Bollier had heard from Yassir' and
went on:

> Bollier's informant, Yassir, also works for the Arab Voice radio
> network. One of his friends works for Arab Voice radio in
> Damascus, Syria. This individual is Mr Zaki, who is also a PFLP-
> GC accountant. The request to send $500 was to have been sent to
> Zaki's PO box in Damascus to cover expenses.[10]

Here, for the first time, was a direct link between Bollier and the PFLP-GC.
Asked how he knew of Mr Zaki's PO box in 1989, Bollier said that Yassir had
told him. Keen was attempting to show that Bollier's real reason for
implicating Libya was his loyalty to the Stasi, a group that had rewarded him
well from the early '70s, in contrast to the Libyans who seemed continually
to owe him money. Bollier admitted that he owed the Stasi money, and that
at the end of his relationship with the Stasi one of his former handlers came
to Zurich and left with Bollier's BMW car, without making any payment.

As he approached the final part of his cross-examination, Keen, for good
measure, drew analogies between Bollier's mystery CIA man and scenes
from Carol Reed's film noir classic, *The Third Man*, set in cold war Vienna:

> *Q*: Was he wearing a mackintosh, by any chance, Mr Bollier?
> *A*: Yes, that is correct. A light-coloured mackintosh.
> *Q*: He didn't happen to have a trilby pulled down over his eyes, did
> he, Mr Bollier?
> *A*: No. He didn't.
> *Q*: No trilby. Do you recall hearing zither music when he
> approached you, Mr Bollier?

A: Music?

Q: There was no zither music?

A: No.

Q: Could you see a Ferris wheel in the distance, perhaps?

A: No.

Q: So it was just a plain mysterious man in a mac?

A: Yes. What you say is correct. Presumably it was somebody from the intelligence people[11]

At the conclusion of his testimony, Bollier called the authors from his hotel in the Netherlands and complained of the treatment he had received at the hands of the defence. He always knew he was going to be in for a rough ride from the Crown, but had regarded himself as someone who was friendly to the defence. Given the information which surfaced during his testimony, along with his attempts to implicate Libya within days of the bombing, it is almost impossible to see why he had reached this view. Bollier obviously had a lot to lose if the Stasi were implicated in supplying the PFLP-GC with one of his timers. The Libyans were in Africa, but a Stasi hit squad was a car ride away. Bollier owed the Stasi money and was owed money by the Libyans.

Bollier's testimony fanned an on-going debate about the quality of the media coverage of the trial, in particular that of the BBC, which had earlier made a very expensive and ultimately unsuccessful legal application to televise the proceedings. On 20 June 2000, it was stated in various BBC news bulletins and on the BBC Online website that Bollier had admitted that the timer used to detonate the Lockerbie bomb was made by his company. In subsequent BBC reports, it was stated as fact that Bollier had manufactured and supplied the timer. As Professor Robert Black pointed out:

> If Bollier had indeed made such an admission in his evidence it would have been of the very highest relevance, importance and newsworthiness. But the simple and incontrovertible fact is that he did not . . . What he does say is that a fragment of circuit board shown to him in court might have been manufactured by Mebo . . . For the BBC to report, as if it were established and incontrovertible fact, that this fragment is part of the timing mechanism of the bomb, and for them to report that Bollier had admitted that it was, are quite egregious errors.

Black pointed out the errors to the BBC on 21 June. Initially the

Corporation accepted the inaccuracy of their reports, but this admission was subsequently retracted and the original inaccurate claims reverted to.

With Bollier's testimony over, it was the turn of three former Stasi officers. Messrs Wenzel, Gerber and Arnold all trooped into the witness box. The Berlin Wall may have come down in November 1989, but the trio still felt the need for anonymity. One by one they were quizzed lightly by Advocate Depute Turnbull on the issue of when, if and how they received timers from Bollier. First to take the stand was Wenzel, the lucky recipient of Bollier's BMW car. On the matter of timers, Wenzel identified an MST-13 from photographs as the type of timer bought by the Stasi. He also made it clear that it was the practice of the Stasi to remove identifying marks from any item supplied to them. One of Wenzel's jobs, he admitted to the court, was making bombs that could be fitted to cars, for use in West Germany.[12] He also told the court that the Stasi suspected that Bollier was supplying timers to both the IRA and the Basque terrorist group ETA. Wenzel said that after the fall of the Berlin Wall he had destroyed everything in the Stasi's storeroom, but he could not be sure that this included all the MST-13 timers supplied by Bollier.

Wenzel's colleague Gerber, one of Bollier's handlers, talked about his time in the Stasi, but had little of relevance to say about the indictment. Finally, Mr Arnold described how the Stasi used Bollier to secure sensitive items not available in the Soviet Bloc. One such item was a cipher machine called an Elcrotel. Bollier had earlier vehemently denied this, claiming that he was asked only to find a manual for the machine.

In an interesting development reported in October 1999, around the time the final indictment was handed down against Megrahi and Fhimah, the CIA agreed to hand over Stasi files to the German government. Under the agreement, the CIA would gradually turn over copies of Stasi files 'that touch on German affairs', German government official Ernst Uhrlau was quoted as telling a Bonn newspaper. Germany had long sought to obtain the secret police records allegedly stolen by the CIA after the fall of East Germany's Communist government in 1989. In October 1999, a spokeswoman for the German government, speaking on condition of anonymity, said the CIA had agreed to return copies of the Stasi records, but she declined to offer details.

Officials believe the files identified as yet undiscovered Stasi spies, including cold war agents in former West Germany. Uhrlau was quoted as saying that the CIA would be handing over CD-ROMs containing the records to the German Interior Ministry. The files were said to contain the code names and real names of former Stasi agents, so it is possible that they include details of Mebo's dealings with Wenzel, Gerber and Arnold.

Another witness who was to prove a problem for the Crown was the Mebo employee Ulrich Lumpert. The Swiss technician worked for the company for 16 years, before leaving to work at IBM in 1994. Would this witness at last confirm that the two timers which went to the Stasi were manufactured on brown PC board, rather than the green boards used to make those sold to Libya? Unfortunately for the Crown he did not, but rather confirmed that both the Stasi and the Libyan timers contained the same green boards.[13] Lumpert came over as a much more credible witness than either of his former employers, and, since he had actually made the timers, he was no doubt best placed to remember the detail of their components.

The second of the Crown's 'Big Three' witnesses took the stand on 11 July. In contrast to Edwin Bollier, 56-year-old Maltese shopkeeper Tony Gauci had kept a very low profile in the 11 years since media reports had first named him as a crucial witness. His court testimony was to be his first public utterance on the case. Gauci was taken through his previous statements by Advocate Depute Campbell. He was asked about his statement, made in September 1989, in which he described a man coming into his shop and buying clothes. In a tense moment, Campbell asked Gauci if he would take a look around the courtroom and see if he could see the man who bought the clothes. Gauci replied, referring to Megrahi, 'He is the man on this side. He resembles him a lot. On this side, on my side.' When asked if he was able to say what day of the week the man purchased the clothes, Gauci replied 'No.'

Gauci confirmed that the customer had bought two Slalom brand shirts. When asked their colour, he replied: 'Brown, bluish. One was blue I think, checked, I think, and the other one greenish. If I see them I will recognise them.' He was shown a sample Slalom shirt and asked to describe its colour. He replied: 'It's greenish and greyish. It's more greyish.' Asked how it compared to the one he had sold to the customer, he said: 'It's – the clothing is very similar. There were two types of colours.' Shown a photograph of the fragment he acknowledged that its colour was 'very similar' to the sample shirt.

The Crown's examination of Gauci was quiet and subdued, but it was widely expected that when Bill Taylor QC rose to his feet he would immediately attack all of the inconsistencies in Gauci's statements. What actually happened was one of the less memorable bits of Taylor's cross-examination. He also took Gauci through some of his oldest statements, made in 1989 and 1990, but did so with no real verve. During a complicated discourse about whether Christmas lights were up in Tower

Road outside Gauci's shop, Gauci appeared to become confused, referring to the lights being up when the police came to interview him, rather than the day the clothes were purchased. Taylor left the matter hanging in the air. Even more remarkably, considering that his client was the one alleged to have bought the clothes, Taylor never raised the matter of Gauci's identification of Mohamed Abu Talb.

Gauci continued to insist that he could not pinpoint the exact date on which the clothes were purchased. The Crown alleged that it was 7 December. What Taylor knew, but did not tell Gauci, was that the following day, 8 December, was the Catholic holiday of the Immaculate conception. Taylor was able to argue in his closing submission that, had the date in question indeed been 7 December, the close proximity to this important holiday would surely have helped Gauci to remember.

Gauci's evidence was, of course, only really relevant to the charges against Megrahi, but Richard Keen QC for Fhimah nevertheless felt it necessary to cross-examine the witness about Mohammed Abu Talb. He reminded Gauci that in an earlier statement, much closer to the actual date of purchase, his brother Paul had shown him a photo of Abu Talb from a newspaper, which he, Tony, considered to be a likeness to the clothes buyer. Referring to one statement in particular, Keen read aloud:

> Mr Bell wrote down a statement from me. I can only say that of all
> the photographs I have been shown, this photograph, number eight,
> is the only one really similar to the man who bought the clothing,
> if he was a bit older. And then, in slightly smaller handwriting:
> 'Other than the one my brother showed me.'[14]

The number eight referred to a photograph of Megrahi and the 'one my brother showed me' was a reference to Abu Talb. Keen also raised a point concerning a discrepancy in dates, when a statement was taken from Gauci on 1 September and not signed until the 2nd.[15]

No doubt Tony Gauci left the witness box with a sigh of relief, after just a day of questioning. Many questions remained unanswered, including the date of the clothes purchase. Gauci could remember that his brother Paul had gone home to watch a football match on TV on that day. It was known that there were matches on both 23 November and 7 December. Paul could, of course, have shed some light on the matter, but the Crown chose not to call him, even though he was in the court building. The reason, no doubt, was that he had pinpointed 23 November as the day he had gone home to watch the match.

Another matter left untouched by Megrahi's defence was the grey Slalom shirt. On the basis of Gauci's evidence the prosecution was able to assert, unchallenged, that the bomb-damaged piece of grey shirt that supposedly contained the crucial fragment of circuit board had been bought from Gauci's shop. However, a glance back through Gauci's statements showed that this assertion was, at the very least, open to question. In his first statement, given on 1 September 1989, he gave a detailed list of the items the man had purchased and their prices. The list did not include any shirts. On 30 January 1990, the police showed Gauci the fragment of grey Slalom shirt and a sample of an identical shirt. In a statement given the same day, he confirmed that he had had such shirts in stock for the past two or three years, and added: 'That man didn't buy any shirts, for sure.' It was not until over a year after making his original statement that Gauci recalled the customer buying two Slalom shirts. Having had no recollection of them for the best part of two years, he could now not only remember selling the shirts, but could also recall their price, LM3.75 and LM5.25. But even this evidence did not fit the Crown case, because according to Gauci neither of the shirts were grey; one was blue-and-white and the other beige.

A further issue never raised with Gauci was the distance from his shop to the Holiday Inn and to the taxi rank by the bay. In 1995 it took the authors, walking at a normal pace, less than three minutes to walk from Mary's House to the entrance of the Holiday Inn, more than four minutes to reach the intersection of the Strand, and a further two to cross the intersection itself to the taxi rank. Considering it was raining, why would anyone walk the distance downhill to get a taxi when the taxi stance is further away than the hotel and Tower Road is a one-way street leading down to, rather than away from, the taxi rank? Like so many aspects of the case, the obvious was ignored in favour of a much more complicated scenario.

Of all the Crown's witnesses, Libyan informant Majid Giaka was the most eagerly anticipated. But before he appeared, the court would have to grapple with a related issue which was to become the greatest point of controversy of the entire trial. It was to blow up spectacularly in the Crown's face and would raise once again the issue of the Crown's approach to the trial and the role of the CIA.

Both Crown and defence had for some time been in possession of heavily censored copies of the CIA cables concerning Giaka. In February 2000, Senior Procurator Fiscal Norman MacFadyen wrote to defence solicitors Alistair Duff and Eddie MacKechnie to inform them that the Crown were in the same position as the defence in relation to the cables and that notations, or commentaries, explaining the blacked-out sections would be provided by William McNair of the CIA, who was responsible for the censorship.

On 22 August, the day the court reconvened after the summer recess, Bill Taylor QC for Megrahi stunned onlookers by revealing to the trial that Turnbull and MacFadyen had seen versions of the cables and that the cables had not been revealed to the defence. Taylor told how the previous day, in the course of a meeting unconnected with the CIA cables, Advocate Depute Campbell had told defence counsel Beckett and Burns that the Crown had seen the CIA cables in a much less edited form. This had occurred on 1 June, when two of Campbell's senior Crown colleagues, Alan Turnbull QC and MacFadyen, had had a secret meeting with CIA officials in the vaults of the US Embassy in The Hague.

The Lord Advocate Colin Boyd then gave his version of events regarding the cables, and in the process made some astonishing revelations. He first of all assumed responsibility for the affair, saying that Turnbull and MacFadyen were acting on his authority. He told the court that a letter was sent to the defence on 5 June 2000, giving fuller annotations of two of the 25 cables, 'as a direct result of the consideration by the Crown Counsel and Mr McFadyen'.[16] He went on to state that in effect the Crown had behaved properly, citing case law. He stated his views to the court in this manner:

> My Lords, the purpose of the consideration by the learned Advocate Depute and the Procurator Fiscal was to consider the following matters – that is, the consideration of the unredacted cables, the largely unredacted cables, in June of this year. First of all, they considered whether or not there was any information behind the redaction which would undermine the Crown case in any way. Secondly, they considered whether there was anything which would appear to reflect on the credibility of Mr Majid [Gaika]. They also considered whether there was anything which might bear upon the special defences which had been lodged and intimated in this case. On all of these matters, the learned Advocate Depute reached the conclusion that there was nothing within the cables which bore on the defence case, either by undermining the Crown case or by advancing a positive case which was being made or may be made, having regard to the special defence.[17]

Judge Lord Coulsfield was clearly not entirely happy with the Crown's view, telling Boyd: 'My concern, as you'll understand, is the Crown making a judgement on relevancy of matters of that kind without the defence having the opportunity to consider the material themselves.'[18] Soon after, another judge, Lord MacLean, also expressed misgivings about Boyd's statement and asked: 'Is there any particular reason why the accused's representatives, at least, should not see for themselves what lies under these redacted parts?'[19] The Lord Advocate replied that the documents were not under his control, but in the control of the United States. After further submissions from the defence counsel, Lord Sutherland invited the Lord Advocate to use his 'best endeavours' to raise the matter with the CIA.

Why did Advocate Depute Campbell tell the defence that the Crown had seen the CIA cables in a far less edited form? Sources within the Crown office, who spoke on condition of anonymity, revealed to the authors the drama that lay behind his decision. Campbell was not immediately informed of the decision to view the largely unedited cables, and although the Lord Advocate accepted responsibility for the Crown's decision, the main motivator behind the move was Senior Procurator Fiscal Norman McFadyen. He in turn solicited Turnbull and contact was made through Brian Murtaugh of the US DoJ. Of all the Crown team, McFadyen had been involved in this case longer than anyone else, earning him the nickname 'Mr Lockerbie'.

As the court would soon discover, the censored passages of the cables were, contrary to the Lord Advocate's assertion, very relevant to the defence case and went to the heart of the credibility of the informer, Giaka. The authors' sources confirmed that both Turnbull and McFadyen knew immediately that the new information made available to them could be very damaging to their case, if the defence got hold of it. As the time for Giaka to appear drew closer, Campbell made it clear that the defence should be informed and he resolved to bring it to their attention. Undoubtedly, as we shall see, the cross-examination of Giaka by the defence would have been much less successful but for the honourable actions of Advocate Depute Campbell.

The splits in the Crown team in fact pre-dated the trial. Crown Office sources have reported that during a meeting ten days before the case opened, a suggestion was made that the Crown might not be able to sustain the case against Fhimah and should consider prosecuting Megrahi alone. According to the sources, McFadyen's reaction to the suggestion was 'apoplectic'. He had, after all, invested the last 11 years of his career in the pursuit of the case against these two Libyans and he was not about to let part of it slip away so close to a trial date.

The affair of the CIA cables continued to simmer away, waiting to boil over. On 25 August, the Lord Advocate intimated to the court that fresh sets of the CIA cables had been handed to the defence. Bill Taylor QC suggested a short recess in order that the defence could discuss the new material. When the court resumed, it was clear from Bill Taylor QC's tone and his words that the defence would need more time to prepare for Giaka's testimony.

Richard Keen QC was forthright in his comments, telling the court:

> It's only been possible to carry out the briefest perusal of the material which has been handed to the defence by the Crown, but even that brief perusal makes it abundantly clear that what is now disclosed is, in many instances, highly relevant to the defence, and I frankly find it inconceivable that it could have been thought otherwise . . . Some of the material, which is now disclosed, goes to the very heart of material aspects of this case, not just to issues of credibility and reliability but beyond. And the defence are now placed in an extremely difficult position. But it is undoubtedly the case that further inquiries will be required and the defence may have to consider their position with respect to the trial.

The Lord Advocate played for time, telling the court:

> I did, however, feel that since I would no doubt be asked to give assurances to the Court about these documents, I myself should take some time to consider carefully the words I might use and also to consult on the terms of anything that I said to this Court.[20]

With those words, it was clear that Giaka would not be making his appearance any time soon and would have to remain in the police compound for at least another week. On the face of it, and judging by the comments made by the Lord Advocate, there might be some explaining to do when the trial resumed. Could it be that the blacked-out information was helpful to the defence? According to Keen, it was much more than that. The air in the back offices of the court was beginning to fill with the smell of rancour. The relationship between the Crown and the defence is by its nature adversarial, but the level of distrust was growing at an alarming rate.

The following Monday the Lord Advocate addressed the court and, for the first time, admitted that criticism of the Crown might be warranted, 'on the basis that it might be suggested that what is revealed [in the cables] ought to have been revealed before'. This was, as the evidence would reveal, a gross understatement of the facts, but it was the closest that the Lord Advocate would come to making an apology to the court.

Boyd's predecessor, Lord Peter Fraser, recounted to the authors an episode around May 1991 when he visited the US Attorney General in Washington DC. During the visit, Fraser reported that he was ready to proceed with indictments in the Lockerbie case. Fraser claims the Americans asked him to 'hold off' as they were developing new evidence. We now know that the 'new' evidence was Giaka.

During the course of several interviews Lord Fraser was asked who he was planning to indict in May 1991. Fraser confirmed that the planned indictments did in fact relate to Megrahi and Fhimah. In an earlier interview, given before the start of the trial, when asked what he thought the verdict was likely to be, he gave the somewhat surprising assessment that he thought it likely that before the end of the trial the judges would abandon the case. Asked if this was because of lack of evidence, he described a situation that he had once encountered personally, unconnected with the Lockerbie case, where a judge had called counsel into chambers and intimated that the charges would not hold up.

Unlike many former Lord Advocates, Fraser did not go on to become a judge and is therefore not bound to stay silent on such matters.

Back in court Colin Boyd admitted that the suggestion that the cables should be reviewed came from his office and explained:

> The examination [of the cables] was not to make available information for the Crown's use at trial, but was restricted to assessment as to whether there existed information which would undermine the Crown case, or which supported any of the incrimination. During this exercise, both the Advocate Depute [Turnbull] and the Regional Fiscal [McFadyen] examined portions of the cables which still had certain redacted portions. They were given an explanation of what lay behind that by the CIA officials. They were not in a position, of course, to demand access to the information, and not in a position to disclose any information, but were to ask the agency whether there was any method by which we could bring a matter which might need to be disclosed to the attention of the defence.[21]

Boyd had chosen his words carefully. Asking the CIA if there was 'any method by which they could bring a matter to the attention of the defence' was very different to actually seeking the CIA's permission to bring it to the defence's attention. What exactly would the Crown have done if the agency had refused permission? Would the undertakings that Turnbull and McFadyen gave the CIA supersede their duty and obligations as officers of the court? The whole exercise left much to be desired.

The issue spilled over into 29 August, when both Bill Taylor QC and Richard Keen QC addressed the judges with their submissions. Neither was satisfied that all the information held by the CIA on Giaka had been released, and both were very concerned that items in the cables, which the CIA's annotations had described as being 'atmospherics', really hid from view information which they considered crucial to Giaka's credibility. Keen submitted that the court should issue an Official Letter of Request to the US government concerning the cables, but the idea was rejected in favour of a request from the judges and an undertaking from the Lord Advocate that he would employ his 'best endeavours' with the CIA.

Giaka, it now transpired, would be returned to his secret location in the USA and would come back to testify on 26 September. The question marks over his credibility came as no shock to those who had some knowledge of Giaka and the cables debacle merely added to the belief that he would prove to be much less of a stellar witness than the Crown and the US DoJ had implied.

Witness number 684, Abdul Majid Abdul Razkaz Abdul Salam Giaka, eventually returned to Camp Zeist under cover of a convoy of the US Marshal's Service. Since 1970 the Service has protected, relocated and supplied new identities for former mobsters, drug dealers and murderers, among the over 6,800 witnesses to have entered the US Witness Security Program (WITSEC), more commonly known as the Witness Protection Program. Since 1991, the programme had provided a haven for the man some believed held conclusive proof of the guilt of Megrahi and Fhimah.

Special arrangements had been agreed in advance regarding Giaka's appearance in court. He would be screened from the public and press, his voice would be distorted on the audio system and the closed circuit TV was ordered not to film Giaka at any time. He was excused from giving his new name or his new address, which was listed on the witness list as 'C/O Department of Justice, Washington DC'.

With these precautions in place, Giaka took the stand. He was now able to see both Megrahi and Fhimah for the first time since he had been spirited out of Malta almost a decade earlier. Examination in chief was carried out by Advocate Depute Campbell who, in his own low-key manner, led Giaka through some of the preliminaries such as his age, place of birth and education. Giaka was 40, from Tripoli and had not completed his university education.

Giaka said that he had first gone to work for the Libyan Intelligence Service (JSO) in January 1984, in the motor pool. He claimed that in December 1985 he was appointed as Assistant Station Manger for Libyan Arab Airlines in Malta, based in offices at Luqa airport and Valletta. He said the job was a cover for his work for the JSO. He was taken through a long and varied set of questions relating to the structure of the JSO and its different divisions, a move obviously designed to establish the extent of his knowledge of the workings of Libya's secret state apparatus.

Giaka was then asked about Megrahi, who, he claimed, headed the Airline Security section of the JSO in 1985 before being moved to the Centre for Strategic Studies in Tripoli in 1987. Giaka recounted that when he went to Malta in 1985 he reported to Megrahi and that the station manager at Luqa was Fhimah. He claimed Megrahi asked him to take care of his friend, Fhimah.

The first truly significant revelation in Giaka's testimony concerned the date of his first contact with the CIA. Advocate Depute Campbell again led the questioning:

> *Q.* Did there come a point in 1988 when you made contact with the American embassy in Malta?
> *A*: Yes.
> *Q.* When was that?
> *A*: In August of 1988.
> *Q.* Was there a particular incident that led to you doing that?
> *A*: Yes.
> *Q.* Describe that incident, please.
> *A*: At some point in August, a telegram from Tripoli arrived and this contained orders to me and Mr Fhimah to leave the station and come back to Tripoli the same day. We were instructed to take the first plane to Tripoli that day. I learned this early in the morning, and I learned it through one of the employees of Libyan Arab Airlines, Aleeb Shad.[22]

Giaka later discovered that a woman passenger had complained about an incident at the airport, he explained, and this was brought to the attention of his bosses in Tripoli. Although the matter seemed fairly insignificant, it appeared to have a significant effect on Giaka:

> *Q.* What was your own reaction to being recalled to Tripoli in connection with this matter?

A: I felt uncomfortable working for the JSO because of its involvement in terrorism and the way it was dealing with dissidents. And this was the straw that broke the camel's back, if you will. I felt that we, as employees in the JSO, really had no weight, in comparison, for example, to a complaint by a pretty Egyptian woman – that we had no influence.'[23]

So a complaint by a 'pretty Egyptian woman' had prompted Giaka to become a snitch. It later became clear that his feeling of unease at being summoned to Tripoli may have had much more to do with his involvement in smuggling and gambling. But whatever the reasons for his defection, the simple yet stunning truth was that Giaka was reporting back to the CIA well before Lockerbie.

Giaka told the court he had bad feelings about terrorism, but denied that he was ever involved in it. He said his 'goal was to leave his job and go to the United States'.[24] He explained that he approached the US Embassy with a woman called Doris, who translated for him. He told the officials there that he wanted to go to the US but, not surprisingly, they wanted him to stay in his position to gather intelligence.

Campbell asked Giaka if he had raised medical issues with the Americans:

> *Q.* Did you, when you became involved with the American authorities, ask them to assist you in getting a certain type of medical treatment?
> *A:* Yes.
> *Q.* Did you require any medical treatment?
> *A:* I had an injury, an old injury in my arm. I considered leaving the JSO, but I was young enough at that time to be called into the military service. So I was trying to get as far away as possible from the JSO. I wanted to lead a normal life, be a normal citizen. So I asked the Americans to help me to aggravate this injury in my arm slightly so that it would be a reason for me to be exempt from military service.
> *Q.* And did that involve you, then, wanting to get some surgery that would give the impression that you were unfit for such service?
> *A:* Yes.
> *Q.* And did you in due course, with the assistance of the American authorities, get such surgery?
> *A:* Yes.

Q. How many surgical operations did you have?

A: I had two surgical operations on my arm.

Q. Did you have any treatment to your back?

A: No, I didn't get treatment for my back, but I did have a medical examination which was conducted by the agency.

Q. And what was the purpose of that?

A: The purpose of this examination was to find an excuse, or something that would serve as an excuse. We were trying to find something that might prove I had a back problem.

Q. And what did you intend to do if a point came where you could leave the JSO and you weren't conscripted for military service? What did you intend to do?

A: I wanted to go into business.

Q. Whereabouts?

A: In Libya.[25]

Giaka had been caught out in a lie. If, as he claimed, he was a JSO operative, he would already be exempt from Military Service. Not only that, but in the course of just a few minutes his goal had shifted from one of moving to the United States to one of running a business in Libya. More erratic testimony was to come.

Campbell now sought to take Giaka through a condensed timetable of his contacts with the CIA. Did he know that the people with whom he was dealing were from the CIA? Not at first, said Giaka, but he found out later. He recalled that his contact 'used to note down the information', but added, 'I don't know how he worked.'[6] Giaka, it appeared, was the only person inside Camp Zeist who was unaware of the CIA cables which had occupied the judges and lawyers for weeks.

Campbell moved onto one of the more contentious elements of Giaka's evidence, the 'explosives in the drawer' saga. He claimed Fhimah told him that ten kilos of TNT had been delivered by Megrahi and that when Fhimah opened his desk drawer he saw two large boxes containing 'yellowish material'. He said that as well as the explosives, Fhimah stored $10,000 in travellers cheques in the office. He claimed the explosives were in the form of bricks, which at one stage were covered with airline rush tags. Asked to describe the size of the bricks he said, rather confusingly, that they were slightly larger than the boxes. According to Giaka, the TNT stayed in the drawer until it was taken away by the Libyan Consul in Malta.

Asked about Megrahi's visit to Malta on 7 December 1988, Giaka said he travelled that day under the name of Abdel Baset Ali. As the testimony continued, the defence objected that Campbell was asking leading questions:

> *Mr Taylor*: He is leading, in my respectful submission, in the matter
> of timing. It's perfectly obvious what he is about, to those of us who
> have read the cables. I am not of course including Your Lordships in
> that, because Your Lordships don't know what is there and what is
> not there. But it is plain that what he is doing is following a path,
> which was well-trodden in the United States, of asking grossly
> leading questions in order to try to pin down times.
> *Mr Keen*: My Lord, I would adopt that part of the objection. One
> can see the matter of timing from the question as it was framed, and
> it's a matter of considerable materiality and indeed a matter of
> considerable debate elsewhere in the evidence.[26]

The defence were clearly concerned that Giaka could not be relied upon to remember details of any of these events without the aide-memoir of the cables. Campbell had continually read out portions of the cables, with Giaka tending to say 'yes' to what was put to him.

The witness was led though the December evening when he claimed to have seen the two accused arrive in Malta on a flight from Tripoli. He described what he said 'looked like a Samsonite suitcase', adding: 'It had the same shape and it was brownish. It was shiny brownish.' He then described seeing Fhimah take the case from the luggage carousel and he and Megrahi take it through customs without it being opened. Malta had the normal 'Green' and 'Red' channels, and those with nothing to declare could conceivably walk through the Green channel without being stopped.[27]

Giaka was next asked if a Libyan named Said Rashid had asked about the possibility of placing an unaccompanied bag on board a British flight at Luqa airport. He said he consulted with a JSO colleague called Salah and they produced a report together saying that it was possible. Giaka claimed that when he raised the matter of the report with Megrahi, his reply was 'Don't rush things.'[28]

The Advocate Depute wound up his examination by asking Giaka to recall a conversation he had with Fhimah.

> *Q*: Did the subject of the destruction of Pan Am 103 come up in
> any of these conversations?
> *A*: Once I asked Lamin to accompany me in travelling to Malta,
> because as a member of JSO I was not allowed to travel without

authorisation, so if Lamin came with me . . . The second time I visited him, he had changed his mind. He said that 'Abdel Basset and I were not allowed or couldn't leave Libya because the American authorities were looking for us'.

Q. You said that Mr Fhimah told you, 'Abdel Basset and I were not allowed or couldn't leave Libya because the American authorities were looking for us'?

A: Yes.

Q. What else did he say about that subject?

A: He said that Abdel Basset was going to get in touch with Abdallah Senussi to talk to him about this matter. And in the second visit to Lamin, he told me that there had been orders from Mr Senussi to him and to Abdel Basset and also to me, and these were instructions not to leave Libya; this was because of the investigations into the destruction of Pan Am 103. He seemed upset during the conversation. He said something that I still remember. He said, 'The Americans are looking for us, and the Americans bombed Tripoli.' This seemed to me to mean that they were not waiting for a reprisal.

Q. When you say, 'This seemed to me to mean that they were not waiting for a reprisal,' can you just explain to me what you mean by that?

A: He said, in a moment when he was upset, and he was very upset during the conversation: 'They bombed Libya, and the matter was not investigated, and they are now waiting for or expecting a reprisal.'

Q. And did he say anything about money?

A: He had an amount of money which had been frozen, he said, in Switzerland. I don't really know anything about that. It was about $200,000, something like that.[29]

It was an odd exchange, not least because of Giaka's almost perfect memory of the conversation. The judge, Lord Sutherland, asked him when the conversation took place. He replied, 'April or May or March 1991, during these three months.'[30]

Giaka's evidence in chief came to an end after just a few hours.

Bill Taylor QC was the first to cross-examine him and he rose to the attack almost immediately, questioning him about his work in the JSO's car pool:

Q. Car mechanics need some training, but hardly, would you agree, great intellectual training?

A: Would you repeat your question, please?

Q. You don't require to be very bright to mend a car?

A: I have not understood your question.[31]

But it was the previously censored portions of the CIA cables that would give the defence their most deadly ammunition. Taylor read one of the cables, written around a year after Giaka had first spoken to the CIA. The contents were devastating:

> Giaka requested reimbursement of 1,000 Maltese pounds, or lira, for a second operation on his arm. He also requested reimbursement of 500 Maltese lira for 20 days of hotel, car rental and per diem expenses encountered on this trip to Malta. The case officer plans to provide the above funding to Giaka at a meeting on 4 September, in addition to the $5,000 salary owed him in the period to August 1989. Giaka will be advised in no uncertain terms, on 4 September, that we will not provide any additional financial assistance for ten operations on his arm. He will also be told that we will only continue his $1,000 per month salary through to the end of 1989. If Giaka is not able to demonstrate sustained and defined access to information of intelligence value by January of 1990, the CIA will cease all salary and financial support until such access can be proven again.[32]

So there it was in black and white. Many months after the Lockerbie bombing, the quality of intelligence supplied by Giaka was of such poor rating that the CIA threatened to stop paying him. How strange that 11 years on he should be able to give testimony which, when taken at face value, appeared to place two close work colleagues at the centre of one of the greatest terrorist plots of all time.

Using the cables, Taylor continued to attack every aspect of Giaka's motivation and character. While doing so, he noticed that Giaka was smiling towards the two US lawyers who sat in court. Reluctant to make eye contact with Taylor, to the annoyance of the defence, when answering questions for which he was unprepared he looked towards Brian Murtaugh and Dana Biehl, the US DoJ lawyers who were seated behind the prosecution team. Taylor asked Giaka if he knew the pair and Giaka confirmed that he did. At one stage, both defence counsel felt that the DoJ lawyers were making facial gestures, prompting Taylor to respond: 'You needn't look at the Crown benches. You'll not get any assistance there, Mr Giaka.'[33] Both defence teams considered raising the matter with the judges, but were content to make their concerns known to the Crown during a recess.

The cables showed that Giaka spent the first few meetings with the CIA in the company of a person referred to as T1, a Maltese friend called Doris Grech who acted as interpreter. Money appeared to be at the heart of Giaka's motives and it was clear he was willing to alter events to suit the circumstances.

His first day in the witness box ended with a grilling about his application to the CIA for money to have sham surgery performed on his arm. Giaka claimed it was an old injury that had become aggravated. The CIA eventually paid for the sugery, unaware that Giaka also managed to get Libyan Arab Airlines to pay for it. The following day Taylor resumed his onslaught, quizzing Giaka about Megrahi's alleged 'don't rush things' comment. He put it to Giaka that, prior to giving evidence at the trial, he was interviewed at least 14 times by the FBI and the CIA, gave evidence at the US grand jury proceedings which gave rise to the indictment against the two accused, and was then interviewed by the Scottish police and that not once during those interrogations did he make this claim. Taylor pointed out that one of the CIA cables, dated 6 September 1989, reported on meetings with Giaka on the previous two evenings, during which he was asked specifically whether any Libyan officials had made any comments in relation to Pan Am 103. The cable stated:

> Giaka could not give any specific comments about what other Libyan officials have said or speculated about Pan Am 103. From Giaka's comments, it appears that Pan Am 103 may be a non-subject with his colleagues. He could not provide any additional information.[34]

Giaka answered, somewhat ludicrously, that he did not tell the CIA for security reasons.

Before handing over to Richard Keen QC, Bill Taylor skilfully got Giaka to accept that, despite his poor recollection of some events, the information contained in the CIA cables was correct. Taylor put it to him that if there was a cable dated 21 December 1988 reporting on a meeting with him on the afternoon of the previous day – just a day before the Lockerbie bombing – then that meeting had indeed taken place. It was the very same afternoon that Giaka claimed to have seen the two accused at Luqa Airport with a 'brownish' Samsonite-type suitcase, yet the following day's cable made no mention of this.

From the moment Richard Keen QC began his cross-examination, it was clear that he too was intent on making mincemeat of Giaka. Referring to the fact that Giaka was once again looking at the US DoJ's Brian Murtaugh and Dana Biehl, his opening question was: 'Can you see me, Mr Giaka?' Keen quickly got the witness to admit that both he and the woman he would marry, Cynthia Mifsud, worked at the Malta airport in 1988 and that both were working on 21 December, with Cynthia involved in baggage check-in. Knowing exactly what was being insinuated, Giaka began to argue about the details of a form showing his signature and the date, 21 December 1988.

Asked why he chose to give his evidence in Arabic instead of English, Giaka said that his English was not good enough for the legal arena. In that case, Keen asked, why was the bulk of his 1991 US grand jury testimony delivered in English? Giaka denied that anyone had suggested he give his present evidence in Arabic.

According to the CIA cables, Giaka had told his handlers that the Libyan leader Colonel Gadafy was a freemason. Keen used the information to reduce the witness to a laughing stock:

> *Q.* How did you discover that Colonel Gadafy is a Mason?
> *A:* Well, was this question put to me before the grand jury?
> *Q.* How did you discover that Colonel Gadafy is a Mason?
> *A:* Was this question among the questions that were asked before the grand jury?
> *Q.* How did you discover that Colonel Gadafy is a Mason?
> *A:* You asked me a question, and I want to know where you found that question, please.
> *Q.* How did you discover that Colonel Gadafy is a Mason?
> *A:* I am asking about the document that you are referring to. Is this question documented? I remember the answer to that question, but I don't want to indulge myself in subjects that are far from the subject we are talking about. You are talking about the grand jury. Was this question one of the questions that were put before the grand jury?
> *Q.* How did you discover that Colonel Gadafy is a Mason?
> *A:* I still insist that you divulge your source of this question, and then I will answer you.
> *Q.* How did you discover that Colonel Gadafy is a Mason?

A: I am asking Your Lordship to intervene with the defence to clarify the document that he is talking about, and then I will answer the question. I have no objection to answering the question after that.

Lord Sutherland: Mr Majid, we are not concerned with where, if anywhere, the defence got hold of this information, but it is a question that they are entitled to ask and I must ask you to answer it.

A: I knew that from a person, but I cannot divulge the name of that person. The person is in Libya, and for security reasons I cannot mention the name of that person.

Mr Keen: Well, in that case, you can simply write it on a piece of paper and pass the name up to his Lordship, and he can then decide if it's to be disseminated to the defence so they can check the veracity of what you are saying. Would you like to do that, please, Mr Giaka?[35]

Following a brief legal argument, Keen returned to the same theme, asking Giaka how the former president of Malta, Guido de Marco, and the former Libyan foreign minister came absurdly to be in a Masonic conspiracy. Giaka said he could not recall. Keen asked if this was the kind of information he was feeding his American masters, prompting the rattled response: 'Don't say my masters. I am a US citizen.'[36]

By now the world's media had cottoned on to the comedy theatre of Giaka's testimony – and there was more to come. According to the CIA cables, Giaka had claimed that he was a relative of Libya's former ruler, King Idris. Giaka denied it, blaming poor translation. Keen responded bluntly: 'Mr Giaka, you are a liar, aren't you? Mr Giaka, you tell big lies and you tell small lies, but you lie, do you not?'[37]

Seemingly caught out on numerous further occasions, Giaka blamed a combination of poor translation and recording by the CIA. The mood in the Crown camp during his cross-examination was described by one insider as 'gloomier than a November evening in Edinburgh'. So riled did Giaka become by Keen's continual use of the phrase 'American masters' that he complained to the judges.

It was obvious from Keen's cross-examination that Giaka had been somewhat less than truthful with the CIA regarding his employment history when he first approached them. He initially claimed he was in the secret files section of the JSO, when in fact he had only been in that section for a matter of days and prior to that had worked as a car painters' labourer for 18 months. He resigned from the files section on discovering that some 400 files had gone missing, fearing that he would be blamed. The CIA had quoted Giaka as saying he had a 'longstanding personal relationship with Senussi', Gadafy's intelligence chief. When questioned about this by Keen, true to form, Giaka denied he had said it. As the cross-examination moved towards the issue of the sham surgery, the exchanges became vitriolic. Discussing the estimated cost of the surgery, Keen asked: 'Couldn't the CIA have broken your arm for nothing, Mr Giaka, if you were so anxious to have your arm broken?'[38]

Keen began Giaka's final day in the witness box, 28 September, with a line of questioning which succeeded in catching the Libyan completely off guard:

> *Q.* Mr Giaka, what did you do after you finished giving evidence yesterday at 5 p.m?
> *A:* I went back to where I am staying.
> *Q.* Then why did you remain in this building until after 7 p.m. last night?
> *A:* You can ask the people who are accompanying me or who are with me about this.
> *Q.* What were you doing in this building until after 7 p.m. last night?
> *A:*I was in a room, and I was waiting to be taken to the place where I am staying.
> *Q.* Have you seen the printout of yesterday's evidence, Mr Giaka?
> *A:* I didn't see anything.
> *Q.* Can you see me, Mr Giaka?
> *A:* Yes.[39]

Implicit in Keen's questions was the suggestion that a post mortem on Giaka's atrocious performance in the witness box had been carried out with the prosecuting counsel and the DoJ lawyers. Giaka had come to the trial with a huge price tag: almost ten years of living comfortably in the United States, never having done a day's work since his departure from Malta in July 1991, and raising a family and driving a vehicle, all courtesy of the US taxpayers.

In a conversation with the authors during Giaka's testimony, the former head of the CIA's investigation, Vincent Cannistraro, called Giaka a 'slug'. The overall picture with Giaka, as it developed under cross-examination, was indeed far from complicated. A former car painters' labourer and low-level intelligence operative, he claimed to earn between 1,000 and 1,200 dollars per month from the CIA prior to fleeing Malta. He was involved in small-time smuggling at Luqa airport and after an incident involving a well-connected young Egyptian woman at the airport was summoned back to Head Office in Tripoli. Fearful of the consequences, he asked his friend Doris Grech to accompany him to the US Embassy in Malta, where he expressed his disillusionment with the JSO because of its terrorist links. He told the CIA variously that he wanted to go to America; to return to Libya to run a business; and to remain in Malta and establish a car rental firm. He adjusted his CV with the CIA and omitted to inform them that for the first 18 months of his work with the JSO he was a car painters' labourer, telling them instead that he initially worked in the 'secret files section'. Had he elaborated to the CIA about his car painting activities, they may have shown him the door.

The car rental business was a rather simpler proposition than the surgery. Giaka needed $30,000 from the CIA to add to the money he had managed to save from his total salary in Malta for two years. During his first couple of years on the CIA payroll, Giaka regaled his handlers with stories of Masonic conspiracies, his family ties to King Idris and his involvement from the outset with Gadafy's revolutionary committees (even though he would have been only six years old when the committees were first established). Well over a year after first approaching the US embassy, he had failed to mention anything that might implicate Libya, let alone Megrahi and Fhimah, in the bombing of Flight 103. Indeed, so disillusioned were his CIA handlers with the quality – or, rather, lack of quality – of his information that they threatened to stop paying him.

Once transported out into the Mediterranean to meet with FBI agents aboard the *USS Butte* in July 1991, Giaka's memory became remarkably more detailed. In the two weeks that followed, statements such as, 'Suitcase, I do not know anything about a suitcase' evolved into, 'Oh that suitcase – that was some time in September, October, November, or December 1988' and finally into 'It was on 20 December that I saw the brown Samsonite-type suitcase carried by Fhimah and Megrahi at Malta airport.' If not the FBI, maybe it was the sea air that had restored the Libyan's memory, or perhaps the fear that, unless he could secure his passage to the US by telling his inquisitors what he thought they wanted to hear, he would be posted back to Libya.

Winding up his masterful cross-examination, Richard Keen QC could not resist one last dig at the hapless Giaka:

Q. While you've been in America, Mr Giaka, have you managed to

dip into any of the gems of America literature, such as . . . short
story writers like James Thurber?

A: I have read some books, but not all authors.

Q: Have you encountered someone called Mitty, first name Walter?

A: I do not recall.

Mr Keen: No further questions, My Lords.[40]

Advocate Depute Campbell bravely attempted a re-examination, but the
miracle required to rehabilitate this witness was not forthcoming.

18. A CASE TO ANSWER?

So, the 'Big Three' witnesses had come and gone and, as the more sceptical observers had always predicted, none had delivered the prosecution's killer punch. There were more witnesses to come but, by the close of the Crown case, many who had followed the trial believed the chances of either accused being convicted were slender.

Richard Keen QC indicated to the court that he would be making a 'no case to answer' submission to the court on behalf of Fhimah. This legal tactic surprised the Crown team, who obviously felt they had produced a viable case against Keen's client. Contrary to expectations, the submission, which was made on 28 November, concentrated on the narrowed area of *mens rea*, or 'guilty knowledge'. Keen argued that even if an explosive device entered the baggage system at Luqa airport, the Crown had produced 'not one jot of evidence' that Fhimah could have known about it. The quality and precision of the submission, which cited many legal authorities in support, completely wrongfooted the Crown, who struggled to give an adequate rebuttal. Advocate Depute Campbell insisted:

> There is a body of circumstantial evidence, coming from a number of sources, which taken together is capable of supporting the inference that Mr Fhimah joined in a conspiracy, or common criminal purpose, with Mr Megrahi and others.[1]

This use of the word 'inference' was one that would be used repeatedly by the Crown in its later closing statement.

Since there was no other evidence as to how the bomb suitcase got on to Flight KM180 from Malta to Frankfurt, Campbell argued, it could be inferred that Fhimah must have assisted in putting it there. Then there was the diary evidence relating to the tags. Depending on the context of the diary entries, they could be seen as vital, or simply innocuous reminders. In addition, there was the damning evidence of Fhimah's friendship with Megrahi. Commenting on the Luqa airport inference, Lord Coulsfield replied: 'Since we don't know how the system was subverted, what is the basis for inferring that it was Mr Fhimah rather than somebody else, like a loader who had been bribed, who actually subverted it?'[2] Not satisfied with Campbell's response to this question, the judge added, highlighting a major deficiency in the Crown case:

> There is no evidence to indicate that the defeating of the system at Malta Airport was something that Mr Fhimah was even in a position to do, because the furthest that the evidence goes, as I understand it, is to indicate that on previous occasions he may have been able to put a bag onto the computer – onto the conveyor belt.[3]

Campbell was forced to admit that the inference was based on no evidence. Referring to the Crown's allegation that Fhimah was at Luqa airport on 21 December, Lord McLean pointed out to Campbell: 'It is accepted . . . that there is no evidence that he was seen at the airport on 21 December.' Campbell conceded: 'I accept that. It's a matter of inference . . . from a number of pieces of evidence.'

The 'no case to answer' submission was undoubtedly a tactical masterstroke by Fhimah's team. They had elicited some very interesting comments from the judges and the narrowness of Keen's approach had undoubtedly given the Crown a headache. In considering the submission, the Court was required to look, not at the quality of the evidence, or the reliability and credibility of the witnesses who testified, but simply at the sufficiency in quantity. It was clear from the outset that the Crown had a huge amount of circumstantial evidence and in their judgement the next day the judges did agree with the Crown that it had met the sufficiency test.

In ruling against the defence submission, the judges made some very telling points, the significance of which were not lost on Fhimah's team. The judges declared:

> We have come to the view that, with regard in particular to certain entries in the second accused's diary [and] his association with the first accused with whom he is charged as acting in concert, and crucially, the evidence of Majid Giaka . . . we are unable to be satisfied that there is no case to answer, and we must therefore refuse Mr Keen's motion.[4]

The judges were not obliged at this stage to consider the quality of Giaka's testimony, but everyone knew that the informant's witness box performance was so appalling that when considering their final verdicts the judges would have no choice but to reject it. On the strength of the ruling, Fhimah's team took the decision to lead no evidence in defence of their client.

There was no credible evidence against Fhimah, but the same could not be said of Megrahi. The Crown had seemingly demonstrated that on the night before the bombing he had stayed in Malta, using a false passport in the name of Abdusamad. Also, although Edwin Bollier's credibility had been savaged by both sides and Majid Giaka had been made a laughing stock, the cross-examination of Tony Gauci was not as wounding as it might have been. Nevertheless, a vigorous defence case should have sealed a not-guilty verdict for Megrahi – or so many observers thought. Speculation mounted as to whether or not Megrahi would give evidence to counter the allegations left hanging in the air by the Crown. If he did, among the issues he would be required to address were the false passport issue, an interview he had given to ABC television reporter Pierre Salinger on 26 November 1991 in which he denied having been in Malta on 20 and 21 December 1988,[5] and his connections to Bollier. In the event, it was decided that he should not take the stand.

Still, Megrahi's team could not afford the luxury of leading no evidence at all, so went ahead with calling witnesses. First into the box was Major Joseph Mifsud, who from 1979 to 1988 headed the Meteorological Office at Luqa Airport. Shown his department's records for the two periods, 23–24 November 1988, he confirmed that there was light intermittent rain at the airport from noon onwards, which by 6 p.m. GMT had produced 0.6 of a millimetre of rain. The records for 7–8 December, by contrast, confirmed that no rain fell at all at the airport, save for a trace at 9 a.m. Mifsud was of the opinion that the weather in Sliema, where Tony Gauci's Mary's House shop was located, would have been very much the same as at the airport (only around five kilometres away from the shop). Asked if he thought that rain could have fallen in Sliema between 6 p.m. and 7 p.m. on 7 December, he said that although there was cloud cover at the time, there was only a ten per cent chance that a few drops might fall, and that that would have been insufficient to make the ground damp.

The next witness was to provide the trial with one of its most significant episodes. FBI agent Edward Marshman had, in November 1989, interviewed PFLP–GC bomb-maker Marwan Khreesat at the headquarters of the Jordanian intelligence service in Amman. Marshman was taken through a formal report of the interview, known in FBI parlance as an 'FD302'. It confirmed much that was already known: that Khreesat was a double agent for the Jordanian intelligence service; that he went to the German town of Neuss in October 1988 to stay with Dalkamoni and his brother-in-law Hashem Abassi; that he and

Dalkamoni had gone shopping for electrical goods with Abassi's brother Ahmed acting as translator; that three Arab men arrived in the Neuss apartment from Sweden; that shortly before the Autumn Leaves raids he had telephoned his handler in Jordan; and crucially, that he had built a series of barometric bombs.

The document's first significant revelation was that prior to the Autumn Leaves raids, Khreesat had met in Yugoslavia with another PFLP–GC operative, whom he called Abu Fuad. He did not know this man by any other name, but, shown a photograph of the late PFLP–GC member Mobdi Goben, he identified him as Abu Fuad. It was Goben who ran the safe house in Krusevac, Yugoslavia, which was found to contain Semtex and detonators, and it was he who wrote the memorandum that had brought the trial to a standstill when it was disclosed a few weeks earlier. According to Khreesat, the pair met in Belgrade and travelled together to a rented house around 200 kilometres away.

The document went on:

> Fuad has been in Yugoslavia for a long time and is married to a Yugoslavian. Fuad's son is in the Yugoslavian army and is also known by the name Fuad. Fuad's automobile is an off-white colour diesel Mercedes-Benz, model 200. The fuel tank is divided and the contraband to be smuggled is put into this tank. Dalkamoni said that the tank is altered in Syria at the garage of a PFLP–GC member by the name of Khaled El Fitti . . . El Fitti is a mechanic by trade, who specialises in these alterations. Dalkamoni challenged anyone to find the hidden compartment. Khreesat speculated that the car was driven between Yugoslavia and Syria by way of Turkey. Fuad was in charge of the Yugoslavian sector of the PFLP–GC.[6]

By far the most extraordinary revelation in the FD302 concerned a name hardly before mentioned in connection with Autumn Leaves. It was the mysterious Abu Elias, which the Goben Memorandum had claimed was the *nom de guerre* of the person who had planted the Lockerbie bomb in the suitcase of the unsuspecting Khalid Jaafar. The report said Dalkamoni had told Khreesat that Abu Elias was 'an expert in airport security'. It also stated:

> Khreesat advised that he did not tell the Germans anything about Abu Elias. Khreesat never saw Abu Elias in Germany, but was told by Dalkamoni that Abu Elias had arrived. [This occurred on 22 October 1988.] Khreesat told the Germans that they should have

waited one more day to make the arrests, as Dalkamoni was on the way to meet Abu Elias when they were arrested. Khreesat did not know the function of Abu Elias in Yugoslavia, nor did he know the purpose of the meeting that was to be held in Yugoslavia.[7]

Khreesat nevertheless reported that Abu Elias had 'all the details about how to get [the bombs] on the aircraft'.[8] Marshman told the court that during the FBI debriefing session, Khreesat had helped make up a composite picture of Abu Elias, which, when finished, he described as a good likeness.

According to the report, shortly before the Autumn Leaves raids Dalkamoni mentioned to Khreesat that:

> Abu Elias had arrived in Germany that day . . . Khreesat asked Dalkamoni why Khreesat was there if Abu Elias was such an expert. Dalkamoni replied that Abu Elias was an expert in airport security and Khreesat was the expert in building the IEDs [bombs]. Abu Elias was of concern to Khreesat because Khreesat felt that he could not render the IEDs inoperable, as Abu Elias would probably know it.[9]

Khreesat confirmed that one of the bombs he had made went missing, saying it had happened one day while he was in the shower. According to the report:

> Dalkamoni knocked on the door and said that he was leaving to go to Frankfurt. After getting out of the shower, Khreesat went back to work on the IEDs. At this time he noticed that the fifth device was no longer in the workroom. He did not pay a lot of attention to this, as he was thinking about the upcoming meeting with Abu Elias. Khreesat speculated that Dalkamoni took the fifth device with him, as only Khreesat and Dalkamoni ever went into the room.[10]

Khreesat was sure that this device, like the one found in Dalkamoni's car on the day of their arrest, was built into a Toshiba radio-cassette player. He was unable to specify the model, but when shown a catalogue of Toshiba products he said it looked exactly like a bronze model RT-F423. Referring to the call Khreesat had made to his case officer before his arrest, the FD302 stated:

> Khreesat told his case officer that he had prepared a device and given

it to Abu Elias. Khreesat advised that he had assumed that the fifth device went to Abu Elias, as related above. After this telephone call, Dalkamoni and Khreesat went to Dusseldorf Airport. They walked around and Dalkamoni picked up several airline timetables. One was for Pan Am, and Dalkamoni also picked up timetables for Swissair and KLM. When Khreesat saw the Pan Am logo, he made the connection to Frankfurt Airport.

Marshman confirmed it was at Düsseldorf Airport that the Pan Am logo was seen. Marshman's evidence passed by with barely a comment from the media, yet the FD302 contained the most extraordinary revelations. For at least a decade, official sources had claimed that the Autumn Leaves raids effectively terminated the PFLP–GC's German cell. Now there was confirmation, from the mole at the heart of the cell, that on the eve of the raids a Toshiba radio-cassette bomb had gone missing (albeit a Toshiba which, according to Khreesat, was different to the one that contained the Lockerbie bomb). Furthermore, he believed it had been passed on to a terrorist specialising in airline security, who had evaded the raids.

The allegations concerning Abu Elias were all the more interesting because they tallied with the claims of the Goben Memorandum. The defence might have been able to make more of this evidence had the Syrian government complied with the Letter of Request seeking its help in securing three missing pages from the Memorandum. But the request was, of course, turned down. It would have been surprising if the Syrian government had responded positively, given that the defence were attempting to implicate a Syrian-based terrorist group.

The third witness called by the defence was another FBI agent, Lawrence Whittaker. David Burns QC led him through the report he had compiled in October 1989, following a visit to Frankfurt airport with Scottish police officer Watson McAteer. The report, discussed in chapter 14, concluded that there was no evidence that any bag had been transferred from KM180 to the Pan Am feeder flight at Frankfurt airport. And it described a potentially significant incident, which Whittaker recounted to the court:

> There was an individual who appeared to be an airport worker. He was dressed in clothing appropriate to the area, carrying a suitcase, to the best of my recollection, a single suitcase, who approached a coding station, or a baggage entry input station, near where we were standing and placed it in one of the luggage bins on the track, used the keypad to encode what I assume was a destination, and sent the

bag on its way. And then he wandered off. I have no knowledge of where he began his journey or where he went after that.[11]

Whittaker further explained:

> The reason that we mentioned it [to the BKA] is there had been, prior to this point in time and earlier in the investigation, a number of discussions about what could possibly have happened, one of them being the theory that a rogue bag had been introduced into the system. The only point we were making at this time was that we had an individual carrying by hand a suitcase who simply came by, and the amount of time required to place it into the system was very small.[12]

Whittaker did not know it, but he was to be the last of the witnesses to testify at the trial. At the end of his evidence and following the reading into the record of a joint minute, Bill Taylor QC told the judges: 'My Lord, that is the case for the first-accused.' A moment or two later Richard Keen QC confirmed: 'My Lord, there is no evidence for the second-accused.' On its seventy-seventh day, the case of 'Her Majesty's Advocate vs Abdelbaset Ali Mohmed Al Megrahi and Al Amin Khalifa Fhimah' had drawn to a close. There remained only the closing submissions and the verdict.

Advocate Depute Alistair Campbell was tasked with closing the case for the Crown. He reminded the court that the case was circumstantial, but insisted the evidence from a number of sources, when taken together, provided proof beyond reasonable doubt of the Crown's four central claims. The first of these claims was that the 270 Lockerbie victims died as the result of a bomb exploding aboard Flight 103. The second was that the bomb was transported in an unaccompanied suitcase from Malta to Frankfurt, aboard Flight KM180 and was subsequently transferred at Frankfurt and Heathrow airports, ending up in luggage container AVE on Flight 103. The third was that each of the accused was involved 'in concert with each other and with others in the commission of the murder'. The fourth and final submission was that there was no evidence to support the special defence of incrimination.[13]

Going on to address his submissions, the Advocate Depute took the court through a painstaking series of chapters, from the aircraft's position and the weather at the time. He spoke at length of the blast-damaged items. When he reached the item of evidence designated PI/995, the piece of fabric in which it was alleged the fragment of timer was embedded, Lord

Sutherland interjected to remind him that there was some cross-examination of this witness about the apparent alteration of the label. Lord Sutherland asked, 'Is there anything you wish to say about that? Is there an issue of DC Gilchrist's credibility and reliability on the recovery of this rather important piece of debris?'[14] To many observers, the re-naming of the fragment of shirt cast doubt on the provenance of the MST-13 timer fragment, which was, after all, the most crucial exhibit in the entire case. But not to Campbell, who replied simply, 'In my submission there is not.'

In making his submissions about the various airports, Campbell began with Malta, but within moments was giving a detailed account of the various baggage procedures at Frankfurt. Referring to the hotly disputed computer printout from the Frankfurt baggage system, he declared: 'From that it may be concluded that a bag from KM180 was transferred as an interline bag from KM180 through the computerised baggage system to Pan Am 103A.'[15] In this one sentence lay the nub of the entire case; if there was no proof that the bomb came in an unaccompanied suitcase aboard KM180, the entire Crown case was destroyed. Yet the Crown could offer no evidence of how the bag was got aboard KM180 in the first place. Maltese baggage loaders had been prepared to testify, yet they were never called as Crown witnesses.

Campbell moved on to Megrahi's alleged membership of the JSO, speaking of it as if it was, in itself, an offence. In doing so he was relying on the descriptions of the organisation's workings provided by Giaka, who was, of course, very much on the bottom rung of the JSO. In attempting to shore up the witness, Campbell made the remarkable claim that 'In any event, upon examination, his motivation in approaching the United States authorities was not a mercenary one.'[16]

Campbell raised the matter of Megrahi's false passports, ignoring the fact that if he was indeed a member of the JSO, then, in common with his counterparts in MI6 and the CIA, these would be essential tools of the trade. In fact, it is likely that several victims of the Pan Am bombing had more than one passport which could be justified by the nature of their government jobs.

Turning to the MST-13 timers, Campbell gamely picked his way through the minefield of Edwin Bollier's evidence, understandably concentrating on those elements favourable to the Crown case and rejecting those which were not:

> The question then arises as to whether there was a supply of any
> MST-13 timers to the Stasi, and in their evidence, each of Bollier,

Meister and Lumpert suggested the MST-13 timers were supplied to the Stasi. In my submission, that evidence should be rejected.[17]

Tony Gauci could hardly provide more of a headache than the other 'big three witnesses', but Campbell still had to overcome the fact that Gauci had never definitively identified Megrahi as the clothes purchaser and the fact that the meteorological evidence from Malta tended to suggest that the date of the clothes purchase was Wednesday 23 November, rather than Wednesday 7 December. Campbell insisted:

> Mr Gauci appeared as a credible witness and a witness whose reliability can be tested by reference to other evidence in the case.

He added:

> As to the date . . . In his evidence Mr Gauci said that he thought it was about a fortnight before Christmas . . . He thought it was on a Wednesday . . . the Wednesday two weeks before would be 7 December. In evidence, Mr Gauci was of the view that the Christmas lights were already on or being put up.[18]

The reality is that Gauci was confused about the Christmas lights being up. Addressing Fhimah's diary, Campbell asserted:

> On 14 December . . . while Abdelbaset was away, Mr Fhimah was obtaining Air Malta baggage tags for him. The list of reminders in the back of Fhimah's diary includes the reminder to take tags from the airport for Abdelbaset. It says: 'Take tags from the airport (Abdelbaset/Adusalam).'

The Crown could feel confident in using that last sentence, as there was no defence mounted by Fhimah. Had there been, his counsel would have led evidence that the Abdelbaset/Adusalam referred to in the diary was not Megrahi, but actually two people, both of whom were Libyan Aran Airlines employees unconnected to Megrahi.

Campbell maintained that the diary entries provided:

> The name of the participants and the dating of the plan at that stage, and the nature of the plan. The evidence demonstrates that over the ensuing days, the person who wrote the diary entry and the

person who is named in the diary entry were constantly in each other's company. Mr Fhimah was expecting Mr Megrahi on 15 December in connection with the tags. And the tags are an essential part of the plan.[19]

There was not the slightest shred of evidence presented by the Crown that came remotely close to proving that the accused were 'constantly in each other's company'.

Still, Advocate Depute Campbell had done his very best in difficult circumstances. Rounding up the Crown's case the following day, he told the judges: 'My final submission, in departing from the matter, is that when Your Lordships carefully and critically examine the evidence, they will be driven to conclude that each accused is guilty of murder. I invite them to reflect that that is the appropriate verdict.'

On 11 January, without much ado, Bill Taylor QC began his closing argument on behalf of Megrahi. Having set out how he intended to proceed, he turned to the Crown's case in respect of Megrahi's alleged membership of the JSO, pointing out that most of the evidence for this came from the CIA informant Majid Giaka. Giaka had claimed that Megrahi had moved in 1987 to the Centre for Strategic Studies in Tripoli, but, as Taylor pointed out, Giaka had never worked there. That being the case, Taylor argued, he could not know what position Megrahi held there.

Turning to the ABC television interview with Pierre Salinger, Taylor submitted that while Megrahi's remarks could 'be seen to be untruths', they had no legal significance in the context of the trial.[20] It was hardly the strongest of arguments, and it seemed to many observers that the alleged lies in the interview would have been better addressed by the accused himself.

Regarding the special defence of incrimination, Taylor pointed out:

1. In October of 1988, there was in Germany a cell of the PFLP–GC who had both the intention and the means to destroy civil aircraft.
2. That cell was interested in American flights. That cell had acquired a Pan Am timetable.
3. The cell had acquired seven unused Lufthansa luggage labels.
4. The differences, and there are differences, between the Pan Am 103 device and the devices of the Neuss cell are not decisive.
5. There was an alternative to Libya as a source of supply of MST-13 timers, namely the Stasi.
6. There are circumstances which may link Mohammed Abu Talb to

the events we are considering, notably in Malta.

7. It is simply not possible or permissible to dismiss the activities and intentions of the PFLP–GC as irrelevant.[21]

Addressing the crucial exhibit PT/35B – the fragment of circuit board allegedly from an MST-13 timer, Taylor asked: 'Can the court be satisfied as to the provenance and history of this item?'[22] He pointed out DC Gilchrist had testified that he had found the piece of Slalom shirt (exhibit PI/995) cloth on 13 January, but that it was not logged at the property store until the 17th, and the label was changed from 'cloth charred' to 'debris'. Correct police procedure required that such alterations should be made in a clear manner, with a single line put through the old word and the new one written below it. In this case, however, the original word had been 'irregularly and inexplicably' overwritten.

Taylor expanded on the theme, reminding the court of the discrepancies in the pagination of Dr Thomas Hayes's notebook and the fact that the 'PT' designation of the item was apparently out of sequence. He suggested there was evidence to suggest that some exhibits 'were interfered with before they reached RARDE',[23] adding: 'I submit that the irregularities and peculiarities which attend this item [PT/35B] are some which the court ought to have some hesitation in being satisfied as to the item's provenance.'[24]

At the core of the Crown's case was the contention that an unaccompanied bag had been put aboard Flight KM180 at Luqa airport and transferred to Fight 103A in Frankfurt. Taylor put it to the court that terrorists planning a major attack such as this would seek to minimise the risk of failure. The fact that the airside area of Luqa airport was guarded by military personnel, he suggested, ruled it out as a viable starting point for the bomb. All bags destined for Air Malta were checked with a 'sniffer' device, which, under the correct temperature condition, could detect the explosive PETN, which is one of the ingredients of Semtex. Furthermore, the baggage reconciliation system at Luqa made it likely that a rogue suitcase would be detected. The court had heard evidence that 55 bags were physically counted on to Flight KM180, which matched the total number of checked in bags recorded by Air Malta's computer.[25] The Crown had declined the opportunity to call the airline's head baggage loader, a Mr Darminin.

Moving on to Frankfurt airport, Taylor meticulously took apart the prosecution's evidence and pointed out that, as with Mr Darminin, the Crown had not called Mr Koca, the baggage loader who had filled in the worksheet which was so central to its case.

The Frankfurt evidence, Taylor suggested, did not exclude the possibility that the bomb had been planted in the luggage of one of Flight 103's passengers. He pointed out that according to Crown witness Yasmin Siddique, Khalid Jaafar had acted very nervously while standing near her in the queue to pass through passport control. The Crown had called Ms Siddique because she had not seen Jaafar with any bags. It was agreed that the manifest of the Frankfurt–London leg of the flight indicated he had checked in two items of baggage, and that his ticket indicated that this was his check-in baggage allowance. Taken together with the fact that two of his bags were recovered intact from the crash site, the Crown had contended, all this evidence was sufficient to suggest that the bomb had not been planted in his luggage.

But the evidence, Taylor maintained, was not as clear-cut as the Crown had made out. He pointed out that Ms Siddique was not certain that Khalid Jaafar was without bags when she saw him in the queue and, holding up the bags recovered from the crash site, told the judges:

> Your Lordships will see that both of these are smallish holdalls, as I described them, and from Your Lordships' experience of flying, Your Lordships will have no doubt seen many times passengers on aircraft with bags of a similar size and description. So . . . one inference that can be drawn from the size is that if a bag is big, then it's unlikely to be cabin baggage.

The evidence also showed that some passengers had checked in more than two items of checked baggage, and that the flight contained more items of luggage than recorded on the manifest.

Turning to Heathrow, Taylor suggested that if a terrorist were able to introduce a bomb suitcase there he would stand a much higher chance of achieving his objective. He reminded the court of the evidence of Heathrow baggage-handler John Bedford, who had recalled a brown, hard-sided suitcase appearing in the luggage pallet AVE 4041. There was compelling circumstantial evidence, he suggested, that this suitcase, rather than any case arriving from Frankfurt, had contained the bomb.

Having dealt with the airport evidence, Taylor turned to address the identification evidence of Tony Gauci, condemning it as utterly unreliable. Regarding the alleged date of the clothes purchase, 7 December 1988, he contended that Megrahi's presence in Malta that day added nothing to the Crown case. Furthermore, Taylor claimed, such evidence as there was tended to suggest that the clothes had been purchased on another date. He went through the ritual of explaining Gauci's statements about the Christmas lights, arguing that Gauci had clearly experienced a degree of confusion, because he could never say whether the lights were up or not when the clothes were bought. The fact that Thursday, 8 December 1988 was the Maltese national holiday of the Immaculate Conception, Taylor suggested, would surely have assisted Gauci's recollection had the clothes been purchased the previous day.

Addressing another of the 'big three witnesses', Taylor described Edwin Bollier as 'an illegitimate arms dealer with the morals to match',[26] and pointed out that he had concealed his dealings with the Stasi, which included the supply of MST-13 timers, until 1993. 'Now, why should they have concealed that matter?' Taylor asked, adding: 'The only logical explanation is that they wanted to focus attention on Libya.'

Before moving on to Giaka, Taylor turned to the issue of Megrahi's false passports. In doing so, he became embroiled in a short exchange with Lord MacLean, which seemed to many of those present to reek of vitriol. The words themselves, we are told, do not do justice to the atmosphere during the altercation, but those present could feel the tension.

> *Lord Maclean:* Could you just confirm for me, Mr Taylor, that the
> coded passport was never used again after 21 December 1988?
> *Mr Taylor:* We don't know that.
> *Lord Maclean:* Yes, I do. It's day 59, 7860, line 7.
> *Mr Taylor:* Thank you. I am corrected. So Your Lordship has asked
> me a question to which Your Lordship already had the answer.
> *Lord Maclean:* But is anything to be derived from that?
> *Mr Taylor:* I will be coming to that in the course of this part of the
> submission.
> *Lord Maclean:* Oh, good.
> *Mr Taylor:* May I arrive at it?
> *Lord Maclean:* Of course.[27]

Did something slip out in these few words that might give an indication of the thinking of at least one of judges? One lawyer present later described having 'that sinking feeling in the pit of your stomach'.

Arriving at Giaka, Taylor had a rather easier time arguing to the court that the witness was so comprehensively discredited that his evidence should be entirely discounted. Completing his submission on behalf of Megrahi, Taylor compared the Crown case to a multistranded cable:

At a superficial glance, the cable might look strong and sure, but on closer inspection, Your Lordships may conclude that it has been revealed that the strands are mere threads; some are frayed, some break during examination, and others have turned out never to have been joined together at all. The cable made up of these strands is simply not one which will bear the weight of a guilty verdict, and I invite the court to find the first-accused not guilty.[28]

Had Taylor's submission been strong enough to convince these three judges? Time would tell.

It only remained for Richard Keen to present his arguments to the court. His opening words were direct as ever:

My Lords, in my submission it has not been established by coherent, reliable or compelling evidence that Lamin Khalifa Fhimah was party to any plot to destroy a civil passenger aircraft and murder its occupants, and it is upon that premise that I come to address my submissions to the court.

Keen pointed out that the Crown had abandoned the claims that Fhimah was ever a member of the Libyan intelligence services and that his business, Medtours, was ever a cover for the activities of the Libyan intelligence services. For reasons unknown, however, said Keen, the Crown continued to suggest that his client would have wished to further the purposes of the Libyan intelligence services by committing mass murder.

Shifting his focus to Luqa airport, Keen submitted that when the Crown explored with the general manager of Air Malta, Wilfred Borg, whether it might be possible to subvert the baggage systems at Luqa Airport, the suggestion was made that it might have been done by a baggage loader. Yet the Crown's theory was that in his capacity as Libyan Arab Airlines station manager, Fhimah had subverted the system and neither Borg, nor any other witness, were asked how he might have done this. The prosecution had adduced evidence that Fhimah had omitted to hand back an airside pass for Luqa airport. Keen pointed out that the Crown had also led evidence that he had used it as a form of general identification when purchasing a new car, which hardly suggested he was secretly retaining the pass for some sinister purpose.

'We have inference upon inference upon inference upon inference leading to an inference,' Keen argued. He added: 'The Crown's wish to try and incriminate Lamin Fhimah, without reliance upon the allegedly additional parts of the evidence, is perhaps not difficult to understand.'[29] Keen pointed out that the discredited Majid Giaka was the only witness to directly implicate Fhimah in the bombing, and that there was no evidence that Fhimah was at Luqa Airport on the day of the bombing.

Addressing the matter of Fhimah's diary entries, Keen maintained that they contained nothing relating to the bombing of Flight 103. The 'taggs' entry of 15 December had no name and the further tags entry in the note section contained only Megrahi's first name, plus another name. As to the Crown's claim that from 15–20 December the two accused were constantly in each other's company, Keen said that aside from the evidence that the pair travelled on the same flight on 20 December, the contention was completely unsupported.[30]

Again on the issue of the Air Malta tags, Keen insisted that any experienced LAA employee involved with passenger travel would know that Air Malta interline tags were available to LAA at Tripoli Airport. Keen also insisted that the word used in the diary was 'obtain', which could be interpreted as obtaining Air Malta tags for use on flights, rather than taking personal possession of them. Keen further argued that the diary entries did not indicate that Fhimah had actually taken possession of Air Malta tags, and no one at Luqa Airport had reported that any were missing. Fhimah had, of course, left the diary in an unlocked desk drawer in Malta for a period of more than two years after the bombing, which, Keen suggested, was hardly the action of a man knowingly implicated in such a horrific crime.

According to the prosecution, Fhimah had used his inside knowledge of Luqa airport to get the bomb on board Flight KM180. Keen pointed out that any knowledgeable insider would know that all baggage for Air Malta flights, unlike that destined for other carriers, was checked for the presence of explosives. Why then would Fhimah risk trying to get the bomb on board an Air Malta flight, instead of one of the other airlines?[31]

Examining Fhimah's movements on the day of the bombing, Keen pointed out that according to the Crown theory, having knowingly assisted in mass murder, he went to view some new office premises. That, said Keen, indicated either the most astonishing sangfroid on the part of his client or a complete ignorance of the crime.

Returning to Giaka, Keen commented that the detailed description he had given of the structure of the Libyan intelligence services did not sit with the fact that he occupied such a lowly position in the organisation. Leading judges through the informant's numerous statements and the CIA cables, Keen commented:

Now, either Majid Giaka is lying about that matter or, so it would appear, the Lord Advocate has been misled by the Central Intelligence Agency of the United States of America . . . because, as My Lords will recollect, the Lord Advocate was able to advise this court that he had received assurances that all relevant cables concerning Majid Giaka had been produced for the purposes of this trial. If there has been a suppression of material evidence in this case, then that in itself is a matter of fundamental concern so far as Your Lordships' verdict is concerned.[32]

Drawing his submissions to a close, Keen set out the central planks of his client's case:

1. There is no evidence that Lamin Fhimah gave luggage tags to the first-accused in December 1988.
2. There is no credible or reliable evidence that Lamin Fhimah was associated with explosives, either at Luqa Airport or elsewhere.
3. There is no credible or reliable evidence that Lamin Fhimah was a party to the bringing of a bomb or bomb components into Malta. And when I say 'was a party,' I mean knowingly did so.
4. There is no credible or reliable basis for inferring that Lamin Fhimah was at Luqa Airport on 21st December 1988, let alone that on such a date he assisted in placing a bag on flight KM180 to Frankfurt.
5. Even if it is to be inferred that Lamin Fhimah did pass interline tags to the first accused, as the Crown theory would suppose, it cannot reasonably be inferred that he was a knowing party to a plot to destroy Pan Am 103. That, as I said before, is to infer too much from too little.
6. If the actings of Lamín Fhimah, as we know them, illustrate anything, it is complete ignorance of the plot upon which the Crown theory depends.

Concluding, Keen declared:

Looking at the Crown case as a whole, no coherent picture emerges from what amounts to a largely untested chain of conjecture and assertion, incapable of establishing complicity on the part of Lamin Fhimah, let alone of eliminating reasonable doubt. I move Your Lordships to acquit Al Amin Khalifa Fhimah of the charge which now remains on the indictment.[33]

With all the submissions completed, it was time for the judges to retire and consider their verdicts. There had been mounting speculation regarding how long the process would take. Behind the scenes, the Office for Victims of Crime were rumoured to be stating that the verdict would be announced during an afternoon, to suit those American relatives who could not attend the trial. Prior to the end of Keen's submission, the authors spoke with Barbara Johnston of the OVC and asked if her office had had any such discussions with the Lord Advocate about the timing of the verdict. She confirmed that informal discussions had taken place about the timing, but would not elaborate on the details.

Lord Sutherland announced that the court would reconvene on Tuesday, 30 January, but made it plain that the judges would not deliver a verdict on that date, adding:

> It is unlikely; but if by any chance we are in a position to deliver or be ready to deliver a verdict, then what we shall simply do on Tuesday will be to intimate that the verdict will be delivered on the Wednesday. What is a more likely scenario, I think, is that come a week on Tuesday, we might be in a position to indicate a date upon which the verdict will be delivered.[34]

The world was then left to wait and wonder.

Back in court on 30 January, Lord Sutherland announced:

> As we indicated at the time of the last adjournment, we do not propose to issue a verdict today. We are, however, able to inform you that we will be in a position to announce a verdict tomorrow. In view of the substantial number of people which can be expected to turn up tomorrow, and with the difficulties of security, the court will sit slightly later than usual, and we shall therefore adjourn until 11:00 tomorrow morning, when the verdict will be announced.[35]

The judges had confounded Sutherland's own predictions. And their lordships were about to confound just about everyone else's.

CONCLUSION

Dressed in traditional white robes and shashiya hats, Megrahi and Fhimah were led into the court at exactly 11 a.m. local time on Wednesday, 31 January 2001. Within a minute the macer was leading in the three judges. When they were seated, the clerk of court asked: 'My Lords, have you reached a verdict in respect of each accused?'

'Yes, we have,' Presiding Judge Lord Sutherland replied.

Referring to Megrahi, the clerk asked: 'Would you give your verdict in respect of the first accused?'

The reply was stunning. 'Guilty.'

There was a gasp from the victims' families. Most of the relatives of the two accused looked straight ahead, with the exception of Megrahi's brother Mohammed who slumped in his seat, wiping away tears.

'Is that verdict unanimous, or by majority?' the clerk asked.

'Unanimous,' Lord Sutherland replied.

The clerk asked the same questions in respect of Fhimah.

The judge's reply was equally stunning: 'Not guilty.' Again, the verdict was unanimous; again there were gasps.

The Lord Advocate rose to his feet to address the court. As he urged the judges to consider the human cost of the bombing before they passed sentence, there was a minor disturbance as one of the onlookers in the public gallery fainted. It was Dr Jim Swire, the man whose hunger for the truth about the murder of his daughter Flora was one of the key factors responsible for this unique trial coming about. He was carried from the court barely conscious, but thankfully made a speedy recovery.

Within half an hour of their arrival in court, Megrahi and Fhimah went their separate ways for the first time since their plane touched down in Camp Zeist 21 months earlier. Fhimah walked to freedom; Megrahi returned to his cell.

The verdicts were greeted with almost universal shock. Among those who had not followed the trial closely, there was shock that one of the accused had been acquitted. Among many of those who had closely observed proceedings, the shock was that either one could be convicted.

Megrahi was brought back to the court at 1 p.m. local time to be sentenced. Since they had found him guilty of murder, the only option open to the judges was to impose a life sentence. Lord Sutherland announced that he would serve twenty years. Their Lordships did not read their judgment to the court. Instead, the written version was published at 2 p.m. In 90 paragraphs, spread over 82 pages, the judges set out the evidence and arguments that had guided them to their verdicts.

The very first sentence of the judgment contained a glaring error: 'At 1903 hours on 22 December 1988 Pan Am flight 103 fell out of the sky.' The bombing had, of course, occurred on 21 December, not the twenty-second. But that howler was nothing compared with what was to follow. Readers who had been shocked by the verdict were left astounded by the amalgamation of selective evidence and eccentric logic marshalled by the judges in support of their verdict. One of the core principles of criminal justice is that guilt must be proven beyond reasonable doubt. Time and again throughout the nine-month trial, doubt had been cast on the prosecution evidence; yet time and again, the judgment seemed to award the Crown the benefit of those doubts.

The entire prosecution case was dependent on it being proved that the bomb had been contained in an unaccompanied suitcase put aboard Flight KM180 at Malta's Luqa airport and transferred to Flight 103A via Frankfurt airport's baggage system. If this element of the case could not be proved, the other evidence against Fhimah and Megrahi, no matter how powerful, was irrelevant. So what was the evidence that any unaccompanied suitcase, let alone one containing a bomb, was loaded onto Flight KM180? There was none. The judgment acknowledged that the security and baggage reconciliation procedures at Luqa airport appeared, 'on the face of them . . . to make it extremely difficult for an unaccompanied and unidentified bag to be shipped on a flight out of Luqa'. It went on to concede:

> If, therefore, the unaccompanied bag was launched from Luqa, the
> method by which that was done is not established and the Crown
> accepted that they could not point to any specific route by which
> the primary suitcase could have been loaded.

The judges accepted that this constituted 'a major difficulty for the Crown case', but added that it was one 'which has to be considered along with the rest of the circumstantial evidence in the case'. It was a rider upon which their Lordships would rely heavily in justifying their verdict.

In the absence of evidence form Luqa airport, the Crown had been forced to concentrate on Frankfurt, in particular the computer printout from the airport's automated baggage handling system and the handwritten work sheet from coding station 206. Even when viewed uncritically, the computer printout, in the words of the October 1989 telex from FBI agent Lawrence Whittaker, showed 'only that a bag of unknown origin was sent to coding station 206 at 1.07 p.m. to a position from which it was supposed to be loaded on Pan Am 103'. It did not show that the bag was actually loaded onto Flight 103, still less that it was an unaccompanied bag previously unloaded from KM180. As for the worksheet, it indicated only that the luggage from KM180 was processed at coding station 206 between 1.04 p.m. and 1.10 p.m. It showed neither how much baggage was unloaded nor to where within the system each item was sent. In other words, the two documents fell far short of proving the Crown's case.

The defence adduced a good deal of evidence that cast further doubt on the Crown's case. Firstly, the timings on the two documents were open to question. They were not automatically synchronised by machine. Indeed, the timings on the worksheet were handwritten by the baggage operator. It only needed the timing on one of the documents to be out by four minutes to destroy the Crown case. It was up to the prosecution to prove that the timings were accurate, and no such proof existed. The judgment acknowledged that there might be discrepancies in the timings, but added: 'The suspect case was recorded [on the computer printout] as being coded in the middle of the time attributed to baggage from KM180, so that the possible significance of such errors is reduced.' Reduced, yes, but not eliminated.

Lawrence Whittaker's anecdotal evidence that bags could be introduced into the Frankfurt baggage system apparently without being recorded, had provided the defence with a second strong line of argument. The judgment accepted that Whittaker 'did not see any record being made', but added that he 'could not be absolutely certain that no record was made'. It was for the prosecution to prove that *all* bags were recorded, not for the defence to prove that the one observed by Whittaker was not.

A third powerful defence point concerned the Frankfurt security procedures of Pan Am's affiliate company, Alert Security. As a result of a warning circulated in the wake of the Autumn Leaves raids, staff there had been told to look out for explosive devices hidden in radio-cassette players. The court had heard statements by the Alert's X-ray machine operator Kurt Maier, who X-rayed the consignment of bags transferred from other airlines to Flight 103A. Although his training was limited, he said that in the course of his work he had taught himself to distinguish various sorts of electrical equipment. Moreover, he said he knew how to tell if explosives were present, from their appearance. But such factors carried no weight with the judges, who pointed to other evidence showing that 'the standard of training given to Alert employees was poor'. The judgment further observed: 'Mr Maier's description of what he looked for does not suggest that he would *necessarily* have claimed to be able to detect explosives hidden in a radio cassette player.' (Emphasis added.)

At the end of the Frankfurt section of the judgment, having set out in some detail these and other compelling defence arguments, the judges offered the extraordinary conclusion that: 'None of the points made by the defence seems to us to cast doubt on the inference from the documents and other evidence that an unaccompanied bag from KM180 was transferred to and loaded onto PA103A.' So the prosecution had 'proved' the presence of the unaccompanied bag from Malta.

But what of the remainder of the evidence? The second main plank of the prosecution case was that the Lockerbie bomb was exploded by an MST-13 timer supplied to Libya by the Swiss company Mebo, whose Zurich offices were shared in 1988 by Libyan firm ABH, in which Megrahi was closely involved. Again, the defence had done much to undermine this claim. First there was the curious matter of the changed label on the piece of shirt found by DC Gilchrist, in which the crucial fragment of the MST-13 timer was later supposedly discovered. The judges acknowledged that:

> There was no satisfactory explanation as to why this was done, and DC Gilchrist's attempts to explain it were at worst evasive and at best confusing.

They then added, however:

> We are satisfied that there was no sinister reason for it and that it was not tampered with by the finders.

Then there were the anomalies concerning the recording of the fragment by the forensic experts at RARDE. Dr Thomas Hayes testified to finding the fragment in the piece of shirt on 12 May 1989. It was his usual practice to make a drawing of the fragments he found and give them separate reference numbers. He had made a note of his examination of the MST-13 timer on page 51 of his notes, but that page contained no drawing and the number PT/35b was not designated to the fragment until a later date. The defence also argued that it was peculiar that Hayes's colleague Allen Feraday had sent a memo in September 1989, enclosing a Polaroid photograph of the fragment which he described in the memo as being 'the best I can do in such a short time'. While they acknowledged it was 'unfortunate that this particular item which turned out to be of major significance to this enquiry despite its miniscule size may not initially have been given the same meticulous treatment as most other items', the judges declared that they were 'nevertheless satisfied that the fragment was extracted by Dr Hayes in May 1989'. Moreover, the totality of the forensic evidence satisfied the judges that the initiation of the explosion was triggered by the use of an MST-13 timer'.

Regarding the evidence of the Mebo witnesses, Edwin Bollier, Erwin Meister and Ulrich Lumpert, the judges stated that: 'All three, and notably Mr Bollier, were shown to be unreliable witnesses.' Nevertheless, the judges went on to accept certain uncorroborated elements of Bollier's evidence helpful to the prosecution, in particular his claim that in 1986 or 1987 he attended air bomb tests in Libya, which utilised MST-13 timers brought along by an associate of Megrahi's called Nassr Ashur.

Turning to the MST-13s supplied to the Stasi, the judges accepted that that two had definitely been delivered, adding that they could not:

> Exclude absolutely the possibility that more than two MST-13 timers were supplied by Mebo to the Stasi, although there is no positive evidence that they were, nor any reasons why they should have been.

The judgment went on,

> Similarly, we cannot exclude the possibility that other MST-13 timers may have been made by Mebo and supplied to other parties, but there is no positive evidence that they were. Equally, despite the evidence of Mr Wenzel that after the fall of the Berlin Wall he had destroyed all timers supplied to the Stasi, we are unable to exclude the possibility that any MST-13 timers in the hands of the Stasi left their possession, although there is no positive evidence that they did and in particular that they were supplied to the PFLP-GC.

It was logical to conclude from this that there was reasonable doubt that the Lockerbie MST-13 was one of those supplied to Libya. But the judges did not reach this conclusion. In fact, they failed to reach any conclusion at all in respect of this matter.

There was one matter on which the judges had no choice but to accept the defence's submissions. This was, of course, the credibility of the informant Abdul Majid Giaka. 'Putting the matter shortly,' their judgment read, 'we are unable to accept Abdul Majid as a credible and reliable witness on any matter except his description of the organisation of the JSO and the personnel involved there.'

The judges entertained no such doubts about Tony Gauci. They wrote:

> In assessing Mr Gauci's evidence, we should first deal with a suggestion made in the submissions for the first accused that his demeanour was unsatisfactory – reluctant to look the cross-examiner in the eye, a strange and lonely man, and enjoying the attention he was getting.

The judges found no substance to the allegations and declared:

> The clear impression we formed was that he was in the first place entirely credible, that is to say doing his best to tell the truth to the best of his recollection, and indeed no suggestion was made to the contrary.

So Gauci was honest, but did his evidence support the two key elements of the prosecution case? The first was that the clothes were bought on 7 December 1988 and the second was that Megrahi was the purchaser. The date of the purchase had, of course, been narrowed down to two Wednesdays, a fortnight apart; 23 November and 7 December. Gauci had said in his evidence in chief that he thought the date of purchase was around two weeks before Christmas, which made 7 December the more likely date. But, as the judges acknowledged, when it was put to him that he had earlier said the sale was before the Christmas decorations went up, he said: 'I don't know. I'm not sure what I told them exactly about this. I believe they were putting up the lights, though, in those times.'

It wasn't simply earlier in his testimony that Gauci had said this. It was in a statement given eleven years earlier, when his memory of events was surely clearer than in the pressure cooker of the Camp Zeist courtroom. At that time, Gauci recalled that the customer had bought an umbrella before he left the shop, because it had started to rain. Eleven years on, the shopkeeper had told the court, 'It was not raining heavily. It was simply dripping.' The judges acknowledged that in the light of the meteorological evidence provided by defence witness Major Joseph Mifsud:

There is no doubt that the weather on 23 November would be wholly consistent with a light shower between 6.30 p.m. and 7.00 p.m,' but they added, 'The possibility that there was a brief light shower on 7 December is not, however, ruled out by the evidence of Major Mifsud.

Mifsud had put the chances of precipitation in Sliema at the relevant time at no higher than 10 per cent and even then, he said, there would not be enough to make the ground damp. So, even if there was a light shower between 6.30 p.m. and 7.00 p.m. on 7 December, it was hardly enough to warrant the use, let alone the purchase, of an umbrella.

It was clear that Major Misfsud's evidence placed more than a reasonable doubt on the prosecution's assertion that the cloths were brought from Gauchi's shop on 7 December. However, having set out all the counter-veiling evidence, their Lordships delivered the extraordinary punchline: 'We have reached the conclusion that the date of purchase was Wednesday 7 December.'

And there was more to come. Concerning Gauci's alleged identification of Megrahi, the judges noted that there were 'undoubtedly problems'. This was something of an understatement. As the judgment acknowledged elsewhere, Gauci had originally described the clothes purchaser as around 50 years old and about six feet tall, whereas Megrahi was five feet eight inches tall and, in December 1988, 36 years old. According to the report of an identity parade Gauci attended in August 1999, he said: 'Not exactly the man I saw in the shop. Ten years ago I saw him, but the man who looks a little bit like him exactly is number five.' Number five was Megrahi, but the words were neither coherent nor conclusive. In court, eleven-and-a-half years on from the time of the clothes purchase, Gauci said of Megrahi: 'He resembles him a lot.' Megrahi was, of course, by then in his late forties. It would have been surprising if Gauci did not recognise him, because during the past nine years his face had been regularly plastered across the media.

The judges insisted that in considering Gauci's identification evidence they had 'not overlooked the difficulties in relation to his description of height and age'. Surely, then, they would accept there was reasonable doubt that Megrahi was the clothes purchaser? No, they would not. 'We are nevertheless satisfied,' the judgment went on, 'that his identification so far as it went of the first accused as the purchaser was reliable'.

In seeking to justify their strange reasoning, the judgement declared:

There are situations where a careful witness who will not commit himself beyond saying that there is a close resemblance can be regarded as more reliable and convincing in his identification than a witness who maintains that his identification is 100 per cent certain.

So there are situations in which someone who says, 'I'm not completely sure it was him I saw,' can be relied on above one who says, 'I'm absolutely positive it was him I saw.' The judges did not elaborate on the type of situations they had in mind.

The judges described Gauci's evidence as 'a highly important element in this case.' It was also clear from reading the judgment that Megrahi's defence team may have made a tactical mistake in not running a full defence, including putting him on the witness stand. This was especially apparent in the section of the document concerning Megrahi's movements in December 1988, his connection to Mebo and his use of false passports. Referring to Megrahi's brief stay in Malta under a false name the night before the bombing and his departure to Tripoli the following morning, the judges observed it was 'possible to infer' that the visit was 'connected with the planting of the device'. They added pointedly: 'Had there been any innocent explanation for this visit, obviously this inference could not be drawn.'

Had Megrahi given evidence, he might have been able to give an innocent explanation. His legal team had decided it was best for him not to because they had rightly concluded that there was insufficient evidence to justify a conviction. But they had failed to anticipate that this was no impediment to the judges delivering a guilty verdict. This was once more amply demonstrated in the judges' concluding argument. While acknowledging that: 'In relation to certain aspects of the case there are a number of uncertainties and qualifications,' they insisted that:

> Having considered the whole evidence in the case, including the uncertainties and qualifications, and the submissions of counsel . . .
> There is nothing in the evidence which leaves us with any reasonable doubt as to the guilt of the first accused.

The 'certain aspects of the case' in which there were uncertainties included all the main planks of the prosecution case. That the judges could set aside those uncertainties was surprising to say the least. But set them aside they had and, in doing so, had chosen to accept a story that was equally, to say the least, surprising. It was a story which posited that Megrahi, a supposed airline security expert, had chosen to despatch a bomb from an airport guarded by military personnel on an airline that not only carried out explosive checks on passenger baggage, but also physically counted the bags to be stored in the hold, to ensure that they matched the number recorded by the check-in counter. By putting the explosive on a plane to Frankfurt, rather than a direct flight to London, he ensured that the bag would be handled by more airport and Pan Am staff, which increased the risk of the bomb being detected. Earlier, Megrahi had bought the clothes for the bomb-carrying suitcase in a manner that was bound to attract attention to himself, and had left the labels in the clothes, thereby maximising the possibility of their remains being traced back to the place of purchase. He had then colluded in the preparation of a bomb incorporating a timer that was not only impractical for the task in hand, but also, to the best of his knowledge, was supplied exclusively to Libya by a manufacturer with whom he had close personal ties.

In short, the judges had accepted that one of the greatest terrorist feats of all time was carried out by one of the most reckless and stupid terrorists of all time.

In the wake of the verdict, a spate of newspaper stories appeared alleging that the orders for the bombing had come from the very highest ranks of the Libyan government. The most detailed story, which appeared in the *Sunday Times*, claimed that the bombing had been ordered by Gadafy and orchestrated by his brother-in-law and intelligence chief, Abdullah Al-Senussi. The evidence reportedly came from two MI6 moles described as 'senior officials' in the Gadafy regime, one of whom was codenamed 'Piebald'. If it was in the *Sunday Times* and sourced to MI6, then surely it must be true!

The article was reminiscent of the 1980s when, time and again in the wake of Middle East terrorist attacks, 'irrefutable' intelligence evidence of Libyan involvement was leaked to a gullible media. On the few occasions the evidence was released for independent scrutiny – for example, the alleged intercepts of the Libyan messages concerning the La Belle Disco bombing – it was found to be phoney. Had it not struck the *Sunday Times* reporters that MI6 might just have a vested interest in trying to bolster the credibility of a highly dubious conviction? And had they forgotten that the evidence of another Libyan supergrass had just been condemned by the Lockerbie judges as entirely lacking in credibility? How could they be so sure that Piebald and his fellow mole did not share the same motivation as the discredited Mr Giaka? Indeed, how could they be so sure that Piebald and his friend even existed?

It was not the first time that the *Sunday Times* had run a Lockerbie story based entirely on anonymous sources. On the weekend following the issuing of the indictments against the two Libyans, the same paper had run a story claiming that an anonymous British businessman, described as 'a former military policeman', had met the two accused in Malta just days before the Lockerbie bombing. The source claimed the two were 'religious fanatics' and had 'boasted they could "destroy America"'. This man would have been a crucial Crown witness and, given his military background, presumably would have felt duty-bound to testify. But if he had, he would have been made a laughing stock of. Because not only was there no evidence that either Megrahi or Fhimah were religious fanatics (Gadafy is not well disposed to militant Islam within Libya), but it was also never disputed that two days before the bombing both the accused were in Libya. So, either the source was wholly unreliable or the story was nonsense spread by spooks who were aware that the indictment was full of holes.

What other evidence was there of Libyan state involvement in the bombing? First and foremost, there was the MST-13 timer. Apart from the question marks concerning the provenance of the timer fragment, there was clear evidence that at least two identical devices went to the Stasi. Although the prosecution adduced evidence that one of the Stasi's timers may have been seized in Togo in 1986 and that the remainder had been destroyed after the fall of the Berlin Wall, this by no means constituted proof that the Lockerbie fragment came from one of those sold to Libya. Indeed, there was compelling counter-veiling evidence, first aired in Channel 4's *Dispatches* programme, that the fragment was from a handmade circuit board. This suggested it was from a prototype MST-13 not sold to Libya.

The second major element in the case against Libya was the evidence that the bomb was contained within a black Toshiba SF-16 radio-cassette player, almost 76 per cent of the world sales of which, in the period from October 1988 to March 1989, were to Libya. Gwendoline Horton gave compelling evidence about the discovery of a charred piece of manual for an SF-16, but when shown it in court she noticed it had changed since she previously saw it. The Crown's case on this point was somewhat undermined by the revelation that RARDE technician Allen Feraday had, in February 1989, declared himself 'completely satisfied' that the bomb was housed in a white model RT-8016, or RT-8026, Toshiba.

Even if bomb was housed within an SF-16 and incorporated in an MST-13 timer, that would not constitute proof that Libya commissioned and executed the bombing. During the 1980s, Libya was a willing quartermaster to many terrorist groups, including the PFLP-GC. It was therefore quite feasible that Libya had provided those items on a no-questions-asked basis. It was a scenario that, for obvious reasons, neither prosecution nor defence was keen to advance at the trial.

The third and final major component of the case against Tripoli was Tony Gauci's identification of the clothes purchaser as a Libyan. The purchaser had done just about everything possible to bring attention to himself save for prancing around naked. He had chosen a small shop, in which he was the only customer, and had bought a random collection of clothes without bothering to try them on. He had then asked for them to be wrapped and, just in case the shopkeeper had not had a proper look at him, returned for the clothes in a taxi. The bombers had then left all the labels in the clothes, increasing the risk of the trail leading back to the island. It was surely not beyond the realms of possibility that they had used a Libyan proxy to buy the clothes and thereby lay a false trail back to Tripoli.

And if it was possible that the terrorists had framed Libya, was it also beyond the realms of possibility that, somewhere within the darker recesses of the American government, a decision was taken to place the blame at the door of Libya and then work backwards to find the 'evidence' and the 'suspects'? Within less than a month of the bombing, the CIA had Edwin Bollier's letter of 5 January tipping them off about possible Libyan involvement. Later that year, the investigators had discovered that the bomb was wrapped with Maltese clothes, apparently purchased by a Libyan. In addition, there was some tenuous evidence that an unaccompanied suitcase from Luqa airport had been transferred onto Flight 103. One of the points of intersection between Mebo and Libya was Megrahi, who, by virtue of his association with Fhimah, had a link to Luqa airport. By good fortune, their work colleague Majid Giaka just happened to be a CIA informant.

There was no evidence of a plot to lay a false trail to Libya, but it is worth exploring how such a plot could have been successfully achieved. It would require just three basic elements. Firstly, and most importantly, the planting of a fragment of Mebo circuit board in a piece of blast-damaged clothing; secondly, a flexible interpretation of Tony Gauci's identification to make the customer match Mebo associate Megrahi; and thirdly, a few lies about Megrahi and Fhimah by the money-grabbing fantasist Giaka.

The fragment was, of course, discovered within six months of the bombing, yet there were no official leaks about Libyan involvement in the crime until over a year later. According to the official story, this was because, subsequent to the fragment's discovery, it took over twelve months to identify it.

If this account was merely a smoke-screen and the spooks had planted the fragment prior to its discovery, knowing full well that it would implicate Libya, why did those leaks not occur a year earlier, in mid-1989? Simply because, given the weight of evidence that had by then emerged implicating Iran and the PFLP-GC, such leaks would have been greeted with scorn. If a false trail was being laid to Tripoli, it may only have been held in reserve, for example, in case it became necessary to divert attention away from further revelations that the bombers had exploited a CIA-protected drug-running operation.

By August 1990 there had emerged a powerful political imperative to shift the spotlight away from the original suspects, namely Iraq's invasion of Kuwait. It was only after the invasion that news of the timer fragment began to leak and the 'Gadafy did it' stories began in earnest. By then, Tony Gauci had made many of his statements identifying the six-foot, 50-year-old Libyan as the clothes purchaser and in February 1991 he gave a further statement confirming that Megrahi resembled the customer (give or take at least ten years and around four inches). A few weeks later the Lord Advocate, Lord Fraser of Carmyllie, no doubt sincerely believing the evidence to be reliable, was ready to issue indictments against the two Libyans. He was urged to delay doing so by his counterparts in the US, who perhaps knew that the FBI were about to gain access to Giaka.

The scenario just outlined would not require any of the official investigators, or law enforcement and prosecuting authorities, to collude in framing the Libyans and there was no suggestion that they did. It would simply require some minor skulduggery by unknown and unseen spooks. The immense political pressure to finger the 'guilty', while not upsetting the post-Gulf War apple cart, would deliver the rest.

It should be emphasised again that this scenario remains entirely hypothetical, but is it really any more outlandish than the official version?

While there may be no evidence that Libya was framed for the bombing, there is evidence a-plenty that the country was falsely accused of other acts of terrorism during the '80s, a decade in which the US ran a massive covert programme to undermine Gadafy. Within two weeks of the bombing, two of the Crown's 'Big Three' witnesses (Edwin Bollier and Majid Giaka) were informing to the CIA, with Giaka dealing directly with the agency from months before. The agency knew from its encounters with the Libyan that his information was of limited value, but nevertheless did not stand in the way when he was called to be a witness against Megrahi and Fhimah.

Moreover, the CIA had censored some of those sections of its own cables that severely undermined his credibility. So, while there can't be said to be evidence that the two accused were deliberately framed, neither can it be said that the CIA played with an entirely straight bat.

The fragment of the MST-13 timer presented further oddities. Normally intelligence information linking crucial items of evidence to suspects arrives after the discovery of the evidence, but in this case Edwin Bollier's tip-off arrived well before the fragment was found. As for the circumstances of its discovery, it was in a piece of shirt, the exhibit label for which was changed inexplicably and against police procedures from 'cloth' to 'debris'. Then, on extraction from the cloth, it was given the irregular 'PT' designation 35B, rather than a straight number, and, in a break with the scientist's normal practise, the examination notes (which were subsequently incorrectly paginated) were not accompanied by a drawing of the fragment. Such anomalies might have passed by unnoticed were it not the case that RARDE forensic explosives personnel had been involved in a series of miscarriages of justice, involving terrorist cases, spanning a period from the mid-70s to the late '80s. Their failure to disclose potentially vital evidence in some of those cases was not exposed until after Lockerbie.

The Lockerbie investigation was hailed as a model of international inter-agency cooperation, yet, according to the official account of that investigation, it took over a year to identify the newly discovered fragment as being from a Mebo MST-13 timer. This despite the facts that the CIA had a sample MST-13 before Lockerbie and that the timer's manufacturer Edwin Bollier had, within weeks of the bombing, alerted the CIA to the possibility of Libyan involvement. Furthermore, the man who supposedly linked the fragment to Mebo, the FBI's Tom Thurman, had subsequently left his position, having been caught out altering colleagues' reports in a manner that made them more favourable to the prosecution case.

The Crown was able to dismiss the question marks over the provenance of the fragment as irrelevant, but its submissions on this matter may have been less easy to sustain had the court heard evidence that the CIA had received replica MST-13 timers from an American manufacturer. As our investigation has shown, the Crown did not probe this matter as exhaustively as might be expected.

If, as the authors contend in this book, the official story of Lockerbie is nonsense, what really happened? We don't claim to have all the answers, but it is our belief that the bombing was commissioned by Iran and carried out by an alliance of Syrian proxy groups in which the PFLP-GC was to the fore and Hizbullah played an important supporting role.

There is compelling evidence that the October 1988 Autumn Leaves raids did not put pay to the PFLP-GC's murderous plans. As we described in Chapter 2, five weeks after the raids, on 1 December, a DIA bulletin warned of the continuing threat of an Iranian reprisal and noted that some Middle Eastern terrorist groups active in West Germany had the infrastructure to conduct bombings. And at around the same time, the State Department's Office of Diplomatic Security received a specific warning that radical Palestinians were planning to attack a Pan Am target in Europe. To this anecdotal evidence we must add the accounts of PFLP-GC members Mobdi Goben and Marwan Khreesat.

The authors further believe that the bomb suitcase was either substituted for, or added to, a suitcase believed by an unsuspecting Khalid Jaafar to contain heroin. The evidence for this scenario comes from a variety of sources, including his relative Jamil Jaafar and PFLP-GC insiders Major Tunayb and Mobdi Goben. Jamil Jaafar's claim that Khalid had been hoodwinked by relatives in Hizbullah, using the bait of an innocent bride-to-be, is partially corroborated by his host in Germany, Hassan El-Salheli, who confirmed that Khalid had a young fiancée about whom he was crazy. While there is nothing to suggest that El-Salheli and Khalid's other associates in Dortmund were in any way involved in the Hizbullah plot, Naim Ali Ghannam's association with Hizbullah, and the conflicting accounts of the changing of Khalid's airline ticket and of Ghannam's whereabouts on the day of Khalid's departure, all raise questions. The discovery of the Hizbullah T-shirt at the crash site is further possible evidence of Khalid's association with the group.

The young man's demeanour at Frankfurt airport, as witnessed by Yasmin Siddique, suggested he was very concerned about something prior to boarding Flight 103. The flight manifesto confirmed that he checked in two items at the airport, and two of his bags were recovered intact at the crash site. At the Camp Zeist trial the Crown argued that these facts, when added to the fact that Yasmin Siddique did not notice Jaafar with any bags, constituted proof that the two checked-in items were the ones found at Lockerbie. Yet those bags were of the small type usually allowed on as hand luggage and it would surely have been very unusual for a passenger embarking on a long transatlantic flight not to have at least one carry-on bag. Furthermore, a few days after the crash Jaafar's father said he was sure his son had only two carry-on bags and did not have any luggage in the hold of the plane.

At least two packages containing white powder were found at the crash site and some police officers assigned to the Tundergarth search area were told to be on the lookout for heroin. They were informed, unofficially, that it was thought to have been carried by a young Arab passenger who, though not named, could only have been Jaafar. Both packages of drugs were undamaged and one was in an intact suitcase. If either was being carried by Jaafar, the bomb suitcase must have been added to, rather than swapped for, the one containing the drugs. The uncorroborated newspaper story that the Lockerbie investigators had found heroin blasted into the debris, if true, suggests a further package of the drug was in or near the bomb suitcase.

There is nothing to suggest that Jaafar's family in America knew anything of his involvement in heroin smuggling, or his unwitting role in the bomb plot. Furthermore, while it remains clear that security at Frankfurt airport left much to be desired, there is no evidence as to who might have actually planted the suitcase, or the exact mechanism by which they did it.

We may never know for sure that Jaafar was carrying heroin but, as Rev John Mosey's experience confirms, there is no doubt that the drug finds seemed to be covered up. The most credible explanation for this is that, regardless of which passenger they belonged to, a public acknowledgement of the finds would lend credibility to claims that the bombers had exploited a trafficking operation.

Numerous intelligence sources have told a variety of investigators, including Juval Aviv, *Time* magazine's Roy Rowan, film-maker Allan Francovich and these authors, that the drug-running operation was protected by the CIA. They also reported that Major Charles McKee was aware of the operation and was heading back to Washington to blow the whistle. Some insisted that the presence of McKee's team on Flight 103 was no coincidence, and was evidence that he had been double-crossed by his own side. It was also suggested that they took the same flight as Jaafar in order that they might return with hard evidence of the drug deals. The discovery of McKee's colleague Matthew Gannon's body close to that of Khalid Jaafar, despite the fact that they were allocated seats at opposite ends of the aircraft, perhaps strengthens these claims. So too does the fact that all the team members made late changes to their diverse travel plans so that they might travel to the US together on Flight 103.

The issuing of a multiple-entry US visa to Jaafar by the American Embassy in Beirut at a time when, according to the US Bureau of Consular Affairs, the embassy was only issuing visas to Lebanese government and Embassy employees, adds weight to claims that he was being used by the CIA. The missing pages from his Lebanese passport and the disappearance of his US passport, which Yasmin Siddique was certain he had with him on departure from Frankfurt, lends credence to speculation that someone wished details of his recent travels to remain secret.

What of the allegations that government officials and VIPs were kept off the plane? There is no proof, but the flight was just a few days before Christmas and was the main transatlantic route of the major US flag carrier. That it should be only two-thirds full suggests that far more people or their staff had steered clear of it than has ever been acknowledged. It is more likely and indeed more probable that these people were made aware of the general warnings about Pan Am, rather than of a specific threat relating to Flight 103. However, a number of sources, including two at the heart of the South African government of the time, have alleged that the country's Bureau of State Security ensured that Pik Botha and a party of senior officials were kept off the flight. The contradictory accounts of the party's travel arrangements provided by Botha's aides only add confusion to their denials of a warning.

There is little doubt that for merely suggesting the alternative version of the Lockerbie disaster might be correct, the authors will be branded in some quarters as 'conspiracy mongers'. It's a catch-all insult most often used by those whose arguments tend to be lead by rhetoric rather than fact. Nevertheless, it is worth taking a moment to consider a different conspiracy; namely that which would be required to have constructed and maintained an entirely fictional alternative version.

A variety of investigators, including Juval Aviv, James Shaugnessy, Roy Rowan, Allan Francovich and these authors, all produced broadly similar findings. If it is to be accepted that those findings were entirely bogus, all those individuals must have either lied or exaggerated about ever actually conducting the investigations in the first place or have been lied to or misled by all their numerous anonymous sources. In addition Jamil Jaafar and PFLP-GC insiders, Mobdi Goben and Major Tunayb, must also have lied, even though making the allegations might have placed them in considerable personal danger.

The legion of liars and those misled or confused must have extended to incorporate the policemen and searchers at the crash scene, who told Tam Dalyell MP, reporter David Johnston and others of, among other things, the drug and cash finds, the American agents tampering with evidence and the marksmen in helicopters. Either that, or Dalyell, Johnston *et al* must themselves have lied. And, as well as embracing this unfounded conspiracy theory, we must also accept that the criminal charges brought against Juval Aviv, John Brennan, Lester Coleman and Joe Miano, and those threatened against David Johnston and William Chasey, were unrelated to the fact that all of those individuals had, in their various ways, threatened the official line on Lockerbie. Not only that, but the failure of most of those prosecutions to obtain a sustainable guilty verdict from a jury must be purely coincidental.

In short, a wholesale rejection of the alternative version requires a suspension of disbelief.

It remains to be seen whether the conviction of Megrahi will be upheld. At the time of writing the case is going to be appealed, with a hearing expected before the end of 2001. It will be heard by a panel of five judges, who will be more junior in rank than the three lords who heard the trial. It would take brave judges indeed to question the verdict of their more senior colleagues, particularly in such a politically sensitive case.

But whatever the decision of the court, Lockerbie will not go away. It may take many more years before the full truth is known, but in the meantime more uncomfortable evidence is bound to trickle out. The most appropriate forum for the facts to be aired would be a full independent judicial inquiry with the power to compel witnesses. Should such an inquiry take place, it must have access to the appropriate state bodies, especially the intelligence services, of Britain, the US and Germany. Requests for cooperation must also be made to Malta, Sweden, Norway, Denmark, Finland, Switzerland, Libya, Syria, Iran and Israel.

We will end this book by setting out 25 areas that an inquiry must address.

1. The number and nature of the warnings received by the intelligence services between the shoot-down of Iran Air Flight 655 and the bombing of Flight 103 and details of how, and to whom, those warnings were distributed.

2. The numbers and identities of all passengers who originally planned to travel on Flight 103 and the circumstances under which they altered their plans. Particular attention must be paid to the South African government entourage led by Pik Botha.

3. The circumstances in which the bookings of Khalid Jaafar, Charles McKee, Matthew Gannon, Ronald Lariviere and Daniel O'Connor were changed.

4. The exact movements of Khalid Jaafar in the six months prior to the bombing.

5. Why Khalid Jaafar was issued a multiple-entry visa by the US Embassy in Beirut in July 1988.

6. The exact movements of Mohammed Abu Talb subsequent to his return from Malta to Sweden on 26 October 1988.

7. The drug and cash finds at Lockerbie and the subsequent official denials.

8. The possibility that there was at least one extra body at the crash site, the name of which did not appear on the official flight manifest.

9. The circumstances that led the Scottish police to give incorrect evidence about Dr David Fieldhouse at the Lockerbie fatal accident inquiry.

10. Why it was that Transport Secretary Paul Channon felt able in March 1989 to brief journalists that the case had been cracked and arrests were imminent.

11. Why Margaret Thatcher blocked the judicial inquiry recommended by Channon's successor Cecil Parkinson in September 1989.

12. The involvement of MI6 in the Iran-Contra hostage deals and with Monzer Al-Kassar.

13. The involvement of the CIA and MI6 in covert hostage deals during the period between the Iran-Contra scandal becoming public in 1986 and the release of the last remaining Western hostages from Lebanon in November 1991.

14. What role, if any, Andrew Green of the Foreign Office played in 12 and 13 above, and his role in handling the international aspects of the Lockerbie affair between 1988 and 1991.

15. Why the investigating authorities failed to interview Juval Aviv, James Shaugnessy and others about the information they had accumulated about the bombing.

16. The contacts between the CIA and Edwin Bollier during the 1980s and '90s.

17. The alleged break-ins at Mebo's Zurich offices.

18. Why it took the official investigation over a year to identify the fragment of circuit board supposedly discovered by Dr Thomas Hayes, given that the CIA: (a) had been tipped off by Edwin Bollier before the fragment was discovered about possible Libyan involvement in the bombing and (b) had a sample MST-13 timer before the bombing.

19. Why according to the defence team the Crown failed to pass on to the defence details of the evidence of Don Devereux and Charles Byers.

20. The circumstances under which Federal prosecutions were brought against Juval Aviv, John Brennan, Joe Miano and Lester Coleman.

21. The removal of PFLP-GC defectors from Norway by the CIA.

22. The movements and activities of Abu Elias from July 1988 to January 1989 and his contact with the US authorities from the 1980s to the present.

23. The break-in at the offices of Fhimah's company Medtours.

24. When, and under what circumstances, the various British and American authorities involved in the Lockerbie investigation and prosecution became aware of the flaws in the evidence of Majid Giaka. Further, why the CIA allowed Giaka to go forward as a witness at the trial and why it censored those parts of its own cables that were helpful to the defence.

25. How and why the Lord Advocate was able to assure the court that the censored sections of the CIA cables were not material to the defence case when the opposite was true.

The Labour party, when in opposition, promised the British victims' relatives that they would order an inquiry when they got into office. It will be to the government's lasting shame if it were to now renege on that promise.

APPENDIX I — INTERVIEW WITH
LAMIN KHALIFA FHIMAH

Souk Al Juma, some 15 minutes drive from the bustle of busy Tripoli, is not a name known to many outside of the Libyan capital Tripoli, but since his acquittal in the Lockerbie trial Lamin Fhimah has been trying to settle back into a normal life in his family home there. Our driver, unsure of the exact address, had only to stop a passer-by and mention the name 'Lamin' and we were given explicit directions. Fhimah's arrival back in Libya, accompanied by close family members and his Scottish lawyer Eddie MacKechnie, was made into something of a national holiday. Massive crowds greeted the arrival of the UN transport plane as it touched down in Libya, with Fhimah being greeted by the Libyan leader Muammar Gadafy.

In the space of two minutes, between 11.04 and 11.06 on 31 January 2001, Lamin Fhimah had heard that his long-time friend Abdelbasset Megrahi had been found guilty of the murders of 270 people, while he was found not guilty. Normality for Fhimah will not be easy, despite the closeness of his family and friends. A large emotional part of him remains in the Camp Zeist prison with his friend Megrahi.

In an in-depth interview with the authors at his home in Souk Al Juma, Fhimah spoke candidly about his feelings about the trial, the Scottish authorities, Majid Giaka and the CIA.

His home has become a very busy place, with friends and family members constantly dropping by to greet him and spend time together. Their happiness was obvious from the moment we arrived, on a warm sunny afternoon. Cousins, uncles, brother and neighbours lined up to welcome us, reaching into the car to shake our hands. Fhimah was deep in conversation on his mobile phone while a young friend hosed down the courtyard. Our driver seemed very excited to meet Fhimah again, as he had been at the airport but had managed to exchange only a few words with him. He immediately embraced Fhimah and the two exchanged warm greetings.

Taking off our shoes, we were shown into the large entrance room, with even more relatives and friends squatting on the colourful cushions set around the edge of the floor. Gathering up an ashtray and his packet of Rothmans cigarettes, Fhimah joined us to talk about his experiences and hopes for the future. Like the authors, he is still puzzled about why Megrahi was convicted while he, who was undoubtedly innocent, was acquitted, considering it was he who was alleged to have put the bag containing the bomb on the plane in Malta. After the judgement, resigned to the fact that he had to leave his friend behind in Zeist, Fhimah vowed to fight on to win Megrahi's freedom. He is in daily telephone contact with him.

Before the interview began, he asked after the man he affectionately refers to as 'the grandfather'. This is his solicitor Eddie MacKechnie, who became a grandfather for the first time during the trial.

Q. Where were you when you found out you had been accused of the bombing?

A: I'd been working abroad in Tunisia and I arrived at my home here in the evening. I was expecting our driver from Libyan Arab Airlines to pick me up from my house, as I was due to work a night shift. When I arrived back at the house I found a lot of people there, so I thought that something had happened to one of my family. Then somebody told me they had announced my name on the BBC and that I had been accused of the Pam Am bombing. I was shocked, because I had nothing to do with Pan Am. I sat with my family, including my mother and father, told them this and tried to calm them down. The next day I went to the police station here in my area and they informed me officially that there was an indictment against me and my friend Abdel Basset.

Q. Tell me, Lamin, what were you feeling just prior to getting on the plane to Ziest? Did you make this decision on your own?

A: Yes, we made our decision voluntarily, me and my friend Basset. There was no pressure from any side. We were happy to go there because firstly we knew we were innocent and also because it would help start to solve this problem. So we were actually happy.

Q. And when did you first meet your Scottish lawyer?

A: We had been in contact with Scottish lawyer, Mr Duff, for a long time, since '93, and then when we moved to Holland, other lawyers began working for us.

Q. And what did you explain to him, when you first met Mr MacKechnie?

A: Our first step with our lawyers was to tell them that we are innocent. Then we started to work with them and we gave them all the paperwork and help they needed. We were friendly and together we did a very good job.

Q. What were conditions like in the prison while you were waiting the trial starting, how were you treated?

A: Actually I would like to thank the people who were with us. Especially the Governor, Mr Ballantine and Mr Gordon. And we were treated very well by the people who were with us. They are very nice, and I would like to thank them now.

Q. What were you feeling like, the night before the trial started, how did you feel on 2 May?

A: As I told you, we were happy because the trial had started. We asked from the beginning – from '91 – [when the indictments were issued] to be heard in court. I mean, we were looking for a real trial. And we were happy that we were there, so that the facts would come out.

Q. Were you nervous at all?

A: I've never been nervous because I've always known that I am innocent and the truth would come out in front of the judges – I knew that then everybody would know the truth.

Q. When did you discover that Majid Giaka was going to be a witness against you?

A: I think '95. We had been informed by some of his friends and his brother-in-law. They informed us that he had fled and was in contact with the CIA. So at that time we knew he was the only witness against us.

Q. When Giaka walked into court, what did you feel like when you saw him?

A: The truth is that when he came into the court at first he didn't want to look at us, and to us this was very important, because he was supposed to be an honest witness. We looked at his face, but because he knew he was lying he did not look at us. I think the CIA advised him not to look at us, because if he had I'm sure that he would have been sunk.

Q. After he finished his testimony and as the trial developed, did you feel confident, did you feel good within yourself?

A: Yes, all the time. As I told you, we were very comfortable, because we knew that we are innocent. And most of the evidence put forward against us wasn't true. So we left the court feeling happy every day. We said: 'OK, we covered this matter, we covered this point, we covered this angle.' We thought it was only a matter of time, that there wasn't any evidence against us.

Q. What about the final day of the verdict, the day before the judges said they would give the verdict the next day? How did you and Basset spend that evening? I imagine you must have been talking a lot.

A: Yes, we did talk to each other. We knew that we were innocent and we were sure it was a fair trial, so we were expecting that we would be released the next day. We even watched a film that night, and we slept well. Whatever happened would be the will of God, so we were very relaxed.

Q. How did you feel the next morning when they announced the verdict?

A: When Basset and I went to the court our bags and belongings were even packed. When we heard the judges' decision I was very sorry. It was a shock for us that Basset had been convicted. That was everybody's feeling.

Q. Do you feel angry about that?

A: I do, yes, I do feel angry. If my acquittal hadn't come as a gift to me from God, I would refuse it and stay with my friend. But it has to be like this.

Q. Who are you angry at?

A: I'm angry because all the evidence put forward against us didn't make any sense. We were the people they wanted to make a case against. I feel so sorry for the Scottish people, because I think the CIA misled them that there was a case against us.

Q. You think the CIA have misled the Scottish authorities?

A: Yes, we are sure of it because the only evidence against us was gathered by the Scots, but I think the Americans were behind it, and they promised the Scots that they had the evidence against us – they told them that they had a witness against us. And when the truth came out there were only inferences. That was what actually happened in the court.

Q. How has this affected your family, your personal life, since 1991?

A: First of all, I was sorry about it because I was a friend to everybody, but when this happened it was as if they showed me another face. I was friendly to everybody and all of a sudden all my friends heard about this problem, so I was personally harmed by it. And my family, they were small children. It affected them, their lives, their studies. I lost my mother because of this case; she had a heart attack. She followed the news every day. It said they were going to send us to America, so she had a heart attack. We are victims of this also. I lost my job because I had a licence which had to be renewed every year. I was running a tour agency in Malta, but that stopped in 1991. All my movements stopped, actually.

Q. Do you want to go back [to Malta] and do that business again?

A: Yes, I would like to go back and work at Libyan Arab Airlines, and then I will start the tour agency again.

Q. Do you fear that sometime in the future, if you are in Malta or somewhere else, the Americans may try to kidnap you?

A: No, they have no right to do this thing. I am not afraid. I am a free man. I'm innocent. Why should they do that? I'm not afraid of them. I will go where I like.

Q. Is there anything else that you would like to add?

A: I would like to thank the Scottish people for the way they treated us. They were – I will say it again – very good to us. And I hope my friend Basset will be released as soon as possible. I recommend that the judges look again at the life sentence and the evidence; that they study them very well. I want them to be free of the involvement of other countries, or political influence. And I hope that I will see my friend as soon as possible.

Q. Have you spoken to him since you left?

A: Yes, I have. We are in contact every day about taking care of his family. I promised myself that I would do my best with his case and his family.

Q. Good . . . thank you.

A: Thank you for visiting my house.

As we said our farewells in the courtyard, Fhimah asked simply that we not forget Megrahi. This book, in its small way, is testament that we shall never forget.

APPENDIX 2 — INTERVIEW WITH EDDIE MACKECHNIE

In an exclusive interview with the authors, Lamin Khalifa Fhimah's Scottish lawyer, Eddie MacKechnie, spoke candidly about his client and the Lockerbie trial. Speaking in his apartment in Glasgow's West End, less than a month from his client's acquittal, MacKechnie was at pains to state that he would not comment on Abdel Basset Al-Megrahi's case due to the pending appeal.

Recalling his feelings when he first became involved, he said: 'I was attracted to the case and have absolutely no regrets in taking on the obvious challenge.' The challenge, of course, was to prepare the defence of a Libyan national accused of mass murder in the largest criminal trial in the UK's history; a challenge, it has to be said, that many large corporate law firms would have shied away from. The fact that McGrigor Donald, the firm where MacKechnie is a senior partner, with its client list of Blue Chip companies, agreed to represent Fhimah says much for their own courage and their respect for MacKechnie himself.

Although undoubtedly happy with the result of the trial as far as his client, Fhimah, was concerned, it was clear that MacKechnie was unused to discussing his clients with journalists. 'Normally, as a lawyer, one might hesitate to comment upon the details of a case or express one's personal views on any aspect of it, but this was a very unusual case.'

The case threw MacKechnie together with a stranger whose English was limited, but he came to like Fhimah as well as anyone outside of his family and developed a very positive view of him: 'I do know Lamin very well and I was, and am, absolutely certain that he is innocent . . . he is a man who could not have been party to any murder, let alone this mass murder.' Anyone who believes that MacKechnie's relationship with his client is simply a hard-nosed lawyer–client one must think again. His warmth towards his client is genuine and deeply felt, and MacKechnie constantly uses adjectives like 'kind', 'sensitive' and 'emotional' to describe him. The son of the manse and the son of the desert were undoubtedly strange bedfellows, but the bond between the two was cemented over many meetings in the court and the prison at Camp Zeist.

Like Fhimah, MacKechnie praises those involved in the trial; the police, the prison service and the Courts service: 'I agree with Lamin that they deserve great credit for the way they conducted themselves.' He also pays tribute to the US DoJ and FBI for their co-operation with him and his team and speaks highly of the professionalism and courtesy extended by other US agencies, principally the Federal Aviation Administration.

In common with his client, MacKechnie has very definite opinions on the role of the CIA and, as he describes them, 'other clandestine bodies'. He explains, 'This case was intelligence driven and the conduct of the CIA and other clandestine bodies had a very significant impact.' Choosing his words carefully, MacKechnie describes 'the supposed evidence' against his client as 'wholly inadequate and contrived'. Central to the contrivance was witness Giaka. Referring to the claims Giaka had made at trial that he never previously made during his meetings with the CIA and FBI, he says, 'Where did Giaka get the meaningful information that he revealed at the trial? Who gave it to him? . . . It was as if they had a jigsaw with a missing piece – along came Giaka and they tried to make him fit.' An apt analogy, considering Giaka's code-name – 'Puzzle Piece.'

Another crucial unanswered question is why did the CIA claim to have revealed all the cables concerning Giaka when it was clear they had not? And MacKechnie believes that the Agency may have held on to further cables which further undermined the informant's credibility.

The toll of this case on MacKechnie's personal life may not be clear for some time yet. In the preparation of the case, he has travelled more miles than most people travel in a lifetime. During a particularly gruelling period in the USA before the trial, he says, 'I was in 11 States in 10 days.'

At a time when MacKechnie should be basking in the glory of a well-deserved victory, one can't help feeling that this sharp, witty lawyer, with a reputation amongst his peers and friends for kindness and generosity, is somehow still adrift in a sea of unanswered questions. Whatever challenges lie ahead, one senses he will be, like his client and friend Fhimah, forever changed by Lockerbie.

NOTES

CHAPTER 1

[1] Scottish mountain rescue team member interviewed by the authors.

[2] Alan Topp evidence to Lockerbie trial.

[3] Robert Chamberlain evidence to Lockerbie trial.

[4] The US government's claim was reported in a press release issued by the British High Commission in Canberra, Australia, on 16 May 1995 in response to the broadcast of the documentary film, *The Maltese Double Cross*.

[5] Steven Emerson and Brian Duffy, *The Fall of Pan Am 103: Inside the Lockerbie Investigation* (USA: G.P. Putnam's Sons, 1990).

[6] Jim Berwick interview in *The Maltese Double Cross*, 1994.

[7] Carlisle airport official interviewed by the authors.

[8] Interview with George Stobbs in *The Maltese Double Cross*.

[9] British High Commission in Canberra, Australia, press release, 16 May 1995.

[10] Emerson and Duffy, *The Fall of Pan Am 103*.

[11] Interview with Tam Dalyell MP in *The Maltese Double Cross*.

[12] Mountain rescue team leader interviewed by the authors.

[13] Police officer interviewed by author.

[14] Interview with Eric Spofforth in *The Maltese Double Cross*.

[15] Alison Collau interviewed by author.

[16] Raynet coordinator interviewed by author.

[17] Former Lord Advocate interviewed by author.

[18] English mountain rescue team leader interviewed by author.

[19] Scottish mountain rescue team leader interviewed by author.

[20] Search volunteer interviewed by author.

[21] David Thomson interviewed by author.

[22] Carl Hamilton interviewed by author.

[23] *Glasgow Herald*, 24 December 1988.

[24] Hansard, written answer 6 March 1995.

[25] Emerson and Duffy, *The Fall of Pan Am 103*.

[26] *Lockerbie – The Real Story* (London: Bloomsbury, 1989) by David Johnston.

[27] Scottish search volunteer interviewed by author.

[28] Police officer interviewed by author.

[29] Emerson and Duffy, *The Fall of Pan Am 103* (USA: G. P. Putnam's Sons, 1990). A similar story appeared in *Private Eye*, 8 May 1992.

[30] Anonymous source interviewed by author.

[31] Interview with mountain rescue team leader.

[32] Interview with Innes Graham in *The Maltese Double Cross*.

[33] Scottish search volunteer interviewed by author.

[34] The story was reported to the authors by one of the police officers involved. A similar account

appeared in David Johnston's *Lockerbie – The Real Story*.

[35] Interview with Linda Forsyth in *The Maltese Double Cross*.

[36] Police officer interviewed by author.

[37] David Johnston, *Lockerbie – The Real Story* and interview with David Johnston in *The Maltese Double Cross*.

[38] Edinburgh *Evening News*, 29 June 1989.

[39] All details of Dr Fieldhouse's story are from an interview with the author as well as his paperwork.

[40] Carlisle airport official interviewed by author.

CHAPTER 2

[1] Defence Intelligence Terrorism Summary, issued by Defence Intelligence Agency's Terrorism Intelligence Branch, 8 November 1988.

[2] John K. Cooley, *Payback: America's Long War in the Middle East* (USA: Brassey's (US) Inc., 1992), p 160.

[3] BBC Radio 4, *File on Four*, 21 December 1993.

[4] Details of this evidence are from 'Tragedy and Terrorism' by David Evans and David Carlson, *San Diego Union-Tribune*, 9 April 1995.

[5] Matthew Cox and Tom Foster, *Their Darkest Day: The Tragedy of Pan Am 103 and Its Legacy of Hope*, (New York: Grove Weidenfeld, 1992), p 19.

[6] Defence Intelligence Terrorism Summary, issued by Defence Intelligence Agency's Terrorism Intelligence Branch, 1 December 1988.

[7] Text of warning circulated by Federal Aviation Authority.

[8] Emerson and Duffy, *The Fall of Pan Am 103*, Chapter 4.

[9] Interview with Jim Berwick in *The Maltese Double Cross* and Emerson and Duffy, *The Fall of Pan Am 103*, Chapter 4.

[10] Report of the President's Commission on Aviation Security and Terrorism, (US Government Printing Office, 1990).

[11] ABC Television 30 November 1989.

[12] Warning revealed in *The Guardian*, 29 July 1995.

[13] Published Israeli sources cited in *Katz, Israel Versus Jibril*, p 205.

[14] David Yallop, *To The Ends of the Earth: The Hunt for The Jackal* (London: Jonathan Cape, 1993), pp 239–240.

[15] Buck Revell interview in *The Maltese Double Cross*.

[16] South African Minister of Justice, parliamentary oral answer to Colin Eglin MP, 12 June 1996.

[17] Evidence to Lockerbie Fatal Accident Inquiry, 25 October 1990.

[18] Memo by Nicholas P. Geier, Staff Investigator, President's Commission on Aviation Security and Terrorism, 2 December 1989.

[19] Transcript of media interview with Ronald Spiers, released by US State Department under Freedom of Information Act

[20] Ambassador John McCarthy, telephone interview with author 8 September 1994.

[21] Transcript of Ronald Spiers interview.

CHAPTER 3

[1] BBC Radio 4, *File on Four*, 21 December 1993.

[2] John K. Cooley, *Payback: America's Long War in the Middle East* (USA: Brassey's (US) Inc., 1992).

[3] Katz, *Israel Versus Jibril*; Cooley, *Payback*, p 164.

[4] Yossef Bodansky, *Target The West: Terrorism in the World Today*, (New York: SPI Books, 1993), pp 7–8.

[5] Al Dustur, 22 May 1989; *The Observer*, 31 July 1989.

[6] Katz, *Israel Versus Jibril*, chapter 11; Emerson and Duffy, *The Fall of Pan Am 103*, chapter 14.

[7] Katz, *Israel Versus Jibril*, chapter 11.

[8] The PFLP-GC's activities in Germany have been widely reported in the British, American and German press and in a number of books, including: David Leppard, *On the Trail of Terror: The Inside Story of the Lockerbie Investigation* (London: Jonathan Cape 1991); Emerson and Duffy, *The Fall of Pan Am 103*; Cox and Foster, *Their Darkest Day*; Katz, *Israel Versus Jibril*. The authors have used these sources as well as press reports and translations of extracts of surveillance logs compiled by the BKA.

[9] Katz, *Israel Versus Jibril*.

[10] Emerson and Duffy, *The Fall of Pan Am 103*, Chapter 10.

[11] Lockerbie trial transcript, 16 November 2000, pp 8,639–8,649.

[12] Lockerbie trial transcript, 11 November 2000, pp 8,697 and 8,736–8,737.

[13] Katz, *Israel Versus Jibril* and Cooley, *Payback*.

CHAPTER 4

[1] *The Times*, 23 December 1988.

[2] DIA Defense Intelligence Summary, 30 December 1988.

[3] Lockerbie trial transcript, 30 May 2000.

[4] *The Times*, 12 September 1989.

[5] Lockerbie trial transcript, 17 November 2000, pp 8,792–8,795.

[6] Lockerbie trial transcript, 10 November 2000, pp 8,191–8,206.

[7] Jim Berwick interviewed by author.

[8] Michael Jones interviewed by author.

[9] 'Syria, Iran and the Trail of Counterfeit Dollars', Executive Summary, Task Force on Terrorism and Unconventional Warfare, House Republican Research Committee, US House of Representatives, 1 July 1992.

[10] Poindexter's comment to congressional hearings reported in 'Syria, President Bush, and Drugs – The Administration's next Iraqgate', staff report by the Subcommittee on Crime and Criminal Justice of the Committee on the Judiciary, 23 November 1992. (US Government Printing Office, Washington DC, 1993).

CHAPTER 5

[1] Fatal Accident Inquiry official transcript.

[2] Fatal Accident Inquiry official transcript.

[3] Rev. John Mosey interviewed by author.

[4] Rev. John Mosey interviewed by author.

[5] *The Independent*, 19 April 1989.

[6] Martin Cadman interview in *The Maltese Double Cross*.

CHAPTER 6

[1] Declassified documents obtained under US Freedom of Information Act.

[2] James Shaugnessy affidavit, 25 September 1992.

[3] Robert Parry, *Trick or Treason* (USA: Sheridan Square Press, 1993) and *The October Surprise X Files: The Hidden Origins of the Reagan-Bush Era* (Virginia, USA: The Media Consortium, 1996).

[4] There have been many published accounts of the Iran-Contra affair. Among those used by the authors are: Bob Woodward, *Veil: The Secret Wars of the CIA* (USA: Simon & Schuster, 1987); Mark Perry, *Eclipse: The Last Days of the CIA* (USA: William Morrow and Co Inc., 1992); David Martin and John Walcott, *Best Laid Plans: The Inside Story of America's War on Terrorism* (USA: Harper & Row, 1988); Ben Bradlee Jnr, *Guts & Glory: The Rise and Fall of Oliver North* (London: Grafton, 1988).

[5] John Loftus and Mark Aarons, *The Secret War Against the Jews: How Western Espionage Betrayed the Jewish People* (USA: St Martin's Press, 1994); 'Syria, President Bush, and Drugs – The Administration's next Iraqgate', staff report by the Subcommittee on Crime and Criminal Justice of the Committee on the Judiciary, 23 November 1992. (Washington DC, USA: Government Printing Office, 1993.

[6] Former CIA officer interviewed by author.

[7] All details of the Pan Am litigation, the surrounding and the various hearings are taken from documents filed with the court.

[8] Joe Miano, e-mail to authors.

[9] James Shaugnessy affidavit, 25 September 1992.

[10] Court documents filed in Michael Hurley's libel action against Bloomsbury Publishing.

[11] Donald Goddard and Lester Coleman, *Trail of the Octopus* (London: Bloomsbury, 1993).

[12] Lester Coleman interview included in *The Maltese Double Cross*.

[13] Drug Enforcement Administration's alleged connection to the Pan Am Flight 103 disaster, transcript of hearing before the Government Information, Justice and Agriculture subcommittee of the House Government Operations Committee, 18 December 1990 (Washington DC, USA: Government Printing Office, 1990).

[14] *Sunday Telegraph*, 15 November 1992.

[15] Con Coughlin, *Hostage* (London: Warner, 1993), updated paperback edition.

[16] *Sunday Telegraph*, 8 November 1995.

[17] Con Coughlin, *Hostage*.

[18] *Sunday Telegraph*, 8 November 1995.

[19] Con Coughlin, *Hostage*.

[20] *Sunday Telegraph*, 15 November 1992.

[21] Con Coughlin, *Hostage*.

[22] *Sunday Telegraph*, 15 November 1992.

CHAPTER 7

[1] *The Times*, 12 September 1989.

[2] Michael Jones interview, included in *The Maltese Double Cross*.

[3] David Leppard, *On The Trail of Terror*.

[4] Police statements by Tony and Paul Gauci.

[5] Translated SAPO documents.

[6] Emerson and Duffy, *The Fall of Pan Am 103*, chapter 17.

[7] Lockerbie trial transcript, 14 November 2000.

[8] Lockerbie trial transcript, 14 November 2000, pp 8,302–8,325.

[9] Translated BKA surveillance logs and translated SAPO documents.

[10] Emerson and Duffy, *The Fall of Pan Am 103* and translated SAPO documents.

[11] Lockerbie trial transcript, 14 November 2000, pp 8,294–8295 and p 8,491.

[12] Leppard, *On the Trail of Terror*; Emerson and Duffy, *The Fall of Pan Am 103*; Cox and Foster, *Their Darkest Day*.

[13] Lockerbie trial transcript, 14 November 2000, pp 8,277–8,281.

[14] Leppard, *On the Trail of Terror*.

[15] Extracts from Abu Talb's interrogation by SAPO.

[16] Lockerbie trial transcript, 5 November 2000.

[17] Cox and Foster, *Their Darkest Day*

[18] Lockerbie trial transcript, 14 November 2000, pp 8,300–8,317.

[19] Jamilla Mograbi interviewed in *The Maltese Double Cross*.

[20] Annika Wallin interview with author.

CHAPTER 8

[1] Juval Aviv interviewed by author.

[2] Jacobo Finkelstein, videotape deposition, 2 November 1993.

[3] Jim Berwick interviewed by author.

[4] All information about the Pan Am litigation contained in this chapter is drawn from legal and court documents, unless otherwise stated.

[5] Noel Koch interviewed by author.

[6] *Fulton County Daily Report* 5 April 1996.

[7] *Fulton County Daily Report* 10 April 1996.

[8] *Fulton County Daily Report* 16 April 1996

[9] Dr Jim Swire interviewed by author.

[10] *The Guardian*, 20 April 1995.

[11] Author interview with Tam Dalyell.

[12] Todd Leventhal, letter to Tam Dalyell, 28 April 1995.

[13] Letter dated 9 May 1995 from Michael O'Brien, Minister-Counseler for Public Affairs, US Embassy, plus attachment, circulated to the British Press; Scottish press release dated 10 May 1995, plus statement, circulated to the British Press.

[14] Press release and attachments issued by the Biritish High Commission, Canberra, 16 May 1995.

[15] *The Guardian*, 13 May 1995.

CHAPTER 9

[1] Steven Donahue interviewed in *The Maltese Double Cross*.

[2] Details from court documents: Donahue vs USA, US District Court, Southern District of Florida, 1993.

[3] Steven Donahue letter to Congressman Larry Smith, 23 March 1989.

[4] Jamil Jaafar interviewed in *The Maltese Double Cross*.

[5] David Clark interviewed by author.

[6] Jamil Jaafar interviewed in *The Maltese Double Cross*.

[7] Letter from Michael Hurley's solicitor, 4 July 1996.

[8] Testimony of PC Ian Howatson, Lockerbie trial, 8 November 2000.

[9] E-mail from US Bureau of Consular Affairs to author, 22 November 2000.

[10] Statement in open court, in the High Court of Justice Queens Bench Division, between Michael Hurley and Channel Four Television, 1996.

[11] 'Trail of Terror', article by Morgan Strong in *Playboy* magazine, 14 November 1993.

[12] Translation of SAPO documents.

[13] Translation of Abu-Talb interview by SAPO.

[14] Dagens Nyheter, 21 December 1989.

[15] *The Times*, 1 November 1989.

[16] Lockerbie trial transcript, 9 November 2000.

[17] Note of conversation between El-Salheli and ABC TV producer Terry Wrong, 1989.

[18] Letter to Beulah McKee, 9 July 1989.

[19] *Focus* magazine, 30 April 1996.

[20] *Sunday Herald*, 16 April 2000.

[21] Lockerbie trial transcript, 25 July 2000.

[22] 'Trail of Terror', article by Morgan Strong.

[23] Fight 103 seating plan in Cox and Foster, *Their Darkest Day*.

[24] Transcripts of Lockerbie Fatal Accident Inquiry.

[25] Ted Gup, *The Book of Honor: Covert Lives and Classified Deaths at the CIA*.

[26] This information was relayed to a British Lockerbie relative interviewed by the author.

[27] Transcript of media interview with Ronald Spiers released by US State Department.

[28] Ambassador John McCarthy telephone interview with author, 8 September 1994.

[29] John McCarthy e-mail to author, 14 November 2000.

[30] John McCarthy e-mail to author, 3 January 2001.

[31] Tiny Rowland statement, 14 August 1994.

[32] Evidence to Lockerbie Fatal Accident Inquiry, 25 October 1990.

[33] *SA Times*, 16 November 1994.

CHAPTER 10

[1] *Sunday Telegraph*, 29 January 1989; *The Times*, 30 January 1989.

[2] David Yallop, *To The Ends of the Earth: The Hunt for The Jackal* (London: Jonathan Cape, 1993) pp 465–466.

[3] *New York Times*, 22 November 1991.

[4] *New York Times*, 15 November 1991.

[5] Hansard, 14 November 1991.

[6] *Sunday Times*, 17 November 1991.

[7] Transcript of State Department Press Conference, 14 November 1991.

[8] Transcript of Lockerbie Fatal Accident Inquiry, 22 October 1990.

[9] Ronald Kessler, *The FBI: Inside the World's Most Powerful Law Enforcement Agency* (London: Corgi, 1994).

[10] Diarmuid Jeffreys, *The Bureau – Inside Today's FBI* (London: Macmillan, 1994.)

[11] Mark Perry, *Eclipse.*

[12] Ted Gup, *The Book of Honor* (USA: Doubleday, 2000) pp 312–313.

CHAPTER 11

[1] Martin and Walcott, *Best Laid Plans*, Chapter 4.

[2] Bob Woodward, *Veil*, p 93; Yallop, *To The Ends of the Earth*, p 539.

[3] Bob Woodward, *Veil*, p 93.

[4] Bob Woodward, *Veil*, pp 126–128.

[5] Bob Woodward, *Veil*, p 93.

[6] Bob Woodward, *Veil*, pp 125–6.

[7] Yallop, *To The Ends of the Earth*, p 541.

[8] Martin and Walcott, *Best Laid Plans*, p 75.

[9] Howard Teicher interview, *The Maltese Double Cross*.

[10] Martin and Walcott, *Best Laid Plans*, p 73.

[11] Mark Perry, *Eclipse,* p 167.

[12] Martin and Walcott, *Best Laid Plans*, pp 73–79.

[13] Martin and Walcott, *Best Laid Plans.* pp 79–80; Bob Woodward, *Veil*, pp 181–183.

14 Martin and Walcott, *Best Laid Plans*, p 80.

15 Bob Woodward, *Veil*, p 186.

16 Yallop, *To The Ends of the Earth*, p 551.

17 Vincent Cannistraro interviewed in *The Maltese Double Cross*.

18 Martin and Walcott, *Best Laid Plans*, pp 80–81; Bob Woodward, *Veil*, p 184.

19 Martin and Walcott, *Best Laid Plans*, pp 259–261.

20 Martin and Walcott, *Best Laid Plans*, pp 262–263.

21 Mark Perry, *Eclipse*, p 165.

22 Martin and Walcott, *Best Laid Plans*, pp 263–264.

23 Martin and Walcott, *Best Laid Plans*, p 265.

24 Bob Woodward, *Veil*, pp 411–412.

25 Martin and Walcott, *Best Laid Plans*, pp 265–266

26 Martin and Walcott, *Best Laid Plans*, p 177.

27 Martin and Walcott, *Best Laid Plans*, Chapter 9; Bob Woodward, *Veil*, pp 414–415.

28 Martin and Walcott, *Best Laid Plans*, pp 267–268.

29 Bob Woodward, *Veil*, p 421.

30 Yallop, *To The Ends of the Earth*, pp 555–556.

31 Martin and Walcott, *Best Laid Plans*, pp 267–268.

32 Bob Woodward, *Veil*, p 431

33 Martin and Walcott, *Best Laid Plans*, p 268.

34 David Yallop, *To The Ends of the Earth*, pp 555–556.

35 Martin and Walcott, *Best Laid Plans*, pp 271–273.

36 Martin and Walcott, *Best Laid Plans*, pp 275–286.

37 David Yallop, *To The Ends of the Earth*, pp 559–560.

38 Martin and Walcott, *Best Laid Plans*, pp 293–295.

39 David Yallop, *To The Ends of the Earth*, p 560.

40 David Yallop, *To The Ends of the Earth*, pp 557–559.

41 Victor Ostrovsky, *The Other Side of Deception*, (USA: Harper Collins, 1994) pp 114–115.

42 Martin and Walcott, *Best Laid Plans*, pp 315–316.

43 *Washington Post*, 5 October 1986.

44 Martin and Walcott, *Best Laid Plans*, pp 319–320

45 Vincent Cannistraro interviewed in *The Maltese Double Cross*; Cannistraro testimony in the trial of Oliver North; Cannistraro testimony to Federal Grand Jury which indicted Dane Clarridge, reported in *Wall Street Journal*, 27 November 1991.

46 *Washington Times*, 21 November 1990.

47 *New York Times*, 21 November 1990.

48 *New York Times*, 21 November 1991.

49 *New York Times*, 22 November 1991.

50 Susan and Daniel Cohen, *Pan Am 103; the Bombing, the Betrayals and a Bereaved Family's Search for Justice* (USA: New American Library, 2000) pp 15 –154.

51 Loftus and Aarons, *The Secret War Against the Jews* (USA: St Martin's Press, 1994) p 466–467.

52 Vincent Cannistraro testimony at the trial of Oliver North.

53 *Newsday*, 19 April 1987; *The Observer*, 3 May 1987; ABC Television (undated transcript of news item).

CHAPTER 12

1 *Daily Telegraph*, 15 November 1991.

[2] Authors' interviews with Mike Jones and Ingrid Olufsen.

[3] *Independent on Sunday*, 6 February 1994.

[4] Lockerbie trial transcript, evidence of Clive Holes, 6 October 2000.

[5] David Leppard, *On the Trail of Terror* (London: Jonathan Cape, 1991).

[6] *The Fall of Pan Am 103* by Steven Emerson and Brian Duffy (USA: G. P. Putnam's Sons, 1990).

[7] Court of Appeal judgement in Judith Ward case, 4 June 1992.

[8] All details of the Maguire Seven case are from the May Inquiry: *Second Report on the Maguire Case* (London: HMSO, 1992) and from transcripts of the Maguires' original trial.

[9] Allen Feraday evidence to the Gibraltar inquest, 1988.

[10] Court transcripts of trial of Danny MacNamee.

[11] Transcript of Dr Thomas Hayes's evidence at trial of Danny MacNamee, 14 October 1987.

[12] David Leppard, *On the Trail of Terror.*

[13] *The Gibraltar Inquest: The Technical Evdence,* report by Dr Michael Scott, 6 April 1989.

CHAPTER 13

[1] All details of Aviv's case are from papers filed with the court.

[2] Indictment: *USA vs John Brennan and US Aviation Underwriters Inc.*, US District Court, Eastern District of New York.

[3] Vivian Shevitz, letter to warden of MDC, 13 January 1997.

[4] Vivian Shevitz, letter to Judge Thomas Platt, 11 February 1997.

[5] Chasey's story is outlined in his book, *Foreign Agent 4221: The Lockerbie Cover-Up* (USA: Promotion Publishing, 1995).

CHAPTER 14

[1] All details cited below are from Tony and Paul Gauci's police statements.

[2] *The Independent*, 30 October 1989; *Sunday Times*, 5 November 1989.

[3] *Time* magazine, 27 April 1992.

[4] Telex, 23 October 1989, from the US Embassy in Bonn to FBI director, Washington DC.

[5] Defence Intelligence Brief DIB 96–89 – *Pan Am 103: Deadly Cooperation.*

[6] Denis Phipps interview, *The Maltese Double Cross.*

[7] These findings are set out in Air Malta Ltd vs Granada Television Ltd, High Court of Justice, Queen's Bench Division Reply, 19 April 1993.

[8] Senior FAA inspector interviewed by author.

[9] Guima Nasser and anonymous employee of Jerma Palace Hotel, interviewed in the *The Maltese Double Cross.*

[10] The Foreign Office leak has been confirmed by a source within *The Guardian.*

[11] *The Guardian*, 22 December 1993.

[12] *The Guardian*, 5 January 1994

[13] Edwin Bollier, interviewed for *The Maltese Double Cross.*

[14] Channel 4, *Dispatches*, 17 December 1998.

[15] Edwin Bollier interviewed for *The Maltese Double Cross.*

[16] *The Observer*, 23 January 1994.

[17] Vincent Cannistraro interview, *The Maltese Double Cross.*

[18] Translations of Joachim Wenzel interview; translation of Spiegel article.

[19] Margaret Thatcher, *The Downing Street Years* (London: Harper Collins.)

CHAPTER 15

[1] *Los Angeles Times*, 16 November 1991.

[2] *New York Times*, 30 September 1993.

[3] *The Guardian*, 14 December 1991.

[4] *The Mirror*, 31 July 1998.

[5] Agence France Presse, 13 July 1998.

[6] *Washington Post*, 27 August 1998.

[7] Vincent Cannistraro, interview with author 14 September 2000.

[8] Vincent Cannistraro, interview with author 14 February 2000.

[9] *The Scotsman*, 17 February 2000.

[10] *Sunday Herald*, 20 February 2000.

[11] *Mail on Sunday*, 20 February 2000.

CHAPTER 16

[1] Trial transcript 3 May 2000.

[2] Trial transcript 3 May 2000.

[3] Trial transcript 24 May 2000.

[4] *Sunday Herald* 28 May 2000.

[5] *Sunday Herald* 9 April 2000.

[6] Trial Transcript 6 June 2000.

[7] Trial transcript 8 June 2000 pp 2,886–2,887.

[8] Trial transcript 8 June 2000 pp 2,945–2,988.

[9] Trial Transcript 8 June 2000 p 3,002.

[10] Trial transcript 8 June 2000 pp 3,004-3,005.

[11] Trial transcript 15 June 2000 p 3,318.

[12] Trial transcript 15 June 2000 p 3,322.

[13] Trial transcript 15 June 2000 pp 3,323–3,325.

[14] Victim's relative, interview with author July 2000.

[15] Trial transcript 12 July 2000.

[16] Trial transcript 24 August 2000 pp 6,349–6,354.

[17] Trial transcript 10 November 2000 p 8,209.

[18] Trial transcript 10 November 2000 p 8,220.

[19] Trial transcript 14 November 2000 p 8,268.

[20] Trial transcript 14 November 2000 pp 8,398–8,400.

[21] Trial transcript 14 November 2000 pp 8,401–8,402.

[22] Trial transcript 14 November 2000 p 8,402.

[23] Trial transcript 14 November 2000 p 8,409.

[24] Trial transcript 14 November 2000 pp 8,411–8,412.

[25] Trial transcript 15 November 2000 p 8,449.

[26] Trial transcript 15 November 2000 p 8,495.

[27] Trial transcript 15 November 2000 pp 8,517–8,519.

[28] Trial transcript 15 November 2000 pp 8,526–8,527.

[29] Trial transcript 15 November 2000 pp 8,526–8,537.

[30] Trial transcript 15 November 2000 p 8,541.

[31] Susan Lindauer affidavit, 4 December 1998.

CHAPTER 17

[1] Trial transcript 19 June 2000 p 3,646.

[2] Trial transcript 19 June 2000 p 3,648.

[3] Trial transcript 19 June 2000 p 3,672.

[4] Trial transcript 19 June 2000 p 3,674.

[5] Trial transcript 19 June 2000 p 3,707.

[6] Trial transcript 23 June 2000 p 4,251.

[7] Trial transcript 23 June 2000 p 4,252.

[8] Trial transcript 23 June 2000 p 4,260

[9] Trial transcript 23 June 2000 p 4,262.

[10] Trial transcript 23 June 2000 pp 4,265–4,266.

[11] Trial transcript 23 June 2000 p 4,246.

[12] Trial transcript 27 June 2000 p 4,363.

[13] Trial transcript 28 June 2000 p 4,434.

[14] Trial transcript 11 July 2000 p 4,828.

[15] Trial transcript 11 July 2000 p 4,827.

[16] Trial transcript 22 August 2000 pp 6,093–6,094.

[17] Trial transcript 22 August 2000 pp 6,096–6,097.

[18] Trial transcript 22 August 2000 p 6,098.

[19] Trial transcript 22 August 2000 p 6,099.

[20] Trial transcript 25 August 2000 pp 6,522–6,524.

[21] Trial transcript 28 August 2000 pp 6,540–6,541.

[22] Trial transcript 26 September 2000 p 6,784.

[23] Trial transcript 26 September 2000 pp 6,787–6,788.

[24] Trial transcript 26 September 2000 p 6,791.

[25] Trial transcript 26 September 2000 pp 6,793–6,795.

[26] Trial transcript 26 September 2000 pp 6,814–6,815.

[27] Trial transcript 26 September 2000 p 6,818.

[28] Trial transcript 26 September 2000 p 6,833.

[29] Trial transcript 26 September 2000 pp 6,836–6,838.

[30] Trial transcript 26 September 2000 p 6,840–6,841.

[31] Trial transcript 26 September 2000 p 6,844.

[32] Trial transcript 27 September 2000 pp 6,944–6,945.

[33] Trial transcript 26 September 2000 p 6,880.

[34] Trial transcript 27 September 2000 p 6,896.

[35] Trial transcript 27 September 2000 pp 6,979–6,981.

[36] Trial transcript 27 September 2000 p 6,988.

[37] Trial transcript 27 September 2000 p 6,989.

[38] Trial transcript 27 September 2000 p 7,040.

[39] Trial transcript 28 September 2000 p 7,044.

[40] Trial transcript 28 September 2000 p 7,045.

CHAPTER 18

[1] Trial transcript 28 November 2000 p 9,107

[2] Trial transcript 28 November 2000 p 9,133

[3] Trial transcript 28 November 2000 p 9,134

[4] Trial transcript 29 November 2000 p 9,149

[5] Trial transcript 20 November 2000
[6] Trial transcript 5 January 2001 pp 9,245–9,246
[7] Trial transcript 5 January 2001 p 9,244
[8] Trial transcript 5 January 2001 p 9, 256
[9] Trial transcript 5 January 2001 p 9, 253
[10] Trial transcript 5 January 2001 p 9, 258
[11] Trial transcript 8 January 2001 p 9,344–9,345
[12] Trial transcript January 2001 p 9,337
[13] Trial transcript 9 January 2001 pp 9, 372–9,374
[14] Trial transcript 9 January 2001 p 9,394
[15] Trial transcript 9 January 2001 pp 9,398–9,399
[16] Trial transcript 9 January 2001 p 9,474
[17] Trial transcript 9 January 2001 p 9, 419
[18] Trial transcript 9 January 2001 pp 9,444–9,445
[19] Trial transcript 10 January 2001 p 9,521
[20] Trial transcript 11 January 2001 p 9,561
[21] Trial transcript 11 January 2001 p 9,575
[22] Trial transcript 11 January 2001 p 9,603
[23] Trial transcript 11 January 2001 pp 9,623–9,624
[24] Trial transcript 11 January 2001 p 9,624
[25] Trial transcript 11 January 2001 p 9,692
[26] Trial transcript 11 January 2001 p 9,587
[27] Trial transcript 17 January 2001 p 10,042
[28] Trial transcript 18 January 2001 p 10,135
[29] Trial transcript 18 January 2001 p 10,147
[30] Trial transcript 18 January 2001 pp 10,151–10,153
[31] Trial transcript 18 January 2001 p 1,0199
[32] Trial transcript 18 January 2001 p1,0219
[33] Trial transcript 18 January 2001 pp 10,229–10,231
[34] Trial transcript 18 January 2001 p 10,231–10,232
[35] Trial transcript 30 January 2001

INDEX

from Frankfurt 98, 103, 121, 166, 351
from Malta 102-103, 115, 120, 121, 166, 225, 351
X-rayed 120-121, 122, 145
Baker, Bill (US) 167, 193, 195
Barr, General William (US) 167, 190
Bartle, Ronald John *see* Ghandanfar
Basset, Abdel *see* Megrahi
Bathen, Terry E (DIA) 119, 121
Bazoft, Farzad (journalist) 115, 157
BBC 27, 232, 233, 310-311
Beckett, John (lawyer) 252, 255, 315
Bedford, John (Pan Am) 283, 343
Beirut 25, 39, 44, 56-57, 63, 126, 147-148
    hostages 25, 26, 43, 62-63, 67, 85, 86, 93
    US arms for hostages deal 99
    US drugs for hostages deal 23, 25, 86-87, 93, 98, 114, 146, 147, 150
    US rescue group 25, 62-63, 85, 98-100, 126, 146
    US Embassy 25, 26, 39-40, 139, 363
Bell, Harry (DCI) 193, 219, 220, 279
Berlin 47, 48, 180
Berry, John (UK businessman) 200, 276
Berwick, Jim (Pan Am) 19, 36, 37, 60-61, 81, 117, 282-283
Biehl, Dana (US DoJ) 255, 325, 327
Black, Professor Robert (QC) 242-245, 247, 280-282, 310-311
Bollier, Edwin (Swi) 165, 231-236, 260, 263, 274, 275, 303-311, 344, 353
    and CIA 304-306, 307-309, 359, 361, 366
    and Libya 303, 304, 308, 310, 353
    and PFLP-GC 309-310
    and Stasi 303, 304, 308-310, 311, 344
bombs, barometric 34-35, 41-42, 50-53, 54, 55, 57-58, 86, 142, 335
bomb-makers 86, 87, 161, 165, 198, 292, 311

bomb-carrier 58-60, 78, 101, 115, 239
    dupes 42, 56, 58, 61, 64, 78, 135-137, 140-141, 143
bomb-making equipment 49-52, 106, 107, 112, 165
    circuit board 167-168, 184, 188, 198-199, 202, 231, 259, 267, 268, 269-273, 278, 312, 342, 352-353, 358
    detonators 264-265, 304
    'stand off distance' 264, 265
    timers, CIA 269, 270, 270-273, 305, 305-306, 361
    from Togo 268, 274, 305
    Libyan 158, 160, 161, 162, 164, 165, 166, 306, 353
    MST-13, 165, 166, 167, 168-170, 199, 231-236, 239, 249, 259, 267, 269, 273, 274, 275, 305, 306, 352-353, 358, 363
    Olympus 303-304
    PFLP-GC 56-57, 161, 164, 239, 341
    in Senegal 159, 160, 161, 162, 169, 183, 184, 188, 274, 304, 305
    Stasi 310, 311, 341, 358
    'Toshiba' 34, 50, 55, 56, 57, 65, 161, 163, 167-168, 336
    see also forensic evidence; warnings
Botha, Pik (SA) 39, 149, 150, 364
Boucher, Richard (US) 163, 241
Boyd, Colin (QC) 250, 253, 255, 260-263, 315, 318
Boyd, John (police) 68, 73
Brennan, John (Pres USAU) 128, 133, 134, 204, 206, 209-210, 364
'Bringold', Willi *see* Aspin, Leslie
British Airways 17, 257
British Embassy, Washington 152, 153
British government, complicity 21, 62-63, 67, 68, 78, 101, 133-135, 140
Buckley, William (CIA) 85, 99, 150, 151-